Human Behavior
in the SOCIAL
ENVIRONMENT

Human Behavior
in the SOCIAL
ENVIRONMENT
A Macro, National, and International Perspective

Rudolph Alexander, Jr.

Los Angeles | London | New Delhi
Singapore | Washington DC

For information:

SAGE Publications, Inc.
2455 Teller Road
Thousand Oaks, California 91320
E-mail: order@sagepub.com

SAGE Publications India Pvt. Ltd.
B 1/I 1 Mohan Cooperative Industrial Area
Mathura Road, New Delhi 110 044
India

SAGE Publications Ltd.
1 Oliver's Yard
55 City Road
London EC1Y 1SP
United Kingdom

SAGE Publications Asia-Pacific Pte. Ltd.
33 Pekin Street #02-01
Far East Square
Singapore 048763

Printed in the United States of America.

Library of Congress Cataloging-in-Publication Data

Alexander, Rudolph.
Human behavior in the social environment: a macro, national, and international perspective / Rudolph Alexander, Jr.
       p. cm.
Includes bibliographical references and index.
ISBN 978-1-4129-5080-0 (pbk.)
   1. Social service. 2. Social problems. 3. Sociology. I. Title.

HV40.A534 2010
361—dc22   2009035664

This book is printed on acid-free paper.

09   10   11   12   13   10   9   8   7   6   5   4   3   2   1

Acquisitions Editor:	Kassie Graves
Editorial Assistant:	Veronica Novak
Production Editor:	Karen Wiley
Copy Editor:	Melinda Masson
Typesetter:	C&M Digitals (P) Ltd.
Proofreader:	Jenifer Kooiman
Indexer:	Rick Hurd
Cover Designer:	Arup Giri
Marketing Manager:	Stephanie Adams

Contents

Preface

After receiving a bachelor's degree in criminology and corrections in December 1981 from Sam Houston State University, I shifted into social work at the University of Houston. In the summer of 1982, I took my first social work course, with a focus on human behavior in the social environment (HBSE). A dynamic professor taught this course, but I was impressed equally with the course's provisions of foundation knowledge for future social work courses. As a result, I have always believed that a course in human behavior in the social environment is critical to truly understanding social work practice, social welfare, and social policy courses. The Council on Social Work Education (CSWE) prescribes the content that must be covered in HBSE courses, as it does for all social work courses. CSWE says HBSE must provide content about theories and knowledge of human bio-psycho-social development, including theories and knowledge about the range of social systems in which individuals live (families, groups, organizations, institutions, and communities). Further, HBSE must provide an understanding of the interactions between and among human biological, social, psychological, and cultural systems as they affect and are affected by human behavior. Moreover, HBSE must provide content on the impact of social and economic forces on individuals and social systems. Furthermore, HBSE must provide content about the ways in which systems promote or deter people in maintaining or achieving optimal health and well-being. In sum, HBSE represents social work's position that human behavior and the environment act upon each other. Individuals positively and negatively impact the environment, and the environment impacts individuals positively and negatively. Equally, other social systems (families, groups, organizations, institutions, and communities) are affected by the environment, and reciprocally the environment affects these systems as well. Most social work programs divide HBSE into two courses within their curriculum—a micro course and a macro course. This textbook focuses on macro HBSE.

ORGANIZATION OF THIS BOOK

As a macro HBSE textbook, this book's primary focus is social institutions, organizations, and communities. The introductory chapter, Chapter 1, provides a foundation by defining social work, social environment, and human needs. It explains why human needs exist and what causes human needs. Additionally, this chapter discusses human needs in the international communities, particularly those extremely poor communities wracked by considerable human rights violations, as defined by the United Nations. At the end of the chapter is the conceptual framework that I have identified as world systems theory. Overall, the book is grounded in world systems theory as it provides, in part, an understanding of core, semiperiphery, and periphery societies, which one researcher has applied to communities and the extent to which communities are core, semiperiphery, and periphery communities. Chapter 2 discusses human needs in more depth, particularly those caused by poverty, race, gender, natural disasters, violence, crime, ethnic cleansings and genocide, and wars. Also, natural disasters are discussed as they have a serious impact on human needs and communities, such as Hurricane Katrina's impact on the New Orleans communities and the mental health impact on residents. Chapter 3 discusses a number of theories that explain macro HBSE, including social systems theory, community theory, social disorganization theory, routine activity theory, migration theory, inequality theory, feminist theory, power theory and social independence theory, social learning theory, reference group theory, role theory, and Black's theory of law. These theories are loosely grouped as community theories, human conduct theories, inequality theories, and group theories. Chapters 4 and 5 contain discussions of social institutions, including the family, education, religion, medicine and health, the news media, and law. Chapter 6 discusses organizations and their impact, good and bad, on human needs. Chapter 7 discusses urban communities, and Chapter 8 discusses rural communities. Last, Chapter 9 has discussions about several developing countries.

OUTSTANDING FEATURES OF THIS TEXTBOOK

First, this book tightly follows CSWE outlines for HBSE. To that end, the primary chapters, those on organizations, social institutions, and communities, include a section on knowledge and theories, followed by one on the impact of economic and social forces on these topics. In its discussion of families, this textbook includes military families and their needs. Because of the wars in Iraq and Afghanistan, numerous veterans have returned with posttraumatic stress disorder and domestic violence issues. This textbook examines the impact of natural disasters on human and community needs, such as a major flooding in North Dakota and hurricanes in Florida and New Orleans. For instance, mental health professionals have documented the rise in suicides and depression in New Orleans following Hurricane Katrina. Moreover, this textbook discusses human rights, ethnic cleansing, and genocide in international communities and their impact on human needs. As an illustration, the genocide that occurred in Rwanda devastated families. However, some female survivors in Rwanda have been able to rebuild farms and increase the yield for coffee beans. In fact, these women are better farmers than their male relatives were. Economically and politically, women in Rwanda have benefited from tremendous advances following the genocide that took many of their relatives. Last, this book provides a theoretical discussion of terrorism or terrorist activities, void of the emotionality attached to it. Many American movies and television programs intended for entertainment comprise plots involving terrorists who seek to harm Americans. As has been said, one person's terrorist is another person's freedom fighter. Social scientists have formulated a theoretical model to predict which countries will have terrorism due to economic and political oppression within these countries.

By reading this book, students will acquire knowledge and theories involving families, organizations, and communities. Students will also acquire an understanding of the economic and political forces impinging on families, organizations, and communities. Equally, students will understand the almost reciprocal nature of these macro institutions' impact on human behaviors.

CHAPTER 1

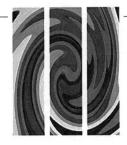

Introduction to Human Behavior in the Social Environment

INTRODUCTION

In Columbus, Ohio, a first-time juror kept a journal during her jury service in a murder trial. The trial lasted a week, and the juror described the social environment depicted from the witness stand and the bonding of jurors during breaks. As revealed in her journal, the judge instructed the jurors to put aside their biases, and when they did, the jury acquitted the defendant ("Murder Trial Thrusts Juror Into Rare Bond With Strangers," 2006). However, the most important aspects of this juror's experience were revealed in what she wrote about the witnesses in the case. This juror, a 52-year-old White female from an upper-class community, wrote that she would never forget "the world in which crime, drugs and social dysfunction run rampant" and that the jury "heard from an array of people whose lives were already in ruin—people hanging on at the fringe of society"—and then lamented that the "case left me feeling sad for the world that so many people inhabit—their social situation, lack of education and inability to see a way out" ("Murder Trial Thrusts Juror Into Rare Bond With Strangers," 2006, p. E1).

This report from a juror in a murder case represents themes presented throughout this book. The juror, who lived less than 10 miles from the defendant's neighborhood, confessed that this neighborhood was a world and an environment that she did not know existed. That she was totally unaware of this environment and its conditions suggests that glaring human needs may not always be reflected in brief news reports. Seeing and hearing real people recount their typical lives and behaviors on the witness stand proved more revealing. Also, if this juror did not know how people lived less than 10 miles from her neighborhood, she was unlikely to know how people lived 10,000 miles away in developing countries. Although not readily apparent, the discussion about this juror exemplifies human behavior in the social environment (HBSE).

Taking a **macro** or broad perspective, this book covers human behaviors within the social environment—that is, how organizations, institutions, and communities impact individuals and families. *Macro* is a prefix, meaning "large, broad, or extensive," and is used to indicate the broadness of an entity, a condition, or a system. Moreover, *community* here includes the international community. A primary focus of HBSE textbooks is to help students become aware of how events and occurrences in one system affect other systems, and HBSE provides knowledge that may be used for social work practice and intervention and social welfare policy analysis.

Human behaviors and natural events are inextricably interconnected, positively and negatively. For instance, when Hurricane Katrina closed the New Orleans port in 2005, Japan, which had purchased corn from the United States, turned to South Africa to buy corn. Japan's purchases reduced the amount of corn available to Africans and also drove up the prices, making corn too expensive for poor African countries to buy and exacerbating famines in some of them (Wines, 2005a). This chain of events shows how a natural disaster in one country can have a negative effect on the fulfillment of human needs on the other side of the world.

Many of us are connected with and benefit from one type of organizational system, corporations. In 2006, Exxon Mobil recorded profits for 2005 of $36 billion. Many corporations have been criticized for exploiting people and environments in developing countries through globalization. According to the Carnegie Endowment for International Peace, "globalization is a process of interaction and integration among the people, companies, and governments of different nations, a process driven by international trade and investment and aided by information technology. This process has effects on the environment, on culture, on political systems, on economic development and prosperity, and on human physical well-being in societies around the world" (Carnegie Endowment, 2007).

However, regular citizens like you and your family benefit from some corporations' exploitive behaviors. We benefit because many of the pension boards that manage our pensions and retirement accounts hold stock in these corporations. The money that goes into retirement accounts is not just put in savings accounts. Instead, the money is invested in corporate stocks, and retirement benefits are tied to dividends. When these corporations underperform, pension boards are pressured to reduce retirement benefits or increase the time a retiree must wait to draw on his or her pension. But when stocks earn considerable profits, like the $36 billion earned by Exxon, shareholders benefit. On the other hand, when companies go bankrupt, the federal government takes over the companies' pension plans, and these pensions are reduced very significantly, impacting the quality of life for retirees. Later in this textbook, we will describe how a number of pension plans from municipalities are in serious trouble and how pensions are reduced significantly when a corporation enters bankruptcy—all negatively affecting human needs and social systems.

SOCIAL WORK

In the United States

According to the U.S. Department of Labor (2005), **social work** is a profession for those with a strong desire to help improve people's lives. Social workers help people function the best way they can in their environments, deal with their relationships, and solve personal and family problems. Social workers often see clients who face life-threatening diseases or significant social problems. These problems may include inadequate housing, unemployment, serious illness, disability, or substance abuse. Social workers also assist families dealing with serious domestic conflicts, including those involving child or spousal abuse. The **Council on Social Work Education (CSWE)**, a social work governing body, asserts that social work is committed to the enhancement of human well-being and to the alleviation of poverty and oppression. Within its general scope of concern, professional social work is practiced in a wide variety of settings. It has four related purposes:

1. The promotion, restoration, maintenance, and enhancement of the functioning of individuals, families, groups, organizations, and communities by helping them accomplish tasks, prevent and alleviate distress, and use resources

2. The planning, formulation, and implementation of social policies, services, resources, and programs needed to meet basic human needs and support the development of human capacities

3. The pursuit of policies, services, resources, and programs through organizational or administrative advocacy and social or political action to empower groups at risk and to promote social and economic justice

4. The development and testing of professional knowledge and skills related to these purposes (CSWE, 2005). The HBSE sequence, as established by CSWE, seeks to impart an understanding of the first of these goals.

Succinctly, CSWE requires that HBSE courses provide students with content on theories and knowledge of human bio-psycho-social development, including theories and knowledge of the range of social systems in which individuals live. Figure 1.1 depicts individuals or human beings and their connections to different systems and social institutions. Human beings are connected to families, groups, organizations, communities, social institutions, and the world. Although Figure 1.1 does not show the reciprocal relationships among these systems and social institutions, reciprocal relationships exist, and all systems impact each other.

In addition, HBSE must provide an understanding of the interactions among biological, social, psychological, and cultural systems as they relate to human behaviors. Furthermore, HBSE must provide content on the impact of social and economic forces on individuals and social systems, as well as the role these systems play in promoting or deterring individuals' optimal health and well-being. These goals, and other CSWE goals, are the focus of micro and macro HBSE courses. This textbook focuses on the macro perspective, conceptualizing community as embracing the international community. An understanding of **human rights** is important to embracing an international perspective of

Figure 1.1   A Configuration of Human Beings' Connection to Various Social Systems

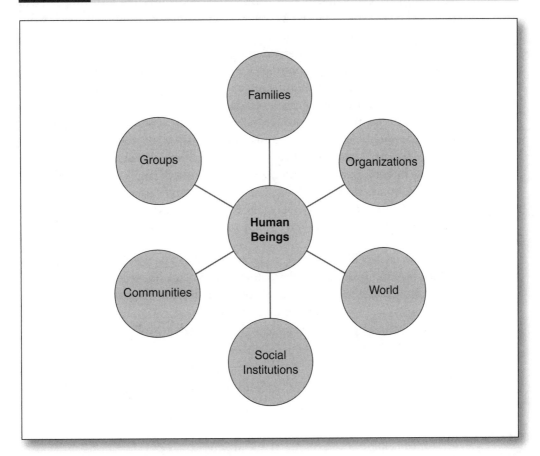

community because serious violations of human rights impede and deter human well-being—which social work strives to prevent and alleviate.

Outside the United States

Social work as practiced in the United States is different from social work as practiced in other countries. Differences in culture, customs, and beliefs prevent the transport of an American model of social work to a developed or developing country. Discussing one recently passed law intended to help African girls who were subjected to virgin testing, Patekile Holomisa, president of the Congress of Traditional Leaders of South Africa, declared that "we will uphold our traditions and customs. . . . There are laws that passed that do not necessarily have any impact on the lives of people. I imagine this will be one of those" (LaFraniere, 2005, p. A1). At the same time, international social work standards require respect for customs and traditions as long as these customs and traditions do not violate *fundamental* human rights. Some South African women believe that virgin testing is a violation of human rights, but other South African women believe it is an important part of their culture and traditions, supported by families and communities. Moreover, the efforts of a single social institution, South African law, may be ineffective in stopping this practice without the involvement of additional social institutions.

In 2004, the International Association of Schools of Social Work (IASSW) and the International Federation of Social Workers (IFSW) met in Adelaide, Australia, to develop the *Global Standards for the Education and Training of the Social Work Profession* (Sewpaul & Jones, 2004). The IASSW and IFSW document defined international social work as follows:

> The social work profession promotes social change, problem solving in human relationships and the empowerment and liberation of people to enhance well-being. Utilising theories of human behaviour and social systems, social work intervenes at the points where people interact with their environments. Principles of human rights and social justice are fundamental to social work. (Sewpaul & Jones, 2004, p. 2)

Moreover, IASSW and IFSW agreed on the core purposes of social work (see Table 1.1).

Table 1.1   Core Principles of International Social Work
1. Facilitate the inclusion of marginalized, socially excluded, dispossessed, vulnerable, and at-risk groups of people
2. Address and challenge barriers, inequalities, and injustices that exist in society
3. Form short- and longer-term working relationships with and mobilize individuals, families, groups, organizations, and communities to enhance their well-being and their problem-solving capacities
4. Assist and educate people to obtain services and resources in their communities
5. Formulate and implement policies and programs that enhance people's well-being, promote development and human rights, and promote collective social harmony and social stability, insofar as such stability does not violate human rights

6.	Encourage people to engage in advocacy with regard to pertinent local, national, and regional and/or international concerns
7.	Advocate for and/or with people the formulation and targeted implementation of policies that are consistent with the ethical principles of the profession
8.	Advocate for and/or with people changes in those policies and structural positions that maintain people in marginalized, dispossessed, and vulnerable positions and those that infringe upon the collective social harmony and stability of various ethnic groups, insofar as such stability does not violate human rights
9.	Work toward the protection of people who are not in a position to do so themselves, for example children and youth in need of care and persons experiencing mental illness or mental retardation within the parameters of accepted and ethically sound legislation
10.	Engage in social and political action to impact social policy and economic development and to effect change by critiquing and eliminating inequalities
11.	Enhance stable, harmonious, and mutually respectful societies that do not violate people's human rights
12.	Promote respect for traditions, cultures, ideologies, beliefs, and religions amongst different ethnic groups and societies, insofar as those do not conflict with the fundamental human rights of people
13.	Plan, organize, administer, and manage programs and organizations dedicated to any of the purposes delineated above

Many similarities exist between social work in America and social work in the international community. Both American and international social work focus on the promotion, restoration, maintenance, and enhancement of the functioning of individuals, families, groups, organizations, and communities. Recognizing the importance of international social work in 2004, CSWE established the Katherine A. Kendall Institute for International Social Work Education. CSWE noted that social work education programs must train their students to live and work in a world where geographical boundaries may be crossed much faster than ever before and where information is readily accessible worldwide. One way to accomplish this task is to internationalize the social work curriculum. As CSWE noted, "the poverty of developing nations, indebtedness, staggering levels of disease, lack of access to health care, employment, clean water, peaceful coexistence with one's neighboring countries, suggests a strong and continuing role on the part of social work programs in educating students and faculties to address these conditions as part of our collective mission in securing the conditions for world peace and stability" (CSWE, 2005, p. 2).

The Katherine A. Kendall Institute for International Social Work Education advances the mainstream development of international content in social work curriculum and boosts cross-organizational partnerships among social workers in developing projects and research. Ultimately, these collaborations will prepare students with the knowledge and skills necessary for a more interdependent global community (CSWE, 2005). Although CSWE requires international content in social work curriculum, Steen and Mathiesen (2005), following an empirical study, concluded that "unfortunately, most schools of social work with MSW [master of social work] programs are failing to infuse human rights contents into core courses and failing to offer human rights electives" (p. 149). Human rights violations are prevalent around the world, and these violations create tremendous human needs and severely impede the first purpose of social work.

HUMAN NEEDS AND SOCIAL ENVIRONMENT DEFINED

In the psychology discipline, Abraham Maslow (1962) described a hierarchy of human needs that have been depicted in many textbooks. At the bottom are physiological needs, which are basic to survival, such as food, water, clothing, and shelter. Safety needs are next. Belonging and love needs follow safety needs. Self-esteem needs are next. Then, at the tip of the hierarchy is self-actualization. According to Maslow, these needs must be satisfied sequentially because, for instance, if a person's physiological and safety needs are not met, his or her self-esteem needs are impossible to address. While self-actualization, or the state and condition of achieving one's highest potential, is the optimal goal, most individuals do not achieve this state. Many individuals, furthermore, may not feel love and belongingness. See Figure 1.2.

One may surmise that a person's environment, while not addressed specifically by Maslow, may determine the extent to which these needs are met. For instance, in a correctional environment, prisoners may get, and are only legally required to receive, the fulfillment of their physiological needs. Safety needs are not ensured. Similarly, in some communities, safety needs are not achieved, and many residents live in fear. Then, for some communities with resources, most of their needs may be met, and they may come close to being self-actualized. But in some developing countries, torn apart by ethnic cleansing and civil wars, many physiological needs are not met, and people starve or die from malnutrition or exposure to the physical elements in those environments.

The *Social Work Dictionary* defines **needs** as "the physical, psychological, economic, cultural, and social requirements for survival, well-being, and fulfillment" (Barker, 2003, p. 291). Further, **social functioning** is defined as "living up to the expectations that are made of an individual by that person's own self, by the immediate social environment, and by society at large. These expectations, or functions, include meeting one's own basic needs and the needs of one's dependents

Figure 1.2   Maslow's Hierarchy of Human Needs

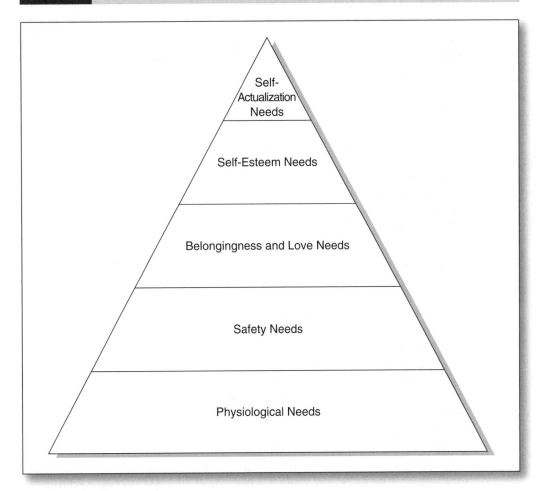

and making positive contributions to society. Human needs include physical aspects (food, shelter, safety, health care, and protection), personal fulfillment (education, recreation, values, aesthetics, religion, and accomplishment), emotional needs (a sense of belonging, mutual caring, and companionship), and an adequate self-concept (self-confidence, self-esteem, and identity)" (Barker, 2003, p. 403).

Zastrow and Kirst-Ashman (2001) provide a very broad definition of **social environment**, including all the conditions, circumstances, and human interactions that surround human beings. In order to endure and flourish, human beings must function effectively within these broad environments. Moreover, the social environment consists of the human beings' actual physical setting. For instance, a person's social environment would include the type of home in which a person resides, the type of work a person does, a person's available income, and the laws and social rules that govern that person. The social environment involves individuals, both intimate and nonintimate; groups; organizations; and communities. It includes all the social institutions affecting an individual, such as health care, housing, social welfare, and educational systems (Zastrow & Kirst-Ashman, 2001).

Both the social and physical environments, conceptualized as components of community attachment, are important to fully understanding some aspects of human behaviors and macro issues (Brehm, Eisenhauser, & Krannich, 2004). For some researchers, **community attachment** consists of the degree of an individual's rootedness in local social relations, but Brehm et al. noted that some theoreticians indicated that the natural environment and the natural setting are an important part of community attachment. As an illustration, these researchers undertook a study to learn how both social and physical aspects of the environment affected the well-being of individuals in communities in the rural Western part of the United States. Their use of the social and physical environments in measuring community attachment supports the content validity of their measurement.

Some Reasons for Inadequate Attention to Human Needs

Whether or not the public perceives that a need or a social problem exists determines, in large part, whether that need or problem is addressed. Various social institutions, such as religious organizations and the news media, have a lot to do with bringing matters to the public's attention. What the public thinks is important, and polling agencies are constantly investigating public opinion. Almost all politicians read polls and respond in some way according to what they perceive the public wants. Of the 15 social problems polled in one survey, 11 appear to positively or negatively affect human needs (see Table 1.2). These 11 include Education, Environment, Drug Addiction, Halting Crime, Problems of Big Cities, Improving Health Care, Improving Conditions for Blacks, Welfare, Mass Transportation, Social Security, and Parks & Recreation. In 2002, nearly 40% of those polled believed that the government spent too much money on welfare, and 64% believed that the government spent too much on foreign aid (New Strategist, 2005).

Gil (2004) states that human needs exist in the United States because the United States is an unjust society. Gil (2004) explained the characteristics of a **just** and an **unjust society**, noting that a just society is characterized by equality, liberty, individuality, collectivity orientation and mutualism, and cooperation, whereas an unjust society is characterized by inequality, domination and exploitation, selfishness and individualism, disregard for community, and

Table 1.2	Americans' Views of Spending to Address Social Needs in 2002

Social Needs	Too Little %	About Right %	Too Much %	Don't Know %
Education	73.3	20.5	5.4	1.0
Environment	58.5	32.4	6.6	2.4
Drug Addiction	57.2	30.2	9.4	3.2
Halting Crime	55.9	34.9	6.6	2.6
Problems of Big Cities	41.5	36.5	13.5	8.6
Improving Health Care	73.7	20.9	3.8	1.5
Improving Conditions for Blacks	30.6	45.8	17.1	6.5
Military	30.5	45.3	21.7	2.4
Foreign Aid	6.5	26.9	63.5	3.1
Welfare	20.6	37.0	39.3	3.0
Space Program	11.1	47.2	35.3	6.4
Mass Transportation	34.8	49.4	10.1	5.7
Highways & Bridges	34.4	49.9	12.2	3.5
Social Security	58.6	33.3	4.5	3.6
Parks & Recreation	34.0	57.2	5.3	2.8

Source: Compiled from multiple tables in *American Attitudes: What Americans Think About the Issues That Shape Their Lives* (4th ed.), by New Strategist, 2005, Ithaca, NY: New Strategist Publications.

competition. Gil (2004) elaborated upon these concepts on three levels—individual human relations, social institutions, and global human relations.

In addition, Gil (2004, p. 34) discusses "**structural violence,**" which emanates from unjust societies:

The function of structural violence is to establish and maintain social, economic, and political inequalities among individuals, social groups, and social classes. Inequalities of rights, responsibilities, and opportunities among people of a society are unlikely to ever be established and maintained voluntarily. Rather, their establishment requires coercion in the form of initiating physical violence which is gradually complemented by a "consciousness of submission" resulting from ideological indoctrination or the colonization of people's minds. Structural violence leads its victims to counterviolence. This counterviolence is not directed at the sources, beneficiaries or actors, furthering injustices. Instead, victims of structural violence tend to perpetrate counterviolence in their own communities through domestic violence, sexual assaults, crime, addictions, mental illness, and suicides.

Although Gil (2004) was discussing only American society, his views can be applied to many international communities. Internationally, human needs exist because of extreme poverty and human rights violations (Human Rights Watch, 1999b, 2003). Sometimes governments in developing countries are insensitive to the needs of their people. They want to stay in power by any means necessary (Human Rights Watch, 2004a, 2005e). Some individuals may want to seize power and may engage in coups to overthrow existing governments. As a result, people who may already have significant needs because of poverty have their needs significantly intensified (Human Rights Watch, 2003), such as women and girls who have been tricked into prostitution in foreign countries (Human Rights Watch, 2002a).

The United Nations Human Rights Declaration and Its Connection to Human Behavior in the Social Environment

The United Nations General Assembly in 1948 issued a report titled the *Universal Declaration of Human Rights* and declared in it that all persons are born free and equal in rights and dignity. Further, no person was to be held in slavery or subject to cruel, inhuman, or degrading treatment, punishment, or torture. All persons have a natural right to

- equal protection of the law;
- liberty to move or travel within one's country, to form a family, and to acquire property;
- freedom of expression; and
- freedom of religion.

These human rights are articulated within 30 articles of the *Universal Declaration of Human Rights,* and these 30 articles help define crimes against humanity and human rights violations (see Appendix B). Moreover, Susan D. Solomon (2003, p. 4), an advocate for human rights, states that "all [30 articles] were also held to be entitled to the indispensable economic, social, and cultural benefits of their country, including an adequate standard of living, employment, education, and health care." The United Nations also has established its Millennium Goals to End Poverty as preventable starvation is a human rights violation (see Appendix A). In addition, Belgium has given itself the right and jurisdiction to prosecute serious violations of human rights wherever they occur in the world (Human Rights Watch, 2005d).

The promotion of human rights is connected to social work and HBSE. Violations of many of these human rights (e.g., Articles 3, 4, 5, 9, 14, 16, 22, 23, 25, 26, and 29) lead to decreased well-being and dysfunction in individuals, families, groups, and communities. Particularly, Article 25 corresponds closely to HBSE. It declares that everyone has a right to a standard of living adequate for individuals' health and well-being and for their families' health and well-being. These needs shall include food, clothing, housing, medical care, social services when necessary, and security affected by unemployment, sickness, disability, widowhood, and old age. In addition, mothers and children are recognized as entitled to special care and assistance, with all children born in or out of marriages given the same social protection. In short, violations of human rights create threats to survival, fulfillment, and well-being, such as those violations illustrated below.

Examples of Human Rights Violations in International Communities and One Community's Response

The 1994 genocide in Rwanda is an example of the effects of structural violence that Gil (2004) described. The root cause of this genocide can be traced to a race theory, advanced in the late 1800s by a British explorer, John Hanning Speke. Speke theorized that all Africans were descendents of a Caucasoid tribe in Ethiopia. The higher-order Africans were tall and somewhat light skinned. Speke believed that all other Africans were subhuman. Invoking Speke's theory, the Belgians, who took control of Rwanda from the Germans in 1916, believed that the taller and somewhat lighter-skinned Tutsis were superior to the shorter Hutus. The Belgians gave the Tutsis administrative duties over the Hutus, and the Belgians and Tutsis severely oppressed the Hutus. The elevation of the Tutsis, who were in the minority, made it easy for Belgium to exploit the country's tea and coffee resources without having a large number of Belgians in Rwanda. The Belgians permitted the Tutsis, but not the Hutus, to receive an education. Only the Tutsis could be employed as civil servants, and the Hutus did all the menial jobs and labor. A rigid classification system was implemented that required citizens to carry identification cards as a Hutu or a Tutsi. While the Belgians classified Rwandans as either Hutu or Tutsi, the classification system was very arbitrary (Temple-Raston, 2005).

Prior to the Belgians entering Rwanda, the Tutsis and Hutus shared similar cultures, language, and religion. Elevated to a conferred superior status by the Belgians, the Tutsis relished their perceived superiority over the Hutus, and the Hutus assumed the role of the oppressed and seethed over their maltreatment. In 1959, the Hutus launched an assault on the Tutsis after a Hutu leader was attacked. Some Tutsis went into exile. In 1961, a Hutu majority vote brought an end to the Tutsi monarchy. Empowered Hutus, suspicious of Tutsis and fearful of their return to power, began to denigrate the Tutsis. Tutsi elements formed the Rwandan Patriotic Front (RPF) to fight the Hutu government. When the Hutu president's plane was shot down in 1994, the Hutus embarked on a genocidal campaign to eliminate Tutsis. Almost 1 million Tutsis and moderate Hutus who were married to Tutsis or who tried to protect Tutsis were slaughtered (Temple-Raston, 2005). Hence, the structure of Rwandan society imposed by Belgium in 1916 precipitated the later genocide in the 1990s. The Hutus did not aim their violence at Belgium but promulgated it within their own communities. This genocide also illustrates a human rights violation and the creation of human needs in the social environment.

During the genocide in Rwanda, some Tutsi women were raped before being killed (Temple-Raston, 2005). Olujic (1995) lamented the use of rape as an instrument of war during the ethnic cleansing and genocide in Bosnia and Herzegovina, noting that rape is harmful not only at the individual, familial, and community levels but also at the international level. Women and girls impregnated as a result of rape are often shunned by their families and communities, which adds to their individual trauma. At the international level, rape violates an individual's human rights, to which many nations have agreed to adhere. Currently, rape during war and conflict has been codified as a human rights violation.

Revealing the societal impact of human rights violations on a community, Kornfeld (1995, pp. 118–119), a member of a human rights mental health agency in Chile, wrote that

> Chile was accused by the international community of violating human rights during the whole period of [Augusto Pinochet's] dictatorship. This "issue" was not only political but also a social, ethical, psychosocial, and mental health problem for the Chilean society. . . . On the one hand, human rights issues were considered by the military regime a part of a conspiracy. . . . On the other hand, human rights violations brought responses from various sectors of Chilean society. Lawyers, social workers, physicians, psychotherapists, Catholic priests, and ministers of other churches turned the defense of human rights into a central issue in their lives. Their efforts entailed a commitment to human life and human beings as well as to their values and

beliefs. That commitment implied to many of them a way of rescuing their own life projects, disrupted by political conditions and political repression. Survivors and human rights workers projected their expectations, wishes, fears, frustrations, impotence, guilt, rage, aggression, sufferings, and losses onto the subject of "human rights." It implied also another way of participating in public affairs.

Kornfeld showed the impact of human rights violations on a community and how community members responded to genocide in their environment.

Moreover, human rights violations often involve the use of torture. According to Kornfeld (1995, p. 116), torture is "the deliberate and systematic application of excruciating pain to a person in an attempt to undermine the will, the affective links and the loyalties, beliefs, and physical and psychic integrity of the individual. Life threats and physical pain are the essence of torture. At a broader level, the reason for torture is to intimidate third parties, thereby ensuring responses of fear, inhibition, paralysis, impotence, and conformity within society." Essentially, torture is intended to subjugate groups and communities.

The lack of sufficient food, or famine, in developing countries has been called a human rights violation. Jenkins and Scanlan (2001, p. 721) stated that food is an essential human need and should be viewed as a universal human right, drawing "on the findings of past studies of social welfare, especially those on the physical quality of life and other basic needs." Moreover, the World Food Programme, a United Nations organization, stated that targeted interventions were needed to help improve the lives of the poorest people in the world. The World Food Programme's policies and strategies aim (a) to save lives in refugee and other emergency situations, (b) to improve the nutrition and quality of life of the most vulnerable people at critical times in their lives, and (c) to help build assets and promote the self-reliance of poor people and communities. To these ends, the World Food Programme (2005) emphasized that women are a key focus for intervention because putting food in the hands of women will benefit children and the entire household and will strengthen women's coping ability and resilience. Simply, women are the primary caretakers of children, and meeting their children's needs is foremost for them, according to assumptions by the United Nations.

While individuals in developing countries generally experience more human rights violations than individuals in developed countries, developed countries have been identified as violating their citizens' human rights too (Human Rights Watch, 2004b; 2006a). Both Human Rights Watch (1999a, 1999c) and Amnesty International (2005, 2006) have accused the United States of human rights violations. In 1999, the United States was accused of human rights violations for embracing capital punishment, particularly capital punishment for juveniles; police brutality against citizens; overincarceration of African Americans for drug offenses; correctional confinement in adult and juvenile institutions; labor violations, especially abuses by American companies doing business in developing countries; violations of gay and lesbian rights; and violations of immigrant rights (Human Rights Watch, 2006a). Several prisons in the United States in particular have been accused of human rights violations. As an example, Human Rights Watch revealed that Connecticut, Delaware, Iowa, South Dakota, and Utah use attack dogs to extract prisoners from cells. If a prisoner refuses to leave his cell when ordered, the attack dogs are brought to the front of the cell. If the prisoner refuses to leave the cell then, the dogs are ordered to attack the prisoner (Human Rights Watch, 2006b). Massachusetts ended its practice of using attack dogs, declaring that there are other ways to remove prisoners from their cells besides sending in animals to rip prisoners' flesh (Fellner, 2006). Human Rights Watch (1999c) has documented practices in super-maximum-security confinement in Virginia that constitute human rights violations. More recently, Human Rights Watch (2004b) has condemned, as a human rights violation, the sentencing of juveniles to life without parole.

In sum, Solomon (2003, p. 4) declared that "experiences such as torture, domestic violence, rape, elder abuse, and child neglect threaten human dignity, liberty, and security. Events like war, political repression, terrorism, genocide, poverty, and disaster deprive individuals of their homes, their families, their work, their schools, their places of worship, and their access to education and health care." In 1995, the World Summit for Social Development (WSSD) recognized that progress in respecting human rights had been made but more still needed to be done worldwide. WSSD noted current problems of social polarization and fragmentation (i.e., community disorganization), expanding disparities and inequalities of income and wealth within and among nations, disrespect for the environment, and marginalization of people, families, social groups, communities, and entire countries. Considerable strain has been placed on individuals, families, communities, and institutions due to rapid social change, economic transformation, migration, and major dislocations of population, especially in places of armed conflict (Solomon, 2003). WSSD further noted that most traumatic experiences are not caused by random, inexplicable events. Instead, many traumatic experiences have their root causes in poverty, unemployment, and social disintegration. Although traumatic experiences that are caused by national disasters may seem to be indiscriminate, "even these events are more likely to be experienced by, and to be traumatic for, individuals and communities with fewer resources" (Solomon, 2003, p. 5). Solomon's comments ring very true for the tsunami that occurred in Asia in 2004 and Hurricane Katrina that affected New Orleans, Louisiana, in 2005.

Natural and Unnatural Disasters Impacting Human Needs

A neglected area in human behavior and the social environment is the impact of natural and unnatural disasters on human behaviors in both rural and urban communities. Human rights violations, such as genocide, ethnic cleansing, and mass rape during civil conflicts, are unnatural disasters negatively impacting humans' well-being. Also, major events such as earthquakes, tornadoes, hurricanes, floods, and terrorist activities can have serious impacts on individuals and communities. Although the federal government and community agencies provide assistance to people who have experienced a natural disaster, the federal government cannot make people "whole" like they were before the disaster. A few researchers have studied the impact of various disasters on individuals' mental health and domestic violence. Thompson, Norris, and Hanacek (1993) studied the impact of Hurricane Hugo, a Category 5 hurricane that killed 70 people and caused almost $14 billion in damages in 1989. They found that middle-aged people experienced the most distress (Thompson et al., 1993). Frasier et al. (2004) investigated the incidents of domestic violence in a North Carolina community after Hurricane Floyd in 1999. They observed that resources were scarce and urged policymakers to be cognizant of subgroups who were more vulnerable to disaster effects. After a flood in St. Louis, Missouri, several researchers found differential effects for types of families (i.e., marital and parental status) (Solomon, Bravo, Rubio-Stipec, & Canino, 1993). After the terrorist attack on New York on September 11, 2001, a group of researchers was interested in the impact of the attack on psychosocial variables for pregnant women who use alcohol and drugs. After 9/11, this sample of pregnant women with a history of alcohol dependence perceived that they had less social support compared to other women. The researchers concluded that their study was the first to investigate the psychosocial impact of 9/11 on pregnant women. Other researchers studied the impact of 9/11 on workers and volunteers for the Red Cross and their use of alcohol after the terrorist attack (Simons, Gaher, Jacobs, Meyer, & Johnson-Jimenez, 2005). This study consisted of 6,055 workers, 64% of whom were women (Simons et al., 2005). The researchers found a functional relationship between posttraumatic stress symptoms and alcohol consumption. An individual's coping with traumatic stress symptoms may manifest itself in decreased or increased alcohol use (Simons et al., 2005).

WORLD SYSTEMS THEORY AS CONCEPTUAL FRAMEWORK

World systems theory is useful in understanding the many issues involved in a macro perspective of human behavior and the social environment. Although world systems theory's initial focus was on systems external to a country, Chase-Dunn (2001, p. 590) asserts that "all the human interaction networks small and large, from the household to global trade, constitute the world system." Chase-Dunn (2001) has used world systems theory to explain human evolution over the past 12,000 years. During these 12,000 years, all large and small world systems have had "culturally different groups trade, fight, and make alliances with one another in ways that importantly condition processes of social change" (Chase-Dunn, 2001, p. 601). Some theorists attribute the development of the modern world systems to Western Europe between 1450 and 1640 (Hall, 2001). Capitalists and merchants during this period sought raw materials, labor, and markets. Their needs spurred increased trade networks and "often led to colonization of many areas of the world" (Hall, 2001, p. 5).

What Is World Systems Theory?

As a framework, the world systems perspective provides an understanding and an explanation for large-scale social change over a very long period of time. At first, its conceptualization was to provide knowledge of the patterns of development involving European hegemony since the 1400s. The world systems perspective has two central propositions:

1. Societies are importantly constrained and affected by their interactions with one another.

2. The modern world system has been structured as a core/periphery hierarchy in which economically and militarily powerful core states have dominated and exploited less powerful peripheral regions as the Europe-centered system expanded to incorporate all the areas of the globe. (Chase-Dunn & Ford, 1999, p. xi)

Simply, modern societies are viewed as core, semiperiphery, and periphery. The **core societies** are the most dominant economically, technologically, and militarily. The **periphery societies** are the least advanced economically, technologically, and militarily. The **semiperiphery societies** are in between the core societies and the periphery societies.

World systems theory may be artificially discussed in terms of "structure" and "dynamics." Structure concerns the characteristics of the system, its components, and the many relationships among these components. Dynamics is the process of structural change. General features of structure include capitalism and the interstate system or political system. In focusing on capitalism, world systems theory principally examines societies based on capitalism. Economic and political relationships emanate from these systems. These relationships within the world system occur among certain key components: economic zones, nation-states, social classes, and status groups. Status groups and social groupings coalesce from cultural identification. Further, religion, language, race, and ethnicity may form the basis for this identification (Shannon, 1992).

As recounted by Chase-Dunn (2001), the dynamics of the interactions among classes shapes the competition among states and capitalists and the amount of resistance put forth by the periphery and semiperiphery societies against dominance by the core societies. Understanding the history of social change as a whole requires knowledge of the strategies employed by the periphery and semiperiphery societies to resist the domination by the core and the strategies employed by the core societies to subdue the periphery and semiperiphery societies. Relatively new, world systems theory has been modified and now addresses issues more central to macro systems. See Figure 1.3 below. These zones could also reflect domestic and international communities.

Figure 1.3   A Perspective on Developed and Developing Societies

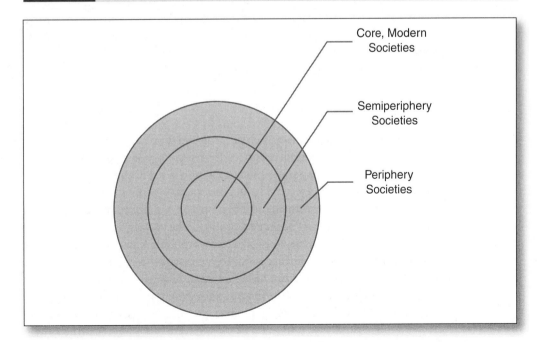

As indicated by world systems theory, the interactions and development of societies are a dynamic process. A society or country may be dominant at one point in history, but its dominance may significantly decline or even disappear later (Anderson & Chase-Dunn, 2005). For instance, Rome or the Roman Empire was once dominant and represented a core state or society. Many years ago, Iraq had a very advanced society with streetlights and sidewalks in its cities when Europe was much less advanced. Egypt, at one time, had a dominant society, and some of the African societies were well advanced, such as Nubia and Ethiopia. In the 1600s and until 1750, England, France, and Spain were the primary hegemonic world powers (Dunaway, 2000). Presently, the core states or societies are the United States, France, Great Britain, and Russia. In 2005, Anderson and Chase-Dunn declared that the semiperiphery consists of Mexico, India, Brazil, and China. The periphery consists presently of most African countries and poor countries in South America and Asia.

World systems' basic structure has not changed much, but it has evolved throughout history. From a world systems perspective, the study of these system dynamics is actually a theory of modern history or an explanation of social changes from early society to modern society. Emphasis is directed at trends, cycles, and an expansion of movement up or down economically by societies in different zones. In a capitalist economy, the fundamental imperative is an incessant effect to amass more capital. One way to amass more capital is to intensify worker exploitation. During periods of economic downturns and lowering profits, the drive to exploit workers increases dramatically due to pressures to keep costs down. As a consequence, capitalists become more creative in developing better exploitation tactics. Thus, the longest trend in capitalist systems is the exploitation of workers, for without exploitation, the world system would not have persisted for over 500 years (Shannon, 1992).

Broadening and Deepening

The exploitation trend consists of broadening and deepening. **Broadening** is the expansion of capitalist economic efforts into new geographic regions. It occurs through the process of incorporation. Incorporation is the extent of a core society including a periphery society within the core society's economic activities. One world systems theorist documented the incorporation of the indigenous population in the southwestern United States, delineating "the nature of the area being incorporated and its people's response to that incorporation fundamentally shaped the incorporation process and its long-term consequences" (Shannon, 1992, p. 129). Dunaway (2000, p. 206), in her study of Cherokee women, stated that "when the capitalist world system incorporates a new frontier, dramatic social changes are set in motion." Detailing some of these effects of incorporations,

Dunaway reported that European trade companies were making 500% to 600% profit on deerskins that were provided by Cherokee hunters who were paid little. Often, the Cherokees were forced into debt peonage, and unpaid debts from one individual were seized from members of the clan (Dunaway, 2000). If a Cherokee died owing debts, those debts became the responsibility of relatives to pay off (Dunaway, 2000). Simply put, Native Americans have never recovered from their incorporation. Their way of life was fundamentally changed, and they were put on reservations where some Native Americans still live today.

Researchers agree that incorporation affected Native Americans, and studies show that tribal conflicts increased as Native Americans came in contact with Whites. Contact and low levels of incorporation led to increased regional violence and made the violence more virulent. As Hall (2001) wrote, incorporation can fragment or amalgamate subordinate groups. The transformation process from an autonomous nonstate society (such as a Native American society) to a subordinate ethnic group is intricate, and identities, cultures, and social organizations are significantly altered (Hall, 2001). In studying the Navajo, Hall (2000) contended that he found similarities with other researchers who studied the incorporation of other Native American groups.

Presently, one might assert that the United States is attempting to incorporate Iraq. Numerous professionals and statespersons, such as former President Jimmy Carter, have stated that the war in Iraq is not about freedom or the freeing of Iraqis from a dictator and tyrant. Instead, it is about the fact that Iraq sits on the second largest supply of oil in the world, which the United States and other industrialized nations need. The people in Iraq who have been labeled as insurgents could be understood from a world systems perspective as resisting domination by a core state, America.

The degree of incorporation functions as a dependent variable and is explained by four independent variables: (a) the relative economic or military strength of the core state in comparison to the area being incorporated, (b) the social conditions (e.g., social structure) and the level of economic development and type of state formation (or lack thereof) in the area being incorporated, (c) the extent and nature of the indigenous resistance to incorporation, and (d) the general level of development of the world system itself at the time of incorporation.

On the other hand, **deepening** occurs when capitalist economic relationships spread to more areas of life within world systems societies. Deepening involves several associated processes—commodification, mechanization, contractualization, interdependence, and increased polarization (see Table 1.3). Commodification is the increased production of goods available as property to be sold, bought, and possessed. Mechanization, the use of more and better machinery to increase the output of workers, facilitates commodification. With deepening exploitation, social and economic relationships are contractualized, or regulated with formal legal agreements. As deepening occurs, a very specialized division of labor emerges to feed the exchange of highly prized goods that traders see as very profitable, resulting in the interdependence of the different labor sectors. As Shannon (1992) put it, deepening causes increased polarization and increased dissimilarity by the periphery and core in the areas of wealth and state organization behaviors. Because of this inequality and different types of exploitation, economic surplus flows to the core and does not stay with the periphery. Moreover, "wage-levels in the core are higher because more workers have had their labor completely commodified so that they are full proletarians whose wages are sufficient to reproduce their labor. Conversely, in the periphery, more of the labor force has been converted into superexploited semi-proletarians. . . . This conversion actually has led to lower real living standards than had prevailed before. The difference in the accumulated wealth and income levels between the core and the periphery has steadily increased" (Shannon, 1992, p. 130).

In the semiperiphery, a lesser degree of industrialization and urbanization exists. Many semiperiphery states have become newly industrialized countries. While some members of semiperiphery countries have enjoyed increased wealth and higher incomes, extreme poverty and landlessness among most of the population still exist in these countries. Ethnic, religious, and regional hostilities are common and sometimes affect political and economic processes. Many semiperiphery states have close relationships with core corporations. Semiperiphery states seek to achieve rapid industrialization. However, when capital and expertise are insufficient to reach that goal, multinational corporations from the core form joint ventures and other collaborative unions with state or local capitalists from the semiperiphery. Then, the state will utilize different types of repressive strategies to keep wages low and ensure harsh working conditions and poor living conditions. These repressive practices explain the need for and the existence of the military to help maintain this hierarchical structure (Shannon, 1992).

The core has long exploited the periphery and made the periphery dependent upon it. This is even more so since the fall of the Soviet Union. Some periphery countries were able to get economic aid from the Soviet Union, but they can no longer do so. During the 20th century, the periphery was forced to solicit economic assistance in the form of loans from the Western core and core-controlled financial institutions. Thus, the periphery has incurred a lot of debt and has been forced by the core to restructure its economic policies to favor the core. As Shannon (1992, p. 101) wrote, "the restructuring policies had a profound effect on living conditions in the most indebted countries." Researchers have documented that restructured policies have led to negative impacts on child survival, childhood immunization, nutrition, economic growth, and urban problems (Shannon, 1992).

Table 1.3	Five Processes Associated With Deepening
Commodification	The increased production of goods available as property to be sold, bought, and possessed
Mechanization	The use of more and better machinery to increase the output of workers
Contractualization	The process of formally sanctioning and regulating exploitation
Interdependence	The dependency between different labor markets to produce goods profitable to the core
Polarization	A schism between the core and the periphery due to deepening of the economic relationship between the two

Use of World Systems Theory in the Literature

Hall (1999) summarized different areas explored by researchers who used a world systems framework. Included in his summarizations were (a) cyclical processes in the world system; (b) the consequences of the collapse of the Soviet Union; (c) cities in the world systems; (d) women, households, and gender in the world economy; (e) the role of culture in the world economy; and (f) subsistence. The latter three have strong implications for human behavior in the social environment. Further supplying linkages to human behavior and the social environment, Kardulias (1999) stressed that the world systems perspective provides scholars from interdisciplinary fields with a framework for studying different cultures, past and present, as they interact(ed) politically, economically, and socially. The world systems model provides a framework to study these cultural interactions, which can be mutually beneficial, but often the results were exploitative.

World systems theory is also referred to as dependency theory. Dependency theory holds that economic differences exist among states in the core and periphery, with states in the periphery dependent upon the more economically developed states in the core (Santos, 1971; Sunkel, 1969). Mullen, Beller, Remsa, and Cooper (2001) wrote an article titled "The Effects of International Trade on Economic Growth and Meeting Basic Human Needs," drawing the connection between world systems theory and human needs. McIntosh (1996) presented statistical evidence on the relationship between world-dependency effects and human needs. McIntosh examined measures of human needs consisting of child mortality, crude death rates, infant mortality, life expectancy, food availability, and immunization. McIntosh (1996, p. 132) found that "dependency lowers the rate of economic growth, illustrating the difficulty low-income countries have in escaping the periphery. At the same time, life chances, measured as life expectancy, infant mortality, and per capita food availability, varied in a manner predicted by the dependency hypothesis." Simply put, the more states in the periphery that are dependent upon more economically developed states in the core, the higher the infant mortality rate and the less food available for people in the periphery.

More recently, world systems theory has been adapted to encompass issues of gender and racism. One proponent of world systems theory found "that as peripheral countries have come to be more integrated into the world economy, women in those countries have come to be more relegated to the least rewarding tasks in the informal sector of the economy. Men, in contrast, increasingly participated in the formal sector as wage laborers and/or in the more remunerative forms of informal sector work" (Shannon, 1992, p. 188). As a consequence, the lower economic status of periphery women is connected to these women's continued high fertility (Shannon, 1992). Economic development of periphery women has exacerbated the relative status of women and produced conditions conducive to higher fertility, which is the reverse of those for women in the core (Shannon, 1992).

Other proponents of the world systems approach have studied the role of women in the households of world systems. Households receive five types of income, consisting of wages, profits from market sales, rental income from property, transfer payments (e.g., state welfare benefits), and products from subsistence activities (Shannon, 1992). As revealed by Shannon (1992, p. 189), "core households tend to receive the greatest proportion of their income from wages transfer payments, although even they receive significant income from the other sources. Peripheral households, in contrast, rarely can even come close to surviving from wages received. Consequently, they employ household members in extensive nonwage income producing activities in the informal sector, including major subsistence activities. These patterns of household income production reflect the differing roles and requirements in the world economy of the periphery, semiperiphery, and core."

Shannon (1992) discussed internal aspects of the periphery, semiperiphery, and core. Within the core, the capitalist class exercises a disproportionate amount of influence but is amenable to influence as long as no radical changes are sought that threaten its interests. As a result, more political participation has occurred among the working middle class. Shannon noted that the middle class in the core plays a significant role in who is elected to political offices. As a result, the middle class can bear upon these elected politicians to enact policies beneficial to them or to block policies that are not beneficial to them. From time to time, the middle classes will support some policies opposed by the capitalist classes. In foreign affairs, the middle class is indifferent, for the most part, but it has opposed military action in the periphery when the military action did not end quickly, such as the French's involvement in Algeria (Shannon, 1992). Shannon's argument is further supported by the Iraq war, which enjoyed very high public support at its commencement in 2003 but very low support in 2007, as the war dragged on with no end in sight.

Rationale for Use of World Systems Theory

Many of the principal proponents of world systems theory are Marxists, and their views of systems issues, especially economic and labor discussions, are critical in nature. But this book uses world systems theory not to coerce students into becoming Marxists but because it provides a useful framework for understanding social institutions, organizations, and communities as well as problems that affect human needs issues that those entities seek to address. Some of the key concepts in world systems theory are the core, semiperiphery, and periphery zones, with most of the power greatest in the core zone and the least in the periphery zone. These zones may be envisioned as similar to social environments. For instance, Shannon (1992) used the concepts of core, semiperiphery, and periphery to study household incomes. One could use these same concepts to understand other macro issues, such as families, organizations, social institutions, and communities within the core, semiperiphery, and periphery. Further, world systems theory provides an explanation for immigration, which is not a new concept and has been occurring since people emerged on this planet, and terrorism, especially terrorism perpetrated by individuals from the periphery. For example, Chase-Dunn (2001) graphed a world systems model that resembles the graph in Figure 1.4.

The Connection of World Systems Theory to Macro Human Behavior in the Social Environment

Shannon's (1992) perspective of world systems theory provides a connection to and understanding of a macro view of HBSE and the discussions that follow. As you recall from the beginning of this chapter, a juror from a suburban community expressed a lack of knowledge about the lives of people who were witnesses in a case that arose from a poor community. In effect, this juror was from the core, and the witnesses were from the periphery. The concepts of core,

Figure 1.4   The Evolution of Societies

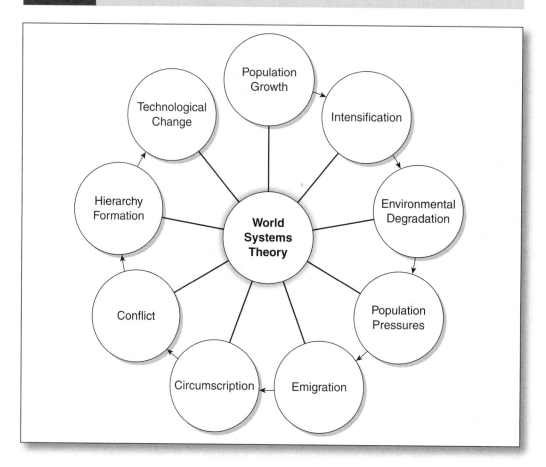

semiperiphery, and periphery zones provide tools for understanding macro systems. Researchers have studied households in the core, semiperiphery, and periphery zones. Within these zones, researchers may examine urban, rural, and international communities. So, we could understand and process data about core, semiperiphery, and periphery zones just in urban areas, rural areas, or international areas or across all three areas.

In a similar manner, communities and neighborhoods may be understood as representing core, semiperiphery, and periphery zones. Communities within the core have more power and influence than communities within the periphery, just like countries within the core have more power than countries within the periphery. Further, world systems theory addresses central issues like conflict (i.e., world wars and civil wars), emigration, and environmental degradation

(Chase-Dunn, 2001; Chew, 2005). As an example, Chew (2005) reported the environmental and climatic changes in Mesopotamia and Egypt from 2200 BC to 700 BC. Bergesen and Bartely (2000) wrote a chapter for a world systems book and had a section entitled Environmental Degradation. In this section, they reported that semiperiphery states have permitted more deforestation historically than periphery states (Bergesen & Bartely, 2000). Immigration may be understood from a world systems perspective, as may the relocation of businesses to Mexico, Central America, and China and the resulting impact on neighborhoods and communities in the United States. For the purposes of this textbook, the macro systems are shown in Figure 1.5.

Chase-Dunn (2001) declared that all small and large human networks from the household to global trade make up world systems theory. Figure 1.5 illustrates how human beings are connected to various systems. An individual

Figure 1.5   The Macro Perspective for This Textbook

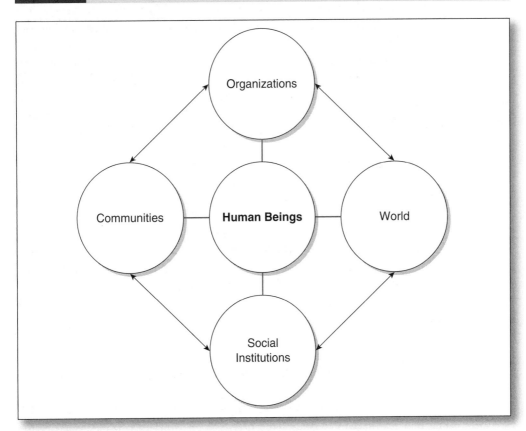

or a human being is connected to his or her family; groups, such as a gang or school band; an organization, such as the National Association for the Advancement of Colored People or the National Organization for Women; and a social organization, such as a church, mosque, or synagogue. Most humans have a connection to all four systems shown in the figure. They affect these systems, and these systems affect them.

This textbook focuses on the macro (social institutions, organizations, and communities) as opposed to the **micro** (individuals, families, and groups), but the family is discussed here as it is a major social institution. As the depiction above shows, however, these systems are interrelated. World systems theory provides a framework for understanding the impact of macro systems on micro systems and vice versa. Take the concept of deepening, which is, in part, the governing of social and economic relationships through formal legal mandates. A growing number of macro institutions consisting of state legislatures (law), concerned communities (communities), and law enforcement agencies (organizations) have adopted and enforced statutes to notify the community when a sex offender moves within a neighborhood. This type of legislation has been hailed as a tool to protect children from sexual predators. Macro laws can affect micro systems, and these laws' impact on micro systems is nebulous and may be ineffective (Cohen, 2003). For instance, the law that outlawed drinking alcohol in 1919, the Volstead Act or Prohibition, provided the economic base for organized crime in America (Jensen, 2000). Further, when Prohibition was repealed, it led to a surge in violence (Jensen, 2000). The sex offender law has led to sometimes deadly physical assaults on individual offenders (Prentky, 1996). More important, research has failed to support the hypothesis that community notification protects children from sexual predators (Berliner, 1996). Some researchers have even postulated that community notification might lead parents to be less vigilant in protecting their children because the sexual abuse of children is more likely to occur from relatives, friends, and trusted community officials (i.e., coaches, priests, teachers, etc.) (Redlich, 2001).

At the same time, macro systems have undoubtedly had a positive effect on micro systems, such as individuals and families. Congress, a macro system, had a tremendous positive effect on alleviating the destitution of individuals during the Great Depression in the 1930s. In the 1960s, Congress passed laws creating Medicare and Medicaid—programs to provide health care for the poor and elderly persons.

President Barack Obama Illustrating the Conceptual Framework

In 2008, a majority of American voters elected Barack Obama as the 44th President of the United States, the first African American to be elected to the

Presidency. In reality, President Obama is biracial as his mother was White and reared in Kansas and his father was African and from Kenya. President Obama represents numerous themes and concepts reflected in this textbook. Principally, this book is about human needs and how these needs are addressed or not addressed by macro social institutions. For instance, President Obama disclosed that when he was a child, his mother received food stamps (Severson, 2008). As a twice-divorced woman, President Obama's mother received help from her parents as well as temporary assistance through the food stamps program (Fornek, 2007). In one campaign speech, President Obama recalled when discussing his mother that "there were times that she didn't have enough money for groceries. And even though she was very proud and very independent, there were a couple of times growing up where she accepted food stamps to make sure we had enough food on the table. It was tough. And it was pretty much tough all the way through my teenage years" (Levey, 2008, p. A-22). Because of these family difficulties, President Obama stated that his maternal grandparents helped rear him, and during his campaign, he often discussed publicly his grandmother. Moreover, President Obama related that his mother had died of cancer, and before her death he heard her on the telephone arguing with her insurance company about paying for her treatment.

President Obama, during the time he was a Harvard law student in the 1980s, worked as the director of the Developing Communities Project on Chicago's South Side as a community organizer. He was 24 years old when he was hired and was paid $13,000 a year in addition to $2,000 for a secondhand car (Moberg, 2007). After his graduation from law school, he continued for a period engaging in community organizing. At the Republican convention, Rudolph Giuliani and Sarah Palin ridiculed the nomination of President Obama by the Democrats, noting that he had worked as a community organizer (Malkin, 2008; York, 2008). Years earlier, a public school administrative aide had asked President Obama why he was wasting his time being a community organizer when he was studying law at such an elite school. President Obama (1990) related the woman's question and his response and explanation in his chapter "Why Organize? Problems and Promise in the Inner City" in Peg Knoepfle's book, *After Alinsky: Community Organizing in Illinois.*

In his chapter, President Obama (1990) discussed the needs of the urban and inner-city poor and how difficult these needs are to address. He noted that the election of a minority mayor, such as Mayor Richard Hatcher in Gary, Indiana, or Mayor Harold Washington in Chicago, does not mean that problems or needs will be easily addressed. A community organizer, according to President Obama, is vital in bringing together churches, block clubs, parent groups, and any other institutions in a given community to pay dues, hire organizers, engage in research, develop leadership, hold rallies, and conduct education campaigns.

Theoretically, community organizing offers a process for synthesizing multiple strategies for empowering neighborhoods. Community organizing assumes (a) that the problems of inner-city communities are not caused by the lack of effective solutions but by the lack of power to employ needed solutions, (b) that the sole way for communities to create enduring power is to organize people and money toward a common vision, and (c) that a viable organization can only be created when a broadly based indigenous leadership, not one or two inspiring leaders, molds the diverse interests of its local institutions (Obama, 1990). These activities are necessary to develop plans to address an assortment of issues, such as securing jobs, improving education, and fighting crimes (Obama, 1990).

Like this textbook, in 1990 President Obama discussed a number of macro social institutions, such as communities, churches, the news media, schools, the political system, and organizations, within his brief book chapter. President Obama (1990) noted that blatant discrimination has been replaced by institutional racism, that companies cannot compete internationally by basing themselves in the inner cities with their multitude of problems, and that the many stressors on families make volunteering by these families extremely difficult. In his 2007 article about President Obama, David Moberg disclosed a number of social institutions reflective of President Obama's history, including his work with faith-based organizations, neighborhoods, and groups. According to Moberg (2007), President Obama had helped train indigenous residents to become leaders, addressed landfills near some Chicago housing projects, helped win employment training services, helped create playgrounds, helped create after-school programs, and helped organized residents demand the removal of asbestos in their apartments and other public amenities.

At President Obama's inauguration, a number of balls were conducted that evening, and the first was called the Neighborhood Inaugural Ball, reflecting the inclusion of neighborhoods and communities in this festive occasion. Reportedly, many of the attendees at the Neighborhood Inaugural Ball were poor and/or homeless, and they were provided with gowns and tuxedos to wear at no charge, along with the renting of rooms at the Marriott hotel at no charge (Montet, 2009). The Stafford Foundation provided much of the assistance to the underprivileged attending the Neighborhood Inaugural Ball. According to its Web site, "the Stafford Foundation is a faith-based non-profit organization founded on promoting the principles of Jesus Christ. We are focused on bringing people of good will together to help the underserved, the marginalized and the distressed and assisting them in helping themselves, and eventually to help others. We believe that by investing in the hopes and dreams, the abilities and the potential of the less privileged, our communities and our nation will benefit. For in the bank of life is not good that investment which surely pays the highest and most cherished dividends?" (The Stafford Foundation, 2009, p. 1). These macro social institutions are reflected in the following chapters.

CONCLUSION

This chapter began with a discussion of how some individuals live in one environment and have no idea about the environments in which other individuals live, although these environments may be only a few miles apart. However, disturbances in one environment may have an impact on other environments, regardless of the distance between them. This chapter defined social work and the requirements of HBSE courses, including CSWE's mandate that international content be included within social work courses. We provided a depiction of the connection of individuals to other systems and stated that the focus of this book is macro HBSE, consisting primarily of social institutions, organizations, and communities, broadly speaking. In addition, a discussion was provided involving human rights and how the violation of human rights falls within HBSE. The world systems perspective was offered as a conceptual framework appropriate for understanding macro institutions' impact on individuals. Finally, this chapter discussed President Barack Obama's early life and his life as a young community organizer to show the numerous macro social institutions reflected in his life and his work.

Key Terms and Concepts

Broadening

Community attachment

Core societies

Council on Social Work Education (CSWE)

Deepening

Human rights

Just society

Macro

Micro

Needs

Periphery societies

Semiperiphery societies

Social environment

Social functioning

Social work

Structural violence

Universal Declaration of Human Rights

Unjust society

World systems theory

CHAPTER 2

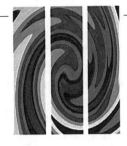

Human Needs and Problems Requiring Responses From Organizations, Institutions, and Communities

INTRODUCTION

This chapter is intended to provide you with a conceptualization of the type and range of problems affecting macro systems. However, this chapter will focus primarily on problems and needs of families, categories, and communities since society's negative effects on groups, organizations, and institutions are relatively minimal. For instance, society does not have a significant impact, economically or socially, on groups such as the Young Republicans on a college campus or organizations such as the American Medical Association or the U.S. Chamber of Commerce. The U.S. Chamber of Commerce exerts a tremendous amount of pressure on the legislative and executive processes (Birnbaum, 2005); it spent $30 million on lobbying in the first half of 2004, prompting Common Cause to state that the system is unfair for the average person who cannot lobby in this manner. Simply, lobbying leads to access to politicians to advocate for an organization's interests, and sometimes donations to politicians are given in exchange for promises to support or oppose legislation. However, society positively and negatively affects families, categories, and communities.

Stolley (2005) distinguishes between groups and categories. A **group** is an assembly of individuals who interact regularly, have a mutual sense of identity, and have a sense of belonging. On the other hand, a **category** is a collection of individuals who share a common status or characteristic(s) (Stolley, 2005). It is rare that society targets and thus increases social and economic pressures on groups like the Young Republicans or a chapter of Mothers Against Drunk Driving. However, throughout history, radical groups and organizations have been targeted, such as the Black Panthers and the Weathermen from the 1960s and 1970s.

The Black Panther Party was formed in 1966 by Bobby Seale and Huey P. Newton. Its early mission was to protect Black people from police brutality and harassment. It also provided free breakfast programs and other social services in the community. Chapters of the Black Panthers spread, and shoot-outs between the Black Panthers and law enforcement occurred in California, Illinois, and New York. Estimates were that over 20 Black Panthers were killed and a number were sent to prison in various confrontations (Robinson, 2004). Consisting of mostly middle-class White females and males, the Weathermen were a violent group that sprang from the Students for a Democratic Society, which severely disrupted the 1968 Democratic National Convention in Chicago. A spokesperson for the Weathermen stated that nonviolence was an excuse for people not to struggle and to acquiesce to the power structure. Members made bombs and blew up more than 20 American structures, including a portion of the New York City Police Department and the barbershop at the U.S. Capitol. Combining with members of the Black Liberation Army, members of the Weathermen robbed an armored car in 1981 of over $1.5 million, which was to help fund the liberation of Black people in America. Both the Black Panthers and the Weathermen fought the perceived power structure, killing some police officers in the process. However, neither of these types of groups really exists in today's society as both advocated for revolution.

Moreover, there is a history of categories of people being targeted for increased burdens and sometimes discrimination. For instance, single mothers receiving public assistance have been demonized. Recall that Ronald Reagan rose to prominence in California by campaigning against the "welfare queen." At one time, gays and lesbians were diagnosed as having mental disorders just for being homosexual. Drug dealers and "crack" users were subjected to significant penal sanctions. Formerly incarcerated felons who had paid their debts to society were barred from voting and disqualified from securing lawful employment. Individuals who are homeless have been harassed by local governments. As an example, city leaders adopted a new policy for addressing the homeless population on Skid Row in Los Angeles. Roughly 50 blocks in size, Skid Row houses between 8,000 and 10,000 homeless persons, and the new policy calls for them not to be rousted from their tents and cardboard homes as long as they remove their homes by 6 a.m. ("L.A. Putting Homeless Issues on Back Burner to Tackle Crime," 2006). Thus, for social work students and professionals committed to social justice, categories may be more important than groups. This is so because a group may contain 10 to 12 individuals or 50. But a category is a significant large collection of individuals, such as all the undocumented Latinos in the United States (i.e., 12 million), all the gay people in the United States, or all the individuals incarcerated for drugs or nonviolent crimes. Intervention aimed at alleviating the burdens of and discrimination against categories of individuals has more of an impact than it does when aimed at a group.

The Americans with Disabilities Act (1990) has been hailed as a vitally important piece of legislation affecting social welfare policy. It can be understood as the product of two social institutions. It can also be viewed as a congressional effort, which was later endorsed by the courts as constitutional, to help a category of individuals who were ignored and discriminated against by society. Congress conducted hearings, listening to individuals and organizations and detailing statistics and findings for this category of citizens. Besides being a social welfare policy issue, the Americans with Disabilities Act was also an effort by Congress to help Americans with disabilities, and this is human behavior in the social environment too. Congress recognized a category of Americans in need and passed legislation to assist them. In addition, the courts got involved and determined whether certain disabilities fell within the parameters of the Americans with Disabilities Act, such as substance abuse or addictions or health problems like high blood pressure (*Hodgens v. General Dynamics Corporation*, 1998) and diabetes (*Darnell v. Thermafiber*, 2005; *Nordwall v. Sears Roebuck*, 2002). Assessments were conducted to ascertain the extent of the helpfulness of this legislation for individuals with disabilities.

Legislation, however, cannot always address the needs of families, categories, and communities because these needs are very difficult to alleviate. Some of these needs arise from nature and can only be explained by physical science or, for some people, God. Some have linked floods and plagues or diseases to divine forces. But modern science offers a more knowledgeable explanation for these phenomena. Regardless of one's belief system, no one can doubt the very destructive forces of major disasters and diseases existing and occurring in the environment. They lead, and have led, to the deaths of millions of people throughout history, destroying families, communities, and societies.

Although natural disasters have caused great misery and destruction throughout human history, the miseries and destruction caused by individuals have been far, far greater. Genocides, wars, ethnic cleansings, slavery, and crimes have been very destructive to humankind. Early social workers were instrumental in persuading Congress to pass legislation barring the sexual exploitation of young women and, in 1910, to pass the White-Slave Traffic Act. Yet, the National Institute of Justice (2005) announced a grant opportunity for a study of a demonstration project in Atlanta, Georgia, involving the commercial sexual exploitation of children, including pornography, prostitution, and smuggling of minors for unlawful purposes. Troubled and victimized in their families or communities, some children in the Atlanta area had been targeted by persons seeking to use them sexually for profit. In some extreme cases, children have been bought and sold in a murky sex industry. The long-term physical and emotional injuries from commercial sexual exploitation of children have implications for these children when they become adults and for the criminal justice system that must deal with some of them should the aftereffects of sexual exploitation lead them to criminal acts.

After World War II, the United Nations declared that it would never allow genocide again. But genocide has occurred, as it did in the 1990s in Bosnia and Africa. Further, women and girls from poor countries in the Balkans and Mexico have been and are being sold as sex slaves. In 2000, Congress passed the Victims of Trafficking and Violence Protection Act. Estimates are that 600,000 to 800,000 victims are trafficked globally each year, and 18,000 to 20,000 are trafficked to the United States (U.S. Department of Justice, 2009). The problem has become so serious that Congress created the Human Smuggling and Trafficking Center. Some of these women have been found in major cities of the United States (Ribando, 2007). Debates have occurred about the causes of human trafficking, and poverty is often cited. However, many social scientists and scholars attribute and link poverty to social inequality, which is a condition created by human beings in positions of power over other human beings.

All of these problems, both natural and human-made, affect families, groups, organizations, institutions, and communities. Lives are lost, homes are destroyed, families are severely disrupted, and communities are made unstable. Terrorism, which at one time was believed to be an international problem, is now a domestic problem as a result of the bombing of the federal building in Oklahoma and the attack by the 9/11 terrorists. While many Americans have put up a brave face and declared that they will not let the terrorists "win" by altering American society, significant changes have occurred. Americans have fewer rights today than they had before the attack on 9/11. Security experts say that they cannot prevent attacks on American soil and that Americans must be aware because it is only a matter of time before another will occur. The effect of this alertness is that Americans are subjected to false alarms and hoaxes (Hays, 2005), elevating their anxieties. Moreover, there are security costs associated with these false alarms and hoaxes that adversely affect organizations—law enforcement, transit, and governing bodies.

Undoubtedly, in the United States, poverty, social inequality and discrimination, crime, disasters, and terrorism have major short-term and long-term effects on the collective mental health of families and communities. Depression, posttraumatic stress disorders, and sometimes suicides occur among direct victims and indirect or collateral victims as a result of these problems. Similar problems in international communities such as poverty, famine, civil wars, genocide and ethnic cleansings, and terrorism have a cataclysmic effect on people in developing countries. Many of these problems constitute violations of human rights as declared and ratified by the United Nations.

Questions have been raised about the appropriateness of using clinical measures on populations in developing countries. Though some of the problems are the same, human beings in developing countries, because of their cultural beliefs, may have different mental health difficulties than people in a highly developed society, such as in the United States. For instance, Sudan militants forced individuals in Darfur to leave their homes, and these individuals who fled were not able to perform burial rituals of murdered relatives according to their customs. Their inability to perform these burial rituals increased their mental anguish. Also, in Bosnia, the Muslim community shunned Muslim women who were raped and impregnated by the Serbs in rape camps after the genocide and ethnic cleansing ended. Similarly, relatives and the community shunned and rejected African women in Darfur after they were raped and impregnated by Arab militia. While women who have been sexually assaulted in the United States have access to medical and psychological services, women in war-torn developing countries have virtually nothing. This chapter explores all these problems and issues, beginning first with the United States and then discussing other countries.

POVERTY IN THE UNITED STATES AND INTERNATIONAL COMMUNITIES

Overall Poverty

In 1964, Mollie Orshansky of the Social Security Administration (SSA) devised a definition to measure **poverty** in the United States. The Bureau of Budget, later to become the Office of Management and Budget, established this definition as the official measure of poverty for statistical use for all federal agencies. This original poverty definition created a number of income cutoffs or thresholds that were adjusted by family size, sex of the family head, number of children under 18 years old, and farm-nonfarm residences. The crux of the definition of poverty was the economy food plan (i.e., the major food groups and the amounts for each) established by the Department of Agriculture for the least costly nutritionally sufficient plan for a family of four. Based on findings from the Department of Agriculture's 1955 Household Food Consumption Survey, one third of the amount spent by a family of three or more after taxes went for food. As a result, the poverty thresholds for families of three or more people were fixed at three times the price for the least costly nutritionally sufficient food plan. For two-person families and single-person homes, different procedures were established to adjust for differences in outlays for food. Using the 1955 survey results, the cost of the nutritionally sufficient food plan for a two-person family was multiplied by a factor of 3.7. For single persons, no multiplier was used, and their poverty was determined by a fixed proportion of the two-person family's threshold. Each year, the Department of Agriculture revised the poverty thresholds based on changes of prices for items in the economy food plan or, stated differently, on inflation as determined by the Consumer Price Index (U.S. Census Bureau, 2004).

Poverty is discussed extensively here because it is correlated with a number of other human needs and often exacerbates other problems. For example, poverty is linked to amputations for people suffering from diabetes and blindness due to diabetes. While middle-class and upper-class persons suffer from blindness and amputations from diabetes, the poor have the highest rate of these maladies. Further, poverty is also linked to the higher rate of infant mortality among the poor. In the area of education, poverty is associated with children dropping out of school. For these reasons, as well as others, different aspects of poverty are presented below to give students full knowledge of the characteristics of poverty in the United States.

The U.S. Census Bureau released statistics for people and families in poverty by selected characteristics in the year 2006. Table 2.1 includes selected characteristics, data in thousands, and percentages. These percentages are based on the total population. For instance, the total number of persons in poverty in 2006 was 36,460,000, and this represented 12.3% of all persons in the United States. About 24% of African Americans and about 21% of Latinos were in poverty. Most of the poverty in the United States was located in the South. Females who did not have husbands had significant poverty, 28%. See Table 2.1.

Table 2.1 People and Families in Poverty by Selected Characteristics for 2006

People	In Thousands	%
Total	36,460	12.3
Family Status		
In Families	25,915	10.6
Head of Household	7,668	9.8
Related Children Under 18	12,299	16.9
Related Children Under 6	4,830	20.0
In Unrelated Subfamilies	567	41.5
Reference Person	229	40.4
Children Under 18	323	44.9
Unrelated Individuals	9,977	20.0
Male	4,388	17.8
Female	5,589	22.2
Race		
White	24,416	10.3
White, not Hispanic	16.013	8.2

(Continued)

Table 2.1 (Continued)

People	In Thousands	%
Black	9,048	24.3
Asian	1,353	10.3
Hispanic Origin, Any Race	9,243	20.6
Age		
Under 18 Years	12,827	17.4
18 to 64 Years	20,239	10.8
65 and Over	3,394	9.4
Nativity		
Native	30,790	11.9
Foreign Born	5,670	15.2
Naturalized Citizen	1,345	9.3
Not a Citizen	4,324	19.0
Region		
Northeast	6,222	11.5
Midwest	7,324	11.2
South	14,882	13.8
West	8,032	11.6
Metropolitan Status		
Inside Metro Statistical Areas	29,283	11.8
Inside Principal Cities	15,336	16.1
Outside Principal Areas	13,947	9.1
Outside Metro Statistical Areas	7,177	15.2

People	In Thousands	%
Work Experience		
All Workers 16 and Over	9,181	5.8
Worked Full-Time	2,906	2.7
Worked Part-Time	6,275	12.6
Did Not Work at Least 1 Week	15,715	21.1
Families		
Total	7,668	9.8
Type of Family		
Married Couples	2,910	4.9
Female Head of Household, No Husband	4,087	28.3
Male Head of Household, No Wife	671	13.2

The data and tables on poverty that follow are older than the data in Table 2.1. But these data are for categories not presented above. They are provided to give a fuller picture of poverty in the United States among categories of people. At the time of the 2000 census, 12.4% of the U.S. population was below the poverty level, 16.1% of children were in poverty, 9.9% of persons 65 and over were in poverty, and 9.2% of all families were in poverty (U.S. Census Bureau, 2005).

Compiled from the U.S. Census Bureau in 2005, Table 2.2 lists the top 10 states and territories for the percentages of various categories in poverty. While social workers are concerned about the overall percentage of people in poverty, they are especially concerned about children under 18 years of age and elderly persons 65 and over. These data show that Puerto Rico has the highest percentage of people in poverty, the highest number of children under 18 in poverty, and the most individuals 65 and over in poverty.

For children under 18 years old, both the rate and the number of children in poverty remained the same from 2003 to 2004 (see Table 2.3 for 2004 poverty rates by state). For each year since 2000 to 2004, both the rate and

Table 2.2 Top 10 States and Territories for Percentages in Poverty for Various Groups

Overall in Poverty		Under 18 in Poverty		65 and Over in Poverty	
Puerto Rico	48	Puerto Rico	58	Puerto Rico	44
District of Columbia	20	Washington, DC	31	Mississippi	19
Louisiana	20	Mississippi	27	Louisiana	17
Mississippi	20	Louisiana	26	District of Columbia	16
New Mexico	18	New Mexico	25	Alabama	16
West Virginia	18	West Virginia	25	Arkansas	14
Alabama	16	Alabama	21	Georgia	14
Arkansas	16	Arkansas	21	South Carolina	14
Kentucky	16	Texas	20	Tennessee	14
Texas	15	Kentucky	20	North Carolina	13

Table 2.3 Poverty Rate for 2004

Place	Number in Poverty	Rate of Poverty (%)
Mississippi	604,000	21.6
Louisiana	845,000	19.4
New Mexico	358,000	19.3
District of Columbia	98,000	18.9
Arkansas	476,000	17.9
West Virginia	317,000	17.9
Kentucky	700,000	17.4
Texas	3,625,000	16.6
Alabama	706,000	16.1
South Carolina	635,000	15.7

Place	Number in Poverty	Rate of Poverty (%)
Oklahoma	520,000	15.3
North Carolina	1,256,000	15.2
Georgia	1,266,000	14.8
Idaho	196,000	14.5
Tennessee	830,000	14.5
Arizona	798,000	14.2
Montana	127,000	14.2
New York	2,641,000	14.2
Oregon	493,000	14.1
California	4,661,000	13.3
Washington	794,000	13.1
Rhode Island	132,000	12.8
Nevada	288,000	12.6
Ohio	1,388,000	12.5
Maine	157,000	12.3
Michigan	1,210,000	12.3
Florida	2,062,000	12.2
North Dakota	73,000	12.1
Illinois	1,474,000	11.9
Missouri	659,000	11.8
Pennsylvania	1,389,000	11.7
Colorado	498,000	11.1
Nebraska	186,000	11.0
South Dakota	81,000	11.0

(Continued)

Table 2.3 (Continued)

Place	Number in Poverty	Rate of Poverty (%)
Utah	256,000	10.9
Indiana	652,000	10.8
Wisconsin	571,000	10.7
Hawaii	129,000	10.6
Kansas	279,000	10.5
Wyoming	50,000	10.3
Delaware	80,000	9.9
Iowa	282,000	9.9
Virginia	682,000	9.5
Massachusetts	570,000	9.2
Vermont	54,000	9.0
Maryland	473,000	8.8
New Jersey	722,000	8.5
Minnesota	412,000	8.3
Alaska	52,000	8.2
Connecticut	257,000	7.6
New Hampshire	95,000	7.6
United States	37,162,000	13.1

Source: Compiled from *Income, Earnings, and Poverty From the 2004 American Community Survey,* by P. Fronczek, 2005, Washington, DC: U.S. Census Bureau.

the number of people in poverty overall increased in the United States. In terms of type of family and poverty, the poverty rate for a married couple increased very slightly—from 5.4% to 5.5%—from 2003 to 2004. There was a slight increase for single-parent females, from 28.0% to 28.4%, and single-parent males remained the same—13.5% (Walt, Proctor, & Lee, 2005).

Poverty and Gender

In 1999, as shown in Table 2.4, of all females in the United States, 7% were below the poverty line, compared to 5% of males. Among young people up to the age of 15, males are more likely to live in poverty. After the age of 15, a shift occurs, and more females live in poverty. A possible explanation for this shift may be the effects of females coming into childbearing age and the accompanying problems of single parenthood and perhaps later divorce.

Table 2.4   Gender and Poverty for 1999

Age (in years)	Male	Female
Under 5	1,743,703	1,668,322
5	354,679	334,985
6 to 11	2,111,555	2,037,018
12 to 14	890,569	863,539
15	297,525	295,849
16 to 17	570,123	578,991
18 to 24	2,198,398	2,900,186
25 to 34	1,833,858	2,714,689
35 to 44	1,789,400	2,446,340
45 to 54	1,263,254	1,556,084
55 to 64	899,124	1,263,847
65 to 74	544,372	1,006,597
75 and over	428,502	1,308,303

Poverty, Race, and Ethnicity in the United States

In 2003, the U.S. Census Bureau made available data for persons living in poverty sorted by race. In Table 2.5, race is divided into three categories—Asian or Pacific Islander, Non-Hispanic White, and Other. Other includes Mexican,

Table 2.5	Percentage of Persons in Poverty by Age Group and Race

	Asian or Pacific Islander		Non-Hispanic White		Other	
	Male	Female	Male	Female	Male	Female
Total	10%	10%	7%	9%	20%	24%
Under 18	12%	11%	10%	10%	29%	29%
18 to 64	9%	10%	6%	8%	15%	21%
65 and Over	14%	7%	5%	10%	17%	25%

Puerto Rican, Cuban, South or Central American, or Other Hispanic/Latino and African American. Twenty-two percent of persons in the Other category, 8% of Non-Hispanic Whites, and 10% of Asians or Pacific Islanders were in poverty. For persons under age 18, 29% were in poverty, as were 10% of Non-Hispanic Whites and 12% of Asians or Pacific Islanders. For persons between the ages of 18 and 64, 18% of Other, 7% of Non-Hispanic Whites, and 10% of Asian or Pacific Islanders were in poverty. For persons 65 and over, 22% of Other were in poverty, as were 8% of Non-Hispanic Whites. Looking just at males, 20% of Other, 7% of Non-Hispanic Whites, and 10% of Asians or Pacific Islanders were in poverty. For males under 18 years, 29% were below poverty, as were 10% of Non-Hispanic Whites and 12% of Asians or Pacific Islanders. For males between the ages of 18 and 64, 15% of Other, 6% of Non-Hispanic Whites, and 9% of Asians or Pacific Islanders were in poverty. For males 65 and over, 17% were in poverty, as were 5% of Non-Hispanic Whites and 14% of Asians or Pacific Islanders. For females, 24% were in poverty, as were 9% of Non-Hispanic Whites and 10% of Asians or Pacific Islanders. For females under age 18, 29% were in poverty, as were 10% of Non-Hispanic Whites and 11% of Asians or Pacific Islanders. For females between 18 and 64, 21% of Other, 8% of Non-Hispanic Whites, and 10% of Asians or Pacific Islanders were in poverty. For females 65 and over, 25% of Other were in poverty, as were 10% of Non-Hispanic Whites and 7% of Asians or Pacific Islanders (U.S. Census Bureau, 2003).

In 2004, the Bureau of the Census conducted a follow-up survey and found that the official poverty rate went from 12% in 2003 to 12.7% in 2004. In actual numbers, there were 37 million people in poverty in 2004, an increase of 1.1 million from 2003. Poverty levels remained the same for African Americans, 25%, and Latinos, 22%, but poverty increased for Whites from 8.2% to 8.6%

in 2004. The only group to have a decrease in poverty from 2003 to 2004 was Asians, from 8.6% to 8.2% (Walt et al., 2005).

Poverty in Developing Countries

Earlier in this chapter, we explained and defined poverty and how poverty is measured in the United States. But poverty in other countries, especially developing countries, is much more severe, and the United Nations and poverty researchers have defined it differently. Sachs (2005) differentiated among three types of poverty. **Extreme or abject poverty** exists when households cannot secure their basic needs for survival. These households are characterized by chronic hunger, an inability to access health care, lack of safe drinking water or sanitation, an inability to acquire education, poor shelter, and lack of basic clothing, especially shoes. According to Sachs (2005), extreme poverty is only seen in developing countries. **Moderate poverty** exists when households just barely secure basic needs. **Relative poverty** exists in households that have income below a specific proportion of some average national income. In high-income countries, these households are characterized by a lack of access to cultural programs, entertainment, recreation, quality health care, and quality education. These households lack opportunities to participate in activities that promote social mobility (Sachs, 2005).

In 2000, representatives of most countries signed the Millennium Declaration, which pledged to liberate men, women, and children from the abject and dehumanizing conditions resulting from extreme poverty, among other goals, by 2015. The goal was to cut extreme poverty in half by the end of 2015. As reported by the United Nations, more than 1 billion people are in abject poverty and live on less than $1 a day. About 2.5 billion people live on less than $2 a day. To address extreme poverty, the United Nations stated that "overcoming the structural forces that create and perpetuate extreme inequality is one of the most efficient routes for overcoming extreme poverty, enhancing the welfare of society..." (United Nations Development Programme, 2005, p. 5). Elaborating further on extreme social inequality and its correlation with extreme poverty, officials of the United Nations wrote that numerous and interlocking layers of inequality produce difficult hardships for people throughout their lives. Income inequalities intermingle with other life-chance inequalities, such that being born into poor families lessens other life chances. Poor women are less likely to receive care while pregnant and more likely to lose their children either before or shortly after birth. For instance, children born in poor households in Senegal or Ghana are 2 to 3 times more likely to die before age 5 than children born into the richest 20% of households in Senegal or

Ghana. Gender in developing countries is one of the strongest predictors for disadvantages. In India, the death rate for girls 1 to 5 years old is 50% higher than the death rate for boys (United Nations Development Programme, 2005).

The World Bank, echoing the sentiments of the United Nations, stated that poverty in developing countries is more than the absence of assets. It declared that "poor people are vulnerable to economic shocks, natural disasters, violence and crime, [and] they are often denied access to education, adequate health services and clean water and sanitation" (World Bank, 2005, p. 1). The World Bank noted that it was involved (i.e., making loans, collecting loans, and consulting) in more than 100 countries and recommended and endorsed the Millennium Development Goals agreed to by the United Nations. These goals articulate a strategy to reduce poverty that involves better coordination between developed and developing countries, improving the environment for stronger economic growth in developing countries, dismantling barriers to trade, scaling up human development, and increasing aid and its effectiveness (World Bank, 2005).

Famine

Famine has been defined by the World Health Organization (2002) as occurring when the severity of critical malnutrition levels affects more than 15% of all children from age 6 months to 59.9 months. The United Nations has a somewhat different definition, declaring that a famine occurs when there is an extreme collapse in the availability of food that leads to widespread deaths from starvation or from hunger-related illnesses. Both definitions are somewhat arbitrary. For instance, 13% to 15% of children in a country may suffer from malnutrition, and some deaths may not be widespread. A declaration of famine triggers international food aid, but people may be hungry and dying though a famine is not declared. The people of Southern Africa have been suffering from hunger for over a decade. The Southern African Development Community reported that the chronic malnutrition (stunning) rate for Zambian children between the ages of 6 months and 59 months in 1991 was 39%. Then, it increased to 55% and remained at that level. The acute malnutrition (wasting) at that time in Zambia was 4.4%. In Malawi, the rate of chronic malnutrition was 49% for its children (World Health Organization, 2002).

Patel and Delwiche (2002) have offered a provocative treatise, suggesting that developed countries, such as Great Britain and the United States, often generate and cause famine in less developed countries. They state that during the 120-year British rule of India, there were 31 famines, but there were only 17 famines over the 2 millennia prior to British rule (Patel & Delwiche, 2002).

According to Patel and Delwiche (2002), famine does not occur spontaneously due to a failed crop season but is the outcome of market forces. Under British rule, India's food was integrated into the world's food market, and the British forbade India's practices of feeding its people during food shortages. As a result, the Indian people were subjected to repeated famines.

Patel and Delwiche (2002) assert that famine is currently caused by poverty and Western policies. The World Food Programme reported that there was not a shortage of food in Lesotho, an African country, in 2002. Two thirds of the people lived below the poverty line, and 50% of the population was considered to be destitute. Because of increasing prices and shrinking incomes, the people of Lesotho could not afford to buy the food that was available. In 2001, the International Monetary Fund ordered the government of Malawi to decrease its grain reserve from 165,000 metric tons to between 30,000 and 60,000 metric tons. The International Monetary Fund justified its order based on costs and the belief that next year Malawi's harvest would increase the stock. When the crop did not meet projections, the people of Malawi experienced a famine and began to die (Patel & Delwiche, 2002).

Some African leaders hold the United States and the European Community responsible for African famines. Transnational food corporations based in the United States and Europe depend upon cheap inputs from some developing countries. According to Patel and Delwiche (2002, p. 8), the United States

has a twenty-year history of first generating hunger through macroeconomic policy that while selling itself as austere, systematically enriches large corporations and impoverishes working families. Then the government hen-feeds the hungry with surplus food this policy produces. This two-step trick was perfected within the United States. In 1981, Congress told the USDA to reduce the storage costs associated with its dairy support program. Simultaneous cuts in welfare provisions for the poor and the incipient recession provided a ready market for the surplus. Now this discipline is being applied in Southern Africa as a way to force open markets for U.S.–produced GM [genetically modified] grain.

GM grains are banned in Japan and the European Union, producing a large surplus that has been increasing. Thus, the United States needs a home for this grain. According to Patel and Delwiche (2002), food aid to African countries is really de facto support for U.S. agriculture businesses. The U.S. Agency for International Development, which distributes food to African countries, buys over a billion dollars' worth of products a year from agricultural businesses in the United States. While some African countries have been leery of the GM grain, they could not withstand U.S. pressure. Only Zambia, concerned over the safety of GM grain and the U.S. food policy, refused to accept GM grain. Secretary of State Colin Powell sought Vatican support to get Zambia to accept the GM grain. Zambia saw the problem as a lack of food available that the poor could afford. So, Zambia purchased grain from domestic and regional sellers (Patel & Delwiche, 2002).

However, not all famines are caused by the West; some are caused by internal conflicts within developing countries. In 1998, the world was shown pictures of emaciated Africans of all ages living in the Sudan. About 250,000 people were at risk for starvation. This famine has been called the Bahr el Ghazal famine of 1998. Experts agree that a 2-year drought caused by El Niño presented conditions conducive to a famine. However, the famine itself was caused by Sudanese government policies. The Sudanese government had backed the Murahaleen, an Arab militia group, to assist it in terrorizing the African population. Long before the famine, the Murahaleen had stolen cattle and grain and had burned crops in an attempt to rid the country of dark Africans. As Africans were driven from the land and away from food and their farms, they were put at risk for starvation (Human Rights Watch, 1999b). Further, the African people living in Darfur, many of them refugees, have become at risk for starvation.

NATURAL DISASTERS

Selected Disasters, Historical and Current

Fires, earthquakes, floods, mudslides, tornadoes, hurricanes, and similar natural disasters all have the potential to kill people and destroy homes. The Federal Emergency Management Agency (FEMA) has defined a major disaster as "any natural catastrophe, or regardless of cause, any fire, flood, or explosion that causes damage of sufficient severity and magnitude to warrant assistance supplementing state, local, and disaster relief organization efforts to alleviate damage, loss, hardship, or suffering" (Young, Ford, Ruzek, Friedman, & Gusman, 2000, p. 1). The President of the United States has the authority to declare an area of the country a disaster area, which triggers federal assistance. Extreme and devastating forces of disasters can have far-reaching consequences for individuals, communities, and society. Although a disaster may last for only seconds, such as an earthquake, or for several days, such as a flood, the impact on individuals and communities can last for months, for years, or forever. Recovery, reconstruction, and restoration may take years. Long-term recovery for people differs significantly because of the intricate interaction of psychological, social, cultural, political, and economic dynamics.

The tsunami of 2004 killed an estimated 174,000 people and destroyed numerous homes, but an estimate from the United Nations was that more than 400,000 persons were killed. Indonesia, Sri Lanka, India, Thailand, Somalia, Burma, Maldives, Malaysia, Tanzania, Seychelles, Bangladesh, South Africa, Kenya, and Yemen were all affected. The most destruction occurred in Indonesia, Sri Lanka, India, and Thailand, where many thousands died. Citizens and vacationers from Germany, Sweden, Britain, France, Norway, Japan, and Italy were also killed (BBC News, 2005). According to the International Action Center (IAC), the United States and Great Britain share responsibilities for the devastation of the tsunami although the weather cannot be controlled. Speaking for the IAC, Sara Flounders and Dustin Langley (2004, p. 1) declared that "the U.S. and British governments owe billions of dollars in reparations to the countries of this region and to all other colonized countries. The poverty and lack of infrastructure that contribute to and exacerbate the scope of this disaster are the direct result of colonial rule and neo-colonial policies. Although economic and political policies cannot control the weather, they can determine how a nation is impacted by natural disasters." Flounders and Langley (2004) demanded money from the United States and the British for human needs, not for wars that they eagerly fund.

In 2005, an earthquake in Pakistan killed nearly 90,000 people, destroyed over 200,000 homes, and decimated entire communities. The death toll in Pakistan was predicted to go up as the cold weather and snow would likely kill more people who were without shelter (Najam, 2006). However, Pakistan had a mild winter immediately after the 2005 earthquake, and relief supplies were able to be transported to the estimated 3.5 million people made homeless. The World Bank called this earthquake the most devastating in Pakistani history. A year after the disaster, about 400,000 people were still living in tents and about to undergo a second winter without permanent shelter.

Worldwide, from 1990 to 2003, earthquakes killed an estimated 111,854 persons (Jan, 2005). In 2005, the United States suffered over 1,000 deaths from Hurricane Katrina and saw the displacement of over 500,000 from the city of New Orleans. Further death and destruction have come from tornadoes and flooding, such as the flooding that occurred in North Dakota in 1997, submerging an entire city under water. Then, 90% of the 52,500 residents had to be evacuated, with 83% of homes and 62% of businesses damaged. Residents had no water for 13 days and no drinking water for 23 days. Of the 22 schools in the Grand Forks Public School District, 16 were seriously damaged, causing $74 million in damages. At the University of North Dakota, 72 buildings were damaged, causing $48 million in damages. Empathizing with the North Dakota citizens, more than 20,000 volunteers from numerous areas came to help clean up and rebuild. About 60,000 tons of flood debris were taken away for disposal at landfills (FEMA, 2008). Today, citizens of North Dakota have mixed views regarding the recovery from its flooding (Ryan, 2009).

In 2005, Hurricane Katrina came close enough to New Orleans to cause a breach in the levee system that protects the city from flooding. People were trapped in their homes and trapped in the Houston Astrodome and New Orleans Convention Center without water and food for several days. Over 1,000 people were killed in Louisiana, many of them from New Orleans. Many people felt that the federal government's very slow response was due to the fact that many victims were Black and poor. Because the entire city was asked to evacuate, New Orleans residents were sent to numerous cities throughout the United States.

David M. Walker (2006), then comptroller general of the United States, testified before Congress that the size and strength of Hurricane Katrina resulted in one of the largest natural disasters in American history and that the damage to the Gulf Coast was exacerbated by Hurricane Rita, which closely followed. In his testimony, Walker defined mass care (housing and human services) and economic assistance and services, both of which involved issues of human behavior in the social environment (HBSE). **Mass care** is the "capacity to provide immediate shelter, feeding centers, basic first aid, bulk distribution of needed items, and related services to persons affected by a large-scale incident, including special needs populations such as those with physical or mental disabilities that need additional attention" (Walker, 2006, p. 18). **Economic assistance and services** are "the capability to meet the demands for cash assistance, human services programs, educational services, and family and child welfare services" (Walker, 2006, p. 19). In both areas, as well as others, federal, state, and local agencies were vastly overwhelmed (Walker, 2006).

All these disasters can disrupt systems and cause considerable collateral damage, such as homelessness and mental health difficulties (Elias, 2005). In addition, there are economic damages. The Commerce Department reported that Hurricane Katrina caused $170 billion in property losses and the Labor Department reported that 279,000 people filed for unemployment insurance benefits because of Hurricane Katrina. A senior economist for Wells Fargo stated that the economic impact of Hurricanes Katrina and Rita will continue to extend far beyond the Gulf Coast and will have national implications for the U.S. economy, such as gas for $3 a gallon. (Gas prices prior to Hurricane Katrina were a little over $2 a gallon.) Personal income, consisting of wages, salaries, rents, interests, and other sources, fell by 0.1% in August 2005, but if Hurricane Katrina had not occurred, personal income would have risen by 0.2% (Henderson, 2005).

TERRORISM

In the United States

Someone once said that one person's terrorist is another person's freedom fighter. Though the United States and the West label Hezbollah, which fought Israel in 2006, as a terrorist organization, Hezbollah is the primary provider of social services in southern Lebanon, including the creation of schools and hospitals. In fact, Tavernise (2006) reported that Hezbollah performed social work. So, differences may exist over who is and who is not a terrorist. Numerous Arab countries believe that America and Americans are terrorists based on their foreign policies. The U.S. Department of State has recognized that no definition of terrorism has gained universal international acceptance. Nonetheless, some terms have been defined to help in an understanding of what terrorism is from an American perspective. **Terrorism** is defined as premeditated, politically motivated violence perpetrated against noncombatant persons or targets by subnational groups or clandestine agents that is usually intended to influence a broader audience. **International terrorism** is defined as terrorism involving citizens from the territory of more than one country. Last, a **terrorist group** is any group practicing or that has significant subgroups that practice international terrorism. The United States monitors terrorism, terrorist groups, and international terrorism based on these definitions. It has identified elements of terrorism in Africa, Asia, Eurasia, Europe, Latin America, and the Middle East. In addition, it monitors countries that purport to sponsor terrorism (U.S. Department of State, 2001).

Oklahoma City Bombing

Before 9/11, the terrorist attack that had shaken the American people the most was the bombing of the federal building in Oklahoma City on April 19, 1995. The bombing by Timothy McVeigh was the worst attack on American soil up to that time, killing 168 people, including 19 infants and toddlers. In addition, hundreds of persons sustained injuries. The resulting requests for mental health services provide an idea of the effects of the bombing on the community. Mental health professionals responded to about 1,500 requests for crisis intervention services. After 2 years, a federal agency had provided services to 9,000 individuals in the form of support groups, crisis intervention, outreach, consultation, and referral (Early & Ludwig, 2003). According to a report by the Oklahoma State Department of Health, about 22 (6.5%) of the 341 survivors were off work for more than a year, and 14% of the survivors never returned to work. Another survey identified 914 survivors, 92% of whom reported that they were injured by the bombing. Of this total, two thirds received psychological counseling and auditory services. The most common complaints were hearing damage, depression, and posttraumatic stress disorder.

9/11 Attack on New York City, Washington, and Pennsylvania

On September 11, 2001, foreign terrorists attacked New York City, Washington, DC, and Pennsylvania. Reports were that the mostly Saudi terrorists had planned and trained for the attack for years. They picked buildings that they believed had great significance to the American people. The smashing and demolishing of two important symbols of America in the media capital of the world was intended to cause the most severe psychological shock to the American people. By destroying the Twin Towers, the terrorists hoped to let Americans know that they were vulnerable, and their vulnerability was magnified by the surprise. Americans everywhere were stunned and bewildered by this attack. Throughout New York City, mental health assessments showed that adults and children were adversely affected mentally by this attack (Herman, Aaron, & Susser, 2003).

Betty J. Pfefferbaum and several colleagues (2005) conducted a review of the literature to assess the psychological impact of terrorism on families and children in the United States. Besides 9/11, they included within their review the bombing of the World Trade Center in 1993 and the Oklahoma City bombing in 1995. They noted that following the 9/11 attacks, exposure to the televised coverage of the bombing was associated with psychological outcomes. However, they acknowledged that little is known about the continuing impact of fear and anxiety on children and that additional research is needed, such as a study of the "pathways to varied outcomes, including conditions other than posttraumatic stress, and to examine coping and resilience" (Pfefferbaum et al., 2005, p. 315).

In 2008, E. Alison Holman and her colleagues conducted a prospective study to examine the impact of 9/11 on a national sample of Americans. Because data had been gathered before 9/11, the authors were able to collect data about 2 weeks after the attack and in the subsequent time period leading up to 3 years after the attack. They found that acute stress responses to 9/11 were associated with a 53% increase in cardiovascular ailments. Because they had pre-9/11 data, they were able to control for preexisting conditions. They found that hypertension increased 1 year after 9/11 by a ratio of 2.15 and 2 years after 9/11 by a ratio of 1.75. Heart problems increased 1 year after 9/11 by a ratio of 4.67 and 3 years after 9/11 by a ratio of 3.22.

In International Communities

According to the U.S. State Department definition of terrorism, a number of terrorist activities have occurred. Some of these attacks have been directed at the United States and some at other countries. Terrorists focus primarily on causing a large loss of life, and terrorism has occurred recently in Kenya and Tanzania, where the U.S. embassies were bombed; in Spain, where the train system was attacked in 2004; and in Great Britain, where the London subway system was targeted in 2005.

On August 7, 1998, one truck loaded with explosives drove up to the U.S. embassy in Nairobi, Kenya, and a second truck loaded with explosives drove up to the U.S. embassy in Dar es Salaam, Tanzania. At about the same time, both trucks exploded. Both attacks were carried out by members of Al-Qaeda. These two attacks were responsible for the deaths of 220 persons and injuries to over 4,000 persons. Most of the dead and wounded were not Americans but instead were Kenyans and Tanzanians (Institute for the Study of Diplomacy, 2005). Four persons involved in the attacks were indicted, convicted, and sentenced to life without parole. One of the persons convicted held dual citizenship as both an American and a Kenyan citizen. Investigative bodies searched for security failures (Institute for the Study of Diplomacy, 2005). The Accountability Review Board within the U.S. Department of State found that the numerous American personnel sent to help with the aftermath of the attack brought problems of coordination and logistical overload and that there were systematic and institutional failures in Washington, DC. The U.S. process for assessing threat levels worldwide was flawed and underestimated the threat of terrorism in Nairobi, and the United States had not appropriated enough funds to build safer embassies (U.S. Department of State, 2001).

The fallout from the bombing in Kenya and Tanzania led to a significant decrease in tourism—the largest import to both countries. Kenya is known for its famous game reserve, the Masai Mara, and Tanzania is known as the home of the Serengeti. Each year, there is a massive movement of wildebeests from the Serengeti through the Masai Mara and then a return trip about 5 or 6 months later, each attracting numerous tourists. As tourism has decreased, the economies of both countries have suffered, increasing unemployment and joblessness. These acts show terrorism in poor countries has major ripple effects that extend to the United States.

In Madrid, Spain, on March 11, 2004, several bombs exploded on commuter trains, killing 191 persons and wounding 1,460. This attack, like the attacks in Kenya and Tanzania, was tied to Al-Qaeda. It occurred 3 days before

Spain's national elections. Spain's socialists charged that the government had provoked the attacks by Al-Qaeda by supporting the United States in its war on Iraq. Others charged that the Spanish government had not been truthful by blaming the attack on a Spanish terrorist group. For one or both reasons, the incumbent government was voted out of office, and a socialist president was elected. The new president promised to return Spanish troops from Iraq when their tour of duty ended in July 2004 (Wikipedia Encyclopedia, 2005). On January 23, 2008, Spain reported that it had arraigned 10 Islamic individuals who were planning the suicide bombing of Spain's transportation systems. Since the 2004 bombing, more than 250 suspected Islamic terrorists have been arrested in Spain (Goodman, 2008).

On July 7, 2005—called 7/7 by some Britons and comparable to America's 9/11—52 persons were killed and 700 persons were injured in London. The persons responsible were Muslims, and they were killed during these multiple bombings in their suicide missions. Katie Friesen (2007) analyzed the effects of these bombings within Britain and Spain. Prior to 2004, both Britain and Spain had experienced some terrorism, but these attacks were internal in nature—acts of the Irish Republican Army (IRA) and Euskadi Ta Askatasuna (ETA). The bombings in Spain in 2004 and the bombing in London in 2005 were the first acts of terrorism carried out by Muslims. After the bombing in London, the Muslim population was targeted for abuse and some violence, the embracing of multiculturalism was questioned, increased ethnic profiling occurred, the level of prejudice against Muslim society increased, and the diminishing of Muslims' rights occurred. In both Great Britain and Spain, public transportation is utilized extensively, and many citizens of these countries now fear it.

CRIME

Overview

The United States uses two primary techniques to measure the incidence of crimes. One is the **Uniform Crime Report**, which gives the number of Part 1 offenses (i.e., serious crimes like murder or manslaughter, aggravated assault, sexual assault, armed robbery, burglary, motor vehicle theft, and arson) reported by almost all cities to the FBI. Another tool for measuring or counting crimes is the **National Crime Victimization Survey** (NCVS). Twice a year the U.S. Census Bureau conducts the NCVS, contacting a representative sample of households and asking if any family member 12 years or older has been the victim of a crime within the past 6 months (Bureau of Justice Statistics, 2005a).

The principal advantage of the NCVS is that it captures unreported crimes. The NCVS does not ask about homicide as homicides are generally accurately reported in the Uniform Crime Report. This chapter uses statistics from the NCVS because they detail crimes that have had an effect upon families and communities. Moreover, the NCVS reports crimes per 1,000 members of a specific age group in the U.S. population. For example, it shows the number of persons in the United States between the ages of 16 and 19 for a particular race and gender and uses that figure to calculate a rate that compares equally different cities and communities, regardless of size.

The Bureau of Justice Statistics collects data on victimizations. In 2004, it reported that there were 25.1 male victims per 1,000 males, compared to 17.2 female victims per 1,000 females, for violent crimes (Bureau of Justice Statistics, 2005a). Violent crimes were defined as homicide, rape, robbery, and both simple and aggravated assault (Bureau of Justice Statistics, 2005c). A more detailed study for the violent crimes defined above revealed that teenagers experienced the highest amount of violent crimes, and that persons 65 and older experienced the least violence. Most homicide victims were male in 2003. African Americans were more likely than Whites to experience property crimes, 191 per 1,000 compared to 157 per 1,000. African Americans were more likely to experience burglaries than Whites, 44 per 1,000 compared to 28 per 1,000 (Bureau of Justice Statistics, 2005b). Realistically, males and African Americans suffer the most from crimes, but research shows that the fear of crime is higher among women (Ferraro, 1995; Lee, 2007). To illustrate, in 2005, the rate of personal crimes for persons 12 years and older for White females was 16.5 per 1,000 persons but for African American females, the rate was 25.5 per 1,000. The rate for White males was 25.5 per 1,000, the same for African American females, and for African American males, the rate was 32.5 (Bureau of Justice Statistics, 2005c).

Fear of Street Crime

Fear is normal. Some events naturally produce fear. To a child, sharp and booming lightning and thunder produce fear. Many natural disasters, such as tornadoes and hurricanes, also produce fear. Some Americans have always been fearful and believe that certain groups want to harm them, such as Native Americans, former slaves, the Japanese, communists, and now the members of Al-Qaeda. Thus, there is a long history of fear in the United States. Another fear, which for some has racial elements, is the fear of crime.

Konty, Buell, and Joireman (2004) believe that fear of crime, which includes the fear of terrorism, serves very important purposes. According to them, a powerful social institution is very capable of producing fear in the population. When individuals are fearful, they become more punitive toward others, less concerned with the welfare of those they punish, and more concerned with their own welfare. What are the powerful interests to which Konty et al. (2004) allude? Many believe that the primary culprit in producing fear in the American people is the news media, which like to sensationalize crime. The more readers and viewers they get, the greater their advertising revenues (Konty et al., 2004). But there are other powerful interests that benefit financially from the fear of crime. One is the gun lobby. Numerous weapons are sold to the American people for self-protection allegedly from home invaders. More affluent citizens can hire security guards to prevent outsiders from coming into their neighborhoods. Home security alarm systems have become big business in America. While women, and especially White women, are the least likely to be assaulted, society, consisting of the news media and other institutions, has made them the most fearful. Makers of pepper sprays, whistles, and self-defense courses market heavily to these women. Companies that sell military hardware have benefited from fear of terrorism. The United States is the most dominant military machine in the world, and it has spent considerable dollars fighting the War on Terror. Airport security has increased. Konty et al. (2004) state not that Americans have no reason to be fearful but that fears have been exaggerated for financial and political purposes.

Numerous researchers have studied the fear of crime from a variety of perspectives (Sims & Johnston, 2004; Tulloch, 2004). Page (2004) found that Congress had used citizens' fears, prejudices, and anxieties to build support for eliminating Pell Grants for prisoners. Fear of crime affects not only individuals but also neighborhoods and the broader society. At the individual level, the fear of crime can have damaging psychological effects when it encumbers personal movement and causes individuals to be distrustful of their neighborhood, community, and life in general. At the neighborhood level, the fear of crime is inversely associated with neighborhood cohesion, attachment, and linkages. At the societal level, the fear of crime may increase problems for areas beset by existing disadvantages and may encumber societal change. Using citizens from Brisbane in Queensland, Australia, McCrea, Shyy, Western, and Stimson (2005) studied fear of crime and predictor variables drawn from individual factors, neighborhood disorder, social processes, and neighborhood structure. They found that individual factors were the most significant in predicting the fear of crime, and neighborhood factors were second (McCrea et al., 2005).

Corporate Crime

While society is more concerned about street crimes, corporate crimes have significant negative effects for families and communities (Shapiro, 1999). These crimes take many forms. Corporate officials' criminal activities led to the collapse of Enron and WorldCom, causing scores of former employees to lose their retirement income because these people had 401(k)s and pension plans with these companies. The collapse affected investors both large and small. Bernie Madoff's massive fraud wiped out the retirement funds of numerous persons and crippled many charitable organizations that had made investments with Madoff. Pension funds throughout the United States held stocks in many of these companies. While some pension funds were not entirely depleted, their losses were still significant. For instance, the State Teachers Retirement System of Ohio lost $60 million when Enron collapsed. Although the Ohio Teachers' Retirement Fund has assets of over $2 billion, the $60 million loss forced cuts in retirement benefits. Because of the number of retirees nearing retirement, the pension fund has stated that it cannot and does not guarantee that future retirees will have health benefits. Smaller investors may not have been able to sustain these losses. In Texas, officials criminally manipulated electricity prices, manufacturing a shortage. The officials were able to raise the electricity rates of people in California, and one Texas official was taped joking and laughing at the situation involving poor elderly people in California who were forced to pay for overpriced electricity. Bernie Ebbers, the chief executive officer of Mississippi-based WorldCom, was sentenced to 25 years in prison for assisting in the $11 billion accounting fraud of the company, causing the collapse of WorldCom and mass losses for shareholders, including money invested by pension boards (Crawford, 2006).

Most corporate crimes are considered "white collar" because they are committed by educated, relatively affluent individuals who often wear suits to work. Babiak and Hare (2006) discussed these individuals as psychopaths who lack consciences, although most people believe that psychopaths are just those individuals who commit heinous violent crimes. Hare is the foremost authority on psychopaths and has developed a widely used scale to measure psychopathy.

HUMAN PROBLEMS IN DEVELOPING COUNTRIES

Central to this section are several major topics that are important to HBSE students in understanding the scope of macro issues in international communities. The first is poverty, described earlier in the chapter. Of course, all societies have poverty, including nations that are core societies. Poverty is a strong predictor for more social problems, such as crime and delinquency or child protection interventions. But in developing communities, poverty is more extreme, making other problems more extreme, such as malnutrition, starvation, and infant mortality. The second is famine, also described earlier in the chapter, because it has the potential to kill a very large group of people. Violent conflicts in developing countries are third, as they have the potential to make other problems worse, such as poverty, displacement from people's homes, and people becoming refugees. Fourth, a more extreme form of some violent conflicts includes genocide and ethnic cleansing, which aim to eliminate completely an entire race or ethnic group. Fifth, **human trafficking** is a form of human rights violation recognized as a worldwide problem. Human traffickers force some desperate individuals into slavery or prostitution after they have been misled about traveling to a different country to secure jobs. Sixth and finally is terrorism, described earlier in the chapter, as it has become a growing problem for the United States, Great Britain, and Spain as well as other countries.

Violent Conflicts

Since 1990, armed conflicts among and within developing countries have directly resulted in the deaths of more than 3 million people, and millions more have died as corollaries of these conflicts. In addition to the obvious human costs, violent conflicts upset entire societies, sometimes causing these societies to revert to previous stages of advancement by several generations. Armed conflicts damage food systems, causing hunger and malnutrition and retarding progress in nascent health and education systems. In addition, about 25 million people are displaced as a result of armed conflicts in developing countries. Although this is a worldwide problem, about 38% of all violent conflicts are in Africa. Further, a disproportionate amount of violent conflicts are within the countries with the most poverty (United Nations Development Programme, 2005).

The United Nations Development Programme (2005) has outlined the human development costs of violent conflict, many of which are less visible. Direct effects of violent conflict are loss of life, wounding, disability, and rape. Not obvious are disintegration of health, economic damages to fledgling poor countries, infrastructure damages, collapsing food production systems, and psychological stress and trauma to victimized communities. The United Nations Development Programme (2005) has developed a **Human Development Index (HDI)** to measure the amount of human development in a country. While one cannot make a causal statement, there is a very strong association between low human development and violent conflict. For sure, violent conflict accelerates movement to the bottom of the HDI and increases the probability of a protracted stay at the bottom of the HDI. Of the 32 countries at the bottom of the HDI, 22 have experienced violent conflicts (United Nations Development Programme, 2005).

Violent conflicts produce losses that negatively affect the economies of countries and impede growth. Poor people may suffer the most from the economic damage from violent conflicts because they have little or no assets and cannot adjust to a loss in income. Further, the World Bank conducted a study and found that a civil war lasts on average 7 years. The rate of economic growth is reduced by 2.2% for each year of the conflict. As a civil conflict goes on, these losses accumulate. For instance, the conflict between the El Salvador government and rebel guerrillas that began in 1992 reduced economic growth by 2% annually. Moreover, countries are usually hesitant to invest in other countries that are engaged in conflicts, and those with existing investments in such countries may choose to withdraw those investments because of the conflicts. Even after a conflict has ended, investments may be slow to recover because of destroyed roads, bridges, and power systems. El Salvador lost about $1.6 billion worth of infrastructure due to its violent conflict (United Nations Development Programme, 2005). Simply, foreign investment significantly decreased in El Salvador.

Violent conflicts devastate educational systems and related infrastructures. One of the key factors in human development is the advancement of education, and strong educational systems help communities progress in other areas, such as health, nutrition, housing, roads, and food production. Violent conflict seriously damages the educational foundation needed for human development and contributes to and sustains conditions conducive to further violence. During conflicts between rebels and government forces, the rebels often target schools because they view schools as part of a corrupt government. For example, during Mozambique's civil war that lasted from 1976 to 1992, the rebels destroyed and forced the closure of about half of the country's schools. The Israeli army destroyed or damaged about 282 schools in the Occupied Palestinian Territory and frequently destroyed the homes of Hamas members who were believed to be terrorists as a matter of policy. In times of civil war, governments spend less on education and increase their spending for the military. Even if some schools are open and not damaged, parents may refuse to send their children to school due to safety concerns (United Nations Development Programme, 2005).

Children also pay further costs as a result of violent conflicts. In some countries, children are abducted and conscripted into the armed forces. In Uganda, the Lord's Resistance Army is reported to have conscripted about

30,000 children for military duty from the start of its conflict with the country's government in 1986 to about 2002 (United Nations Development Programme, 2005). Some children, however, are coerced to join armies with the promise of money for their poor parents or just to escape the poverty in their communities. Worldwide, the estimates are that violent conflicts have among their combatants about 250,000 child soldiers (United Nations Development Programme, 2005).

When violent conflicts break out, most of the dead are children. Wars and their aftermath make children more vulnerable to diseases and death. Most of the 2 million children who die from violent conflicts die of preventable diseases such as acute malnutrition, diarrheal diseases, measles, respiratory infections, and malaria. Prior to the conflict in 1995, Bosnia and Herzegovina had vaccinated about 95% of the children against various diseases. After the violent conflict began, this rate plummeted to less than 25%. In Russia, from about 1994 to 1996 the tuberculosis rate was 90 per 10,000 persons, but in Chechnya, a war-torn area, the rate was 160 per 10,000, including both children and adults (United Nations Development Programme, 2005).

Although everyone suffers when violent conflicts occur in a region, women and adolescent girls are more vulnerable than others. Many females experience rape, sexual exploitation, and abuse during and after the conflict. The use of rape as an instrument of war has been documented in Bosnia and Herzegovina, Cambodia, Liberia, Peru, Somalia, Sierra Leone, and Uganda (United Nations Development Programme, 2005). However, this problem has been evident since countries began invading other countries. Women in refugee camps are sometimes coerced to trade sexual favors for basic goods. Professionals note that many women and girls who have been sexually victimized suffer from both physical and mental health problems, and some of them are rejected by their families and communities (United Nations Development Programme, 2005). Rejection is especially likely to occur if these women become impregnated by opposing forces.

As stated, most violent conflicts involving governments and rebels or guerrillas have occurred in countries with high levels of poverty. However, the United Nations Development Programme (2005) contends that wealthy countries should care about what happens in poorer areas. Poor countries in armed conflicts typically sell their resources to help finance their military or terrorist activities. In some cases, these resources include drugs, which may reach the United States and other rich countries. Cocaine has come from Central America, heroin from Afghanistan, and marijuana from Liberia (United Nations Development Programme, 2005). But there are other reasons for rich, developed countries to be concerned about violent conflicts within developing countries. According to the United Nations Development Programme (2005), rich countries, in their own self-interest, should do more to address the challenges presented by violent conflicts in unstable countries. A century ago, countries could establish their security by building up their military, strengthening their borders, and maintaining themselves as islands protected from the world. This is no longer the case as globalization has made countries more connected. Violent conflicts transcend a country's security measures and don't need passports to enter a country. In 2005, then UN Secretary-General Kofi Annan concluded that collective security is impossible based solely on a single country (Human Development Report 2005, 2006). Collective security

> links people in rich countries directly to communities in poor countries where lives are being devastated by conflict. International drug trafficking and illicit arms transfers provide the financing and the weapons that fuel violent conflicts in countries such as Afghanistan and Haiti—and they create profound threats to public welfare in rich countries. When health systems collapse because of violent conflict, rich countries as well as poor countries face an increased threat of infectious disease. The breakdown of immunization systems in Central Africa and parts of West Africa is a recent example. When violence uproots people from their homes, the flows of refugees and displaced people, and the export of conflicts to neighbours, create challenges for the entire international community. When weak states tip over into violent conflict, they provide a natural habitat for terrorist groups that pose a security risk to people in poor ones. Above all, when rich countries, through their indifference, display a tolerance for poverty and violent conflict, it challenges the hope that an interconnected world can improve the lot of everyone, including the poor, the vulnerable and the insecure. (Human Development Report 2005, 2006, p. 152)

Violent conflicts may or may not involve human rights violations. It is possible for a country to have a civil war that does not target civilians specifically. But some violent conflicts have as their goals the elimination or destruction of a race or an ethnic group. This is **genocide**, the most serious human rights violation.

Ethnic Cleansing and Genocide

Following the Holocaust and the killing of 6 million Jews and other targeted groups during World War II, the United Nations promised that it would never let this happen again. The United Nations and some specific countries declared that genocide is a crime against humanity. An arm of the United Nations prosecuted war criminals and brought them to justice. Within the U.S. Department of State, the Office of the Special Envoy for Holocaust Issues exists and assists in the apprehension of war criminals and the provision of restitution for victims if possible. The office is concerned not merely with the past but also with the future, warning against contemporary discrimination and intolerance, which may lead to genocide (Schwartz, 2003). The United Nations sanctioned the bombing of Bosnia and Herzegovina to stop the genocidal practices that the Serbians were committing upon other groups.

However, the United Nations did not act in Rwanda to stop militant Hutus from killing almost 1 million Tutsis and moderate Hutus in a little more than a month in 1994. Hutus implemented a systematic strategy of genocide that some observers compared to the Nazis' systematic program of genocide against Jews. Hutus believed that using guns to kill Tutsis would be too expensive. So, the Hutus purchased large numbers of machetes from China. In the first week of the genocide, Hutus drove Tutsis out of their homes and into government offices, churches, schools, or other public sites, where they then massacred everyone present. A planned strategy was implemented once the killing started. Hutus went door to door in some neighborhoods, systematically killing Tutsis. Government supporters set up roadblocks to detain and then kill any Tutsis trying to escape. Toward the end of the month, the militant Hutus employed a new strategy called pacification. They decided to stop mass killings and simply arrest Tutsis, who would then be taken somewhere else and killed. Near the end of the massacre, the Hutus shifted strategy again, tracking down Tutsis and killing them (Human Rights Watch, 1999d). Human Rights Watch (1999a) recapped the changes that had been made since the 1994 genocide and noted that the United Nations Security Council established the International Criminal Tribunal for Rwanda to try and punish those who led and encouraged the genocide. In 2002, the International Criminal Court was created to address and deter future genocidal practices. Several countries, including France and Belgium, apologized to the Rwandan people for not stopping the genocide. Also, in 1998, U.S. President Bill Clinton apologized for not interceding to stop the genocide against the Tutsis.

Yet, a different type of genocide is currently occurring. Some call it "ethnic cleansing," while some consider it a crime against humanity like genocide. **Ethnic cleansing** is defined as the rendering of an area ethnically homogeneous by force or intimidation. Similar to forced population removal, ethnic cleansing involves the use of terror-inspiring violence. Some people may be killed or forced to flee for their lives. Repeatedly, the United Nations has declared that ethnic cleansing is a violation of international humanitarian law and those leaders who inspire it must be brought to justice. The effort in the former

Yugoslavia to militarily cleanse ethnic groups from certain areas is a recent example of ethnic cleansing.

Another tactic used in ethnic cleansing is rape and impregnation (Allen, 1996). While rapes have occurred since the beginnings of wars and conquests, the Serbians stooped to a new low (Halsell, 1993). Not only did the Serbians rape very small children; they also raped females capable of having children in rape camps that they had established (Halsell, 1993). Their goal was to impregnate Muslim women and have them bear Serbian babies for a "Greater Serbia." Estimates were that the number of Bosnian women raped ranged from 20,000 to 100,000 (Halsell, 1993). Serbians believed that these children would be Serbians and not Muslims. They hoped to shame these women and to ensure that Muslim men who survived the killings would not want women who had Serbian babies. Thus, the overall Muslim population would be adversely affected. In another part of the world, the practice of using rape as ethnic cleansing has appeared again in Darfur. In the Sudan, the Janjaweed, a militia group supportive of the Arab-led government, have been raping African women and declaring, "We want to make a light baby" (Wax, 2004, p. A01).

Human Trafficking

In 2004, Wendy Patten, a representative of Human Rights Watch, testified before Congress. She noted that Human Rights Watch had been monitoring and studying human trafficking for over a decade and that during that time trafficking in women and children had occurred between Burma and Thailand, Nepal and India, Thailand and Japan, Eastern Europe and Greece, and countries of the former Soviet Union and Eastern Europe and postconflict Bosnia and Herzegovina. Recently, trafficking in children for agriculture labor and domestic help occurred in Togo. Refugee women from Bhutan who were residing in refugee camps in Nepal were victims of sex trafficking (Patten, 2004). Human Rights Watch (2002a) reported that the trafficking of women in Bosnia and Herzegovina appeared in 1995—the year in which the conflict ended with the signing of the Dayton Peace Agreement. During the 3 years of ethnic cleansing, women were subjected to abuse in rape camps and detention centers. But another form of abuse quickly appeared after the end of the conflict. The United Nations, after studying the problem, estimated that 227 nightclubs and bars in Bosnian cities were involved in human trafficking. Another UN estimate suggested that 25% of the women working in these nightclubs were trafficked and more than 2,000 women were trapped and working in brothels. Typically, these women were looking for work or higher incomes. In the process of making arrangements to travel to places with the promise of jobs paying high wages, they were forced into prostitution and forced to work off the debts for their travel. In the brothels, they were charged for basic items and thus never able to pay off their debts (Human Rights Watch, 2002b). This type of abuse is very similar to African Americans who sharecropped on land owned by Whites in the late 1800s until the late 1950s or 1960s. Sharecropping came after slavery in which Whites owned land but did not have money to pay wages. Although African Americans did all the work, they could never get out of debt for seeds and farming supplies, as their debt increased each year (PBS, 2008).

CONSEQUENCES AND IMPACTS OF DISASTERS AND HUMAN RIGHTS VIOLATIONS ON HUMAN BEHAVIORS

Overall Effects

All of the problems discussed above have consequences for families, groups, organizations, and communities. For example, a hurricane, such as Katrina in 2005, can have ripple effects, causing deaths, separation from family members, destruction of homes and neighborhoods, and relocation to new areas. Different groups are affected adversely by such events. In the case of Hurricane Katrina, poor people were unable to leave the city or unable to return due to lack of resources. The planned rebuilding does not provide for adequate low-income housing, preventing poor African Americans from returning. According to a Bush housing appointee, the rebuilt New Orleans will not be as Black as it was before when African Americans constituted about 67% of the population. Drug addicts were also adversely affected. As reported by the news media, some persons repeatedly tried to break into a hospital. The reported reason for these invasions, according to the mayor of New Orleans, was that illicit drugs had been permitted to flow easily into New Orleans before the hurricane but the addicts were not able to get any drugs while in shelters. So, they went to hospitals looking for drugs. Further, some communities were destroyed, such as the Ninth Ward in New Orleans, while others were severely disrupted. Also, communities in Baton Rouge, Louisiana, and Houston, Texas, took in huge numbers of hurricane refugees, stretching their resources. Such disasters strain organizations, such as the Red Cross and FEMA, to their limits. Another organization, the New Orleans Police Department, was affected by Hurricane Katrina in that numerous police officers went AWOL (absent without leave) during the crisis, thus making it easier for looting to occur. Hurricane Katrina and its impact on New Orleans damaged the image of the United States in many international communities. Numerous countries expressed shock at the ineptitude of the United States in responding to the disaster.

The United States has fought two wars in Iraq since the 1990s. The National Veterans Foundation (2005) has gathered data on these conflicts and states that more than 360,000 soldiers have returned from Iraq and Afghanistan. Since March 2003, 40 Army personnel and 9 Marines have committed suicide in Iraq, and 43 more from both branches have committed suicide since they returned to the United States. Prior to the United States going to war with Iraq, a domestic violence hotline for military spouses averaged about 50 calls a month. Shortly after the first Iraq war, the number of calls averaged 500 a month (National Veterans Foundation, 2005). The National Veterans Foundation (2005) suggests that, based on statistics from the Vietnam War in the 1960s, these numbers involving service personnel from Iraq may get worse in the long term. About 3.4 million persons served in various capacities in the Vietnam War. Of this total, over 110,000 have committed suicide since the end of that conflict, and over 500,000 have suffered from posttraumatic stress disorder. Some of these mental health difficulties result in homelessness. One in three homeless men in America is a veteran, and of all homeless veterans, 42% are Vietnam veterans (National Veterans Foundation, 2005).

The most common consequence as a result of crime, natural disasters, terrorism, genocide, civil wars, U.S. military conflicts, and sex trafficking is the development of trauma and posttraumatic stress. Mental health professionals assert that terrorist attacks, house fires, car accidents, and traumatic events produce similar mental health difficulties. Individuals may experience sleeplessness, anger, and weepiness. Some survivors of Hurricane Katrina exhibited anxiety, sleeplessness, and increased incidence of domestic violence—all behaviors that had not manifested themselves prior to the hurricane hitting the Gulf Coast (Associated Press, 2005). The most common occurrence is that families, groups, and communities may develop severe depression and posttraumatic stress disorder. Further, suicides may occur. Some New Orleans residents who were stranded during the flooding and several New Orleans police officers committed suicide. A year after the flooding, the community had experienced an increased number of suicides, and community depression was extremely high.

Some mental health professionals have identified four types of victims of disasters. **Primary victims** are individuals who were directly exposed to the effects of a disaster. **Secondary victims** are individuals with close family and personal connections to primary victims. **Tertiary victims** are individuals whose occupations require them to respond to a disaster. **Quaternary victims** are concerned and caring members of communities beyond the impact of the disaster (Young et al., 2000).

In 1989, the United States was so concerned about the effects of trauma on soldiers that it created the National Center for Posttraumatic Stress Disorder within the U.S. Department of Veterans Affairs (2008). PSTD has been studied among service members (Solomon & Shalev, 1995), victims of violent crimes (Falsetti & Resnick, 1995), disaster victims (McFarlane, 1995), industrial and accidental injury victims (Best & Ribbe, 1995), and torture survivors (Vesti & Kastrup, 1995). Moreover, PTSD has been studied with regard to specific racial groups, including African Americans (Allen, 2001), Native Americans (Robin, Chester, & Goldman, 2001), Asians and Asian Americans (Abueg & Chun, 2001), and Latinos (Hough, Canino, Abueg, & Gusman, 2001). Further, poverty, oppression, and discrimination have negative consequences.

The United States, for an industrialized country, has a very high infant death rate that is traced to poverty. According to the Centers for Disease Control and Prevention (2008), the infant mortality rate, defined as the rate in which babies less than 1 year of age die, has declined in the United States from 26 per 1,000 live births in 1960 to 6.9 per 1,000 live births in 2000. In 1998, the United States ranked 28th in the world in infant mortality. The Centers for Disease Control and Prevention (2008) attributes the U.S. ranking to disparities among various racial and ethnic groups, particularly in the African American community. Interestingly, the Central Intelligence Agency (CIA) tracks infant mortality rates worldwide. In its latest update in 2008, the CIA states that Angola has the highest infant mortality rate, 184.44 per 1,000 live births, and Singapore, ranking 221st, has the lowest, 2.30 per 1,000 live births. In this ranking, the United States is 180th with 6.37 infant deaths per 1,000 live births. Among the countries with lower infant death rates than the United States are South Korea, Cuba, Italy, New Zealand, Greece, Ireland, the United Kingdom, Portugal, the Netherlands, Canada, Australia, Belgium, Denmark, Spain, Switzerland, Germany, Norway, Finland, France, Hong Kong, Japan, and Sweden (Central Intelligence Agency, 2008).

The consequences of oppression and discrimination may be depression and suicide. Researchers have documented the high rate of suicide among young gays who have been oppressed and have encountered discrimination as a result of their sexual orientation, prompting preventions to help gays feel better about their sexual orientation and to take pride in being gay. Because of its ubiquity, the next section discusses PTSD in more detail because trauma can have far-reaching effects, often causing secondary stress and trauma for friends and relatives of victims of primary trauma.

Secondary traumatic stress involves the behaviors and emotions occurring as a result of the knowledge that a loved one has experienced a trauma. This stress may occur from knowing, helping, or attempting to help a significant other who has experienced a trauma (Figley & Kleber, 1995). Figley and Kleber (1995) defined secondary traumatic stress as stemming from an individual's knowledge that a traumatizing event has occurred to a significant other. Significant others can be the spouse, children, or relatives of the victim. Friends and neighbors may be significant others. Colleagues from work may be significant others. Further, helping professionals may be significant others, such as rescue workers, emergency personnel, social workers, nurses, physicians, and psychologists. For individuals who are close to, devoted to, or intimate with a victim, the knowledge of a significant other's trauma may produce feelings of powerlessness and disruption.

Figley and Kleber (1995) have theorized about the causes of secondary trauma. Empathy, they argue, requires that members of systems connect with the victims of trauma and their suffering. They seek answers for themselves to the questions that victims generally have. For instance, victims of trauma and their significant others want to know: What happened? Why did it happen? Why did I act as I did then? Why have I acted as I have since? If it happens again, will I be able to cope? Systems around the victims attempt to secure these answers in order to help change the victims' negative behaviors. However, the search for these answers sometimes causes secondary systems to exhibit behaviors similar to those of the victims. These may include visual images of the event that caused the trauma, sleeping problems, depression, or other symptoms resulting from visualizing the victims' trauma, having contact with the victims, or both (Figley & Kleber, 1995).

Military Service and Posttraumatic Stress Disorder

Since the end of the Vietnam War, the literature on the psychological aspect of wars has grown immensely. Both clinical literature and empirical literature have provided very strong evidence that war has a serious effect on combatants, military support personnel, and families. Professional clinicians have identified the symptoms that characterize combat-related stress behaviors and have developed etiological models that show the beginning and course of stress-produced symptoms. Moved in the 1980s by the numerous reports of the psychological problems of Vietnam veterans, the American Psychological Association embraced **posttraumatic stress disorder** (**PTSD**) and included it as a mental disorder within the *Diagnostic and Statistical Manual of Mental Disorders* (American Psychiatric Association, 2000). The official recognition of PTSD stimulated researchers to seek a greater understanding of the disorder so as to treat the veterans trying to recover from their combat experiences (Weathers, Litz, & Keane, 1995). In Israel, a country with a military that has been on alert and engaged in combat regularly since being founded in 1949, mental health professionals recognize PTSD and a related disorder, **combat stress reaction (CSR)** (Solomon & Shalev, 1995). In many ways, the study of trauma emanating from the combat environment has provided a paradigm for understanding other trauma caused by rape or natural disasters (Weathers et al., 1995).

Since the Vietnam War, the wars in Afghanistan and Iraq have been the most prolonged periods of combat for U.S. forces. Mental health professionals believe that these wars will produce a new generation of veterans with serious mental health problems (Litz, 2005). Hoge et al. (2004) estimated the PTSD risk for veterans who fought in Afghanistan at 11% and for those who fought in Iraq at 18%. As a matter of fact, some Gulf War veterans have encountered serious problems with the criminal justice system, which is not to suggest they suffered from mental health problems as a result of serving in the first Iraq war. For instance, Timothy McVeigh, who was executed for blowing up the federal building in Oklahoma City, was a veteran of the Gulf War. In addition, John Muhammad, one of the DC snipers who is currently under a death sentence in Virginia and likely to receive a second death sentence in Maryland, is a veteran of the Gulf War. In 2003, the federal government executed Louis Jones, Jr., a veteran of the Gulf War, for the rape and murder of a servicewoman. Jones attributed this violence to his experiences in the Gulf War, including exposure to Iraqi nerve gas (Mayfield, 2003).

Some might conclude that Louis Jones may have been attempting to use the Gulf War to excuse his criminal behaviors. However, data from a 2005 survey of soldiers who have returned from serving in the Iraq war provide support for Jones's claims. More than 3,700 veterans returning from Iraq in 2005 reported concerns that they might hurt someone or fears that they might lose control with someone (Zoroya, 2005). About 1,700 soldiers said that they had thought of harming themselves and that they might be better off dead, and more than 20,000 reported having nightmares or difficulties processing war recollections (Zoroya, 2005). While the majority of veterans do not have significant problems, the survey found that 25% (about 50,000) of returning veterans do have significant physical and mental health issues (Zoroya, 2005).

In 2008, *The New York Times* published an article detailing veterans returning from Iraq and Afghanistan who had been involved in violent acts upon their return to the United States. Examining a period from 2001 to 2007, the *Times* found an 89% increase in veterans who had committed or had been charged with homicides. In this study, 121 veterans had been charged with homicides, and 13 veterans had committed suicide. Most of these 121 veterans had no mental health screenings when they departed for Iraq or Afghanistan or upon their return to the United States. They were diagnosed with PTSD after they were charged with homicides. Although the military attempts to gauge the mental health needs of veterans, it acknowledges that the military mental health system is overburdened, understaffed, financed poorly, and undermined by the stigma of a diagnosis of PTSD. According to a military expert, early treatment might help veterans to avoid problems like depression, substance abuse, and criminal justice system involvement (Sontag & Alvarez, 2008).

Violent Crime, Adverse Effects, and Posttraumatic Stress Disorder

Violent crimes and the fear of violent crimes contribute to mental health problems and posttraumatic stress disorder. Hanson, Kilpatrick, Falsetti, and Resnick (1995) explored the considerable toll of violent crimes on individuals' mental health and lifestyles. Reviewing previous studies, they noted that PTSD is the most common psychological disorder that occurs from exposure to violent crimes. Individuals may experience PTSD due to other factors in their lives, but being the victim of a crime, such as a sexual or physical assault, increases the rate of PTSD by 3 or 4 times. In addition, other mental health problems occur as a result of being exposed to violent crimes. These may include substance abuse, anxiety disorders, depression, relationship problems, and sexual dysfunction. As a result of being victimized by violent crimes, individuals may experience lifestyle changes like moving to a new residence, decreased productivity at work, and restricted social involvement. Even just the fear of being a victim entails considerable adjustment in individuals' lives. People have reported that they do not shop or work late because of their fears of violent crime. Women are more likely than men to report that their fear of victimization restricts their activities (Hanson et al., 1995).

Hanson et al. (1995) described the risk and protective factors at three levels—individual, family, and community. Risk factors in this context were past victimization, young age, and a diagnosis of active PTSD. **Protective factors** operating at the individual level come from developmental psychopathology. Children who are exposed to parental psychopathology, poverty, or warfare are at greater risk for mental health problems. Protective factors were temperament, gender, and IQ. Further, perceptions involving cognitive processes of appraisal and attribution are related to adjustment to violent acts. Falsetti and Resnick (1995) found differences in causal attributions for sexual assault victims with depression and/or PTSD and individuals who had not been sexually assaulted. Sexual assault victims, given a hypothetical question, rated the scenario as more unstable than persons who had not been sexually assaulted. These victims also rated hypothetical positive events as more unstable than nonvictims. In addition, these victims rated hypothetical negative events as more internal than nonvictims.

In sum, victims are more likely than nonvictims to make attributions that convey no control over positive or negative events (Hanson et al., 1995).

Family factors that serve a protective function are family cohesion, supportive family members, absence of family dissension, no neglect, and a positive parent-child relationship. However, a history of mental health and substance abuse negatively affects a family member who is experiencing symptoms of PTSD. Grounded by social disorganization theory, Hanson et al.'s (1995) research hypothesized that low levels of neighborhood organization, such as involvement in community activities, community support networks, and community services, would help prevent exposure to violence and PTSD. Specifically, social disorganization theory holds that the degree of disintegration in a community is determined by the strengths within that community. This hypothesis was supported. Social ties external to family are extremely helpful in improving individuals' mental health. The degree of social support in a community has been shown to be associated with a variety of benefits (Hanson et al., 1995).

Mental Health Effects of Rape as a War Strategy

The United Nations, because of the aim and consequences of rape during ethnic wars in Bosnia and Rwanda, has decided that rape is a violation of human rights. In a place like Darfur, rape is especially difficult for cultural reasons. When rape is used as a weapon of war, it is "aimed at terrorizing and subjugating entire communities, and affects the social fabric of communities" (Human Rights Watch, 2005c, p. 1). One woman was raped by seven Janjaweed and became pregnant. She had the baby, and everyone in the community knew that the father was a Janjaweed. The woman stated that she did not want the baby. In the very conservative culture of Darfur, the stigma accompanying rape is almost impossible to overcome. As one raped woman said, no one would marry a raped woman in her country. Compounding the problem, many community members in Darfur believe that a conception can occur only from consensual sex, never during a rape. As a consequence, a raped Darfur woman who becomes pregnant is often blamed for the pregnancy and shames her family. However, this view is not universal, and communities have responded in different ways. Some communities encourage a cousin to marry a raped relative as a means of protecting the honor of the family, but it is only a ceremonial marriage. Some men leave their wives and children after their wives are raped. Some raped young women believe that they will not have an opportunity to marry because they are *khasrana* (damaged). One young woman believed that she was *mashautana* (possessed) because she would wake up screaming at night. The family did not talk about what happened, and the young woman's father withdrew (Human Rights Watch, 2005c).

CONCLUSION

This chapter has discussed the myriad circumstances emanating from poverty, natural disasters, crime, and human rights violations—all of which adversely affect human behaviors. First, this chapter discussed poverty extensively with data detailing the incidence of poverty. Poverty prevented many persons in New Orleans from leaving the city after Hurricane Katrina, and poverty will prevent many persons from returning, according to a New Orleans developer. Then, this chapter discussed crime and who is most likely to be a crime victim, as well as discussed natural disasters and terrorism on American soil. Internationally, this chapter discussed famine, civil wars, and violent conflicts in African countries. Genocide and ethnic cleansing were addressed with discussions of the Serbian behaviors against Muslims in Bosnia and African women in the Sudan. Particular focus was put on the use of rape as a form of ethnic cleansing in both Bosnia and Africa. The sex trafficking of women from poor countries in Europe and Mexico was addressed. Some of the women who have been sold as sex slaves are in brothels in the United States. Last, this chapter indicated that many of these problems, both domestically and internationally, have implications for human behaviors. Particularly, crime, natural disasters, terrorism, civil wars, genocide, and ethnic cleansing all have implications for systems. Considerable emphasis was placed on PTSD, depression, and suicide within the U.S. population, service personnel returning from Iraq and Afghanistan, and people in developing countries.

Key Terms and Concepts

Category

Combat Stress Reaction (CSR)

Economic Assistance and Services

Ethnic Cleansing

Extreme or Abject Poverty

Famine

Genocide

Group

Human Development Index (HDI)

Human Trafficking

International Terrorism

Mass Care

Moderate Poverty

National Crime Victimization Survey (NCVS)

Posttraumatic Stress Disorder (PTSD)

Poverty

Primary Victims

Protective Factors

Quaternary Victims

Relative Poverty

Secondary Traumatic Stress

Secondary Victims

Terrorism

Terrorist Group

Tertiary Victims

Uniform Crime Report

CHAPTER 3

Theories to Explain Macro Systems

INTRODUCTION

The aftereffects of the shootings at Virginia Tech in 2007 and Northern Illinois University in 2008 have been to bring increased attention to students with mental health problems and counseling centers on college campuses. The Center for the Study of Collegiate Mental Health at Penn State University gathered first-of-a-kind data from students who had visited mental health centers at various colleges and universities. Ben Locke, the executive director of the center, stated that "mental health affects every aspect of a college student's functioning" and "the earlier you intervene in mental health issues, the more likely you are to be successful in treating it" (Armas, 2009). Locke's statements could be understood as expressing two theories. Stated differently, Locke is saying (a) that the quality of mental health (the independent variable) is related to the degree of college students' functioning (the dependent variable) and (b) that the time of intervention with mental health problems (the independent variables consisting of a measurement that would reflect early and late) affects the type of outcome (the dependent variable with success vs. no success). Validated through sound research studies, theories thus help us understand human behaviors and what causes them regardless of the social environments. Theories provide an understanding of families, social institutions, organizations, and communities.

The purpose of this chapter is to help you learn of some theories that would explain problems and behaviors described in Chapter 2 and subsequent chapters. While some theories have both micro and macro applications, we've chosen theories based on their ability to help us understand macro issues (Rössel & Collins, 2001). No social theory explains 100% of the cases representing a phenomenon; one deviant case is not necessarily adequate evidence to refute and invalidate a theory. A theory is supported and validated when statistical evidence indicates that the theory explains most cases—maybe 60% or 70% of the phenomenon. For instance, a theory might state that children who grow up in an abusive home are more likely to be abusive parents. However, it is always possible that some children who grow up in an abusive home will not become abusive parents, whereas some children who grow up in a nonabusive home will later become abusive parents. Take the hypothetical example in Table 3.1, where we show what a statistically significant relationship might look like. We see that 62% of the individuals who grew up in an abusive home became abusive parents, compared to 29% of the individuals who did not grow up in abusive homes, supporting perhaps social learning theory. But as we can see, 38% of individuals who grew up in abusive homes did not become abusive parents. That 38% does not refute or invalidate social learning theory. We would conclude, nevertheless,

| Table 3.1 | Hypothetical Example Showing the Relationship Between Growing Up in an Abusive Home and Being an Abusive Parent |

	Whether Individual Grew Up in an Abusive Home	
Whether Abusive Parent	*Yes*	*No*
Yes	62%	29%
No	38%	71%

Note: $X^2 = 24.56$, p < .005

that social learning theory is supported and that those who grow up in abusive homes will be abusive parents. A theory is supported and validated when statistical evidence indicates that the theory explains most cases—more than 50% or maybe 60% or 70% of the phenomenon. We might reformulate social learning theory to provide a deeper understanding of why those who grew up in abusive homes did not become abusive parents, indicating some other crucial variables in this phenomenon. But we will still likely have some deviant cases and likely will not be able to explain 100% of this phenomenon.

While theories help guide the acquisition of knowledge, we should keep in mind that a theory, following a meticulous and carefully conducted investigation, may not be supported. Still, the investigation can provide useful and valuable knowledge when a theory has not been supported. For instance, the former president of Harvard University, Lawrence Summers, theorized that there are fewer women than men in math and sciences for genetic reasons. Summers's position was quickly criticized as sexist, but one could view it as a theory. If a researcher tested this theory and found it to be unsupported, knowledge has been provided. Numerous theories have been proposed to explain the behaviors of minorities, like Latinos and African Americans, as well as gays, lesbians, and bisexual and transgendered persons. Although these may be extreme examples where some theories may be found to be unsupported, research studies based on neutral theories that are not supported still may provide knowledge. Someone may theorize that students enter social work because they care about oppressed people and social justice. But a study that shows that this theory is untrue or partly true provides knowledge. It might be that most social work students, who are mostly White females, care more or most about other White women whom they believe to be oppressed and victims of numerous injustices.

There is strong empirical support to suggest that the selection of theories presented here explains families, groups, categories, organizations, institutions, and communities. We begin with systems theory, including world systems theory. Then, we discuss community theory, social disorganization theory, routine activity theory, and migration theory. We classify these as theories that explain systems and community behaviors. The next classification of theories explains inequality and oppression, and these theories include inequality theory, feminist theory, and power theory and social independence theory. We then discuss social learning theory, reference group theory, and role theory as they may be used to help students understand communities. Finally, we introduce Black's theory of law, which explains law and social control agents (such as some social workers). Table 3.2 provides the theories presented and a brief description of them, followed by a more detailed explanation. You will note that some theories, which have different names, have similar explanations of human behaviors.

Table 3.2   Theories to Explain Macro Systems

Theories	Brief Explanation
1. Systems Theory & World Systems Theory	Systems are related and connected, and disequilibrium in one system affects other systems.
2. Community Theory	A community is a system of interconnected and interacting subsystems, and each community engages in boundary maintenance.
3. Social Disorganization Theory	Social disorganization, or social problems, occurs due to a failure of rules, normlessness, cultural conflict, or breakdown.
4. Routine Activity Theory	Crimes occur due to (a) suitable targets, (b) motivated offenders, and (c) the absence of capable guardians.
5. Migration Theories	Factors that come into play when a person or group considers whether or not to migrate include (a) factors associated with the area of origin, (b) factors associated with the area of destination, (c) intervening obstacles, and (d) personal factors.
6. Inequality Theory	Perceived inequality involves a person's sense of relative deprivation, which is a feeling that there is a discrepancy between what is perceived to be and what is perceived should be or a discrepancy between an achievement and an expectation of achievement.
7. Feminist Theory	Women's position in life is caused by external factors created by a male-dominated society.
8. Power Theory and Social Independence Theory	Power or social independence is derived from (a) having resources, (b) having alternative sources for obtaining needed services, (c) the ability to use force against others, and (d) the lack of need for services.
9. Social Learning Theory	Deviant behavior is caused by imitation, definition, differential association, and differential reinforcement.
10. Reference Group Theory	Individuals form their attitudes in reference to groups and their self-evaluations by choosing unusual points of reference.
11. Role Theory	Role theory concerns the explanation of characteristics of persons performing jobs and tasks within various social contexts. In addition, it explains processes that produce, explain, or are affected by these behaviors.
12. Black's Theory of Law	The quantity of law is determined by the amount of social control, the quantity of respectability, the direction of law between differences in respectability, and the magnitude of differences in respectability. Often, the quantity of law is used as the dependent variable and the other variables are independent.

THEORIES TO EXPLAIN SOCIAL INSTITUTIC
ORGANIZATIONS, AND COMMUNITIES

Systems Theory

A number of disciplines have embraced systems theory, including social work and sociology. Miller (1955) articulated a definition of general system theory that is generally accepted in social work. According to Miller, general system theory encompasses a number of related definitions, assumptions, and postulates about all types of systems, including atomic particles, atoms, molecules, crystals, viruses, cells, organs, individuals, small groups, societies, planets, solar systems, and galaxies. Hearn (1979) took general system theory and reformulated it as systems theory to explain the areas that specifically concern social work, such as working with individuals, groups, organizations, and communities. Each is a complete system, but each is also related or connected to other systems. This configuration also reflects the mandate of human behavior in the social environment to include theories and knowledge about the range of social systems in which individuals live (families, groups, organizations, institutions, and communities).

Drawing from general system theory, Hearn (1979) explained the concepts that are important for understanding systems theory. First, some systems are living, and some are not. For instance, an individual constitutes a living system, but a planet does not. A system has an environment, which is everything external to the system. Systems have various degrees of **entropy**, which is the amount of disorganization in a system. Systems strive to maintain a condition known as a steady state or **homoeostasis**. Viewed in this manner, a system, when it has been disrupted, seeks to return to its predisruption state. Another important concept is that of **equifinality**, which refers to obtaining the same results from different initial conditions. For instance, skilled mental health professionals may be persons with graduate degrees in social work, counseling, psychology, or nursing. There are multiple ways to become a skilled counselor.

A system may be opened or closed. A closed system limits inputs and outputs, but an opened system facilitates inputs or outputs. One may further understand **opened and closed systems** as a vent that permits air flow in and out, which would be opened. A closed vent impedes air flow. Borrowing from physics, systems theorists use the concept of **holon**, which is a component that is simultaneously a whole and a part. Every system, except for the smallest system, has subsystems. Another important concept is that of the **focal system**. It is the system that is of primary interest at a given time. Hearn (1979) summarized the system concepts that are used in assessing and intervening with various systems. The most prevalently adopted concepts are boundary definition and maintenance, feedback, open system, entropy, input-throughout-output, steady state, equifinality, interdependence, homeostasis, wholeness/holism, interrelatedness, holon, and synergy and environment.

Hearn (1979) then distinguished between opened and closed systems. A closed system does not permit the following dynamics. For instance, an opened system exchanges energy and information with its environment. An opened system, compared to a closed system, is self-regulatory. As an illustration, when an opened system is disrupted, it returns to its previous state automatically. Opened systems operate as functional processes. This means that all parts of a system perform harmoniously so as to maintain homeostasis. Opened systems facilitate **feedback**, which is defined as a feature that adjusts future conduct by past performance, and feedback helps maintain a system's steady state.

As related above, a family is a system, and systems theory has been used to provide a theoretical basis for family therapy (Fraser, Hawkins, & Howard, 1988; Lord & Barnes, 1996; Michaels & Green, 1979; Sutphen, Thyer, & Kurtz, 1995). According to Hearn (1979, p. 336), "a family may be identified as a focal system. If viewed as a holon, attention must be given both to its members and to its significant environments, such as schools, community, work organization, other families and the neighborhood. Merely to look at the interactions among family members (the family as a whole) ignores the functions of the family as part." For instance, Henggeler, Halliday-Boykins, Cunningham, Shapiro, and Chapman (2006) conceptualized an intervention for violent juvenile offenders that they called multisystemic treatment, which was based in part on systems theory. According to them, just working with a violent juvenile on probation was insufficient. Instead, the intervention had to include the juvenile's family, extended family, school, and neighborhood and maybe the neighborhood gang. Figure 3.1 shows how systems are nested.

Figure 3.1   A Juvenile Delinquent Nested Within Other Systems

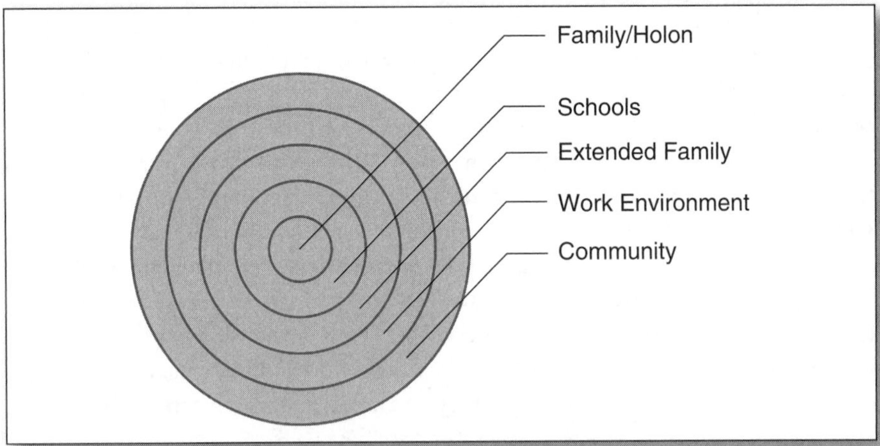

- Family/Holon
- Schools
- Extended Family
- Work Environment
- Community

A contemporary family consists of many arrangements. These arrangements include nuclear families (i.e., families that consist of only parents and unmarried children), single-parent families (i.e., families of one parent and one or more children), common law relationships (i.e., a man and a woman who live together with or without children), reconstituted families (i.e., a husband and wife with children from a previous marriage), blended families (i.e., a man and a woman who are not married with children from one or both of the spouses' previous marriages), extended families (i.e., parents, unmarried children, and other relatives, such as uncles, aunts, and grandparents), consanguine families (i.e., a family organized around blood relatives, such as several sisters or brothers living together); conjugal families (i.e., a family consisting of just a husband and wife), and same-sex couples with or without children.

Each family, regardless of its type, provides various instrumental and expressive functions for each member, such as socialization, safety, procreation, care, and social support. According to Andreae (1996, p. 606), "the family system represents a subsystem of the larger community of which the following assumptions may be made":

- The whole is greater than the sum of its parts.
- Modifying one system will lead to changes in other systems.
- Over a period of time, families organize and evolve.
- For the most part, families are opened systems that receive information and exchange it with other family members and with outside systems. The degree of openness of a family differs according to circumstances and the life of the family.
- Individual dysfunction emanates from an active emotional system. Often, a symptom in one member diverts attention from another part of the system.

A systems perspective may be used, as stated, to illustrate the interconnection of all systems, but we describe here a world systems perspective because it explicitly includes a discussion of globalization and how to think about international issues.

World Systems Theory

World systems theory involves all the small and large human interaction networks, from the household to global trade (Bailey, 2001). As described by Christopher Chase-Dunn (2001, p. 591),

the main idea is simple: Human beings on Earth have been interacting with one another in important ways over broad expanses of space since the emergence of ocean-going transportation in the 15th century. Before incorporation of the Americas into the Afroeurasian system, there were many local and regional world systems (intersocietal networks). Most of these were inserted into the expanding European-centered system largely by force and their populations were mobilized to supply labor for a colonial economy that was repeatedly reorganized according to the changing geopolitical and economic forces emanating from the European and (later) North American core societies. This whole process can be understood structurally as a stratification system composed of economically and politically dominant core societies (themselves in competition with one another) and dependent peripheral and semiperipheral regions, some of which have been successful in improving their positions in the larger core-periphery hierarchy, while most have simply maintained their relative positions.

Globalization and internationalism have been the subject of considerable recent debate. Barker (2003, p. 180) defines **globalization** as "the movement to make economic and cultural activity worldwide in scope and application." This definition involves the internationalization of corporations, which means their reach extends throughout the world (Barker, 2003). Some theorists contend that globalization is a new phenomenon (Sadowski-Smith, 2002), but other theorists believe that it is not new (Chase-Dunn, 2001). (We will discuss globalization more in Chapter 9.) A group of macrosociologists has begun to write about world systems theory and has placed globalization and internationalism within this theory.

The development of the modern world system is driven by the accumulation of capital and geopolitics involving states and businesses competing for power and wealth. A critical point to understand is that "competition among states and capitals is conditioned by the dynamics of struggle among classes and by the resistance of peripheral and semiperipheral people to domination from the core" (Chase-Dunn, 2001, p. 591).

Community Theory

A **community** is a system of interacting and interconnected member subsystems. The system survives as long as the subsystems stay in systematic relationships. Each community, to maintain its character as a distinct system, engages in a pattern of conscious and unconscious processes that are called **boundary maintenance**. A boundary maintenance process may be the construction of spatial boundaries, the establishment of norms, or the development of colloquialisms. According to Bridger, Luloff, and Krannich (2002, p. 9), boundary maintenance alone, however, was not enough to ensure the systemic relationship among different parts of the community. Internal and external changes constantly threatened to disrupt well-established patterns of life. Somehow, though, most communities managed to function relatively smoothly. According to systems theory, the concept of equilibrium made this possible. Except in the rarest of circumstances, such as war or famine, a community was always in a state of equilibrium.

Following World War II, social, economic, cultural, and technological changes transformed life within the United States at the local level, and communities began to change as a consequence. As communities became more dependent on extralocal institutions and sources of income, a major regression in autonomy and local solidarity occurred. Put in research terms, there is a negative relationship between the need for extralocal institutions and sources of income and the degree of autonomy and local solidarity. In other words, the more a community depends on extralocal institutions and sources of income, the less autonomy and local solidarity exist in the community (Bridger et al., 2002).

The key factor in this theory is the progressive expansion of communities' need for extralocal institutions and corporate systems into community affairs. As a result, the locus of decision making transferred from local officials to individuals and areas far removed from the community. As these extra controls took root, communities were undergoing internal changes due to advances in transportation and technologies. These advances have greatly increased people's interactional opportunities. People can shop in one community, work in another, go to a physician in a third, and live in a fourth. Although these changes appear to have given people more freedom, they have come at a price— weakening localized or horizontal linkages (i.e., residents' ties), eroding local solidarity, and "leaving community bereft of the resources necessary to counter the macrostructural shifts" (Bridger et al., 2002, p. 11) that have occurred as described above. By macrostructural shifts, Bridger et al. are referring to the changes and transformations that occur at the macro level that impinges upon local citizens. For example, the building of the interstate highway system within the United States had a major, negative impact upon some small towns as it rerouted traffic. Also, the North American Free Trade Agreement (NAFTA) had a major, negative impact on some small communities when companies left these small communities to open plants in Mexico. Latino activists state that NAFTA has worsened the immigration problem within the United States. Shifts at the macro level impact communities, and local residents in these communities are basically powerless to combat these shifts.

In 1963 Roland Warren articulated this theory, calling it the "Great Change" (Warren, 1970). The **Great Change** states that the community as a unit of social organization has diminished significantly. Local autonomy has been supplanted by a dependence on external organizations and authorities. Consequently, residents and local organizations are more cognizant of affairs and behaviors in the larger society, and they are less concerned and less occupied with community affairs. The Great Change represents a theoretical understanding of the transformation of community life. This transformation has occurred in several spheres: (a) the division of labor; (b) the differentiation of interests and associations; (c) the increasing systemic relationships within the larger society; (d) the bureaucratization and impersonalization within the community; (e) the transfer of functions to profit enterprise and government; (f) the urbanization and suburbanization of the outer rural community; and (g) changing values (Bridger et al., 2002).

This theory has implications not only for what happens in rural and small communities but also for developing communities. Globalization is not a recent phenomenon that was initiated with the election of President George W. Bush. It goes back to the very beginning of colonization as some countries went into other countries for economic reasons and began to make decisions from abroad that impacted community life in colonized countries.

Social Disorganization Theory

Social disorganization theory emerged after World War I. The country had undergone change as a result of migration, urbanization, and industrialization. These societal changes caused or accelerated a host of social problems, such as crime and delinquency, mental illness, drug addiction, alcoholism, and other deviances (Rubington & Weinberg, 1995). As the theory grew from its inchoate stage, early sociologists created different versions of social disorganization theory, but they all agreed that social problems occur as a result of social disorganization (Rubington & Weinberg, 1995).

Social organizational theory explains society as a complex, dynamic social system where parts of the system are synchronized. When actions impact one aspect of the system, adjustments must be made to other parts of the system in order to maintain harmony. When adjustments do not occur or are inadequate, social disorganization occurs. **Social disorganization** is defined as a failure of rules, normlessness, cultural conflict, or breakdown. Social change is the root cause of social disorganization. Hence, social change leads to social disorganization, which leads to social problems (Rubington & Weinberg, 1995). As an illustration, Sampson and Groves (1989) used a community version of social disorganization theory to hypothesize that low economic status, ethnic heterogeneity, residential mobility, and family disruption lead to community social disorganization, which then leads to more crime and delinquency. This hypothesis was supported.

HUMAN CONDUCT THEORIES

Routine Activity Theory

Sociologists have proposed most of the theories used to explain crime and delinquency in society. They have identified several structural conditions that have been reported to cause crime. In the 1960s, a paradox arose that caused many sociologists to reconsider preexisting theories. Despite the generally accepted belief that certain structural conditions (i.e., poverty and lower social class) cause crime, there was a very significant increase in crime beginning in the 1960s when structural conditions did not get worse and in fact structural conditions were lessened. This prompted Cohen and Felson (1979) to develop **routine activity theory**, which they contend explains direct-contact predatory crimes and property and violent crimes. Sociologists are very interested in the concepts of space and time and frequently write on spatial and temporal dimensions of social behaviors. Simply, the minimal requirements for a predatory crime are (a) suitable targets, (b) the absence of capable guardians, and (c) motivated offenders. In essence, these authors contend that three variables must be present for predatory crimes to occur. By stressing that these are the minimal requirements, Cohen and Felson have left room for an expansion of their theory to include other significant variables.

Routine activity theory can be used to explain a variety of predatory crimes (Hipp, Bauer, Curran, & Bollen, 2004; Mustaine & Tewksbury, 1997, 2000; Tewksbury & Mustaine, 2003). It has been used to explain why some communities have more crimes than other communities (Bryant & Miller, 1997). It can explain domestic violence (Kelley, 1994), sexual assaults, child molestation, burglaries and larceny (Massey, Krohn, & Bonati, 1989; Mustaine & Tewksbury, 1998), armed robberies (Felson, 1987), hate crimes (Felson, 1987), workplace violence (Lynch, 1987), stalking (Mustaine & Tewksbury, 1998), and many homicides (Tischler, 1996). One might question this theory by suggesting that some establishments get robbed although they have a security guard, but the theory says *capable* guardians. An armed security guard who is 70 years old might not be a capable guardian, and neither might a woman, though armed, who is 4 feet, 11 inches and weighs 95 pounds. One frequently robbed convenience store stopped all robberies by hiring three security guards. One armed guard stood next to the cashier at the cash register, another armed guard stood behind the counter with a visible shotgun, and a third armed guard stood about 15 feet away. The amount of firepower reduced robberies to zero, but the price of this security was passed on to customers. Also, routine activity theory would suggest that small children are more likely to be sexually molested than older children, and this is especially the case when a motivated person is alone with a child. Simply, a child is more of a suitable target than a grown woman.

Migration Theory

People have migrated from one area or region to another throughout recorded human history. *The Columbus Dispatch* reported that the state of Ohio lost 126,452 residents from 2000 to 2004, and the number-one reason for this migration was the lack of jobs (Doulin, 2006). Also losing residents for economic reasons were New York, California, Illinois, Massachusetts, New Jersey, Michigan, Louisiana, Kansas, and Utah (Doulin, 2006). Recently, the illegal immigration of Latinos from Mexico and South America to the United States has been a hotly debated and contested social issue (Connelly, 2006). In the 1800s, social scientists began to write scholarly articles on the laws of migration. In 1966, Everett Lee provided a systematic theory of migration that has many testable hypotheses for a broad range of movements by individuals.

Broadly speaking, **migration** is the permanent or semipermanent change of one's residence. According to Lee's (1966) theory, every act of migration consists of an origin, a destination, and a set of intervening obstacles, regardless of the distance or difficulties involved. Further, the theory predicts migration regardless of whether a move is across town, to a different city or state, or to a different country. The factors that come into play when a person or group considers whether or not to migrate include (a) factors associated with the area of origin, (b) factors associated with the area of destination, (c) intervening obstacles, and (d) personal factors. According to Lee (1966, p. 50), "we can never specify the exact set of factors which impels [or] prohibits migration for a given person, we can, in general, only set forth a few which seem of special importance and note the general or average reaction of a considerable group." A favorable factor for one person, such as a neighborhood with good schools, may be a disincentive for another person, such as a retired couple without children or grandchildren, or may be an indifferent factor for a third person.

Lee's (1966) theory is broadly applicable. It can be used to explain the movement of professors from one area of the country to another area. One of the obstacles to moving is the expense of transporting one's belongings. A new college or university (the destination) makes it easier for professors to move by paying their relocation expenses. The theory may explain your move to attend college if you came from out of town or from another state. One critical obstacle for many students is paying for their education, and the availability of a full scholarship may remove the financial obstacle and cause a student to move across the country. Further, this theory can explain why some people will move from certain states (i.e., hurricane-prone areas) and not return and why many people from New Orleans who experienced Hurricane Katrina and relocated to other states will not return. The international chapter at the end of this book discusses refugees, and Lee's (1966) theory explains why some people who were living in the Sudan "moved" to Chad in 2005. The theory can also explain the exodus of Jews from Egypt to Palestine from 1917 to 1939, as well as why some Jews migrate to Israel.

INEQUALITY THEORIES

Inequality Theory

Writing in the early 1960s, John Stacy Adams (1965) lamented that other than philosophers, political scientists, politicians, jurists, and economists, few people were professionally concerned with the just distribution of wealth, power, goods, and services in society. To Adams (1965, p. 267), this lack of interest was strange because "the process of exchange is almost continual in human interactions." An important aspect of exchange processes is that once an exchange has occurred, the people involved in the exchange determine whether its outcomes are being just or unjust. Researchers have noted that some individuals are unhappy when they believe that they have been treated unjustly. Adams wanted to extend these concepts surrounding justice into a broader theory and postulate other outcomes besides dissatisfaction when individuals believed that they had been subjected to inequality. Although Adams's theory may appear to be applicable to micro systems, it has the potential to apply to macro systems. At the macro level, it can explain the behaviors of members of the military, minority groups, and workers, as well as group cohesiveness in general. Johnson, Selenta, and Lord (2006) used principles from Adams's (1965) theory to explore organizational justice because an understanding of it could promote a sense of fairness among workers.

Adams (1965) eschewed the term *justice* and preferred to discuss his theory in terms of inequality. First he discussed **relative deprivation** as a concept and conceptualized **distributive justice theory** as a foundation for understanding inequality theory. Simply, relative deprivation is the perceived unfair violation of expectations. Stated differently, relative deprivation is a feeling that there is a discrepancy between what is perceived to be and what is perceived should be or a discrepancy between an achievement and an expectation of achievement (Adams, 1965). Relative deprivation was first introduced in the 1940s to explain seemingly contradictory findings from a study of soldiers after World War II. The study found that soldiers with a high school education were not as satisfied as soldiers with less than a high school education, although soldiers with a high school education had better opportunities for advancement in the military. A similar finding showed that soldiers in the Army Air Corps, who had better promotional opportunities, were not more satisfied than soldiers in the Military Police, who had lesser promotional opportunities. To explain these findings, the concept of relative deprivation was introduced into the academic discourse.

Distributive justice has been discussed in economic terms. Individuals in an exchange relationship experience distributive justice when the profits of individuals are proportional to their investment. Profits are determined by the amount received minus the costs. Costs are those things that a party gives up in the exchange and may include risk, loss of reward, or psychological discomfort. Investments that are brought to an exchange are skills, effort, education, training, experience, age, sex, and ethnic background.

According to Adams (1965, p. 273), "when an inequality between the proportions exists, the participants to the exchange will experience a feeling of injustice, and one or the other party will experience deprivation. The party specifically experiencing relative deprivation is the one for whom the ratio of profits to investments is the smaller." Importantly, the theory of distributive justice explains situations involving two or more persons when each receives rewards from a third party, such as employees in an organization who are being evaluated by a director. While Adams used designations such as Person and Other to denote a human exchange, those designations may also "refer to groups rather than to individuals, when a class of jobs (e.g., toolmakers) is out of line with another class (e.g., lathe operators), or when the circumstances of one ethnic group are incongruous with those of another. In such cases, it is convenient to deal with the class as a whole rather than with individual members of a class" (Adams, 1965, p. 280). As theoretical concepts, distributive justice and relative deprivation identify some of the conditions that produce perceptions of justice and, complementarily, the conditions that lead individuals to feel that their relations with others are just.

Adams (1965) focused on the concept of inequity to emphasize the causes and consequences of the absence of equity in human exchange relationships.

For heuristic purposes, Adams chose to focus on common employee/ employer exchanges. However, equity or the lack of equity applies to any social situation involving an exchange between teammates, teacher and student, lovers, child and parent, patient and therapist, opponents, enemies, and so forth. Before defining inequity and equity mathematically, Adams detailed the antecedents of inequity. Inputs are those attributes that an individual has, including education, intelligence, experience, training, skill, seniority, age, sex, social status, and ethnic background. Outcomes are the results of exchanges, such as pay, promotion, satisfying supervision, or parking space.

Feminist Theory

The modern feminist movement began in the 1960s, and during its infancy, feminist theory emerged. Feminist theory sought a comprehensive examination of all environmental factors that oppress women. Later, feminist theory emerged as an independent explanation for women's condition and problems. It sees women's maladaptive behavior, if it occurs, as resulting from external factors, such as oppression, instead of internal factors, such as personal sickness (Rosewater, 1990). Later, feminist theory evolved into a series of feminist theories and perspectives (Dutton-Douglas & Walker, 1988).

Jackie Stacey (1993, p. 50) describes feminist theory as

a body of knowledge which offers critical explanations of women's subordination. . . . It also tends to operate at some level of abstraction, using analytical categories which move beyond the merely descriptive or anecdotal, and at some level of generalisation moving beyond the individual case. . . . Typically, feminist theory offers some kind of analysis and explanation of how and why women have less power than men, and how this imbalance could be challenged and transformed.

Ann A. Abbott (1995) used feminist theory to explain women and substance abuse. Abbott linked the role of inequality in society, differential power between the genders, and the effect of this system on women's self-esteem and their susceptibility to substance abuse. White men in particular possess a highly disproportionate share of societal power, and they determine what is valuable and important. Because women are made to feel worthless, a condition is established where they seek a need to feel complete and in control. Women may use substances to compensate for their sense of powerlessness and frustration. Abbott (1995, p. 262) proposes that

> by using alcohol and other drugs, women seek a paradoxical solution. They initially feel power over the decision to use a substance and seize the opportunity to control their intake of that substance to help them escape their social plight. In the process, as dependence on and tolerance of the substance develop, women are once again controlled by an external force, becoming powerless against it.

Conarton and Silverman (1988) used feminist theory to challenge Erik Erikson's (1980) five stages of human development and the appropriateness of this conceptualization for women. They theorized that women undergo nine phases instead of five: bonding, orientation toward others, cultural adaptation, awakening, separation, the development of the feminine, empowerment, spiritual development, and integration. Conarton and Silverman did not see these phases as stages through which women systematically pass. Instead, they saw these phases as cyclical and explained that women reexperience these phases throughout their lives.

Nes and Iadicola (1989) distinguished three models of feminism, namely liberal, radical, and socialist. Liberal feminism maintains that men and women possess a similar capacity to achieve. However, this capacity for women has been impeded by the social conditions impinging upon women. Some inequality among individuals, however, is expected because of differences in motivation and potential. So, inequality that appears to approximate a bell-shaped curve, irrespective of gender, is natural. However, should such distribution be skewed toward males, then a problem exists. For adherents of the liberal perspective, the issue is not male oppression but the denial of equal opportunity and full liberty for women. Women can prosper socially and economically within the current patriarchal system. Men's attitude and behavior are what needs to change, not men's nature. The change that women need to make is to be more competitive, assertive, individualistic, and self-directed.

Radical feminism views men's and women's natures as being different. Proponents of this perspective believe that women's nature is superior to men's and that men should be more like women. The social order mirrors males' nature and need to dominate and control. Patriarchy was once based on biological factors. Now, it rests upon ideology, law, and violence against women. The male need to dominate and control women gratifies men's ego. Male children come into a society that teaches them to oppress females. Radical feminists seek the total destruction of patriarchy and a new social order based on women's values.

Social feminism involves varied viewpoints. While all feminists agree that women are oppressed by men, the source of that oppression is the subject of different views. Some believe the oppression is based on class, others believe it is based on sex, and some believe it is based on variations of both. Class oppression is based on men's and women's relative ability to produce things, while sex oppression is based on men's and women's relative ability to produce human beings. Another important concept in social feminism is that of human nature. Human nature is based on human needs. Humans have physical or natural needs like all animals (i.e., food, clothing, water, sex, and shelter). Humans also have needs that are specific to their species, such as the ability to think, create, and imagine.

According to feminists, women are restricted in terms of their human needs. Men control and exploit the two spheres of production and reproduction—the workplace and home. According to social feminists, "the primary factor that perpetuates sex inequality . . . is that the modes of production and reproduction and the articulation of these two modes form the foundation of the social order" (Nes & Iadicola, 1989, p. 15). Therefore, a key strategy is to raise women's consciousness so that they would know that their physical and species needs for nurturance, love, and companionship can be realized in a relationship without dominance or submission (Nes & Iadicola, 1989).

Other feminist theorists have examined the application of feminist theory to specific problems that women have. For instance, Rosewater (1990) states that women tend to have problems with depression, substance abuse, anxiety disorders, and violent victimization. Wallace (1995) also indicates that Latino and African American women have more problems than White women with the criminal justice and child welfare systems because of their drug problems. However, White women with drug issues, especially those in the middle class and upper class, do not have the same experiences as minority women with drug problems in the lower social class.

Power Theory and Social Independence Theory

Blau (1964, p. 117) defined power as "the ability of persons or groups to impose their will on others despite resistance through deterrence either in the form of withholding regularly supplied rewards or in the form of punishment, inasmuch as the former as well as the latter constitute, in effect, a negative sanction." Blau's definition carries three limitations. First, the concept of power does not refer to the influencing of others on a single issue but refers to a group or individual's ability to impose its will repeatedly on others. Second, the threatened punishment for resistance makes power a commanding force. However, there is an element of voluntarism in power. Punishment may be selected instead of compliance, distinguishing power from direct physical coercion. Third, power is intrinsically asymmetrical and is the net ability to administer punishment and block rewards. Net ability is that which remains after restraints have been unsuccessfully applied. If persons or groups are interdependent and have equal strength, then neither can exercise power over the other, and there is a lack of power, essentially.

A person or group establishes power over others by providing the services they demand. If some persons continually provide needed services to others that they cannot get elsewhere, those receiving the services become dependent and beholden to those persons for these needed services. If these persons provide benefits that produce interdependence, they are less subject to dependence and obligation. Individuals or groups can also achieve power over others by threatening to deny needed benefits that they currently provide unless those receiving the benefits submit to demands. The threat of punishment occasions the dependence that is the origin of power. It is an indirect exhibition of power. Direct exhibition occurs when recurrent, essential rewards are withheld. As Blau (1964, p. 118) notes, "the government that furnishes needed protection to its citizens, the employer that provides needed jobs to his [or her] employees, and the profession that supplies needed services to the community all make the others dependent on them and potentially subject to their power."

Blau (1964) reformulated Emerson's (1962) power-dependent relations schema to delineate the circumstances that create an imbalance of power. Emerson's schema, in effect, can also be used to explain the conditions of social independence, the requirements of power, the issues of power conflicts, and the structural implications of power. According to Blau's reformulation, four alternatives exist for individuals who need a service that another person has to offer. First, they can be provided with a service that they want enough to be convinced to provide a service in return. Second, they may obtain the needed service elsewhere. Third, they can, if capable, coerce the person to furnish the service. Fourth, they can decide to do without the service. If they are not able or willing to choose any one of these alternatives, they must comply with the wishes of the person. Simply, the person can condition the continued supply of services for others' compliance. The supply of services ultimately creates power. Essentially, the absence of the exercise of alternatives delimits the conditions of power.

As stated, Emerson's (1962) schema also provides an understanding of social independence. The necessities of social independence are characterized by the opposite of power-dependent relations. First, strategic resources promote independence. A person who has resources is insulated from becoming dependent on others. Money and wealth are insulators against dependence. However, money does not guarantee independence. Fame and love may make one dependent, despite wealth and money. Second, having alternative sources for needed services helps cultivate independence. However, a commitment to a social relationship has a degree of dependence. An employee generally stays with an employer because either the second alternative (i.e., a less rewarding job or no job) is less attractive or the employee feels that he or she has invested a lot in the current job. An employer can change the dynamics of a job by making it less attractive to an employee and making the distance between the current job and the alternative lesser. An employer decreases his or her power by making the employee less dependent (e.g., decreasing the distance between the job and the alternative). An employee can decrease his or her dependence by taking fewer benefits from an employer. Another way of viewing this proposition is that the more benefits that an employer gives to the employee, the more power the employer will have. Generally speaking, "the greater the difference between the benefits an individual supplies to others and those they can obtain elsewhere, the greater is his [or her] power over them likely to be" (Blau, 1964, p. 120). Third, social independence is enhanced by a person's ability to use coercive force. Of course, normative behavior might prevent the use of unlawful force. But there is strength in numbers, and creating a coalition might force demands on others who exercise power. The fourth condition of social independence is the lack of need for services. An individual who has few wants and needs is unlikely to be a very dependent person.

This fourfold schema provides strategies necessary to attain and sustain power, which complement the conditions for social independence. Blau (1964, p. 121) stated that "to achieve power over others with his [or her] resources, a person must prevent others from choosing any of the first four alternatives, thereby compelling them to comply with his [or her] directives as a condition for obtaining the needed benefits at his [or her] command." First, to gain power a person must remain indifferent to the benefits that others can offer in exchange for the person's benefits. For example, power strategies that reflect indifference are denying others access to resources that are vital for the welfare of them. This means preventing or limiting others access to government, acquiring needed benefits from outside sources, creating unions, and encouraging competition among suppliers for essential services. A second requirement for maintaining power is to ensure the continued dependence of others on the services one has. The third requirement for maintaining power is to prevent others from using coercive force. The fourth requirement for maintaining power is to preserve people's needs for the benefits that the powerful individual provides.

GROUP THEORIES

Social Learning Theory

One of the most dominant and empirically supported theories to explain crime and delinquency is social learning theory (Adams, 1996; Britt & Gottfredson, 2003; Krohn, 1999; Tittle, 2004). It has been used also to explain the connection between adolescent fire setting and murder (Singer & Hensley, 2004), police misconduct (Chappell & Piquero, 2004), gambling (Skinner, 2003), substance abuse by college students (Capece & Lanza-Kaduce, 2003), drinking and readiness to change (McIntyre, 2003), a comparison of the victimization of adolescent sexual offenders and nonsexual offenders (Burton, Miller, & Shill, 2002), conflict tactics of Arab siblings living in Israel (HajYahia & Dawud-Noursi, 1998), computer crimes by college students (Skinner & Fream, 1997), marital violence (Mihalic & Elliott, 1997), divorce mediation (Stuart & Jacobson, 1986), dating violence (Tontodonato & Crew, 1992), adolescent smoking (Akers & Lee, 1996), exercise-related health needs of elderly persons (Schuster & Petosa, 1993), fertility control of adolescents (Eisen, Zellman, & McAlister, 1992), and alcohol use by the elderly (Akers, La Greca, Cochran, & Sellers, 1989). Very applicable to social work, social learning theory has been advocated as a way to understand human behaviors in the social environment (Thyer & Myers, 1998) and as a conceptual framework for social work education (Thyer & Wodarski, 1990).

Social learning theory states that both conforming and deviant behaviors involve the same learning process, functioning within a context of situation, social structure, and interaction. The direction of this learning process within the context determines whether a behavior is conforming or deviant. Whether a behavior is conforming or deviant is not determined by an all-or-nothing process or either-or process but rather is determined by the balance of influences on behavior. The balance is typically stable over time, but it can change under certain circumstances. Social learning theory acknowledges that the principles in operant and classical conditioning explain conforming and deviant behavior. But social learning theory says that the principal mechanisms of learning are that part of the learning process in which differential reinforcement and imitation produce cognitive and overt behaviors that serve as cues for conforming and deviant behavior. Social learning theory emphasizes four major concepts in this process—imitation, definition, differential association, and differential reinforcement (Akers, 1998).

Imitation

Besides direct conditioning, another way in which behavior develops is through imitation or modeling (Akers, Krohn, Lanza-Kaduce, & Radosevich, 1979). **Imitation** is the duplication of a particular behavior by an individual after viewing another individual who had performed the same behavior. Two explanations have been offered to explain why imitation occurs. First, an individual who imitates does so because he or she has been vicariously reinforced after viewing another individual being rewarded for a particular behavior. Second, an individual who imitates does so because of operant conditioning. That is to say, imitated behavior occurs because it has been directly reinforced (Akers, 1973). An abundance of evidence, gathered from experimental studies in laboratories, shows that children will often imitate or model behavior (Bandura, 1977; Gadon, Sprafkin, & Ficarrotto, 1987; Hicks, 1971; Hilgard, Atkinson, & Atkinson, 1979; Rimm & Masters, 1979; Schultz, 1976; Tryon & Keane, 1986). Most important, the likelihood of an adolescent imitating behavior is stronger when the model is admired (Akers, 1973, 1985). As an illustration, Evel Knievel, the motorcycle stuntman, was blamed for several children sustaining fractured limbs after trying to jump obstacles with their bicycles following one of Knievel's highly publicized stunts. Lionel Tate, then a 12-year-old boy who was somewhat large for his age, killed a 7-year-old girl by jumping on her in an attempt to imitate a wrestling move. He was sentenced to life imprisonment as a 14-year-old but was given 10 years' probation after his murder conviction was overturned. He subsequently robbed a pizza deliveryman, had his probation revoked, and was sent back to prison for 30 years (Aguayo, 2006).

Definition

Definitions and learning-specific techniques are necessary components in the commission of crimes and a major component of differential association. Before a person can commit a crime, the person needs to learn definitions, which would make him or her willing to violate the law. Moreover, the person needs to learn specific techniques unique to law violating, such as breaking into a safe or counterfeiting. In his reformulation of differential association, Akers (1973) accepts that if definitions are important in learning to commit crimes, then they are also important in learning deviant behavior. Therefore, definitions in a deviance sense refer to normative statements about right and wrong (Akers, 1973). For example, before a person will smoke marijuana on a regular basis, he or she must believe that smoking marijuana is righteous or proper. DeYoung (1989) has provided an example of how important definitions are in the maintenance of deviant behavior by describing how the North American Man/Boy Love Association (NAMBLA) normalized pedophilic behavior in its newspaper. NAMBLA published accounts proclaiming that sex between an adult and a child is beneficial in helping the child learn about his sexuality or in freeing the child from a totalitarian society.

Differential Association

Differential association is the process by which an individual aligns himself or herself with the group that controls the individual's major source of reinforcers. The most important of these groups are one's peer group and family. However, other groups are also important, including school, church, and social groups (Akers et al., 1979). For instance, an adolescent who is a heavy marijuana smoker who moves to a new community is going to align himself or herself with a group that is going to provide reinforcers for his or her behavior.

Differential Reinforcement

Differential reinforcement is the process by which deviant behavior becomes dominant over conforming behavior. By illustration, given two modes of behavior that are both reinforced, the one that is reinforced in the greatest amount, more frequently, and with the highest probability will become dominant (Akers, 1973). An adolescent who is presented with the choice of smoking marijuana or not smoking marijuana will manifest the behavior that is reinforced the most, more frequently, and with the highest probability.

Aware of the strong evidence from psychological research involving learning, Burgess and Akers (1966) revised this theory of differential association into a theory of deviance and renamed it social learning theory. This theory more closely resembles the reinforcement theories of Bandura (1977) and Rotter (1975) than pure Skinnerian theory because pure Skinnerian theory rejects mentalistic processes. Moreover, Akers's (1985) social learning theory differs from Bandura (1977) and Rotter's (1975) social learning theories in that Akers theorized that "the principal behavioral effects come from interaction in or under the influence of those groups which control individuals' major sources of reinforcement and punishment and expose them to behavioral models and normative definitions" (Akers et al., 1979, p. 638).

Although similar to Sutherland's (1939) nine statements of how criminal behavior is learned, Akers (1985) contends that his seven reformulated statements are a new theory. His theory says:

1. Deviant behavior is learned according to the principles of operant conditioning.

2. Deviant behavior is learned both in nonsocial situations that are reinforcing or discriminative and through that social interaction in which the behavior of other persons is reinforcing or discriminative for such behavior.

3. The principal part of the learning of deviant behavior occurs in those groups that comprise or control the individual's major source of reinforcements.

4. The learning of deviant behavior, including specific techniques, attitudes, and avoidance procedures, is a function of the effective and available reinforcers and the existing reinforcement contingencies.

5. The specific class of behavior that is learned and its frequency are a function of the reinforcers that are effective and available and the deviant or nondeviant direction of the norms, rules, and definitions that in the past have accompanied the reinforcement.

6. The probability that a person will commit deviant behavior is increased in the presence of normative statements, definitions, and verbalizations that have acquired discriminative value for behavior in the process of differential reinforcement of such behavior over conforming behavior.

7. The strength of deviant behavior is a direct function of the amount, frequency, and probability of its reinforcement. The modalities of association with deviant patterns are important insofar as they affect the source, amount, and scheduling of reinforcement.

These seven propositions constitute social learning, but the heart of the theory is the first sentence in proposition 7: "The strength of deviant behavior is a direct function of the amount, frequency, and probability of its reinforcement." From these seven propositions, Akers (1985) has deduced four independent variables that he says will explain any conforming or deviant behavior. These are the extent of an individual's imitation of admired models (which is deduced from proposition 2), the extent of an individual's definitions of certain behaviors (which is deduced from proposition 5), the extent of an individual's differential association (which is deduced from proposition 5), and the extent of an individual's differential reinforcement (which is deduced from proposition 3).

Reference Group Theory

Many sociologists, social psychologists, and cultural anthropologists adopt the view that a person's reference group shapes attitudes and conduct. A reference group is defined as any group that shapes the attitudes and behaviors of individuals. Moreover, the individual's self-appraisal, feelings, and conduct emanate from his or her position in his or her reference group and the reference group's position within a social hierarchy (Hyman & Singer, 1968). The most unique contribution of reference group theory is that individuals form their attitudes in reference to groups and their self-evaluations by choosing unusual points of reference. Of course, behavior may occur without guidance from a reference group. Also, some persons in particular statuses have incongruent self-image because they have other statuses. These status sets influence the process. In addition, some persons within a group may depart from a group because they have memberships in other groups. Still, reference group theory explains which memberships and which statuses govern a person. An example of the explanatory power of reference group theory is reflected by the following proposition: The probability of death within a year is predicted by locating an individual in a certain reference class (e.g., 21 years of age).

Festinger (1968) argued that the drive for self-evaluation involving an individual's opinions and abilities has implications for understanding the behavior in groups as well as the processes of group creation and changing group membership. Given that self-evaluation only occurs when a person compares himself or herself with other people, the urge for self-evaluation constitutes a force impinging upon individuals to belong to groups and to relate with others. In a subjective sense, individuals' need to feel correct in their opinions and feel unquestionable in their assessment of their performance of abilities provides a sense of satisfaction from relating with other people. Surely, individuals receive other pleasures from being associated with a group, but the drive for self-evaluation is considerable.

As Festinger (1968, p. 143) declared,

> people, then, tend to move into groups which, in their judgment, hold opinions which agree with their own and whose abilities are near their own. And they tend to move out of groups in which they are unable to satisfy their drive for self-evaluation. Such movement in and out of groups is, of course, not a completely fluid affair. The attraction to a group may be strong enough for other reasons so that a person cannot move out of it. Or there may be restraints, for one or another reason, against leaving. In both of these circumstances, mobility from one group to another is hindered.

Festinger (1968) delineated several specific hypotheses and derivatives from a theory of social comparison processes. These hypotheses are used to study how processes determine appraisal, evaluation of ability, and opinions. Festinger stated a number of hypotheses and corollaries, which were followed by explanations and rationalizations. These hypotheses and corollaries are mostly testable through experimental research.

Role Theory

Role theory concerns the explanation of characteristics of persons performing jobs and tasks within various social contexts. In addition, it explains processes that produce, explain, or are affected by these behaviors. The explanation of patterned human behavior or roles is central to role theory. Roles are connected to social positions or statuses. Generally speaking, a social position identifies a commonly recognized set of persons. Titles, such as physician, schoolteacher, janitor, professional athlete, hermit, grandmother, juvenile delinquent, and social worker, represent a particular set of persons. Each title represents a social position. For instance, a physician, schoolteacher, and janitor are expected to behave in certain ways. A physician writes prescriptions and conducts physical examinations. A schoolteacher lectures and grades papers. A janitor empties wastebaskets and sweeps floors. Each social position features a characteristic role (Biddle, 1979).

According to Biddle (1979, p. 8), role theory "is as broad as the ocean and as shallow as a mud puddle." It has been called "a set of plastic concepts that can be applied to the superficial analysis of any individual and social system" (Biddle, 1979, p. 8). The fluidness of role theory contributes to its popularity with some social scientists. These social scientists define role, social position, and exception. Role could be an identity, a set of characteristic behaviors, or a set of expectations. Expectations could be descriptive, prescriptive, or evaluative.

Some of the basic propositions of role theory are as follows:

1. Some behaviors are patterned and are characteristic of persons within contexts (i.e., from roles).

2. Roles are often associated with sets of persons who share a common identity (i.e., who constitute social positions).

3. Persons are often aware of roles, and to some extent roles are governed by the fact of that awareness (i.e., expectations).

4. Roles persist, in part, because of their consequences (functions) and because they are often imbedded within larger social systems.

5. Persons must be taught roles (i.e., must be socialized) and may find either joy or sorrow in the performances thereof.

But these propositions are basic. Biddle (1979) discusses a multitude of concepts related to role theory, such as context, functions, social systems, **role playing, role taking, self-concept, role conflict,** and **role overload.** Roles are partialized into role differentiation, role set, role complement, and role integration. Affecting role integration are complementary interdependence and reciprocity.

Because Western society is complex, quickly changing, and crisis laden, a number of positions and roles exist. These positions and roles are both positive and negative. Some of these negative roles are unpleasant, demanding, and anxiety provoking. A changing, stressful society may require individuals to adjust to new roles and positions. Individuals who do not adjust easily experience maladjustment. Role theory provides an explanation for individuals' adjustment.

Adjustment has many definitions. It refers to adaptation, ability to perform, flexibility, and satisfaction. In the therapeutic environment, adjustment refers to the absence of unhappiness or neurotic symptoms. In other environments, adjustment represents a person's ability to cope with others' demands. Taking the common definition, one might say that adjustment is an individual's ability to accommodate the social position or positions that the individual has and the expected roles for this individual. According to Biddle (1979, p. 322),

the adjusted person likes his or her identities and enjoys and performs well the roles that are expected of him or her. Persons are maladjusted when they are unhappy with their positions or dissatisfied with or unable to perform well roles that are expected of them. To be maladjusted is not necessarily a bad thing. Creative scientists and artists are often dissatisfied with the expectations of earlier generations. But maladjustment is always associated with tension, hence it is assumed to be problematic for the person. Maladjusted persons are motivated to do something about the condition, thus maladjustment predicts both personal and social change.

Adjustment or maladjustment may be caused by structural problems such as status, role conflict, role ambiguity, role overload, role discontinuity, and role malintegration. All may pressure a person. For the most part, persons with low status are more likely to be maladjusted than persons with high status. Role conflict is the common or attributed polarized dissensus that presents problems for individuals. **Dissensus** is the condition when nonconsenual expectation exists or is presumed to exist. For instance, a mother and father might have different norms for their daughter's behavior. If parents disagree, this disagreement would be called common dissensus. If the daughter believes her parents hold different views, then this would be attributed dissensus. Role ambiguity occurs when shared specifications linked to an expected role are insufficient or incomplete to inform an individual of what is desired or how to do it. Role overload is simply a role set that is too complex for an individual. Role discontinuity is a lack of integration in the roles that a person is asked to do in sequence. Role malintegration exists when a person cannot reconcile roles that require tremendous physical strength with those roles that require mental acuity.

Then there are personal problems affecting adjustment, such as role skill and self-role congruence. Role skill is a person's ability to perform a complex role. Some characteristics associated with role skill are intelligence, flexibility, and emotional maturity. Self-role congruence occurs when there is a match between a person's expected role and personal characteristics. Individuals who experience stress because of their positions or expected role undergo role strain. As a coping strategy, persons who have difficulties with their position or expected role may alter their involvement and role distance. Involvement is the extent to which an individual invests effort into a role performance. Biddle (1979, p. 326) adds that "these concepts do not exhaust the subject of adjustment to roles."

Donald Black's Theory of Law

Reality manifests itself through behavior. As such, all realities behave or manifest themselves differently when forces impinge upon them, such as molecules, organisms, planets, and personalities. The same may be said for social reality, such as families, organizations, cities, revolutions, conversation, friendships, and government. Social reality or social life varies according to stratification, morphology, culture, organization, and social control (Black, 1976).

Stratification involves the vertical layering of social life with the most privileges of life resting with individuals at the top and few or no privileges resting with persons at the bottom. **Morphology** entails the horizontal spreading of people and their degree of integration or intimacy. **Culture** is the unique patterns of a group. **Organization** is the collective action of a group. Last, **social control** involves the normative facets of social life and determines what constitutes deviant behavior. Social control also determines whether such deviant behavior will be disapproved, prohibited, compensated, or punished. It emanates from a number of institutions, such as the family or church (Black, 1976).

Social control also explains other facets of social life. Accepting that individuals respond to the expectations of other individuals, one may explain variations in conduct by variations in social control. Accordingly, one may assume that legal authorities, as well as other persons, will respond to the expectations of others. Law, therefore, may be explained by other forms of social control, such as control provided by the family, church, neighborhood, and school (Black, 1976).

Theory of Law Variables

This representation of the theory of law involves several variables. These are the quantity of law, the amount of social control, the quantity of respectability, the direction of law between differences in respectability, and the magnitude of differences in respectability. Often, the quantity of law is used as the dependent variable, and the other variables are independent.

According to Black (1976, p. 3), the quantity of law is "known by the number and scope of prohibitions, obligations, and other standards to which people are subject, and the rate of legislation, litigation, and adjudication." As such, it can be measured in a variety of ways. For instance, any complaining to a legal authority is more law than no complaining and represents the quantity of law. The legal authority may be a police official, a call or visit to a regulatory agency, or the court to bring a lawsuit. Also, the accepting or investigating of a complaint is more law than rejecting or not investigating (Black, 1976).

In criminal law, an arrest is more law than no arrest, a search of a person on the street is more law than no search, a search of a person's car is more law than the waiving of a car search, and an interrogation is more law than no interrogation. The setting of bail is more law than no bail. A higher bail is more law than a lower bail. A conviction is more law than no conviction. A conviction for a felony is more law than a conviction for a misdemeanor. A prison sentence is more law than probation. In family court, a juvenile's detention before a hearing is more law than a release to his or her parents (Black, 1976).

In civil law, a verdict in favor of the plaintiff is more law than a verdict on behalf of the defendant. This is so because of the increase of obligations upon the defendant and no obligation upon the plaintiff. The more money awarded to the plaintiff, the more law for the defendant. An appeal by the plaintiff is more law, and a successful appeal is more law. At the same time, a decision in favor of the defendant is less law (Black, 1976).

The amount of social control is a quantitative variable. One setting (i.e., family, community, organization) may have more social control than another, and each setting may have more social control than a similar setting. For instance, a family may have more social control than a neighborhood, and one family may have more social control than another family. Also, a private setting, such as a military or Catholic school, may have more social control than a public setting, such as a public school (Black, 1976).

Respectability is a normative status and represents a variable of importance to the theory of law. People have various degrees of respectability, which are enhanced or hurt by individual and group affiliation. In part, respectability is determined by the amount of social control imposed upon individuals. The more social control imposed, the less respectable an individual is. Singularly or as a whole, different types of social control determine respectability. Moreover, unrespectable individuals, among themselves, have less law than respectable individuals, among themselves. For instance, thieves are less likely than white-collar professionals to invoke law among themselves (Black, 1976).

The direction of law between differences in respectability is a normative direction. According to Black (1976, p. 114), "a deviant act has normative direction if the offender is less respectable than his victim, or vice versa. The normative direction of law is opposite that of the deviant act. Thus, if a deviant act is from less to more respectability, the normative direction of law is from more to less." Thus, an offense has normative direction if the victim and the offender do not have equal amounts of respectability.

Last, the magnitude of the differences in respectability is the degree of difference between one person and another. For instance, a president of a major university likely has more respectability than a store clerk. At the same time, the store clerk likely has more respectability than a homeless person. The magnitude of difference between the president and the homeless person is greater than that between the president and the store clerk. Given these variables, Black (1976) has proffered some propositions for empirical testing.

Theory of Law Propositions

According to Black (1976, p. 107), "law varies inversely with other social control." So, as the family or neighborhood loses social control, there is more law. Also, "law varies directly with respectability" (Black, 1976, p. 112). That is to say, the more respectable a person is, the greater the quantity of law. Black (1976, p. 114) states that "law is greater in a direction toward less respectability than toward more respectability." This proposition refers to deviants and how they are controlled. Last, according to Black (1976, p. 117), "in a direction toward less respectability, law varies directly with normative distance." However, in a direction toward more respectability, law varies inversely with normative distance.

A number of problems related to law and social work can be studied with Black's theory of law. For instance, the proposition that "law varies inversely with other social control" (Black, 1976, p. 107) can be used to study the decisions of family court judges who decide child welfare issues. Law could be operationalized as a decision to place a child in the custody of children's services versus a decision to leave the child with the family. The amount of social control may be operationalized by several variables, such as the amount of parental control, the amount of control by relatives, the amount of neighborhood control, and the amount of church control. An investigator would hypothesize that there is a negative relationship between the amount of law and each of the social control variables.

Another study in the same area could investigate the amount of law and the amount of social control by zip code. That is, different neighborhoods have different amounts of social control. The theory of law would hypothesize a negative relationship between the amount of social control and the amount of law. Neighborhoods with high amounts of social control would have less law, and neighborhoods with low amounts of social control would have more law.

The second proposition in the theory of law is that "law varies directly with respectability" (Black, 1976, p. 112). Here, law could be operationalized as whether or not a social worker in child protection recognizes a complaint of child neglect. In the family chapter, there is an admission about the Connecticut Department of Children and Families that low- and middle-income families are treated differently because many middle-income families react aggressively and hire attorneys. The degree of respectability would be operationalized as whether the complainant is more or less respectable. The investigator would hypothesize that social workers are more likely to recognize a complaint when the complainant is respectable than when the complainant is less respectable.

The proposition that "law is greater in the direction toward less respectability than toward more respectability" (Black, 1976, p. 114) may be tested by studying social workers or family court judges. The proposition states that less respectable people are more likely than more respectable people to have law imposed upon them by social workers and family court judges. Social workers can increase the quantity of law by validating a complaint of child neglect, and judges can increase the quantity of law by ruling against a family.

The last propositions may seem complex, but they can be studied in the social work arena. They state that "in a direction toward less respectability, law varies directly with normative distance, but in a direction toward more respectability law varies inversely with normative distance" (Black, 1976, p. 117). These propositions suggest that the amount of respectability is a control variable, dichotomized into less and more respectability. Law, as previously used, is dichotomized into more and less law. Normative distance is operationalized as the amount of distance among persons. It has advantages when its direction is from a high-class offender and a lower-class accuser. For example, suppose a female hospital custodian accuses a famed heart surgeon of sexual harassment. If viewed as a contest between these two individuals, the heart surgeon has an advantage.

Normative distance may be measured by using, for instance, a modified version of Hollingshead and Redlich's (1958) hierarchy of classification to measure social class. It has a range of one to seven major classifications with some classifications having subheadings. The first category consists of executives of major corporations, and the seventh category consists of sharecroppers. If the distance between persons is represented by one person having 1 point and the other person having 5, then normative distance is represented by 5 points with 5 being the most normative distance. So, in a direction toward less respectability, there is a positive relationship between law and normative distance. But in a direction toward more respectability, there is a negative relationship between law and normative distance.

So, an investigator would hypothesize that the less respectable a person is in comparison to a witness, the greater the likelihood that a positive relationship between law and (undesirable) normative distance exists. But the investigator would also hypothesize that the more respectable a person is to a witness, the greater the likelihood that a negative relationship exists between law and (desirable) normative distance. In other words, the more desirable normative distance, the less law one will find.

These hypotheses may be tested in a number of ways. One way is to study the social worker as a witness in a child abuse case against a less respectable person and a more respectable person. Normative distance would be measured by the distance between the social worker witness and a person on welfare. Toward the person on welfare, there is a positive association between this normative distance and the quantity of law. But toward an executive director, there would be a negative association between normative distance and the quantity of law. This is so because, according to Black (1976), in a direction toward less respectability, law varies directly with normative distance. However, in a direction toward more respectability, law varies inversely with normative direction.

CONCLUSION

All the theories selected in this chapter are provided to explain the macro systems and discussions that follow. As you know, these are social institutions (i.e., family, religion, education, the news media, the law, and medicine), organizations, and communities or neighborhoods. The chapter began with a reminder that no social theory is likely to explain 100% of a phenomenon and that there are always deviant cases. Always, some individuals are going to defy the odds and present themselves differently from what a theory would say, such as growing up in an abusive home and not becoming an abusive parent or being sexually molested as a child and not displaying delinquent behavior as an adolescent. We then discussed a number of theories that were classified under the headings of theories to explain systems and community behaviors (systems and world systems theories, community theory, social disorganization theory, routine activity theory, and migration theory), theories to explain inequality and oppression (inequality theory, feminist theory, and power and social independent theory), theories to explain groups and categories of behaviors (social learning theory, reference group theory, and role theory), and one theory to explain law and social control agents (Black's 1976 theory of law). In many of these theories, numerous hypotheses were presented to help us see and understand that supported hypotheses from theories generate knowledge.

Key Terms and Concepts

Boundary Maintenance	Entropy
Community	Equifinality
Culture	Feedback
Definitions	Focal System
Differential Association	Globalization
Differential Reinforcement	Great Change
Dissensus	Holon
Distributive Justice Theory	Homeostasis (Steady State)

Imitation

Migration

Morphology

Opened and Closed Systems

Organization

Relative Deprivation

Respectability

Role Conflict

Role Overload

Role Playing

Role Taking

Routine Activity Theory

Self-Concept

Social Control

Social Disorganization

Social Disorganization Theory

Social Organizational Theory

Stratification

CHAPTER 4

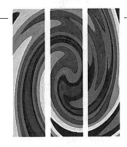

Major Social Institutions Impacting Human Behaviors

Families and Marriages, Education, and Religion

INTRODUCTION

The Chicago Tribune published an interesting story about a unique family system (Casillas, 2009). The Husicks, who had two biological sons and two adopted sons, learned that a church member was about to lose her five children to the child welfare system due to abuse and neglect. Intervening, the Husicks took the three girls to provide foster parenting. The two boys, a baby and an 8-year-old, were placed with the Broscheits, who also had children. Attempting to maintain the bonds among the siblings, the social worker arranged for the siblings to meet at the child placement agency. However, the Husicks and Broscheits elevated the siblings' meetings and strengthened the bonds not only among the siblings but also between the two families. Without directions from the social workers, they met at McDonald's for one sibling's birthday and scheduled other social visits, becoming one large extended family. When one sibling was upset or had good news, one mother would call the other siblings and let them talk. The children were also having visits with their biological parents, from which the two families helped each other deal with the emotional fallout. Mrs. Husick and Mrs. Broscheit became good friends, offering support to each other as one or the other lost a family member to death, unemployment, or other negative life situations. Ultimately, the Husicks and the Broscheits adopted the children. One girl is graduating from college in 2009, another is a sophomore in college, and the third is a high school senior. The boys are still with their adopted family. One girl stated that the Husicks are her family but that she is also a part of the Broscheit family. The Husicks and Broscheits started a support group for similar foster and adoptive families, and the Husick and Broscheit fathers started one just for other fathers with such arrangements (Casillas, 2009). This story shows the involvement of multiple social institutions.

Society is made up of numerous social institutions that are formed to meet human needs (Ballantine, 2001). Stolley (2005) identifies seven major social institutions: family, medical system, military, religious system, political system, economy, and educational system (Stolley, 2005). Newman (2002) provides a list of social institutions similar to Stolley's but adds law. Johnson and Rhoades (2005) divided social institutions into the political economy, consisting of the economic system and the political system; governmental social systems, consisting of the social welfare, education, and criminal justice systems; and nongovernmental social institutions, consisting of the health care, religion, and mass media systems (Escobar-Chaves et al., 2005). Given the definition of social institutions provided by Johnson and Rhoades (2005), several more institutions can be identified that meet social needs. These include such entertainment institutions as sports, vacation spots, movies, clubs, and the arts.

Further, many social institutions are interconnected, such as the home, school, and community (Epstein & Sanders, 2000). Also, some social institutions partner with other social institutions to impact public policy, such as the Becket Fund for Religious Liberty, which is a nonprofit, nonpartisan public interest law firm that protects the free expression of all religions and provides equal protection of religious people in public life and public benefits (*Beard v. Banks,* 2006).

In 2005, New Strategist, a political organization, published the extent to which individuals had confidence in various social institutions (see Table 4.1). Most people had a great deal of confidence in medicine and the least confidence in television.

Table 4.1	Confidence in Various American Institutions in 2002			
Institutions	*A Great Deal*	*Only Some*	*Hardly Any*	*Don't Know*
Banks & Financial Institutions	22.0%	58.2%	18.3%	1.4%
Major Companies	17.3%	62.8%	17.9%	2.0%
Education	24.9%	58.9%	15.6%	0.7%
Executive Branch of Government	26.7%	50.0%	21.2%	2.1%
Medicine	37.0%	51.3%	11.2%	0.5%
Scientific Community	36.8%	48.2%	8.9%	6.0%
Television	9.5%	47.0%	42.5%	0.9%
U.S. Supreme Court	35.2%	49.9%	11.4%	3.5%
Organized Labor	11.1%	60.4%	23.1%	5.5%
Organized Religion	18.5%	56.2%	23.8%	1.5%

Source: Compiled from multiple tables in New Strategist (2005).

The major social institutions relevant to this textbook are the family, education, medical systems, religion, media, and the law, with the first three discussed in this chapter and the second three in the following chapter. While the law, consisting of laws enacted by Congress, state legislatures, city council ordinances, and court decisions, may not be viewed often as a social institution, its impact is considerable. Congress has long passed laws that significantly impact human behaviors and societies (Belkin, 2005), such as the Civil Rights Acts of 1871 and 1964, the Violence Against Women Act, and the Americans with Disabilities Act. Equally, the U.S. Supreme Court has decided landmark cases, such as *Plessy v. Ferguson* (1896), which upheld the concept of "separate but equal," and *Brown v. Board of Education* (1954), which reversed *Plessy* and outlawed racial segregation in schools. In the area of criminal justice, the U.S. Supreme Court issued the rulings in *Gideon v. Wainwright* (1963), which provided attorneys to indigents charged with felonies, and *Miranda v. Arizona* (1966), which compelled law enforcement to advise citizens of their rights when they are arrested. In death penalty cases, the U.S. Supreme Court has ruled in *Atkins v. Virginia* (2002), which barred the execution of persons with mental retardation, and *Roper v. Simmons* (2005), which barred the execution of juveniles under the age of 18. In the area of the right to privacy, the U.S. Supreme Court has ruled in *Roe v. Wade* (1973), which gave women the right to terminate their pregnancy in the first trimester; *Gonzales v. Oregon* (2006), which gave Oregonians the right to assisted suicide and which has the potential to spread to other states; and *Lawrence v. Texas* (2003), which held as unconstitutional laws banning sodomy.

Recently, courts have considered whether governmental agencies may prevent same-sex persons from marrying. A Massachusetts court ruled that same-sex persons may marry (*Goodridge v. Department of Public Health*, 2003), but a New York court ruled that they may not (*Hernandez v. Robles*, 2005). In 2004, 11 states passed laws preventing same-sex persons from marrying. Thus, both the legislative branches of government, which pass laws, and the courts, which decide the constitutionality of laws, have major impacts on social behaviors and therefore are a major social institution.

Although most social work programs view family as a micro system, the family has been called the most important social institution (Caputo, 2001; Garbarino & Abramowitz, 1992; James, 2005; Lareau, 2002; Stoller & Gibson, 2001). In 1852, the U.S. Supreme Court stated that the great basis of human society throughout the civilized world is marriage and legitimate offspring (*Gaines v. Relf,* 1852), which form families (Fields, 2003). Although this case is over 150 years old, it still informs the legal views of current justices, judges, and state legislatures. Thus, we focus a lot on families, marriages, and same-sex relationships in this chapter. Given the current wars in Iraq and Afghanistan, the chapter also addresses military families, for significant social forces impinge upon them.

Figure 4.1 depicts the six social institutions discussed in this chapter and how they impact each other. Families can impact other institutions, such as when they force the media to cancel an offending television program, and can

Figure 4.1 Major Social Institutions

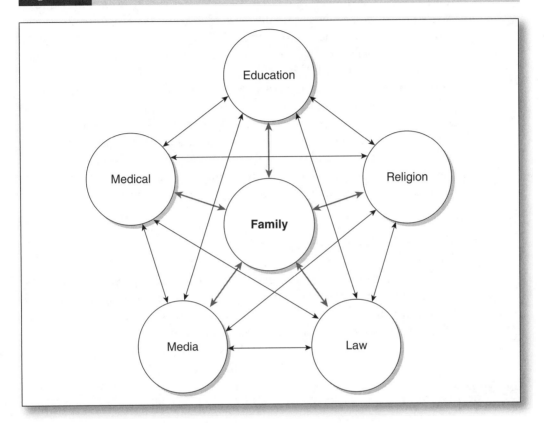

influence the passage of laws, such as community notification of sex offenders. The discussions that follow clearly show that social institutions are interconnected. Further, the discussions will show that some laws, though most in society believe them to be helpful, have negative discriminatory impacts.

THEORIES AND KNOWLEDGE ABOUT FAMILIES AND MARRIAGES

The American family has evolved on many levels, and this evolution has had broad implications for society. When society was mostly agrarian, many relatives lived together on farms, with households consisting of a husband, a wife, children, and perhaps grandparents and parental siblings (MacKinnon, 2004). In 1850, 70% of elderly people lived with their children, and 11% lived either with a spouse or alone (Ruggles & Brower, 2003). By 1990, 16% of elderly persons lived with their children, and 70% either lived with a spouse or alone (Ruggles & Brower, 2003). Further, Ruggles and Brower (2003) studied the changes in the family and family definitions from 1850 to 2000. As society advanced and became more industrialized, family structure changed (Heuveline & Timberlake, 2004) and became more nuclear, or a family consisting of parents and their children in one household (Dozier & Schwartz, 2001). The 20th and 21st centuries have brought a significant increase in single parents with children and in divorces and a growing acceptance of gay and lesbian families with children conceived either through third-party sperm donation, in a laboratory, or via adoption. In the 1960s and 1970s, an increase in divorces led to the breakup of some families and an increase in single-parent families. Also, during this period, the number of single-parent homes where women were having children without being married increased.

Statistics on Contemporary Families

Table 4.2 describes the different family types as reported by the 2000 census. The average family size in the United States in 2000 was 3.14 persons. All together, there were 71,787,347 families in the United States. In terms of single parents with children, 2,190,989 households were headed by men, and 7,561,874 were headed by women (U.S. Census Bureau, 2003).

Table 4.2   Various Family Types as Reported by the 2000 Census

Geography	Average Family Size	Total Families	Married-Couple Families	Female-Headed Households With Children Under 18 Years
United States	3.14	71,787,347	54,493,232	7,561,874
Alabama	3.01	1,215,968	906,916	141,057
Alaska	3.28	152,337	116,318	17,243
Arizona	3.18	1,287,367	986,303	129,511
Arkansas	2.99	732,261	566,401	76,774
California	3.43	7,920,049	5,877,084	834,716
Colorado	3.09	1,084,461	858,671	102,113

Geography	Average Family Size	Total Families	Married-Couple Families	Female-Headed Households With Children Under 18 Years
Connecticut	3.08	881,170	676,467	91,114
Delaware	3.04	204,590	153,136	22,975
District of Columbia	3.07	114,166	56,631	24,561
Florida	2.98	4,210,760	3,192,266	437,680
Georgia	3.14	2,111,647	1,548,800	258,006
Hawaii	3.42	287,068	216,077	23,619
Idaho	3.17	335,588	276,511	27,091
Illinois	3.23	3,105,513	2,353,892	315,957
Indiana	3.05	1,602,501	1,251,458	160,311
Iowa	3	769,684	633,254	64,367
Kansas	3.07	701,547	567,924	62,757
Kentucky	2.97	1,104,398	857,944	110,565
Louisiana	3.16	1,156,438	809,498	161,546
Maine	2.9	340,685	272,152	32,352
Maryland	3.13	1,359,318	994,549	159,342
Massachusetts	3.11	1,576,696	1,197,917	163,550
Michigan	3.1	2,575,699	1,947,710	283,758
Minnesota	3.09	1,255,141	1,018,245	111,371
Mississippi	3.14	747,159	520,844	106,203
Missouri	3.02	1,476,516	1,140,866	156,571
Montana	2.99	237,407	192,067	21,201
Nebraska	3.06	443,411	360,996	39,685
Nevada	3.14	498,333	373,201	50,675

(Continued)

Table 4.2 (Continued)

Geography	Average Family Size	Total Families	Married-Couple Families	Female-Headed Households With Children Under 18 Years
New Hampshire	3.03	323,651	262,438	27,257
New Jersey	3.21	2,154,539	1,638,322	196,809
New Mexico	3.18	466,515	341,818	56,133
New York	3.22	4,639,387	3,289,514	573,384
North Carolina	2.98	2,158,869	1,645,346	227,351
North Dakota	3	166,150	137,433	13,639
Ohio	3.04	2,993,023	2,285,798	323,095
Oklahoma	3.02	921,750	717,611	94,403
Oregon	3.02	877,671	692,532	83,131
Pennsylvania	3.04	3,208,388	2,467,673	298,021
Rhode Island	3.07	265,398	196,757	31,703
South Carolina	3.02	1,072,822	783,142	131,010
South Dakota	3.07	194,330	157,391	17,645
Tennessee	2.99	1,547,835	1,173,960	165,842
Texas	3.28	5,247,794	3,989,741	564,288
Utah	3.57	535,294	442,931	40,329
Vermont	2.96	157,763	126,413	14,792
Virginia	3.04	1,847,796	1,426,044	186,591
Washington	3.07	1,499,127	1,181,995	146,920
West Virginia	2.9	504,055	397,499	42,304
Wisconsin	3.05	1,386,815	1,108,597	128,952
Wyoming	3	130,497	106,179	11,604
Puerto Rico	3.41	1,004,080	682,804	131,584

Source: From U.S. Census Bureau (2003), *Current Population Survey, March 2002.*

Grandparents With Primary
Responsibility for Their Grandchildren

When Congress passed the Personal Responsibility and Work Opportunity Reconciliation Act of 1996 (PRWORA), it directed the U.S. Census Bureau to include in the 2000 census questions to determine the extent to which grandparents were caring for their grandchildren and whether this parenting was temporary or permanent. Individuals were asked for the first time if they had grandchildren living in their homes, whether they were the primary caregivers for these children and meeting these children's basic needs, and how long this relationship had been occurring—less than 6 months, 6 to 11 months, 1 or 2 years, 3 or 4 years, or 5 years or more (Simmons & Dye, 2003). Congress mandated census information about grandparents due to the large number of parents who were not caring for their children due to drug problems, criminal justice issues, and child protection interventions.

Table 4.3 shows that in 2003 a number of grandparents in the United States were responsible for their grandchildren. Some grandparents lived with their grandchildren but were not responsible for their basic needs. The "percentage of coresident" provides the percentage of grandparents who lived with their grandchildren and had primary responsibility for providing their basic needs. Racially, the percentages are as follows: White (41.6%), African American (51.7%), First Nations and Alaska Native (56.1%), Asian (20%), Native Hawaiian and Pacific Islander (38.7%), and Latino (34.7%) (Simmons & Dye, 2003).

In terms of gender and age, as shown in Table 4.4, 905,675 (37.3%) grandfathers were responsible for their grandchildren compared to 1,521,005 (62.7%) grandmothers. The largest age group of grandparents who were responsible for their grandchildren is 50 to 59 years (35.1%). Members of this same age group were more likely to have had their grandchildren for 5 years or more (40.3%) (Simmons & Dye, 2003).

The census data do not indicate why grandparents had primary responsibility for their grandchildren, but research literature and news reports tell us why. Reports have emerged that some parents have serious drug issues, have died of AIDS, or have been imprisoned (Urbina, 2006b). Consequently, some parents are unable to care for their children, forcing grandparents to take custody. In one case a 62-year-old grandmother in Washington, DC, took custody of her 10- and 12-year-old grandsons after their father was incarcerated and their mother was assessed as too depressed to care for them (Urbina, 2006b). Of course, other issues, such as mental illness or death, can prevent some parents from being able to care for their children.

Table 4.3 Grandparents Caring for Grandchildren by Race

	White	African American	First Nations & Alaska Native	Asian	Native Hawaiian & Pacific Islander	Latino
No. Responsible for Grandchildren	1,340,809	702,595	50,765	71,791	6,587	424,304
% of Coresident	41.6	51.7	56.1	20	38.7	34.7
Less Than 6 Months	12.6	9.8	13	13.6	12.7	14.6
6 to 11 Months	11.6	9.3	10.5	11	8.4	11.2
1 to 2 Years	23.8	21.2	22.5	25.2	23.8	25.1
3 to 4 Years	15.8	14.6	13.9	17.6	11.7	15.8
5 Years or More	36.3	45.2	40	32.7	43.3	33.3

Table 4.4 Grandparents Caring for Grandchildren by Gender and Age

	Sex		Age					
	Male	Female	30 to 39	40 to 49	50 to 59	60 to 69	70 to 79	80 +
No. Responsible for Grandchildren	905,675	1,521,055	161,652	708,049	850,877	508,757	172,471	24,924
% Responsible for Grandchildren	37.3	62.7	6.7	29.2	35.1	21	7.1	1.0
Less Than 6 Months	38.4	61.6	14.8	39.4	27.9	12.9	4.3	0.7
6 to 11 Months	38.7	61.3	11.9	37.3	30.7	14.8	4.6	0.6
1 to 2 Years	38.3	61.7	10.5	37.8	31.6	15	4.5	0.6
3 to 4 Years	38	62	5.0	32.8	36	19.4	6.0	0.9
5 Years or More	35.7	64.3	1.0	17.1	40.3	29.5	10.7	1.5

The boxed feature "The Case of Marie and Her Sons" tells partly of a grandmother's failed attempt to care for her grandchildren, but it is mostly about the difficulties of a single mother with drug issues. This family illustration depicts systems theory, Black's theory of law, and human environments—all previously discussed in the text.

The Case of Marie and Her Sons

Daniel Bergner (2006b), a reporter for *The New York Times,* wrote a lengthy article about a Puerto Rican woman and her five boys, all of whom had been taken from her. The cover of this magazine was adorned with an African American caseworker with a master's in social work (MSW) who was employed by the Connecticut Department of Children and Families and was agonizing over seeking parental termination. Marie had her first child when she was 13 years old, and she had five boys in all. Most of her boys were born with drugs in their system. Three of the men who fathered the boys were involved with drugs, and the home was chaotic. The oldest boy stated that his mother hit him and made him miss school to watch his siblings while she was out using drugs. The boys were initially placed with their grandmother, who had used drugs too but who had stopped. However, the grandmother brought the boys to the Connecticut Department of Children and Families, saying that they were too much trouble, and thus they were placed with different foster families. Marie had entered drug treatment and had apparently been clean for a while. But she had lied to her caseworker on two occasions—in one case she claimed to have been robbed and beaten, but her boyfriend had assaulted her. Then, she claimed that someone hit her car, but the police report stated that she was under the influence of drugs and/or alcohol and hit another vehicle. Annette Johnson, the caseworker, had considerable work and related life experiences. She had worked in marketing for Procter & Gamble before returning to school to get her MSW. Her youngest brother had worked for a drug dealer and died when a balloon burst in his stomach. Further, she had six cousins who had died from heroin overdoses and AIDS contracted from sharing needles. Despite this family background, Annette was not eager to seek parental termination and adoption. But

(Continued)

(Continued)

she was concerned for the boys. In addition, Marie was pregnant with her sixth child at the age of 29. Though Marie was doing better, the concern was that the pressures from parenting the boys, one of whom was diagnosed with an attention deficit disorder, would cause her to relapse. Against this background, the commissioner of the Connecticut Department of Children and Families informed the staff that the department had 6,300 children in its custody and 24% were African Americans, twice the percentage in Connecticut, and 35% were Latinos, 3 times the percentage in the state population. These numbers aside, the caseworker indicated that she would seek termination of Marie's parental rights.

Author's Analysis

You can see systems theory operating within this situation: the mother; the grandmother; the boys; the Connecticut Department of Children and Families; foster families; the police department, which is called upon to help social workers remove children from homes when parents resist; and the legal system. Various environments are obvious too: the drug culture and drug treatment programs.

Also stated by the MSW supervisor was that "investigated White families are broken apart least often then [sic] Black families, then Hispanic . . . Families that obtain aggressive legal counsel can influence the way the department wants to proceed with a case and with the overall outcome of our interventions. We may examine the information a little closer if the family is high profile or wealthy, given that we know they will most likely vigorously oppose the department's decision" (Bergner, 2006b, p. 53). This admission supports Black's theory of law, which states that less respectable individuals receive more law than more respectable individuals.

Marriage Theory

Qian, Lichter, and Mellott (2005) explained marital search theory, which is an extrapolation of the theory of the matching of job applicants and employers in the labor markets. In the labor market, job applicants search for the best possible job, given the number of jobs opened (opportunities) and personal liabilities (constraints). In any given prospective job offer, some jobs are going to be desirable to the job seekers, and some are going to be undesirable. The reasons for some jobs being undesirable are varied, including low pay, unacceptable working hours or days, or environmental or organizational shortcomings. To find an especially desirable job is time consuming and costly. For instance, a job seeker might be under pressure to find a job quickly to meet pressing financial obligations, or an employer hiring for a desirable position may hire for that position very quickly. Therefore, job seekers mentally establish a minimally acceptable match between themselves and employers. This is called the "reservation wage," but it is not strictly a dollar amount and can consist of other factors that job seekers believe are critical. Job seekers reject offers below the reservation wage and accept the first job offer at or above the reservation wage. It follows then that if everything is equal, "the lower the reservation wage, the more likely searchers will find a job quickly" (Qian et al., 2005, p. 475).

Extrapolated to how people make decisions about marriages, the principles and concepts are the same, despite the popular belief that people fall in love and then get married (Jacobs, 2004). This principle applies equally to individuals who live together without being married. Individuals wanting to get married or to cohabitate with someone will seek the best possible partner given candidates' qualifications and constraints. Qualifications are beauty or physical attractiveness, education, amount of salary earned, or amount of trust fund an individual has. Constraints are all those qualities that one might call "baggage," including the number of children one has or whether these children were born out of wedlock. Women who want to get married, similar to the job seekers setting a reservation wage, establish mentally a "reservation quality partner." The reservation quality partner is the minimally acceptable partner for marriage or cohabitation. Marital search theory states that when there is a scarcity of men with pleasing qualities, women will cast a wider net. Theoretically, they are lowering their reservation wage or lowering their reservation quality partners. As a result of lowering their reservation quality partners, a mismatch occurs, analogous to a mismatch between a newly hired employee and an employer.

Qian et al. (2005) tested marital search theory with a study of disadvantaged African American, White, and Latino unwed mothers. The sample also included men who fathered children out of marriage, but the focus was on unwed mothers because the aim of PRWORA in 1996, as part of welfare reform, was to encourage poor women to get married as a means of reducing their dependency on welfare or public assistance. Controlling for education and age in this longitudinal study involving 102,722 women, they found that cohabitation and out-of-wedlock children negatively affected the quality of women's partners and that women who have had children when they were not married are more likely to remain single. For White and African American women, the odds that they would marry rather than cohabitate was 30% lower than for childless single women, but for Latino women, the odds were stronger—56% lower than for childless single women (Qian et al., 2005).

Web sites, such as Match.com and MySpace.com, that provide information on men and women searching for relationships display elements of marital search theory. For instance, Yahoo! has a relationship site for individuals who have Yahoo! e-mail accounts. Men and women state their qualities and wants in categories like race and ethnicity, age, level of education, salary level, number of children, and prior marital status. These represent constraints and qualities. One woman stated that her age range for a partner was 14 to 99, any race, no specific education level, and no minimum salary the man earned. Theoretically, she was casting a very wide net. Some women will specifically state that they are only interested in serious, marriage-minded guys and those that play "head games" should not contact them. Further, some women state that they do not have any baggage, that they have children who are grown and not living at home, or that they are not "high-maintenance women." According to some women who post their information and revise it from time to time, some men use the Web site as a cyber playground and are not interested in serious relationships. Some men claim to be single but are not or do not have the type of job or level of education that they claim to have. These types of men are outside women's reservation quality partners and thus are excluded according to the marital search theory. A cursory study between women's and men's wants shows gender differences in what each seeks in a partner, which supports what Qian et al. (2005) suggested in their study.

Same-Sex Marriages

In 2004, the mayor of San Francisco ordered the issuance of marriage licenses to gays and lesbians in San Francisco. Numerous couples, as a result, got married and then sought the benefits afforded to individuals in heterosexual marriages. According to the federal government, there are 1,049 rights and responsibilities afforded to heterosexual married couples and numerous societal and business benefits. However, recently married gay and lesbian couples in San Francisco learned that they were not entitled to these benefits, such as discount for spouses for car insurance (Marech, 2004). Later, the California Supreme Court ordered San Francisco to stop issuing marriage licenses to same-sex couples until it had ruled on the constitutionality of the law (*Lockyer v. City and County of San Francisco*, 2004). In 2008, the California Supreme Court ruled that the state's designating same-sex couples as domestic partnerships but opposite-sex couples as marriages violated the California Constitution (*In re Marriage Cases*, 2008).

Similarly, the Massachusetts Supreme Judicial Court ruled that the Massachusetts Constitution does not ban gays and lesbians from marrying. A few other state courts have been willing to follow Massachusetts' lead, such as Vermont, Iowa, and Connecticut. Further, state legislatures, state referendums, and Congress have been unanimously unwilling to sanction gay and lesbian marriages.

Same-sex couples and those who support their rights believe their civil rights are violated when they are not allowed to marry. They equate this issue with the issue of interracial marriages, which the U.S. Supreme Court allowed in *Loving v. Virginia* (1967). In New York law, 316 benefits have been identified as accruing to opposite-sex couples in marriage (*Hernandez v. Robles*, 2006). Among the more important benefits are that married people have significant tax advantages, rights in probate and intestacy (i.e., dying without a will) proceedings, rights to support from spouses during the marriage and following a divorce, and rights to obtain insurance coverage and make health care decisions. Symbolically, their union is recognized and sanctioned by the state. Because same-sex couples cannot marry in New York, they are denied these 316 benefits, and their unions are not recognized or sanctioned by the state (*Hernandez v. Robles*, 2006).

Gays and lesbians have encountered a number of setbacks over the issue of same-sex marriage (Belluck & Reuthling, 2006). Several state courts have ruled against issues surrounding same-sex marriages (*American Civil Liberties Union of Tennessee v. Darnell*, 2006; *Andersen v. King County*, 2006; *Citizens for Equal Protection v. Bruning*, 2006; *Perdue v. O'Kelley*, 2006), stressing that it is up to the legislative branches to extend marriage to same-sex couples. The issue of same-sex marriages has encountered stiff opposition in state legislatures and Congress (Bradley, 2005; Wardle, 2005), and the general public has strongly endorsed the proposition that marriage is defined as a union of a man and woman (*Citizens for Equal Protection v. Bruning*, 2006). In 2008, California voters adopted a constitutional amendment that banned same-sex marriages (Archibold & Goodnough, 2008).

Gay and Lesbian Family Issues

Within the last few years, gays and lesbians have made considerable advancements in society (Butler, 2005; McDonald, 2004; Portelli, 2004) and have openly and proudly declared their homosexuality and formed families. Gays and lesbians have been able to form civil unions in some states and to foster and adopt children or to have their own children via artificial insemination. In addition, they have created stepfamilies by leaving heterosexual families and entering same-sex families when a parent realizes that he or she is gay or lesbian (Lynch, 2004). While some courts have ordered a same-sex partner to pay child support when a relationship has ended, same-sex couples cannot marry. They get the "burdens" of child support, like heterosexual married couples who have divorced, but not any of the many benefits afforded to married couples (Baskerville, 2004; Glenn, 2004; Lind, 2004).

In child welfare, the legal system is concerned with the best interests of children (Richman, 2005). When most of society ceased to view homosexuality as dysfunctional, it could not be viewed as detrimental to children who may have had a parent who entered a same-sex relationship and still wanted to be a parent to his or her child (Golombok, 1999; Muse, 2003). Also, court decisions have indicated that gays and lesbians have the same right to foster and adopt children as heterosexual couples or singles (Downs & James, 2006). When children were involved, the court seemed to be concerned with the best interest of the children and not societal objections. For example, in *Finstuen v. Edmondson*, (2006), a lesbian couple had twins in New Jersey, and thus they were a family. After moving from New Jersey to Oklahoma, they were not viewed as a family under Oklahoma law. A federal judge ruled that an Oklahoma law forbidding recognition of same-sex parents was a violation of the two women's fundamental rights to make decisions regarding the care, custody, and control of their children. The court referenced previous decisions when an adoption created families but the state sought to break up the families without evidence that the parents were unfit or that the children's best interests were not being served (*Finstuen v. Edmondson,* 2006). Hence, the ruling in *Finstuen v. Edmundson* seems to have legally recognized same-sex families, which states cannot break up.

Same-sex couples with children have some of the same issues that heterosexual couples have (Liptak, 2006). In Virginia, two women were involved in a same-sex relationship in 1990 and traveled to Vermont to enter a civil union. The following year, they decided to have a child and selected a sperm donor. When the child was born, the mother's partner was in the delivery room lending her support for the birth. The child was born in 2002, and both women were listed as parents on the child's birth certificate. But in 2003 the couple decided to separate, ending the relationship or union. The birth mother decided that she was no longer a lesbian and did not want her former partner to see the child. The Vermont Supreme Court ruled in favor of the noncustodial parent and upheld her parental rights (*Miller-Jenkins v. Miller-Jenkins,* 2006). However, this issue may not have been settled because the birth mother lives in Virginia and Virginia does not recognize civil unions.

Further, the birth mother is being represented by Liberty Counsel, a public interest law firm that defends traditional marriages, and its position is that the issue should ultimately be decided by the U.S. Supreme Court because it represents a conflict between Virginia and Vermont laws (Liptak, 2006).

Legal Attempts to Define a Family

All levels of government have some power to protect the morals, safety, and well-being of a community—a right referred to in the law as **police powers** (Alexander, 2003). Local governments have the right to establish zoning laws, which, for instance, may restrict the location of a fraternity house or group homes. In doing so, communities have had to decree what a family is and is not. This has been a long-established right of a community, and this power provokes clashes with individuals and families when they feel that their individual rights are being trampled. In 1977, the U.S. Supreme Court held as unconstitutional a city of East Cleveland ordinance that essentially barred nonnuclear families from living together. Although the justices held the ordinance as illegal, they upheld the authority of the city of East Cleveland to define a family (*Moore v. City of East Cleveland*, 1977).

For zoning purposes a community may define what is and is not a family, and several communities have done so (Moore, 2006b). A community in Black Jack, Missouri, a suburb of St. Louis, refused to amend its ordinance prohibiting unmarried and unrelated families from continuing to occupy a house that the couple had purchased in the community. Black Jack zoning law prohibited more than three unrelated individuals from living together and assessed a $500-a-day penalty for violations. One couple had lived together for 13 years and had two children together. The woman had an older daughter from a previous relationship who referred to the man who lived with her mother as "father" (Moore, 2006a). The $500 fine would accumulate each day, and at some point, the Black Jack government could proceed to seize the couple's assets and have them legally evicted. The only solution to this issue would be for the couple to get married, which they decided was a violation of their Fourteenth Amendment right to liberty. Liberty means, in part, the right to marry or not marry and to have children or not have children, but the Black Jack government was indirectly trying to force this couple to marry. The American Civil Liberties Union (ACLU) of Eastern Missouri filed a lawsuit on behalf of the family on August 10, 2006, and on August 15, 2006, the city council of Black Jack voted to change its definition of what constitutes a family (ACLU, 2006). The above scenario supports Heuveline and Timberlake's

(2004, p. 1215) observations that "the presence of children has brought cohabitation into public discourse, leading concerned policymakers to propose incentives to incite unmarried cohabitation partners to marry."

Marriage

Normally, when governmental and legal authorities discuss the family, they refer to an institution produced by marriage that has resulted in children, and marriage is deemed a contract between a man and a woman. In *Maynard v. Hill* (1888), the U.S. Supreme Court stated that marriage creates the most important relation in life and has more to do with the morals and civilization of a people than all other institutions. The U.S. Supreme Court noted that marriage is an institution regulated by the various legislatures, which establish the age at which individuals may marry, the duties and obligations that marriage creates, property rights issues, and the grounds upon which a marriage may be terminated (*Maynard v. Hill,* 1888). A Massachusetts court analyzed the intent of the Massachusetts legislature and stated that society and the government have a strong interest in promoting and protecting heterosexual marriage as the social institution that best forges a connection among sex, procreation, and child rearing. Continuing, the Massachusetts court stated that marriage regulates heterosexual behavior, brings order to the resulting procreation, and ensures a stable family structure for rearing, educating, and socializing children (*Goodridge v. Department of Public Health,* 2003). Although the Massachusetts court recognized the historical context of marriage, it strongly urged the Massachusetts legislature to change its definition of marriage in order to recognize that this social institution has changed. Later, the Massachusetts legislature passed a bill sanctioning same-sex marriage. A New York court, by contrast, indicated that the definition of marriage as a union between a man and a woman communicates an important, long-standing public policy decision supporting procreation, child welfare, and social stability—all legitimate state interests (*Hernandez v. Robles,* 2005).

Social and Economic Forces on and by Families and Marriages

Snyder and McLaughlin (2004) studied changes in the American family residing in metro, nonmetro, and suburban areas from 1980 to 2000. During this 20-year period, economic changes occurred that impacted families. By 2000, both nonmetro and suburban areas had similar percentages of family households, about 71%, whereas the percentage in metro areas was 61%

(Snyder & McLaughlin, 2004). Further, changes had occurred in the number and percentage of single-parent homes from 1980 to 2000. Female-headed households with children increased by 18% in metro areas, 10% in suburban areas, and 11% in nonmetro areas (Snyder & McLaughlin, 2004).

A number of professionals have argued that there have been dramatic changes in family structures, which suggests that the family is in serious trouble (Currie & Skolnick, 1988; Jones et al., 1991; Melton, 1995; Parkman, 1995). Melton (1995) listed a number of changes since the 1960s that he believes have ominous signs for the family. These are a decline in the fertility rate and in the percentage of men as the sole breadwinner, and an increase in the number of children living with a single mother, especially within the African American family; in the number of births to unmarried women; in divorces; in the number of couples living together without being married; in the number of single people living alone; and in the median age before marriage (Melton, 1995). Currie and Skolnick (1988) discussed the consequences of family disruption for children and society. Other professionals have questioned the perceptions of some individuals concerned with the family, such as those who fret over the high divorce rate in the United States. Rather than seeing a high divorce rate as a negative, it might be positive in that being married and miserable has long-term effects on the well-being of individuals (Hawkins & Booth, 2005). As stated by Connolly (2002, p. 343), "the family still holds a sanctified place in contemporary society, and the model of a married, heterosexual couple with children is the (fictive) norm. This traditional family unit interacts with other social institutions (such as the schools, the work environment, the law, and the medical profession) in an expected manner."

Positive Aspects of Families and Marriages

Some couples cannot have children, but the law and society permit childless couples to adopt children to form their families. Recently, society and the law have permitted gay couples and single gays to adopt children. We view the adoption of children to form a family in a positive light. As one California court wrote, the adoption of a child is an act of compassion, love, and humanitarian concern whereby the family or parent assumes enormous legal, moral, social, and economic obligations (*Michael J. v. Los Angeles County Department of Adoptions,* 1988). Additionally, some families have adopted children when they could not conceive them, when they wanted more children but did not want to conceive them, or when a spouse had children before marriage occurred. Probably, the most controversial areas in adoption have been transracial adoption of African American children by Whites and adoption of children by gays and lesbians. However, the furor over transracial adoption has subsided, and the legal system has sanctioned adoption of children by gays and lesbians.

Gay and Lesbian Parenthood and Adoptions

Gays and lesbians have been permitted to be foster parents and adopt children. Gays and lesbians as single parents are permitted to adopt children in many states. This issue, while controversial in some states, presents different legal issues for gays and lesbians. For instance, one parent during a divorce proceeding or just before a divorce proceeding may come out as gay or lesbian. Thus, he or she may have biological ties to children, which cannot be easily terminated based just on sexual orientation. In addition, gay and lesbian individuals, with the assistance of biology, medicine, or a surrogate, can conceive children. Hence, they also have biological ties to a child. But even though gays and lesbians can have children in a relationship, they are not totally free from discrimination and some legal problems.

For example, **second-parent adoption**—when a person adopts his or her spouse's children—is sometimes legally prohibited for gays and lesbians (Connolly, 2002; Richman, 2005). Normally, any spouse may adopt another spouse's children, but this is not always the case for same-sex couples. For instance, a same-sex couple, Jeanine and Nichole, moved from Tucson, Arizona, to Santa Clara, California, because in Arizona Jeanine could not adopt Nichole's son (Innes, 2006). In New York, a lesbian was successful in securing second-parent adoption status, but it was not easy. She interviewed about a dozen same-sex couples who had been successful. As the Arizona couple realized, there is no universal standard across states, and barriers remain.

Reports are that one of the barriers to overcoming full family recognition comes from social workers (Connolly, 2002; Downs & James, 2006). Connolly (2002, p. 326), a lesbian, wrote,

> I had fought (and lost) the "family" issue with both our attorney and the certified social worker and was not willing to jeopardize the judge's signature on the final forms by repeating "the law did not make us a family." What I had said earlier to the attorney and a social worker was that, until the adoption, the law had denied us the same rights to parent as heterosexuals have had—to enjoy the same duties and obligations to our child as were realized by heterosexual parents. Lucas had enjoyed life with two mothers, only one of whom had the legal ability to make binding

decisions. The adoption would expand that number to two; but it did not make us a family. Though I celebrated the event as a victory both for us personally and for other gay and lesbian parents who wished to have their relationships with their children legally recognized, the legal process ignored our reality as both lesbians and parents.

International Adoptions

About 20,000 children from abroad are adopted each year by American parents (Gross, 2006). Ortiz and Briggs (2003) reported on why many White parents prefer to adopt internationally rather than from the foster care system in the United States. First, White parents feel more comfortable adopting from other countries, especially in Europe, because children there are more receptive to adoption than American children. Second, discussions about "crack babies" made some parents interested in adoption fearful. Third, conservative politicians' attempt to abolish Aid to Families with Dependent Children (AFDC) was another factor. Congress was successful in replacing AFDC with a program called Temporary Assistance for Needy Families (TANF). According to Ortiz and Briggs (2003), these factors push American families to prefer to adopt children from predominantly White European countries.

However, many of these Eastern European children come from institutions and have significant health problems. For instance, many children in orphanages and institutions from the former Soviet Union are diagnosed with fetal alcohol syndrome. As a result, a growing number of adoptions involve medical adoption experts who conduct screenings of children's medical records. One of the first agencies to conduct medical screening of children waiting to be adopted in institutions abroad was the International Adoption Clinic at the University of Minnesota. In 2005, about 2,000 children were assessed by the International Adoption Clinic by the examination of medical records, photographs, and video (Gross, 2006). In addition, the adoption clinic assessed about 500 children in person after they were brought to the United States, with 100 of these children receiving mental health services (Gross, 2006). One medical adoption expert stated that the longer a child is in an institution, the more likely this child is to have problems. A child with relatively low developmental and cognitive potential in a family environment with high expectations can produce considerable family dysfunctions (Gross, 2006). However, many children from abroad work out well in American families. Medical experts report that the best orphanages, understood as human interactions and care, are found in Ethiopia, China, and Guatemala (Gross, 2006).

With respect to China, Johnson (2002) noted that the number of girls in Chinese orphanages is due to China's family policy. Particularly, China has a limit on the number of children a family may have, and sex discrimination favors boys. Thus, a family who has a girl may choose to give her up to an orphanage and try again for a boy. For the United States, this policy means that there are likely to be plenty of girls available for adoption in this country, but it has had negative social impacts for China, which is currently trying to correct this. According to a *60 Minutes* broadcast in 2006, there is a serious shortage of females in China with males outnumbering females. This has meant that it has become very difficult for young men to find wives. It also means that young girls have become economically valuable for poor families willing to sell them. Often, girls are sold to later become wives (Schorn, 2006). Hence, China's girl problem shows that economic and social forces impact human behaviors and may have international consequences, such as a steep decline in the number of girls available to be adopted by American families.

Negative Aspects of Families and Marriages

A number of economic and social forces impinge upon families (Bankruptcy Services, LLC, 2005). The Council on Social Work Education tells us that we should know how economic and social factors hinder and/or assist social institutions, and the family is a prime example to illustrate these positive and negative influences. Prodded by advocates, Congress has passed a number of statutes to assist families, such as Aid to Families with Dependent Children, the Family and Medical Leave Act, and so forth. Undoubtedly, these laws have had a positive effect on families, easing the financial burdens on many families and recognizing the importance of family support during a medical crisis.

At the same time, economics have worked against many low-income families. In 2006, the Brookings Institution, a nonpartisan think tank, released a report detailing the hidden taxes on low-income families. The report advocated for changes and policies in the economic market that would assist these families, without increasing taxes or creating new social programs. The Brookings Institution found that reducing the cost of living by 1% would put more than $6.5 billion into the pockets of lower-income families (Fellowes, 2006). This windfall could come from eliminating the overcharges that lower-income families pay.

Generally, lower-income families pay more for the same consumer products than higher-income families pay (Fellowes, 2006). As examples, lower-income families who buy homes pay more for their mortgages than higher-income families, and lower-income families pay more for car loans than higher-income families (Fellowes, 2006). Moreover, lower-income families pay excessive fees for furniture, appliances, and electronics, and lower-income families pay more for basic services, such as financial services, groceries, and insurance (Fellowes, 2006). Surely, many businesses want to make as much profit as they can, and some are known to gouge the public, including both low-income and middle-income families. But lower-income families are gouged a lot more than middle-income families. Lower-income families pay more for basic necessities, including food, insurance, mortgages, and financial and tax services (Fellowes, 2006). Many low-income families shop in stores in their neighborhoods where prices are higher, and if they go to a discount store out of their neighborhoods, then there is added cost, such as transportation to those sites. Lower-income families pay more for car insurance, and they pay more for check cashing services and tax refund services. Lowering these taxes and making strategic investments (i.e., seeding the growth of businesses such as large grocers in low-income areas and programs to assist low-income families such as job training) would help those low-income families by providing them with more money to spend on themselves and their families' needs (Fellowes, 2006).

The response to these charges has been that crime in low-income neighborhoods drives out many businesses, but this is more perception than reality. Take car insurance. It is a myth that more cars are stolen in poor neighborhoods than in middle-class neighborhoods. Most car thieves are White (Arizona Criminal Justice Commission, 2004), and professional car thieves want nice cars to take apart and sell. A professional car thief is not going to go to a poor neighborhood looking for a rundown car to steal. This thief is going to go where the nice cars are—the better neighborhoods, shopping areas, and businesses. Thus, the insurance industry does not sustain more losses from auto thefts in poor neighborhoods compared to higher-income neighborhoods (Arizona Criminal Justice Commission, 2004). For instance, the Phoenix, Arizona, area had the most automobiles stolen in the United States, and most of these thefts occurred in shopping center parking lots (Arizona Criminal Justice Commission, 2004). In terms of accidents, the more expensive a car is, the more it costs to repair. The more expensive cars are going to be involved in accidents in the more expensive areas, which is basic sociology. A person who drives a BMW is not likely to be involved in a fender bender in a poor neighborhood. Even something like life insurance cannot be explained honestly. While the life expectancy in poor neighborhoods is shorter than that in other neighborhoods, most poor families cannot afford life insurance, and if they do hold a policy, it is likely to be just enough to pay for a funeral. Insurance companies do not lose money on life insurance in poor neighborhoods. The million-dollar life insurance policies or even $500,000 policies are held by individuals in higher-income families. In fact, most insurance companies have fraud units to investigate accidents involving these high-benefit policies because that is where the fraud is.

Theft is a fact that many businesses address, and this theft may come from customers or from employees. But we must be skeptical about the suggestion that more thefts occur in poor neighborhoods than in higher-income neighborhoods. A lot of people from all social classes and races steal and shoplift. A trip to an electronics store, such as Best Buy, shows that stores like Best Buy are concerned about shoplifting; many items are locked or attached to chains to prevent people from stealing them. Even Barnes & Noble bookstores, which are sometimes located in the suburbs, have theft detection devices in exit doors to prevent customers from stealing books. In addition, some college bookstores employ armed guards at the beginning of the school year. Thus, a supermarket chain that expresses reluctance to open a store in a poor neighborhood because of fears of losses from shoplifters is biased, prejudiced, or misinformed. Thefts occur across the socioeconomic spectrum—not just in poor neighborhoods.

The fact of the matter is that, on the whole, poor families are not well educated and are easy prey for many businesses. The Brookings Institution emphasizes this point.

Posttraumatic Stress Disorder and Its Effects Within Families

Researchers have found that one traumatized family member, because of how a trauma affects the feelings and behaviors of him or her, can profoundly affect everyone in the family (Carlson & Ruzek, 2005). When a traumatized family member's symptoms are severe and remain untreated, they can cause major disruptions within the family system. It is very unsettling for a family to see that a loved one has experienced a trauma. Further, severe trauma and its impact on a family member can make that person hard to live with and may cause the family member to withdraw—both of which have a major impact on the family unit. Carlson and Ruzek (2005) conceded that different individuals react differently to trauma, and likewise, families react differently too. A family may experience a variety of behaviors in reaction to a trauma, or it may experience only a few. Typically, these family behaviors may include sympathy, depression, fear and worry, avoidance, guilt and shame, anger, negative feelings, drug and alcohol abuse, sleep problems, and health problems. Carlson and Ruzek (2005) indicated that both the traumatized family member and the family unit or systems within the family unit may experience some of these problems. For instance, if a traumatized family member is having trouble sleeping, then other family members may also have trouble sleeping. Also, if a traumatized family member begins using drugs and alcohol to cope, other family members may also resort to drugs and alcohol.

Boss (2004), a family theorist and clinician, is very interested in the effects of ambiguous loss on families. She was very involved in working with families in Kosovo following the genocide there in 1999, as well as with families in New York after 9/11. According to her, a useful theory would be applicable locally, nationally, and internationally if it focused less on normative structure and more on events and situations shared by all families. Loss is one such shared experience. Boss (2004, p. 563) writes that loss "lies at the root of human pain and family conflict, and if complicated by ambiguity, has the potential to cause family and marital problems for generations." Children with missing parents caused by war, the Holocaust, ethnic cleansing, kidnapping, exterminations, and terrorism are traumatized and, when they become adults and are married, carry the scars into their families. Boss (2004, p. 563) stated that

in the United States, people struggle with the aftermath of ambiguous loss suffered after the attempted annihilation or assimilation of Native American Indians, and the slavery of Africans brought to our shores. People on both sides of World War II are still struggling with the aftermath, as are children of those lost in the Holocaust, Cambodia, Rwanda, Kosovo, and the Korean and Vietnam Wars. In Central and South America, terrorists kidnap family members so often that the term *desaparecido* (the disappeared) is now common vocabulary in Argentina, Brazil, Colombia, Chile, Panama, Peru, and Mexico. In the war-torn region of Kosovo, 4,000 families still search for their missing. National disasters add to the list of those who vanish without a trace.

Focusing on African Americans, J. D. Leary (2005), a social worker, echoed Boss (2004) and indicated that many African Americans suffer from **posttraumatic slave syndrome** stemming from their years in slavery in America.

Family Issues Involving Veterans

Whealin and Pivar (2005) stated that when a family member is called to prepare to go to war, the impact on the family system can be frightening. Considerable uncertainty exists about the degree of danger a family member will face and when he or she will return. These uncertainties may be increased as the news media focus on the possible dangers, such as what occurred during the first Iraq war when considerable attention was given to possible chemical or biological attacks by Saddam Hussein, Scud missile attacks, and environmental destruction. Family adjustments must be made while family members live in constant fear that their loved ones may not return home alive. Whealin and Pivar (2005) argue that the deployment of a loved one can produce a number of emotions, such as pride, anger, fear, and bitterness. In fact, they argue that there is a cycle of emotions impacting the family unit:

1. The cycle begins with a short period of intense emotions, such as fear and anger, when news of deployment is released to the family.

2. As departure grows closer, a period of detachment and withdrawal may occur. In preparation for the physical separation, family members may experience intense emotions.

3. A period of sadness, loneliness, and tension begins at the time of departure; this can last several weeks or longer.

4. Following the first weeks of deployment, families begin to adjust to a new routine without the deployed service member.

5. As the end of the deployment period draws near, tension increases as the family anticipates changes related to the return of the service member.

After deployment has occurred, family members left at home could experience a number of problems and increased stress. If a family had existing communication problems prior to deployment, these problems may be aggravated during times of stress and have a tendency to add strain to a family. The family structure changes and parental roles are different when one parent leaves for military combat. During Operation Desert Storm, more than 40,000 soldiers were women, and thousands of them left dependent children at home (Whealin & Pivar, 2005). Children who are left at home may have considerable stress and fear, which may manifest in a variety of environments. Children's reactions may include (a) increased irritability and difficulties being soothed; (b) tearfulness, sadness, and talking about things that frighten them; (c) anger toward people and targeting different ethnic or minority groups; (d) increased agitation and fighting with others; (e) wakefulness at night and changes in sleep pattern; (f) more clinging behaviors at home and not wanting to go to school; and (g) complaining about physical problems and wanting more attention (Pivar, 2005).

The National Center for Posttraumatic Stress Disorder (PTSD) has issued a number of reports on issues related to veterans and families from the wars in Iraq and Afghanistan (Ford, 2005). It discussed the overall impact on the family when a family member goes to war. Among the dynamics impacting the family are the uncertainty about the dangers for a loved one in a war zone and the uncertainty about when he or she will be returning home. Robinson (2004) stated that the personal mental health burdens upon soldiers and their families are enormous, and these burdens have consequences for communities and the nation as well if the needs of these soldiers and their families are not met. Robinson (2004) reported that about a year after combat began in March 2003, there were 13,263 medical evacuations from Iraq, 6% of which were for psychiatric problems, but these were only the soldiers who were so severe as to require evaluations. There were more soldiers remaining in the field who had serious psychiatric problems. Some soldiers refused to admit to having psychiatric problems because the military culture scorns perceived weaknesses. As troops return to the United States due to scheduled rotation, they are "met by communities that often have no concept of how to help reintegrate them into society" (Robinson, 2004, p. 6). The diagnosis and treatment of mental disorders is crucial for returning soldiers and their families, as well as for broader communities. National Guard and Reserve soldiers are especially vulnerable because they must reintegrate into their communities and return to their civilian jobs, unlike active-duty soldiers who are under more observation and who are closer to available resources. A superior officer may observe a soldier with mental health difficulties and order him or her to obtain a psychiatric evaluation and treatment. But a Reserve officer may have to rely on his or her family to notice the problems he or she is having (Robinson, 2004). The U.S. Department of Veterans Affairs reported that more than 23,889 soldiers from the Iraq and Afghanistan wars requested help for mental health issues (National Veterans Foundation, 2005), and a study of inpatients at the U.S. Department of Veterans Affairs facilities revealed that 85% of those patients had incomes less than $15,000, with nearly half of these veterans with incomes below the poverty line (National Veterans Foundation, 2005).

The National Center for PTSD (2005) noted that military personnel in war zones have serious reactions to their war experiences and may bring these reactions home to their families. These reactions are connected to posttraumatic stress and include nightmares or difficulties sleeping, unwanted distressing memories or thoughts, anxiety and panic, irritability and anger, emotional numbing or loss of interest in activities or people, and problems abusing alcohol or drugs to cope with stress reactions. Importantly, the National Center for

PTSD (2005) described how traumatic stress reactions can affect families of individuals who had traumatic experiences from wars:

1. Stress reactions may interfere with a service member's ability to trust and be emotionally close to others. As a result, families may feel emotionally cut off from the service member.

2. A returning war veteran may feel irritable and have difficulty communicating, which may make it hard to get along with him or her.

3. A returning veteran may experience a loss of interest in family social activities.

4. Veterans with PTSD may lose interest in sex and feel distant from their spouses.

5. Traumatized war veterans often feel that something terrible may happen "out of the blue" and can become preoccupied with trying to keep themselves and family members safe.

6. Just as war veterans are often afraid to address what happened to them, family members are frequently fearful of examining traumatic events as well. Family members may want to avoid talking about the trauma or related problems. They may avoid talking because they want to spare the survivor further pain or because they are afraid of his or her reaction.

7. Family members may feel hurt, alienated, or discouraged because the veteran has not been able to overcome the effects of the trauma. Family members may become angry or feel distant from the veteran.

According to the National Center for PTSD (2005), the family has a crucial role in helping in the recovery of a traumatized veteran. For sure, the primary source of social support for a mentally wounded veteran is his or her family. Families can impede the veteran's withdrawal from others. Families can let the veteran know that they are willing to listen if he or she wants to relate what war is like. They can give companionship and a sense of belonging, and these supports can counteract, reduce, or eliminate the veteran's sense of separateness that develops from his or her experiences of war. As normal life stresses emanate, families are in a position to provide immediate support. In the event that a veteran is receiving mental health treatment, a family, provided that the veteran agrees, can participate in treatment. A family can impart in therapy how the trauma is affecting other family members, which the veterans may not be able to discern, and learn how the family can help (National Center for PTSD, 2005).

THEORIES AND KNOWLEDGE ABOUT EDUCATION

The formulation of a definition of education requires an understanding of past and present educational systems and the common characteristics of the past and present. In ancient Greek and Roman societies, the purpose of education was to train individuals to subordinate themselves obediently to the collectivity and to become a product of society. A historical study of the establishment and development of educational systems shows that they depend on religion, political organization, the degree of development of science, the state of industry, and so forth. The objective of educational systems is the training of children and adults. Considering these factors, "education is the influence exercised by adult generations on those that are not yet ready for social life. Its object is to arouse and to develop in the child a certain number of physical, intellectual and moral states which are demanded of him [or her] by both the political society as a whole and the special milieu for which he [or she] is specifically destined" (Durkheim, 1956, p. 71). Pallas (2000) reviewed the contemporary research literature and concluded that the educational effects of schooling significantly impact one's later adult life, experience in the workplace, socioeconomic status, cognitive development and knowledge, political and social participation, values, leisure time management, psychological well-being, physical health, and mortality.

Americans have high and often contradictory expectations of contemporary schools. They believe schools should prepare students cognitively, emotionally, and socially. Schools are expected to lay a foundation for students to become mature adults capable of succeeding in higher education, making a living, and establishing a family. This process begins in elementary school. Before a person can ultimately perform complex and sophisticated job skills, he or she builds upon what is taught in elementary school—reading, writing, and calculating (Bills, 2004). Bills (2004, p. 143) contends that "whatever its [sic] roles in the building of community and passing on of moral and public values, elementary schools probably contribute more to the human capital stock of a society—postindustrial as well as earlier forms—than any other segment of the school system." In sum, next to the family, the most authoritative influence in terms of socialization is the school (Newman, 2002).

Schools have been studied from a broader perspective. Like many areas, sociologists are interested in understanding the social structure of schools. Social structure consists of social institutions, organizations, groups, statuses, roles, values, and norms. Applied to the educational system, the social structure includes organizations (e.g., the National Education Association, National Teachers' Association, and state and local school boards); groups (e.g., faculty, students, classes, custodial staff, and athletic personnel); statuses (e.g., teacher, student, principal, coach, counselor, social worker, and nurse); roles (e.g., teaching, learning, disciplining, coaching, and administering tests); cultural beliefs (education is important for later life, or minorities are not that interested in being educated); and institutionalized norms (e.g., respect for educational authorities, no cheating, and drug-free schools; Newman, 2002; Saunders, 1991). This conceptualization of the social structure of schools provides a map for understanding either a micro or macro investigation of the educational system (Saunders, 1991).

However, the school system, pressed by a variety of factors and developments, has changed over time. In the 1940s, teachers stated that the major disciplinary problems in schools were chewing gum, talking without being recognized first, running in the hall, cutting in lines, dress code violations, littering, and making noise. By contrast, in the 1990s, the problems identified by teachers were drug abuse, alcohol abuse, pregnancy, suicide, rape, robbery, and assault. Garbarino (1995) has named this current environment socially toxic. Specifically, children's social context and their social world are poisonous to their development. Further, children who are vulnerable already incur the most damage from a socially toxic environment.

Mooney, Knox, and Schacht (2002) identified current problems in the American educational system, and these included low levels of academic achievement, school dropouts, violence in school, inadequate facilities and personnel, and deficient teachers. Hoping to explain low levels of academic achievement, Marrett (1990) described two social networks involving schools, those within the schools and those linking schools to the broader communities. Social networks consist of connections among students, teachers and administrators, and staff. In the school network, learning is affected by the social context and especially the strength of relationships in that context. Community networks are connections among those within the school network and the wider community, including parents. As an illustration, parents in a Cleveland, Ohio, suburb objected to a freshman research assignment in high school about Internet pornography, which was subsequently cancelled after parental protest and the news media showed up at the high school. The superintendent stated, "We value the partnership we have with the community . . . and we take that very seriously" ("School's Pornography Assignment Prompts Parental Outcry," 2006, p. C7). Community networks can affect learning. Research on oppositional culture theory provides an example. Researchers have used this theory to explain the peer pressures on African American students to not perform well in school (Downey & Ainsworth-Darnell, 2002; Farkas, Lleras, & Maczuga, 2002).

Positive Aspects of Education

A number of positive aspects exist regarding the social and economic influences on education. First, a free public education is available to every child, although the quality of that education has been criticized in many quarters. Retired childless couples and single individuals must pay taxes in most areas of the country to support education because society believes that those with the means must help educate society members for the betterment of society as a whole. Even a college education is within the reach of most individuals. While college students sometimes complain about the rising cost of tuition, at public colleges and universities, students only pay a small portion of the true cost of their education. Money from taxpayers helps supplement the cost of going to college and getting a degree. Further, at the graduate level, universities provide considerable financial support in the form of scholarships. The government provides low-interest loans to help students pay for a college education. These efforts reflect the belief that education benefits society. Research that benefits society comes from an educated populace.

Negative Aspects of Education Law

The problem of inadequate facilities and personnel has been illuminated by several court cases in which individuals sued because of poor schools and facilities. In these cases, the justices made references to the importance of schools and their historical connection to bettering society. These cases reflect the politics, as alluded to by the justices, involved in how schools are funded and how poor communities are ill served. In a case involving school funding, the justices of the Ohio Supreme Court, who had different opinions about the legality of the case, stated that they all agreed with the fundamental importance of education for the children and citizens of Ohio, stressing that educated, informed citizens maintain the strength of democratic institutions.

The Ohio Supreme Court ruled that Ohio's elementary and secondary public school financing system violated the Ohio Constitution, which required a thorough and efficient system of common schools throughout the state. A thorough system was defined as one in which all school districts had enough funds to operate, and an efficient system was defined as one in which every school district had an ample number of teachers, sound and safe buildings, and sufficient equipment so that all students had an educational opportunity. In some schools, which were mostly in rural areas, basic supplies, such as paper, chalk, art supplies, paper clips, and even toilet paper, had to be rationed. Also, some students had no textbooks. Thus, the manner in which Ohio schools were funded violated the constitutional mandate. Specifically, property taxes were the primary means for financing school budgets, which created unequal funding because some communities are more affluent than other communities. The Ohio Supreme Court ordered the state legislature to fix the manner in which schools were funded. However, the legislature did not, and the Ohio Supreme Court essentially terminated the case. In dissent, one justice strongly disagreed with the manner in which the Ohio Supreme Court dropped the case in what was a compromise. She claimed that the legislature merely tweaked the system and called it new and improved, but it was the same system that the court twice ruled was unconstitutional (*Derolph v. State of Ohio*, 2001, 2002).

In Texas, there was a similar problem with similar inaction by the Texas legislature. The Supreme Court of Texas began its decision by stating exasperatingly that once again it was being asked to determine whether the funding of Texas public schools violated the Texas Constitution, which also involved a tax issue that was forbidden by the Texas Constitution. Borrowing from President Thomas Jefferson, the father of the U.S. Constitution, the Texas Constitution further states that a general diffusion of knowledge is essential to the preservation of the liberties and rights of people. Texas had a little over 4.3 million children in its schools in 2003, with 72,500 more children being added each year. In 2003, more than half of Texas students qualified for federally subsidized free or reduced-price lunches. As a result, these children were considered to be economically disadvantaged. Texas children in property-poor districts do not have access to adequate educational revenue. Consequently, property-poor school districts have not provided adequate facilities for students, and these districts are characterized by substandard conditions such as overcrowded schools and classrooms; out-of-date buildings, equipment, and fixtures; and inadequate libraries, science labs, cafeterias, gymnasiums, and other school facilities. Further, in 2003, Texas ranked last among all states in the percentage of high school graduates at least 25 years old. More than half of Latino students in the 9th grade dropped out of school before reaching the 12th grade, and for African Americans the dropout percentage was 46%. Projections were that in 2040, two thirds of the population of Texas would be Latino or African American. According to experts, if these dropout numbers were not reversed, Texas would have a population that not only was poorer and less educated than that of any other state but also would be in need of numerous forms of state services that would be less competitive than those of any other state in the international labor and other markets (*Neeley v. West Orange-Cove Consolidated Independent School District*, 2005).

In both of these cases, the Ohio and Texas legislatures were accused by their highest courts of not having the political will to fix the funding problem, which deprives many students of a proper education. Further, both courts pointed to other states that had similar problems and fixed their problems, such as Michigan, Minnesota, Kentucky, and Vermont.

Sexual Orientation and Education Issues

In education, one of the issues that provokes many individuals is the treatment of gay, lesbian, bisexual, and transgendered students. Macgillivray (2004) advocates for a neutral education policy regarding heterosexual and GLBTIQ (gay, lesbian, bisexual, transgendered, intersexed, or queer/questioning) students. According to Macgillivray (2004, p. 164), "school nondiscrimination policies include sexual orientation and gender identity through prohibiting the exclusion of GLBTIQ students' voice. Given the current inability of GLBTIQ students to speak out because of fear of retribution, coupled with the exclusion of GLBTIQ people and perspectives from the curriculum, schools have not assumed a neutral stance. Not talking about GLBTIQ people and perspectives, when schools currently talk about heterosexual people and perspectives, does not equal neutrality—it equals exclusion." Historically, specific groups have criticized the exclusion of their group from history and advocated for the inclusion of their group in school curriculum. Chinese people helped build railroads to the West and were intentionally left out of pictures depicting the workers. African Americans and Latinos complained about their exclusion from history books. Women have complained about their exclusion as well. Now, gays and lesbians are complaining about their exclusion. While African Americans, Latinos, and women have succeeded, at least at the college level, in creating programs that offer degrees in their areas and have been able to impact primary and secondary public schools, gays and lesbians may have a more difficult time influencing primary and secondary public schools, which is what Macgillivray (2004) targeted in his research study. Some advocates for gays and lesbians seek to have content included in their curriculum on homosexual persons' contribution to society and homosexuality in general. However, strong resistance has emerged from the religious and conservative segments of society, much more than resistance to the inclusion of content on racial minorities and women.

THEORIES AND KNOWLEDGE ABOUT RELIGION

At one time, the most dominantly discussed religions were Protestantism, Catholicism, Judaism, and Islam. In recent years, America has seen an increase in the emergence of other religions and variations of the above four religions as a result of immigration. Present in America now are Salvadoran Catholics, East Indian Hindus, Korean Presbyterians, Cambodian Buddhists, and Pakistani Muslims among many others. In the United States, there has been an increase in Mosques, temples, and ashrams. However, the largest increase in immigration has brought individuals from Latin America and the Philippines, and these individuals are mostly Christians (Smith & Woodberry, 2001).

Religion, as a sociological interest, is those processes and institutions that attempt to make the social world comprehensible and that tie individuals commandingly to the social order. Religious phenomena include magic, rituals, and myths, as well as traditional religions. In primitive religion, humans comprehended their natural environment through a system of magical beliefs (Turner, 2005). Classical sociology focused on the effect of the capitalist economy and the extent to which organized Christianity controlled extremist working-class politics. Methodism, which spread in the 18th and 19th centuries among the working and lower classes, was prominent during the Industrial Revolution. Religion has played an important role in promoting social justice. Some religious organizations were instrumental in opposing slavery (Smith & Woodberry, 2001). Later, the church provided sanctuary to persons fleeing oppressive governments (Smith & Woodberry, 2001). Contemporary sociology focuses on religion's impact on globalization, the conflict between religious fundamentalism and modernity, and the role religion plays in providing an ideological institution for angry and frustrated youths (Turner, 2005). Modern religion presents two important phenomena: Pentecostalism and Fundamentalism. Another important issue that deserves discussion is the issue of the separation between church and state, which people understand in different ways. These differences have an effect on human behavior.

Some churches exert considerable influence in society through what are called megachurches and religious television shows. Persons involved in these churches use another social institution, the media, to get their messages across. One of the most popular religious shows is *The 700 Club*, which is hosted by Pat Robertson and has an estimated 1 million viewers a day. In one episode, Robertson suggested that God gave the Israeli prime minister a stroke for giving up the West Bank to the Palestinians ("Robertson Suggests God Smote Sharon," 2006). Another religious television personality is T. D. Jakes, a best-selling African American author, who has a megachurch in Dallas, Texas. Another best-selling author is Rick Warren, who wrote *The Purpose Driven Life,* which has sold more than 20 million copies.

Some religions interpret current events as the fulfillment of biblical prophecies. For example, in 2005, some expressed apprehensions about the Asian bird flu and its potential pandemic effects. The Jehovah's Witnesses (2005) published a story about the Spanish flu of 1918 and 1919 that killed millions of people worldwide, the Asian bird flu, and their connections to biblical prophecies. The prophecies addressed pestilences and deadly plague. The Jehovah's Witnesses (2005) also discussed the future, reminding the faithful that God spared Noah during the great flood and promised to spare all believers of the upcoming vast destructions. As the Jehovah's Witnesses (2005, p. 10) analyzed it, the survivors will have God with them, and "he will wipe out every tear from their eyes, and death will be no more, neither will mourning nor outcry nor pain be anymore." The Jehovah's Witnesses (2005, p. 11) concluded that "our future need not appear bleak. If you learn about God and come to trust in him fully, you have a bright future ahead of you." From a sociological perspective, the Jehovah's Witnesses, like all religions, make the world comprehensible and help maintain order, in this case, in the face of potential pandemic disaster.

According to New Strategist (2005), a survey of persons 18 years and older in the United States in 2002 revealed that 57% of individuals were reared as Protestant, 30% were reared as Catholic, 2% were reared as Jewish, 7% were reared with no religion, 4.3% were reared as belonging to another religion, and 0.2% did not know. As far as their current religious preference, 53% identified as Protestant, 25% identified as Catholic, 1.7% identified as Jewish, 14% identified as belonging to no religion, 6.8% identified as belonging to another religion, and 0.1% did not know. Regarding the intensity of their religiosity, 24% of individuals attended religious services once a week or more, 23% attended services one to three times a month, 13% attended services several times a week, 14% attended services once a year, 7% attended services less than once a year, 19% never attended services, and 0.8% didn't know (New Strategist, 2005). With respect to the frequency of prayer, 26% prayed several times a day, 31% prayed once a day, 11% prayed several times a week, 9% prayed once a week, 22% prayed less than once a week, 0.5% never prayed, and 0.7% didn't know (New Strategist, 2005).

A survey of youth aged 13 to 17 utilizing data from the National Study of Youth and Religion revealed that 16% of these youth participated in more than one religious congregation. These youth would go to church with their parents and then attend other churches with their friends. In 2005, more than 4,000 young people regularly attended one megachurch in Colorado (Banerjee, 2005). According to Banerjee (2005, p. 1), "a number of Christians are regularly attending different churches in the course of a week or a month, picking and choosing among programs and services, to satisfy social and spiritual needs."

Currently, Pentecostalism is experiencing rapid growth worldwide, with about 250 million believers (Turner, 2005). In Africa and Latin America, Pentecostalism targets persons among the respectable poor (i.e., perceived deserving poor) who aspire to enter the modern world, offering them hope, social inclusion, and welfare services. In West Africa and Southeast Asia, Pentecostalism targets the middle class, while in Nepal, the Andes, and inland China, it targets social minorities (Turner, 2005).

Pentecostalism is important in modern religions because it has very similar characteristics to Methodism, which was prevalent during the Industrial Revolution and promoted a strong work ethic, which was critical to the success of early capitalism. Methodism emphasized discipline, teetotalism, and literacy—all characteristics espoused in modern Pentecostalism. Pentecostal values include betterment through education, self-discipline and -control, social aspiration, and responsibility and hard work, producing socially mobile individuals. In addition, Pentecostalism provides psychological liberation. Devolved, voluntary, and local, Pentecostalism uses a religious market that provides spiritual uplift, social success, and emotional gratification (Turner, 2005). Just as Methodism provided the work ethic for early capitalism, Pentecostalism "is relevant to the work skills and personal attributes of the postindustrial service economy, especially self-monitoring and a refusal to accept social failure" (Turner, 2005, p. 396).

Religious Theory Explaining Family Decline and Political Behaviors

Brooks (2002) reviewed a number of studies conducted by sociologists to formulate the following theory of the effects of religion on family processes and attitudes that affect political behaviors. The influential nature of religion is conveyed by three distinct processes: denominational membership, rates of church attendance, and exposure to denomination-specific influences. Denominational membership represents differential effects of specific denominations. All denominations provide reservoirs of established ideas, authority, and organizations, which differ on the importance of beliefs and ideas. For instance, evangelical Protestantism differs from mainline Protestantism regarding what it believes is wrong with the world. Other denominations, such as Judaism, Islam, and Buddhism, differ. The rate of religious service represents the frequency of exposure to religious messages. Individuals who go to church several times a week are more likely to be affected and motivated by a religious message than individuals who go once every 3 months. Denomination-specific influences are different from denominational membership in that they represent the extent to which a denomination highlights specific issues for its congregation. For example, some congregations are frequently told that gay and lesbian marriages threaten the sanctity of traditional marriages, which is different from just being a member of a specific denomination. Essentially, Brooks's (2002) three variables represent religion's effect on family processes and attitudes that affect political behavior and are the independent variables.

The concept of family decline in Brooks's (2002) theory involves the number of divorces, the number of single-parent families, the extent of children's socialization, and the amount of child poverty. These are the dependent variables. There are also intervening or independent variables. The outcome variable or dependent variable in Brooks's (2002) scheme is whether individuals voted Republican or Democratic, which Brooks hypothesized was caused by beliefs in family decline, which were caused by religion. Brooks (2002) tested this theory and found that all the religious variables affected individuals' beliefs about the decline in the family, which then affected how they voted in presidential elections.

Social and Economic Forces on and by Religion

Separation Between Church and State

One of the most contentious issues involving religion is the concept of separation between church and state (*Americans United for Separation of Church and State v. Prison Fellowship Ministries*, 2005; *Boyd v. Coughlin*, 1996; *O'Connor v. California*, 1994; *Word of Faith Fellowship, Inc., v. Rutherford County Department of Social Service*, 2004). The courts have considered whether a justice on the Alabama Supreme Court can legally display the Ten Commandments on the court's property (*Kuhn v. Thompson*, 2004), whether religious Christmas symbols can be displayed on state property, and whether correctional treatment programs can compel the adoption of religious principles (*Kerr v. Farrey*, 1996; *Scarpino v. Grosshiem*, 1994; *Warner v. Orange County Dept. of Probation*, 1994). Some religious figures have argued that students cannot pray in schools, which is not correct.

Because of the history of religious persecution and religious condemnation, including the infliction of torture and cruel deaths in England when the church was in charge of government, the persons who came to America decided that they wanted to prevent the church from coercing religion on people and to ensure that people would be able to freely choose or not choose religion without fearing punishment. Hence, the First Amendment includes what has been called the Establishment Clause. In 1947, the U.S. Supreme Court explained the demands of the Establishment Clause this way:

> Neither a state nor the Federal government can set up a church. Neither can pass laws which aid one religion, aid all religions, or prefer one religion over another. Neither can force nor influence a person to go to or to remain away from church against his [or her] will or force him [or her] to profess a belief or disbelief in any religion. No person can be punished for entertaining or professing religious beliefs or disbelief, for church attendance or nonattendance. No tax in any amount, large or small, can be levied to support any religious activities or institutions, whatever they may be called, or whatever form they may adopt to teach or practice religion. Neither a state nor the Federal government can, openly or secretly, participate in the affairs of any religious organizations or groups and vice versa. (*Everson v. Board of Education*, 1947, pp. 15–16)

What the Establishment Clause means is that the government or its agents cannot be involved in religion to the extent that the government forces religion on citizens. Students may bring Bibles on school property and read them during recess or lunchtime. They may also pray before taking tests. However, the teacher, who is a government employee, may not lead students in these activities. Also, correctional treatment officials, who are government agents and who may include religion in treatment programs, such as some Alcoholics Anonymous programs that acknowledge God, may not punish an inmate for refusing to participate in treatment. Some prison officials have threatened prisoners with negative reports to the parole board or have increased prisoners' security levels when those prisoners did not participate in religious activities. These negative repercussions, and many others, violate the First Amendment, which says that the government cannot establish or endorse a religion. People may come or not come to religion; the government may not force religion on citizens.

A recent illustration of the issue of the separation between church and state involves the fight over the inclusion of discussions about "Intelligent Design" in biology courses in competition with the theory of evolution (*Kitzmiller v. Dover Area School District*, 2005). Intelligent Design is the philosophy that human life and the universe are so complex that a higher power had to be involved in their creation. The Dover Area School District in Pennsylvania decreed by a vote of 6 to 3 the following statement to read to ninth-grade students taking biology, a required course:

The Pennsylvania Academic Standards require students to learn about Darwin's Theory of Evolution and eventually to take a standardized test of which evolution is a part. Because Darwin's Theory is a theory, it continues to be tested as new evidence is discovered. The Theory is not a fact. Gaps in the Theory exist for which there is no evidence. A theory is defined as a well-tested explanation that unifies a broad range of observations. Intelligent Design is an explanation of the origin of life that differs from Darwin's view. The reference book, *Of Pandas and People,* is available for students who might be interested in gaining an understanding of what Intelligent Design actually involves. With respect to any theory, students are encouraged to keep an open mind. The school leaves the discussion of the Origins of Life to individual students and their families. As a Standards-driven district, class instruction focuses upon preparing students to achieve proficiency on Standards-based assessments.

Some parents objected and filed a lawsuit, arguing that Intelligent Design is really the theory of creationism and violates the principle of the separation between church and state. Hearing evidence from both sides, a U.S. District Court ruled that Intelligent Design was a Christian religious view that was being passed off as a scientific theory. As such, it violated the First Amendment and the Establishment Clause (*Kitzmiller v. Dover Area School District,* 2005).

Positive Aspects of Religion

Religion provides a moral anchor for many individuals and may have more influence on an individual than the law. It also inspires many individuals to help fellow individuals. For instance, Jehovah's Witnesses witness worldwide in countries like Peru, the Netherlands, Mozambique, Korea, and Ukraine. In Amsterdam, Netherlands, Jehovah's Witnesses board ships coming into the harbor to witness to the crews and follow up with them upon return trips. In Alaska, Jehovah's Witnesses use a jet plane to reach remote villages to witness and bring the word of God. Some religious persons canvass the neighborhoods to spread the word of God (Watchtower Bible & Tract Society, 2002). In other reachable communities, Jehovah's Witnesses go door-to-door to witness, linking their community activities to the Bible. One witness (S. Fritz, personal communication, December 17, 2005) points to specific portions of the Bible, such as Acts 20:20: "How I kept back nothing that was helpful, but proclaimed it to you and taught you publicly and from house to house." This biblical reference commands Jehovah's Witnesses to go out in the communities to bring the word of God. In addition, Jehovah's Witnesses are quick to provide relief to people suffering from the results of natural and human-made disasters.

In 1995, a devastating earthquake hit Kobe, Japan, killing more than 5,000 people and leaving more than 300,000 homeless. In 1992, Hurricane Andrew devastated parts of Florida. In Rwanda in 1994, over a million persons were made refugees as a result of the genocide of the Tutsis and moderate Hutus. Jehovah's Witnesses were in all those locations providing assistance and relief (Watchtower Bible & Tract Society, 2002). A number of churches provide social welfare activities to their communities, and their motivation to do so often is driven by their religion.

Negative Aspects of Religion

As stated above, many persons' religion prompts efforts to alleviate suffering in their community. At the same time, religious beliefs have prompted negative and discriminatory efforts against individuals. Religious fundamentalism can be dangerous. In the mainstream media, fundamentalism is associated with radical Islam, and Islam is said to be hostile to modernity, restricting roles for women and promoting a very literal interpretation of religious sources. However, similar types of fundamentalism exist in Judaism, Christianity, and other religions. Fundamentalists stress the relevance of the literal interpretation of the scriptures to contemporary issues. They advocate for purity in what they consider to be an impure world, and they reject any accommodations between the sacred and the profane. Fundamentalism utilizes "confrontation with the secular world, by violent means if necessary, and a worldview that understands the modern world in terms of an endless struggle between good and evil" (Turner, 2005, p. 296). For instance, Christian fundamentalists, such as Jerry Falwell and Pat Robertson, have expressed violent rhetoric toward others. Robertson recently advocated the assassination of a Central American leader, and Falwell has called Mohammed, the founder of Islam, a child molester. Christian fundamentalists have killed in the name of their religion, such as when Paul Hill was convicted of murder and sentenced to death for killing a physician working at an abortion clinic (*Hill v. State of Florida*, 1997). Fundamentalist groups recruit core members and leaders from the urban social classes that are educated but alienated from their societies.

They represent frustrated science teachers, disillusioned physicians, underemployed engineers, unpaid civil servants, and many others. In this contemporary period, religion has become politicized as a response to the secular advancements of globalization. In America, Christian fundamentalists have become a very powerful force in the rise of right-wing politics. In Israel, Jewish fundamentalists have influenced secular politics in their country, such as new home construction on the West Bank, a source of conflict with the Palestinians. In Arab countries, fundamentalist Islam has become a significant means of expression of social and political protest against both perceived internal government corruption and Western dominance (Turner, 2005).

Further, some discriminatory beliefs about gays and lesbians stem from individuals' religious beliefs. In 2007, the coach of the Super Bowl champion Indianapolis Colts, Tony Dungy, stated that he is against same-sex marriages because his God is against same-sex marriages and he must follow God's will (Gilgoff, 2009; Zeigler, 2007).

CONCLUSION

This chapter described three institutions: family and marriage, education, and religion. We discussed knowledge and theories regarding these three social institutions and likewise the social and economic impact of the same three social institutions. We put considerable emphasis on the family as it has been called the most important of all social institutions. Differences exist regarding communities' position on what a family is. For zoning purposes, a community has the right to define and restrict areas for families and thus has the authority to define a family. We described a number of cohabitating family types. We discussed current family issues, including gay and lesbian family issues and family formation by child adoption, domestically and internationally. Lastly, we discussed PTSD and its effects on families, including military families given the current war in which the United States is involved.

Key Terms and Concepts

Police Powers   Second-Parent Adoption

Posttraumatic Slave Syndrome

CHAPTER 5

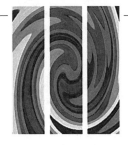

Major Social Institutions Impacting Human Behaviors

Medicine, Mass Media, and the Law

INTRODUCTION

Near the end of the 2008–2009 term of the U.S. Supreme Court, Justice David Souter announced his retirement from the Court after nearly 20 years (Sherman & Feller, 2009). The importance of the U.S. Supreme Court is reflected in a multitude of cases. For instance, in 2000 the presidential election was extremely close between George W. Bush and Al Gore. A dispute arose about the counting of votes in a few counties in Florida, which turned into a legal issue for the U.S. Supreme Court. By a 5-4 vote, with Justice Souter in the minority, the Court stopped the recounts, which effectively gave the White House to President George W. Bush. President Obama stated that he would name a replacement for Justice Souter who possessed empathy and understanding with an outstanding legal background. President Obama declared, "I will seek someone who understands that justice isn't about some abstract legal theory or footnote in a case book. It is about how our laws affect the daily realities of people's lives" (Sherman & Feller, 2009, p. A3). The latter statement suggests that the law affects positively and negatively the lives of individuals. Subsequently, President Obama nominated Judge Sonia Sotomayor to serve on the U.S. Supreme Court—a woman who grew up in a housing project in New York and graduated from Princeton and Yale universities. Standing next to President Obama at his announcement of her nomination, Judge Sotomayor stated that she has never forgotten how her decisions as a judge impact the daily lives of individuals.

Chapter 4 presented the first three major social institutions that impact human behavior (i.e., the family, the education system, and religion). Chapter 5 continues the presentation of the major social institutions that were initially justified in Chapter 1. These social institutions are medicine, mass media, and the law. These three social institutions impact human behaviors but not as intimately or directly as the family, education, and religion. Medicine especially is very broad. According to *Webster's New World College Dictionary* ("Medicine," 2006, p. 842), **medicine** is "the science and art of diagnosing, treating, curing, and preventing disease, relieving pain, and improving and preserving health." In our discussion of medicine, we consider insurance because for many individuals the lack of insurance means inadequate access to medicine. Health care or the lack thereof is critically important to the well-being of adults and their children. According to a survey, 60% of workers reported that health insurance was the most important benefit that their employers offered (Christensen, 2002). Employees see health insurance as extremely important because it protects them and their families from severe financial losses as the result of an injury or a serious illness. Employers provide health care benefits to promote employee health, to increase employee productivity, and to recruit and retain employees (Employee Benefit Research Institute, 2003). Mass media include radio, television, the movies, newspapers, and magazines. The media both provide individuals with knowledge, information, and entertainment and carry messages, both positive and negative. In 2004, Al Gore suggested that President Bush used the news media to frighten Americans into supporting the war in Iraq (Gore, 2004). At one time, the movie industry, at the urging of law enforcement, agreed not to produce movies in which criminals got away unpunished. Instead, criminals were always caught and punished, or they died at the end of the movies. This agreement was called the "Hollywood Code." Television also plays a powerful role in providing information to citizenry, and news programs help determine when the public focuses on some social problems, such as increased public attention of poverty in the 1960s. In short, government institutions manipulate the media to their own ends. The legal and political systems that make laws also have a significant impact on society. The resolutions of some lawsuits help shape social policies involving the family, parent-child relationships, and the securing of medical treatment or medical coverage. For instance, individuals who purchase their own medical coverage may have their policies terminated after filing one claim. Further, the legislative branches of government enact laws that impede or further the happiness of some citizens, such as laws allowing or prohibiting same-sex marriages and permitting citizens the right to keep weapons on their persons while taking public transportation. All in all, these social institutions play vital roles in human behaviors and the social environment.

KNOWLEDGE AND THEORIES ABOUT MEDICINE

Health is synonymous with well-being (Albrecht, 2005). Broadly speaking, a healthy person is one who is sound of mind and body. Put another way, a healthy person is integrated and whole. Also, health can be extrapolated to specific body parts, such as having a healthy heart or a healthy personality. Albrecht states that an environmental perspective can assist with understanding health. A healthy environment is one that values and promotes human rights, clean air, adequate water, a sense of security, and freedom of expression (Albrecht, 2005). However, one's view of health is determined by one's culture. Current Western medicine, for example, determines a person's health by a battery of tests. Medical personnel test a person's blood and urine or conduct a pap smear to determine whether the results fall within the normal range. In addition, physical examinations are made of an individual, such as a digital examination for an enlarged prostate for men. If the various tests, combined with various physical examinations, do not indicate a problem, then the physician will pronounce the person as healthy and in need of no medicine or other health care treatment at that time.

In non-Western or nontraditional societies, health may be determined by a designee of the community. A medicine man, shaman, or holy man might see a reputed ill person and diagnose the illness as stemming from problematic social relationships in the community or with the deity. In this example, "health ultimately resides outside the individual and is situated in the social structure and relationships in the community or inside the individual expressed through dreams and hallucinations about spirits and ancestors" (Albrecht, 2005, p. 267). This phenomenon may be seen in some Western ethnic communities within the United States. Numerous African Americans believe in the power of "root doctors" to diagnose and cure illnesses, which these Americans believe are often caused by an enemy or enemies. Aches, pains, and major illnesses, including psychiatric problems, are believed to be caused by someone "working roots." Likely, the Hmong and Somalians who reside in the Midwest have their own traditional views of health and illnesses. Susan Robbins, in preparation for conducting her dissertation, lived on a Native American reservation in Florida in the 1970s, and she reported that many Native Americans believe that the presence of certain animals can make one sick (Robbins & Alexander, 1985).

Attention to workers' health has its roots in the 1870s, when railroad, mining, and other nascent industries provided doctors to workers. In 1910, Montgomery Ward, a department store no longer in business, was the first to purchase a contract to provide health services for its employees. Before the 1940s, few workers and individuals had health insurance. If one had health insurance, it covered basic medical services, such as a hospital room, board, and ancillary services. Following World War II, the provision of health insurance increased. At that time, the National War Labor Board froze wages to assist the war efforts, and a shortage of workers forced employers to compete for scarce workers. To attract workers in this environment, more employers began to offer health benefits. The provision of health insurance was an effective means of recruiting and retaining workers. Health insurance was popular with employers because unions supported it and benefits were not taxed (Employee Benefit Research Institute, 2003). The majority of Americans continue to receive health insurance mostly from their employers. In 1987, 76% of American workers had their health insurance through their employers, but this percentage has been decreasing due to changes in the economy (Employee Benefit Research Institute, 2003). From 2000 to 2005, the percentage of employers who offered health benefits for their workers dropped from 69% to 60% (Frostin, 2006). Of the businesses with fewer than 200 employees, only 59% provided health insurance (Frostin, 2006).

Health insurance plans usually consist of a combination of insurance policies. This combination may cover the costs of hospitals and physicians, vision care, and dental care. Formerly, health insurance that paid for medical stays and surgeries was called comprehensive or major medical. Presently, the term *major medical* is not used as the health care field has changed, and now we have health maintenance organizations (HMOs) and other plans.

Social and Economic Forces on and by Medicine

Although the United States was one of the leaders in the Industrial Revolution, it lagged behind other industrialized nations in the creation of the welfare state. Great Britain and Germany created social security and unemployment insurance decades before the United States. The New Deal in the 1930s created several major social programs, but a system of health care and sickness insurance was conspicuously absent. After World War II, the federal government began to fund medical research and facilitate the building of hospitals. In 1965, Congress, over the opposition of the American Medical Association due to concerns about governmental control, created **Medicare**, a health program for persons over 65, and **Medicaid**, a program for the medically indigent (Zussman, 1990). Medicare is a health insurance program for individuals age 65 or older, individuals under 65 with certain disabilities, and all individuals with kidney problems who require dialysis or a kidney transplant. Medicare consists of four components: Part A (Hospital Insurance), Part B (Medical Insurance), Part C (Medicare Advantage Plan), and, since January 1, 2006, Prescription Drug Coverage (Part D).

About 35 million Americans ages 65 and older and about 6 million younger adults with disabilities have Medicare benefits (Powell, 2003). Estimates are that by 2031, the number of persons with Medicare benefits will reach 77 million (Powell, 2003). In 2002, the U.S. government reported that 24% of Medicare recipients had no prescription drug coverage (Powell, 2003). The remaining portion had coverage through several employer-sponsored or state programs. Employer-sponsored health plans covered 32.9%, Medicaid covered 12.3%, **Medigap** (also known as Medicare Supplemental Insurance, which provides supplemental health insurance for individuals receiving Medicare) covered 14.8%, **Medicare Advantage Plan** (part of the Medicare program that represents a number of different plans, provided by a private HMO or insurance company) covered 10.6%, and other supplemental programs covered the rest (Powell, 2003). Medicare, Medicaid, and Social Security accounted for 42% of all federal spending in 2003, which has prompted governmental concerns about cutbacks and revisions (Powell, 2003).

Many younger Americans lack insurance coverage. Nationally, 30% of young people aged 18 to 24 lack insurance coverage. Children, who are covered by their parents' insurance, are terminated from coverage at about 19 unless they are in college and taking a full load of courses. As a result, a number of states are passing laws requiring insurers to cover young adults longer, which the insurers are often willing to do because they can increase the amount they charge for coverage (Ramer, 2006). In a scientific poll, nearly

40% of participating Arizona residents reported that they are concerned that they will be unable to afford health care or their prescription drugs. As a result, there is strong support in Arizona for government-aided health care (Crawford, 2006). Frequent reports indicate that the cost of health care is out of control, representing 16% of the nation's economic output (Kaufman & Stein, 2006). Professionals in business, economics, politics, and medicine worry that health care costs will overwhelm the American economy, with business leaders arguing that the costs of benefits for employees and retirees make them less competitive (Kaufman & Stein, 2006).

For reasons suggested above, inequality in health has been a regular focus of researchers. Researchers have identified the importance of social capital, which is linked to race, ethnicity, culture, and social class (Scarpitti, Anderson, & O' Toole, 1997). Social capital is the amount of social resources and networks accessible to persons that assist them in defining and coping with life problems, including health problems. Research suggests that the more social capital an individual has, the less likely that individual is to have a disability, and the higher the individual's level of support and quality of life. Further, research on social equity has emphasized the necessity of examining multiple system levels and of considering "individuals in their environment and as members of a community and nation" (Albrecht, 2005, p. 277).

Albrecht (2005, p. 277) discussed the meaning of a number of sociological findings resulting from studies of organizational factors and health:

> Studies of national health care services, multiple hospital systems, assisted care facilities, hospices, support groups for those with HIV/AIDS and the environment within which these organizations operate have led to important findings about how the organization of health care directly impacts the cost, access and quality of care. This work is now expanding to important sets of cross-national studies that are examining the essentials of effective health care systems, how different organizational models may produce similar results and how the mix of populations served interact with the organizational structures of the delivery system to yield variable results. In other words, the organization of health care needs to be tailored to the needs of the population and local culture and environment. That is why there is persistent interest in comparable health care system research between Scandinavian countries, other European countries, the UK, the United States, Canada, Cuba, and Japan.

Albrecht's (2005) conclusion emphasizes several major points for a macro understanding of human behavior in the social environment as it relates to health care. The organization of health care is a particularly independent or predictive variable. This variable, in multiple studies, has been found to influence the cost of, access to, and quality of health care. More important, these variables have implications for cross-cultural research and international comparative studies. Albrecht stresses that significant knowledge is provided about health care when countries are compared to each other in studies.

Positive Aspects of Medicine

The secretary of the Department of Health and Human Services regularly reports to the president and Congress on the health status of the population of the United States. In 2006, the report prepared by the secretary was over 500 pages long and included massive amounts of data on the population, health insurance and expenditures, health risk factors, morbidity and activity limitation, health care utilization, mortality, and pain management. According to the secretary, the health of Americans has improved in most of the above areas because of significant resources allocated for public health programs, research, health care, and health education (National Center for Health Statistics, 2006). Life expectancy in the United States has continued a long-term upward trend. Many diseases have been controlled, and the related mortality and morbidity have been significantly lowered. Control of infectious diseases and progress in addressing diseases have advanced public health. The decontamination of water has led to control of typhoid and cholera; extensive vaccination programs have controlled polio, diphtheria, pertussis, and measles; and the fluoridation of water has led to better dental care. In addition, laws governing seat belt use and motorcycle helmets have helped reduce incidents of health trauma and deaths. Further, improved medications have led to fewer heart attacks. The National Center for Health Statistics (2006, p. 3) states that "advances in medical technologies, procedures, and new prescription drugs have extended and improved the quality of countless lives."

Two groups have been the primary focus of improved health outcomes—the young and the old. For very young children, such as babies, experts have advised mothers to place their babies on their backs when the babies take a nap to prevent sudden infant death syndrome, and even before these children are born, experts advise mothers to seek prenatal care and refrain from certain activities, such as smoking. Obesity has become a national problem among Americans in general, and the problem has increased in children (Carmona, 2005). African American girls and Latino males are at a higher risk for type 2 diabetes, which is triggered by being overweight (Carmona, 2005). The Surgeon General stated that programs such as We Can! are the latest initiatives to improve the health and well-being of children. We Can! strives to prevent obesity in youth ages 8 to 13 by providing resources and community-based programs that stress healthful eating, physical activity, and less sedentary time. Developed by the National Institutes of Health, We Can! seeks to help parents and caregivers teach children how to live healthier by eating less high-fat and inadequately nutritious foods (Carmona, 2005).

Among the elderly, "improved medical care and prevention efforts have contributed to dramatic increases in life expectancy in the United States over the past century" (Centers for Disease Control and Prevention and the Merck Company Foundation, 2007, p. iii). The elderly, like many other groups, are less likely to die from infectious diseases and acute illnesses and are instead living longer and dying from chronic diseases and degenerative illness (Centers for Disease Control and Prevention and the Merck Company Foundation, 2007). Presently, about 80% of the elderly are living with at least one chronic condition. Because of increased life span as a result of medical advances, by 2030 there will be 71 million elderly, constituting 20% of the U.S. population (Centers for Disease Control and Prevention and the Merck Company Foundation, 2007). Presently, a number of programs exist for elderly persons. Some programs are geared toward keeping the elderly in their homes. To that end, elderly persons are visited in their homes by home care workers who perform household chores. Technology helps in this effort by way of devices that alert outside monitors when an elderly person has fallen. In many other cases, elderly persons are not able to live at home, and assisted care facilities exist for them.

Negative Aspects of Medicine

Health is associated with income and systems problems. Kleinfield (2006b), a reporter from *The New York Times*, reported statistics about diabetes within the Upper East Side and East Harlem in New York. New York has the highest rate of diabetes in the United States (Kleinfield, 2006b). About 1% of the individuals who live on the Upper East Side have diabetes, compared to 16% in East Harlem. When individuals need to be hospitalized for diabetes, the rate for the Upper East Side is 84 of every 100,000 residents compared to 828 of every 100,000 residents of East Harlem. Ten of every 100,000 residents of the Upper East Side have died from diabetes compared to 47 per 100,000 residents of East Harlem. Sociological data reveal that 84% of the residents of the Upper East Side are White and have a median income of $74,446. For East Harlem, 88% are Latino or African American with a median income of $20,111 (Kleinfield,

2006b). The differences in outcomes for people suffering from diabetes support world systems theory and its description of core and periphery communities. For instance, diabetes differentially impacts individuals in New York along race and class lines. Individuals in the core have fewer amputations and fewer deaths than individuals in the periphery communities.

Diabetes is mostly preventable, and if diabetics change their eating habits and lifestyles they can avoid many of its repercussions (amputations, blindness, kidney failure, strokes, and heart attacks). Medical and insurance systems exacerbate the problem because insurance companies will not pay to care for preventable illnesses and hospitals cannot make money from preventable intervention but do make money from the numerous operations that diabetics will eventually have. For instance, insurers refuse to pay $150 for a diabetic to see a podiatrist, which could prevent the need for an amputation later, but will pay the roughly $30,000 that an amputation will cost. Diabetes causes roughly 2,000 amputations a year. Insurers gamble that they will save money now and not have to pay amputation costs years later (Urbina, 2006a). Further, some New York hospitals that attempted to create units staffed with nutritionists to educate people about diabetes had to shut down these units because they lost money (Urbina, 2006a). Because of the increase of diabetes in New York, more than 100 dialysis centers have opened. Some patients need about two or three sessions a week, at a cost of $315 per session (Urbina, 2006a).

The city of New York devotes three staff persons and a budget of $950,000 to diabetes. In its efforts to combat tuberculosis, which affects about 1,000 New Yorkers per year, the city created a staff of 400 persons with a budget of $27 million (Kleinfield, 2006a). Diabetes affects more than 1 million individuals. The New York legislature has considered numerous bills to address the health care problems associated with diabetes, but insurance and health care interests exert pressure to ensure that these bills die. As Kleinfield (2006a, p. A18) wrote, "the health care system tinkers with new models of dispensing care and then forsakes them, unable to wring out profits. Insurers shun diabetics as too expensive. In Albany, bills aimed at the problem go nowhere."

Insurance determines who gets medical care and how much they get. Most individuals receive insurance coverage through their employment, but some individuals purchase their own insurance coverage independently, especially when these individuals are self-employed or starting their own businesses. Estimates are that about 16 million Americans purchase their insurance in the individual marketplace (Appleby, 2007).

Writing for *USA Today*, Julie Appleby (2007) provided a detailed exposé on how some individuals who have purchased insurance are stripped of their coverage. One should keep in mind that most insurance companies are in business to make money, not to help someone receive medical coverage. The best customers are those who pay their premiums and do not file claims. If individuals file too many claims in the eyes of the insurance carrier, their policies will be canceled, and this applies to automobile insurance, home liability policies, and medical insurance. Policies purchased by large companies are unlikely to be cancelled if a few employees have more claims than other employees. The insurance company can simply increase the cost of the insurance to the employees' companies, with some of the added costs being passed on to employees in the form of higher premiums and higher deductibles. However, individual policies are much more susceptible to cancellation.

The process begins when an individual submits an application and discloses his or her medical history. One attorney states that insurance questionnaires are worded in such a fashion as to provide justification for the insurance carrier to cancel a policy under the guise that the applicant lied or gave incomplete information (Appleby, 2007). When claims are filed, the insurance carrier peruses the application for information with which to cancel the policy should the need arise. As an example, one family, consisting of a husband, a wife, and three children, paid $700 a month in premiums for the entire family. The wife was rushed to the hospital one evening for a perforated ulcer and had emergency surgery. Before paying the hospital claim, the insurance company requested some additional information and learned that the wife had seen an ob-gyn for heavy menstrual bleeding, which was not disclosed on the application. As a result, the insurance carrier cancelled the family's policy and refused to pay the $30,000 hospital bill (Appleby, 2007). Another woman was asked on the application when her last menstrual cycle was, and she provided a date. Later, the woman became pregnant, and her child was born with severe brain damage. The insurance company reviewed the application and concluded that the woman had provided the wrong date for her last menstrual cycle and cancelled the policy, leaving the family $140,000 in hospital debt. Another woman had a lump behind her ear and did not initially see a doctor. She purchased an insurance policy, and her lump was later diagnosed as cancer. Her policy was cancelled as the insurance company stated that any prudent person would have seen a doctor immediately about the lump. She was left with about $30,000 in medical bills. Another woman had a rash that was later diagnosed as cancer, and the insurance company cancelled her policy, concluding that she had an existing medical disease at the time of the issuance of the policy. The woman was left with over $100,000 in bills to pay for chemotherapy (Appleby, 2007).

The insurance industry's defense is that it issues a large number of policies and only a very small fraction are revoked. In response, one legal advocate says that current practices give the insurance companies leeway to cancel policies when the insured files a large claim or has too many claims. One attorney said that "anyone who fills one out [an application form] would make a mistake. . . . They have compound questions, confusing questions, ambiguous questions. There's no place to answer 'I don't remember' or 'I don't know'" (Appleby, 2007, p. 2A). As such, insurance companies can find a reason in any application to cancel a policy and not pay the claim.

Robert Pear (2007) reported the story of a 50-year-old real estate agent in Salisbury, North Carolina. As an independent contractor, Vicki Readling had to purchase her own medical insurance, but after being diagnosed with breast cancer, no affordable insurance company would cover her. In 2007, Pear reported that nearly 47 million Americans like Readling had no health insurance. Many of these individuals were middle-class, independent contractors such as Readling, who made about $60,000 in 2006. One insurance carrier was willing to issue a policy to Readling, but the policy was expected to cost more than $27,000 a year. Another insurance carrier boasted that it would provide policies to anyone, including those individuals with preexisting medical problems, but the premiums and deductible were set so high that no middle-class individuals could afford the insurance. Readling was advised by one insurance professional to go back to her former job at a furniture store where she had insurance or to remarry her first husband who had insurance (Pear, 2007). One of the primary factors in the dilemma facing individuals in the insurance market is that they do not have anyone to negotiate for them; nor do they have the leverage of a big corporation like Microsoft or Toyota (Pear, 2007).

Robert Pear's (2007) above account and revelations show the differences in treatment from a systems perspective. Macro systems, such as an insurance corporation, impact individual systems, and as shown in this section, this impact is negative. Individual systems have little reciprocal impact on insurance corporations. Other macro systems, such as the law, may be able to influence the behaviors of the insurance corporations through legislation. But often, another macro system, such as a large organization, is able to influence insurance corporations and negotiate outcomes that individual systems cannot.

African Americans and Their Suspicion of Medicine

African Americans voice more distrust of medicine—and especially medicine linked to the government—than any other racial group (National Public Radio, 2008). Stephen B. Thomas (2000), a researcher from Emory University, conducted a study of African Americans in five cities and reported that nearly one third of them indicated that AIDS was created to harm African Americans. Prominent

African Americans, such as Reverend Jeremiah Wright, created considerable controversy in 2008 for saying that AIDS was an illness created by the U.S. government to control African Americans (Fox News, 2008), an idea ridiculed by many Whites. Harriet Washington (2007), however, published a book in which she chronicled the medical mistreatment of slaves and African Americans and other minorities until the 1970s. Among the stories Washington discussed was that of James Marion Sims, deemed the father of gynecology. Sims, believing women from Africa did not experience pain like White women, operated on slave women without anesthesia in order to seek a treatment for vesico-vaginal fistulas, a condition involving a leaky bladder. Many of these women died from infection, and though Sims has been referred to as "a butcher," a statue was erected of him in 1894 in New York for his pioneering work. Washington (2007) also discussed the Tuskegee Experiment, in which African American men with syphilis were experimented on from the 1930s to the early 1970s. Then, she recounted a Mississippi physician who operated on the brains of institutionalized African American boys and published an article about it and a physician who injected plutonium into an African American male who had been in an automobile accident and was believed to be facing death within 24 hours. The plutonium had nothing to do with treating the injuries of the African American male. Washington (2007) disclosed other medical mistreatment of African Americans in her book, concluding that the medical abuse of African Americans by White institutions has fostered a condition in many African Americans that she called **Iatrophobia**, or a fear of medicine. This fear causes African Americans to refuse some medications, delay or avoid medical examinations, and refuse to participate in ethical medical research trials that may benefit them.

Baker (1999) has discussed minority distrust of medicine and indicated that specific focus on comparing minorities' health to that of the majority or Whites has not been productive. Baker also highlighted some of the ethical problems involving medicine from Nuremberg to the Tuskegee experiment involving African American men in Alabama from the 1930s to 1972 when this study was halted after public disclosure. Since the disclosure of the Tuskegee experiment, many African Americans have become more suspicious of disease and medicine. Even more suspicion has occurred as a result of the epidemic involving HIV/AIDS. Sometimes, African Americans are accused of being paranoid regarding their beliefs about HIV/AIDS (Fox News, 2008). Moreover, Africans have been blamed for HIV/AIDS because the emergence of this disease has been located in Africa (Walters, 2004). One theory is that a disease similar to HIV exists in monkeys and, when an African hunter cut himself, monkey blood infected his wound. As a result, while it might not be explicitly stated by mainstream individuals, Africa is blamed for HIV/AIDS (Walters, 2004).

However, a very controversial but plausible theory supports the view that HIV was caused by an influential Polish American physician in a race to develop a polio vaccine. HIV was first isolated in 1983 by a team at the Pasteur Institute in France, and the source of this disease was then traced to Africa. In chimpanzees, a disease exists called SIV, or simian immunodeficiency virus, and it has been identified as the ancestor of HIV. In the 1950s, a search was on to develop a vaccine for polio, and two of the leaders in polio research in the United States were Jonas Salk and Hilary Koprowski, a physician who migrated from Poland. Salk's oral vaccine was accepted, but there was some caution about it after several children died. Koprowski was developing and testing his polio vaccine using orphans in New York and ran into political problems after it was disclosed that he was conducting experiments on children. As a result, Koprowski and his team went to the Belgian Congo and set up a laboratory there (Chappell & Peix, 2004). Apparently, there were no ethical concerns about conducting experiments on people in Africa.

This vaccine was developed by a process of using monkey kidneys. The kidneys were cut up and put in a flask with live polio virus. The liquid was filtered out, and a virus suspension occurred. Then, the virus was killed with formaldehyde, and the solution became a polio vaccine, which was injected into patients. Koprowski and his team then injected thousands of Africans in the Belgian Congo, Rwanda, and Burundi in a massive testing program. Supposedly, the safest monkey kidneys to use were from monkeys from India and the Philippines. Chimpanzees were unsafe because of the diseases that these monkeys carry, including SIV. Two journalists have charged that Koprowski and his team introduced HIV when testing this polio vaccine. Koprowski denied that he used chimpanzees' kidneys in the development of his vaccine. Almost the entire medical community in Great Britain, France, and the United States has rejected the theory that HIV emerged as a result of Koprowski's polio vaccine development. However, pictures exist showing this laboratory in the Congo jungle with numerous chimpanzees in cages, and African workers have stated that they killed chimpanzees for the harvesting of their kidneys for Koprowski's team. Other evidence shows that HIV emerged in those African regions where Koprowski's vaccine was used (Chappell & Peix, 2004).

The resistance to the polio vaccine theory, as opposed to the hunter theory, created fear among some health care professionals that the public will become suspicious of vaccines, impairing the health of individuals (Chappell & Peix, 2004). Bill Hamilton, a preeminent evolutionary biologist who embraced the polio vaccine theory and who died of malaria, was attempting to prove the theory correct and stated that there was a "paranoid rejection" among many scientists toward the polio vaccine theory (Chappell & Peix, 2004). But a more powerful reason for the resistance is tied to race—to accept this theory is to accept that White people were responsible for the development of HIV in humans and exploited a poor African population in this development. Further, Joffe (1992) conducted a qualitative study of Black and White South Africans regarding the cause of AIDS. He found that Whites blamed Africa and Blacks blamed the West. Joffe concluded that the power relations in society determine who is blamed for AIDS. Given that Africans have no power, blaming them is much easier than blaming the scientific community and a drug company.

HIV and AIDS have devastated Africa, and AIDS has killed people worldwide. Thus, large pharmaceutical corporations that backed Koprowski and funded his research in Africa may be financially liable for the devastation that HIV has caused if the polio vaccine theory is accepted. As a result, governments, scientists, and drug companies have generated considerable resistance to the theory that Koprowski's polio vaccine caused HIV. Instead, there is a further exploitation of Africa by blaming it for HIV and declaring that a careless African hunter is responsible for HIV. Nevertheless, proponents of the hunter theory cannot explain why HIV developed just in the 20th century and not 5,000 years ago. More important, in 2006 an international team of scientists concluded after examining chimpanzee feces that a chimpanzee virus indeed was the cause of HIV (Altman, 2006). These droppings from the chimpanzees were found in southern Cameroon, which is very close to the Congo. These scientists agree that HIV appeared in humans about 50 to 75 years ago and the first documented case came from the then-Belgian Congo in 1959 (Altman, 2006). HIV emerged 1 year after Koprowski vaccinated over a million Africans, and it emerged in the same area where the vaccinations had taken place (Chappell & Peix, 2004). The scientists in the study of chimpanzee droppings did not attribute HIV to the polio development theory, but their findings lend further support.

Last, Cecil Fox, a pathologist with the National Institute of Allergy and Infectious Diseases, stated that many vaccines today are still made with animal parts but this practice should have stopped in the 1960s when scientists first gained the knowledge to make vaccines synthetically. Simply, pharmaceutical companies did not want to spend the money to make the necessary conversions (Chappell & Peix, 2004).

KNOWLEDGE AND THEORIES ABOUT MASS MEDIA

The media consist of the institutions and practices of recording and broadcasting representations, encompassing the postal service and telegraph, telephone, satellite, and computer networks. The mass media typically consist of radio, television, movies, newspapers, and magazines, which also are known as the Big Five (Peters, 2001). The news media, which include the Big Five, are one of the most powerful social institutions in American society, and it has become even more powerful in the age of globalization (Bartlett, 2004; Gamson, 2004). Generally speaking, a major role of the news media is to bring information to the public, and depending on the nature of the news event, they can bring public attention, or a response, to social problems (Jenkins, 1992). The most popular role for the news media is to focus on American politicians and politics. There is a general belief that the news media can keep politicians honest by reporting on unsavory political events and "keeping politicians' feet to the fire." Also, reporters believe that under the First Amendment the public has a right to know what its governmental officials are doing. In fact, some states, to further this role, have given reporters in their states a privilege against disclosing news sources. But in some states and jurisdictions, reporters do not have this privilege and sometimes are jailed for not responding to an investigatory process initiated by a prosecutor or a grand jury. Although the news media frequently ground their insistence on protecting their sources under the First Amendment freedom of the press, they are legally bound in many areas to disclose criminal activities, just as ordinary citizens must.

Barber and Axinn (2004) studied the impact of the mass media as a social change agent that shapes individual behaviors. They presented a theory of the behavior of the media on contraception behaviors in rural Nepal. As a developing society involved in rapid social change, Nepal was ideal for studying the impact of the media because the mass media in Nepal were in the infancy stage. Researchers were able to conceptualize a broad dependent variable consisting of individuals' first contact with various forms of media in addition to their exposure to and experience of other aspects of social change. They used "this comprehensive measurement of social change and ideational variation to demonstrate that mass media influence behavior independent of numerous other mechanisms of change" (Barber & Axinn, 2004, p. 1181). The behavior of interest to these researchers was childbearing behavior in rural Nepal, including the size of the family, the degree of preferring sons, and attitudes about contraceptive use. Following their analyses of the data, they concluded that the evidence showed that their primary hypothesis, which is stated below, was supported in that

> media exposure affects attitudes about childbearing and contraceptive use, which are likely to shape fertility limitation behavior in this setting. Both premarital and lifetime exposure to mass media are associated with higher rates of permanent contraceptive use. In addition, individuals exposed to

mass media sources prefer smaller families, have weaker preferences for sons, and are more positive toward contraceptive use. Lifetime exposure is more strongly related to both attitudes and behavior than premarital exposure, suggesting that the relationship may be much stronger than the conservative premarital exposure models would suggest. (Barber & Axinn, 2004, p. 1198)

Two researchers from the United States and two researchers from Germany compared public discourse in both countries using the abortion controversy. However, their framework could be applied to welfare reform or workers' rights. As they defined public discourse, it is public communications surrounding issues and parties involving and favoring a particular policy domain or the values and broader interests associated with the topic. Public discourse involves not only argumentation by interested parties and information they provide but also images, metaphors, and other illuminating symbols. Prominent in these researchers' theoretical analysis is the role of mass media, which they say is the most important factor (Ferree, Gamson, Gerhards, & Rucht, 2002).

Public discourse occurs in a number of forums, depicted by Ferree et al. (2002) as resembling a sports arena. On the field, the individuals engage in discourse. The fans or spectators are seated in the stands, which are called the gallery. Discourse and decisions are made in a backstage area outside the view of the gallery. "A forum includes an arena in which individual or collective actors engage in public speech acts; an active audience or gallery observes what is going on in the arena; and a backstage, where the would-be players in the arena work out their ideas and strategize over how they are to be presented, make alliances, and do the everyday work of cultural production" (Ferree et al., 2002, pp. 9–10). A number of public forums exist in which public discourse occurs, such as mass media, parliaments, courts, party conventions, town hall assemblies, scientific conferences, and even the streets. All of these public forums constitute the public sphere.

According to Ferree et al. (2002, p. 10), "in the current era, there is one forum that overshadows all others, making them sideshows. For various reasons, general-audience mass media provide a master forum. The players in every other forum also use the mass media, either as players or as part of the gallery." In their depicted model, mass media are placed in the center and enlarged (see Figure 5.1). The spokes from the mass media forum lead to other forums, including the legal forum, social movement forum, religious forum, and political party forum. All the outside forums use the mass media forum. Further, the mass media forum is the major site for politics due to all the players, rightly or wrongly, believing that considerable power exists in mass media to convince others to adopt their points of view. The participants from

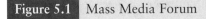

Figure 5.1   Mass Media Forum

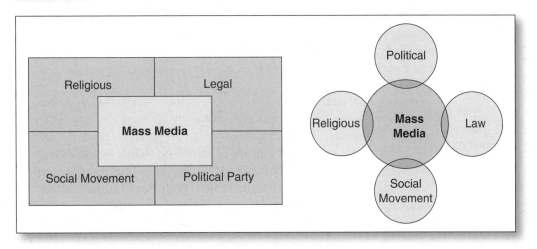

other forums use mass media to evaluate the effectiveness of their efforts. For example, the legislature forum might look to whether its bills are featured in *The Washington Post* and discussed on the evening news. In conclusion,

> the mass media forum is not simply a site where one can read relative success in cultural contests. It is not merely an indicator of broader cultural changes in the civil society but also influences them, spreading changes in language use and political consciousness to the workplace and other settings in which people go about the public part of their daily lives. When a cultural code is being challenged, a change in the media forum both signals and spreads the change. To have one's preferred framing of an issue increase significantly in the mass media forum is both an important outcome in itself and carries a strong promise of a ripple effect. (Ferree et al., 2002, p. 10)

The arena, gallery, and backstage of mass media deserve further elaboration. In the arena, participants employ different forms of speech. Their speeches convey a message about the organizations with which the speakers are associated. Commentary seeks to frame issues favorably and to promote the preferred point of view in the mass media arena. In the arena, journalists perform dual parts— they are gatekeepers who decide which quotations and paraphrases to publicize. Also, they are players themselves. However, carefully chosen comments by journalists can help indicate what is important and frame the issues.

The individuals in the gallery represent different collective identities or solidarity groups of which they are a part. One professional referred to this concept as imagined communities (Anderson, 1991), such as women, workers, Christians, environmentalists, conservatives, Latinos, the Left, or the Right. Because a single individual has multiple identities, he or she represents multiple imagined communities. As Ferree et al. (2002, p. 13) summarized,

> imagined communities are not collective actors. They can only speak through some form of organization or advocacy network that attempts to generate, aggregate, transform, and articulate their concerns. These carriers attempt to represent and make claims on behalf of the interests and values of particular communities that become their constituencies. Often rival carriers compete for the same constituency offering different and even contradictory claims about the "real" interests of the general public or some more specific constituency such as women or Christians.

The backstage of mass media consists of organized production centers for spokespersons who speak for collective actors as opposed to individual speakers in the arena. In short, some speakers are essentially alone in the arena, while other speakers represent collective actors. Those who represent collective actors have assistance in the backstage from organized production centers. Their organizations supply material resources, knowledge of the playing that goes on in the arena, skills to maximize effective use of the media, and alliances with others to help frame their issues. Those speakers who do not have skillful and knowledgeable individuals in the backstage are at a severe disadvantage when competing against those speakers who do.

Positive Aspects of Mass Media

The media provide a mechanism for imparting large amounts of news and information to society. For instance, the U.S. Department of Health and Human Services utilized the media, along with health professionals and the public, to reach out to the U.S. population to improve Americans' health literacy and the capacity of an individual to access, understand, and use health information and services to make better-informed health decisions (Carmona, 2005). This collaborative effort shows the linkages among organizations (U.S. Department of Health and Human Services), the media, and health care professionals. More recently, AMBER Alerts have notified citizens when a child is missing. Television, radio, and highway alerts let citizens know to be on alert and to call law enforcement if the missing child is seen. A criminal justice researcher, Timothy Griffin of the University of Nevada, Reno, concluded that in cases involving the taking of a child by a relative or babysitter AMBER Alerts are effective, but they are less effective with the more dangerous offenders (Jacobs, 2007).

Negative Aspects of Mass Media

Another important role of the news media is to focus attention on problems that they perceive to be in the public interest. From time to time, the news media will discover a social problem, such as poverty among Whites in Appalachia in the 1960s. Further, while persistent hunger exists in Africa, the news media focus attention on famine only occasionally, generating worldwide relief efforts from time to time by showing emaciated children. The news media have latitude in choosing when to report events and bring them to the public attention, which illustrates one of the criticisms of the news media as a powerful social institution. For instance, Doctors Without Borders has criticized the news media for not reporting that nearly 4 million people in the Congo have been killed since war broke out there in 1998 (Szabo, 2006). According to Charles Davis, a journalism professor at the Missouri School of Journalism, "news corporations find it easier and cheaper to focus on the mundane and the trivial, the celebrity-driven news over the real needs of real people" (Szabo, 2006, p. 7D). As an illustration, the news media have an insatiable interest in Paris Hilton. After leaving jail for a brief stay, Hilton was interviewed on *Larry King Live* to let the public know what she went through (CNN, 2007).

As Professor Davis insinuated, the news media are interested in sensational news that attracts people to their newspapers or television news shows. Some of the most popular news items in 2005 were crimes or alleged crimes against White females. A White female from the middle or upper class who was missing or who suffered a serious crime received a high amount of news coverage, while minority women were virtually ignored. A White female addicted to crack cocaine and prostitution who is kidnapped or injured on the street will not be on any of the news shows. The same is true for minority women. Media outlets devoted considerable news coverage to the "Runaway Bride" from Georgia who faked her alleged kidnapping, the White Alabama teenager who went missing in Aruba, and the court hearing to determine who fathered Anna Nicole Smith's baby. African Americans, Latinos, and Native Americans, who also go missing in a high percentage of cases, criticized the news media for their selective attention, but this was quickly termed "playing the race card." In addition, Court TV (renamed truTV in 2008) was criticized for showing primarily murder cases resulting from domestic violence that involved White women as victims, such as Laci Peterson. One attorney who was being interviewed for comments on the Scott Peterson case and domestic violence began her response by stating that she hoped that Court TV would devote the same type of attention to domestic violence cases involving Latino and African American women.

Charles Browne (1967) stated that the media also have on some occasions been used to promote wars by reporting inflammatory stories urging Americans to go to war. As an example, Browne wrote that the Hearst newspapers helped create the Spanish American War by reporting inflammatory stories leading up to this war. Sometimes the media are given erroneous information, which they fail to verify, as a way of mobilizing wars. Prior to the Gulf War, it was reported that a young woman from Kuwait testified before Congress, relating how Iraqi soldiers stole incubators for babies and Kuwaiti premature babies died on the floor. This story was false and was related only to shock Americans and garner support for going to war against Iraq (Center for Media and Democracy, 2006). Kuwait spent millions on public relations firms that used the media to convince Americans to support the war against Iraq and drive the Iraqis out of Kuwait. For the next Iraq war, numerous politicians and news commentators convinced the public with the help of the news media that Iraq had weapons of mass destruction and would give them to a terrorist group to use against the United States (Stevenson, 2003).

Although the media are generally insulated from government pressures and have constitutional protection within the First Amendment, they can, nonetheless, be pressured to distort news and mislead the public. As an example, Steve Wilson and Jane Akre, both investigative reporters for Fox TV, wrote a story about Posilac, a bovine growth hormone that causes significant increases in milk production but has numerous negative effects for humans who consume milk. Posilac is made by Monsanto, a large corporation that manufactures a number of products for human consumption and use. As a result, Monsanto, like many other large corporations, spends huge amounts to advertise its products. The company's advertising was said to be worth billions to Fox TV. A week before the story on Posilac was to air, a lawyer for Monsanto contacted Fox and threatened Fox executives and the two reporters. Fox decided to kill the story, and when the two reporters balked, Fox insisted that they sign a confidentiality agreement promising not to discuss Posilac, Fox's decision, or Monsanto's threats. At one point, Wilson and Akre stated to Fox executives that the public had a right to know the potential risks of drinking milk with Posilac in it, but according to them, a Fox executive told them that Fox determined what was news. The reporters refused to sign the agreement, and Fox attempted to rewrite the story with the help of lawyers.

According to Wilson and Akre, Fox made 83 revisions to their story, removing or changing all the words that Monsanto and Fox did not like. For instance, a study of Posilac indicated that it had cancer risks, but that was changed to "possible health implications." Eventually, Fox TV fired the two reporters (Achbar, Abbott, & Bakan, 2005).

KNOWLEDGE AND THEORIES ABOUT THE LAW

The law, flowing from the legislative, executive, and judicial branches of government, has a powerful effect on human behaviors. Sometimes, human behaviors have an effect on these law-producing institutions as well. For instance, a popular strategy for some groups is to find or create a test case in order to get a court to rule on a social issue. The sodomy case *Lawrence v. Texas* (2003) appeared to have been created in order to get the issue into court and hopefully the U.S. Supreme Court. In Texas in 2003, someone called the police to report a weapon crime, and when officers arrived at the home, they found two men in the bedroom having sex and charged them with sodomy. The men were convicted and fined, setting up a case in which the U.S. Supreme Court held Texas sodomy and deviant sex laws unconstitutional (*Lawrence v. Texas,* 2003). In another case, a U.S. district court denounced that a conservative public interest law firm had influenced the Dover (Pennsylvania) Area School District to pass a policy promoting Intelligent Design in biology courses as a test case. Nominated by President Bush, the judge angrily noted that some judges are called activist judges but he was not and that he was forced to rule on this case. He indicated that activists were the individuals who sought a fight based on unconstitutional principles (*Kitzmiller v. Dover Area School District,* 2005).

As you will recall from Chapter 3, Donald Black's theory of law helps provide understanding of the application of law in various situations and who is more likely to have law imposed upon them. Law also manifests itself in the form of statutes and case rulings by Congress, state legislatures, state supreme courts, and federal courts, including the U.S. Supreme Court. Congress has passed a multitude of laws that have impacted families, categories, organizations, and communities. Listing even 5% of the state and federal statutes and state and federal court decisions would be quite overwhelming. We will discuss two federal statutes here in which Congress recognized and passed legislation to address a human problem and need. Congress conducted hearings on the problems experienced by individuals with disabilities and found that "disability is a natural part of the human experience [and individuals with disability deserve the right] to fully participate in and contribute to their communities through full integration and inclusion in the economic, political, social, cultural, and educational mainstream of United States society" (Americans with Disabilities Act of 1990, 42 U.S.C.S. § 15001). Because of its findings, Congress passed the Americans with Disabilities Act of 1990. The law requires employers to make reasonable accommodations, but the law does not force an employer to keep someone who cannot do his or her job. As health care cost pressures rise, an employer can say that certain tasks, which may be too much for an employee with a disability, are reasonable for a job (Belkin, 2005). For example, Wal-Mart, the largest retailer in the United States, has tried to weed out applicants who may have a disability that will increase its medical costs (*EEOC v. Wal-Mart Stores, Inc.,* 2007). In one case, Wal-Mart paid a person with a disability $300,000 for refusing to hire him ("Wal-Mart to Pay $300,000 to Rejected Job Applicant With Disability," 2007).

Later, Congress conducted a hearing on difficulties families experience with their employment when these families have a sick family member. After hearing witnesses and gathering statistics, Congress passed the Family and Medical Leave Act in 1993 (29 U.S.C.S. § 2601). The Family and Medical Leave Act provides unpaid leave to an employee so that he or she can help take care of a sick family member. Yet, this bold and innovative program does not eliminate all the strain on individuals and families with an ill family member. The Family and Medical Leave Act applies to companies with 15 or more employees (Belkin, 2005). This restriction means that small businesses that employ fewer than 15 workers, where the working poor tend to be employed, are exempted.

Maryland passed an interesting law regarding health care and Medicaid, which may provide a precedent for the entire country. The law also provides a rich case study of the collision of several social institutions. Wal-Mart, the largest retailer in the United States, has been accused of underfunding its medical insurance program for employees. In Maryland, Wal-Mart has 53 stores and employs 17,000 people. However, many Wal-Mart employees were on the rolls of the state Medicaid system in 2006 and previously, and Wal-Mart was accused of dumping many of its employees' health benefits on Medicaid during this period. So, in 2006, the state legislature passed a law that any employer in Maryland with over 10,000 employees must pay at least 8% of its payroll for health coverage or pay the difference to the state for its Medicaid program (Barbaro, 2007). The law was passed in 2006, but the governor, who received a campaign contribution from Wal-Mart, vetoed the bill. In 2006, a second bill was passed and the governor vetoed it again, but the legislature overrode the governor's veto and the bill became law. Passage of the bill in 2006 was attributed to the heavy-handed tactics Wal-Mart employed. The company hired 12 lobby firms, threatened not to build a warehouse that was supposed to provide 1,000 jobs in one Maryland district, and purchased false and misleading television and radio advertisements stating that the bill would harm small businesses. Last, Wal-Mart threatened to sue the state of Maryland in the courts, declaring that its rights were being violated. Advocates for both sides stated that this new state law and the resulting legal challenges in court may provide a precedent for other states (Barbaro, 2006). However, the law was subsequently held by a U.S. district court in Maryland to be unconstitutional (*Retailer Industry Leaders Association v. Fielder,* 2006) and this ruling was upheld in 2007 by the Second Circuit Court of Appeals (Barbaro, 2007).

Positive Aspects of the Law

An impartial administration of the law provides stability among citizens so that disputes have a forum by which they are decided. But the most positive aspects of the law are those laws that have been passed by Congress throughout the years to improve the health and well-being of citizens. The list of these laws is too long to cite in full here, but we will mention a few major laws passed over the past 100 years (see Table 5.1).

Table 5.1   Major Laws Passed Over the Past 100 Years

Congressional Laws	Purpose
Civil Rights Act of 1871	Bans violations of one's civil rights
Food and Drugs Act of 1906	Provides federal oversight of food and drugs
Civil Rights Act of 1964	Bans discrimination in public accommodations
Fair Housing Act of 1968	Bans discrimination in housing
Voting Rights Act of 1965	Protects African Americans' voting rights
Sex Discrimination Act of 1975	Bans discrimination based on sex
Equal Pay Act of 1963	Bans discrimination in pay based on sex

(Continued)

Table 5.1 (Continued)

Congressional Laws	Purpose
Title IX of the Education Amendments of 1972	Bans discrimination in athletics
Pregnancy Discrimination Act of 1978	Bans discrimination based on pregnancy
Civil Rights Act of 1991	Revised Civil Rights Act of 1964 by stripping states of their immunity based on the Eleventh Amendment to the U.S. Constitution.
Family and Medical Leave Act of 1993	Confers the right to leave from a job for family medical reasons
Americans with Disabilities Act of 1990	Bans discrimination based on a disability
The Matthew Shepard Hate Crimes Prevention Act of 2009 (Amended)	Enhances punishments for crimes against the gay, lesbian, bisexual, and transgender population

The U.S. Supreme Court, interpreting the U.S. Constitution, has ruled on cases that have had major effects on society. These cases are not without controversy, and some individuals through the years have criticized these decisions. For instance, when the U.S. Supreme Court reversed the "separate but equal" doctrine in *Brown v. Board of Education* (1954), African Americans and others hailed this decision as a major step forward in combating segregation and discrimination. But large numbers of the public, including some members of Congress, were highly critical of *Brown*. Former Chief Justice Earl Warren was vilified for this decision, and former President Dwight Eisenhower, who had appointed Justice Warren to the U.S. Supreme Court, reportedly stated that his decision to appoint Justice Warren was "the worst damn decision" that he had ever made ("Supremely Liberal," 2009). Thus, U.S. Supreme Court decisions are often not popular and are often viewed negatively by large numbers of the population. We list the decisions in Table 5.2 as positives, but others may disagree.

| Table 5.2 | Positive Decisions of the U.S. Supreme Court |

U.S. Supreme Court Decisions	Ruling
Helvering v. Davis, 301 U.S. 619 (1937)	Upheld Social Security Act
Brown v. Board of Education of Topeka, 347 U.S. 483 (1954)	Segregation violates equal protection; reversed "separate but equal" doctrine
Miranda v. Arizona, 384 U.S. 436 (1966)	Required that citizens be informed of their constitutional rights before being arrested for a crime
Roe v. Wade, 410 U.S. 113 (1973)	Gave women the sole right to terminate pregnancy in the first trimester
Atkins v. Virginia, 536 U.S. 304 (2002)	Banned death penalty for defendants with mental retardation
Roper v. Simmons, 543 U.S. 551 (2005)	Banned death penalty for defendants under 18

Negative Aspects of the Law

While Congress and some states pass legislation with beneficial and helpful impacts on categories of people, families, and communities, some federal and state laws have harmful effects toward which these legislative bodies seem to be indifferent. We suggest that this indifference occurs because African Americans and Latinos and their communities bear the brunt of these harmful laws. For example, in the "War on Drugs," Congress passed in the 1980s a law that punished offenders in the federal criminal justice system for possession of small amounts of "crack" cocaine more severely than for possession of a large amount of powdered cocaine. For the most part, African Americans are more likely to possess crack, and Whites are more likely to possess powdered cocaine. African Americans and some Whites severely criticized these differences in punishment, but Congress has been indifferent to changing the laws. While members of Congress contend that they did not want to be "soft on crime," they refuse to elevate the penalty for powdered cocaine to that of crack. Congress's unwillingness to increase the penalty for powdered cocaine suggests that it wants to protect Whites from severe penalties.

Justification for this assertion is provided by the fact that since the 1980s, African Americans have lamented the disparity between punishments for "crack" cocaine and those for powdered cocaine. The punishment for 5 grams of crack is equal to the punishment for 500 grams of powdered cocaine (Alexander & Gyamerah, 1997). African Americans are more likely to be arrested for crack, and Whites are more likely to be arrested for possessing powdered cocaine (Alexander & Gyamerah, 1997). Yet, Congress has refused to change the law and make the punishments equal. In 2002, the U.S. Sentencing Commission issued a report that recommended changes in the drug penalties because there was a perception in society that race was a factor in drug sentences. Particularly, 85% of all defendants tried in federal courts for crack cocaine were African American (*Kimbrough v. United States*, 2007). In 2006, a federal judge, who had been a strong advocate of harsh penalties for crack as a drug policy advisor under the first President Bush, stated that the policy regarding punishment for crack cocaine "had gone too far and was undermining faith in the judicial system" (Apuzzo, 2006, p. A7). Moreover, the judge stated that "federal laws requiring dramatically longer sentences for crack cocaine than for cocaine powder were 'unconscionable' and contributed to the perception within minority communities that courts are unfair" (Apuzzo, 2006, p. A7).

In 2006, all 50 states, the District of Columbia, and Congress passed another questionable drug law. This law involved an increased penalty for selling drugs near schools, day care centers, parks, or housing projects. This law, as well as many criminal laws, is based on deterrence theory. Deterrence theory, which has its roots in the Classical School of Criminology made popular by Cesare Beccaria in the 1700s, says that people commit crimes because the pleasures anticipated from criminal acts are greater than the perceived punishment. So, if people are thinking about committing sexual assaults, armed robberies, murders, thefts, or illegal drug sales, they are more likely to commit these crimes if the benefits or pleasures seem greater than the punishment. So, if society wants fewer sexual assaults, armed robberies, and murders and less drug selling, society needs to increase the punishment. A multitude of studies have been conducted to determine the validity of deterrence theory. For sure, legislators seemingly believe in deterrence theory because every year there is rhetoric that society needs to get tough on crime and criminals, and every year there are increased penalties for certain crimes.

Allegedly to protect children from drug sellers, all the states, Congress, and Washington, DC, passed legislation creating drug-free zones around schools, parks, and day care centers. Simply, anyone caught selling drugs in these areas was subjected to increased penalties. While the first drug-free zone was created in the 1980s during the War on Drugs, until recently no one had conducted a comprehensive study of the effects of these drug-free zones. In 2005, the Justice Policy Institute undertook a comprehensive study of drug-free zones in several states. The New Jersey Commission to Review Criminal Sentencing examined this issue and found that (a) in urban areas where schools, parks, and public housing developments are numerous and closely spaced, overlapping zones turn entire communities into prohibited zones; (b) by blanketing densely populated African American and Latino communities, the laws were creating unwarranted racial disparity in the use of incarceration for people convicted of drug offenses, and this law had a devastatingly disproportionate impact on New Jersey's minority community; and (c) the laws had failed entirely to accomplish their primary goal of eliminating drug activity near schools and children (Greene, Pranis, & Ziedenberg, 2006).

The above evidence was gleaned from data from Dorchester, Massachusetts. For instance, a comparison was made between African Americans and Latinos and Whites arrested in drug-free zones and eligible for enhanced punishment (see Table 5.3). Interviews with police officers about how charging decisions were made repeatedly revealed that a key factor in how offenders were charged was whether the individuals were "good kids" or "bad kids" (Greene et al., 2006). It is not a stretch to conclude that officers considered Whites to be "good kids" and African Americans and Latinos to be "bad kids." One prosecutor has stated that drug-free zones and enhanced penalties do not drive dealers from schools, and the primary benefit has been to pressure charged offenders into waiving their right to a jury trial because most of them plead guilty in a plea bargain (Greene et al., 2006).

Table 5.3	Race and Whether Charges Were Filed in Cases Involving Drugs Near Schools	
	White	*African American/Latino*
No Prior Record	14% Charged	58% Charged
Less Than 1/8 Gram	11% Charged	41% Charged
More Than 1.5 Grams	26% Charged	94% Charged
Carriers	20% Charged	45% Charged
Drivers	23% Charged	67% Charged
Overall	15% Charged	52% Charged

Judy Greene and her colleagues (2006) were hopeful that state legislatures and Congress would realize the ineffectiveness of these laws and their harmful racial impact. A few legislators have commented that they were surprised by the findings from this study and that they had hoped that the laws they had passed would deter drug sellers from selling near schools. However, judging from what occurred with the furor over the differential impact of crack and powdered cocaine in the 1980s, it is unlikely that there will be any real movement nationally to change these laws.

Laws punishing crack-related crimes more harshly than powdered cocaine–related crimes and laws punishing drug selling in drug-free zones serve an unspoken goal and have benefits. They help keep minority communities impotent and help rural areas politically. African Americans and Latinos who are incarcerated for drug crimes are taken out of their communities, and when they return, they are more likely to be unable to vote. In addition, when they are incarcerated, they are more likely to be incarcerated in rural areas. While prisons in rural areas have not been found to produce job and economic activities, these prisons do have benefits in that they increase the population of rural areas, and these rural areas benefit from receiving state and federal grants based on their population as well as in terms of the political representation of a district, which also is based on population (Alexander, 2005b).

SPECIAL INSTITUTION: CORRECTIONS

The institutions described above are social institutions, but there is one physical institution that deserves discussion here in this chapter. The reason this institution is special is because it is the largest state expenditure in many states and takes money from many of the social institutions discussed. This institution is correctional or prison institutions, and it is important for the following reasons. The United States incarcerates a very high number of persons, negatively affecting families and communities. Further, corrections have huge budgets. For example, for fiscal year 2007–2008, the California Department of Corrections and Rehabilitation (2007) was allocated nearly $10 billion. For fiscal year 2008–2009, the operation budget for the Texas Department of Criminal Justice (2008) was nearly $3 billion. The budget for 2005–2006 for the Ohio Department of Rehabilitation and Correction (2004), which has the largest budget of any agency in the state, was $1.64 billion.

As discussed in the section on education, Texas and Ohio currently underfund education. One reason may be that corrections command very large budgets and take money away from other competing systems and social institutions. Also, prisons have become the new asylum and now hold more persons with mental illness than mental institutions. Corrections facilities and their populations affect many social institutions. The media frequently use crime to boost viewership and readership. Legislators and congresspersons frequently use crime or being tough on crime to attract votes, sometimes leading to ineffective and counterproductive laws. Families, especially Latinos and African Americans who make up a large percentage of the incarcerated, are affected by the separation of fathers and mothers from families and the communities. Many former prisoners cannot vote or the legislatures have made voting difficult, and their inability to vote weakens minority communities in the political arena. In the Texas school funding case, the Texas Supreme Court acknowledged that more than 50% of Latinos and about 46% of African Americans drop out of school, and in 2040 these two groups will constitute two thirds of the population in Texas. There was a reference to these groups needing state services and the difficulties for the state in providing these services, which were very likely prison services.

In 2002, the director of the Ohio Department of Rehabilitation and Correction, Reginald A. Wilkerson, submitted written testimony to the U.S. Senate Judiciary Committee on the criminal justice system and mentally ill offenders. Wilkerson (2002) testified that nationwide 283,800 persons with mental illness were incarcerated in 1998. In 2000, the Bureau of Justice Statistics stated that 114,400 were receiving psychotropic medications and 18,900 were in 24-hour care. In five states—Maine, Montana, Nebraska, Hawaii, and Oregon—20% of inmates were receiving psychotropic medications (Beck & Maruschak, 2001). The television show *Frontline* presented an illustration of treatment and processing of inmates with mental illness in Ohio, reputed to be a model for the country of how to provide mental health services to prisoners with severe mental illness. It showed the revolving door for many prisoners with severe mental illness (Navasky & O'Connor, 2005).

CONCLUSION

This chapter discussed how advances in medicine have led to more Americans living longer and how technologies have increased the quality of life of persons with chronic health problems. At the same time, this chapter noted that insurance policies negatively impact human needs, such as increasing dialysis for persons suffering from diabetes and canceling policies of individuals and families who purchase their own insurance. The mass media provide information and entertainment for Americans, with both positive and negative effects. Individuals can pressure sponsors and sponsors can pressure the media to change or alter programming. But the media have negatively influenced some individuals and can selectively decide to present or not present information to viewers. As described earlier, a major corporation, which may not be making safe products, can pressure the media not to report certain stories by threatening to take its advertising dollars to a competitor. The law, representing state legislatures, Congress, and the courts, can also have positive and negative effects. Congress and state legislatures have passed legislation that has contributed to the well-being of society, but some legislation has had harmful and negative effects on minority communities. Further, some legislation has produced counterproductive policies.

The mass media tend to focus on problems and issues related more to the core than to the periphery communities. The "Runaway Bride" and the legal hearing regarding Anna Nicole Smith's baby and the baby's father, which was shown live on CNN, are examples of the concern for the core. Last, Black's theory of law states that the law treats defendants and plaintiffs differently depending on whether they are respectable or unrespectable. This is similar to whether defendants and plaintiffs come from the core or the periphery.

Key Terms and Concepts

Latrophobia	Medicare Advantage Plan
Medicaid	Medicine
Medicare	Medigap

CHAPTER 6

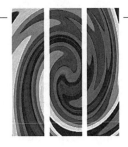

Organizations Affecting Human Behaviors

INTRODUCTION

Human Rights Watch, an organization dedicated to stopping abuse of oppressed and marginalized groups, is involved with a number of children's rights, including child labor, child soldiers, HIV/AIDS, juvenile justice, orphans and abandoned children, refugees and migrants, street children, education, and violence against children. Regarding the latter two categories, Human Rights Watch opposes the paddling of children in public schools and seeks to end this practice. As stated in a special report on the issue, "African–American students and students with mental or physical disabilities receive corporal punishment at disproportionately high rates, creating a hostile school environment in which these students may struggle to succeed" (Human Rights Watch and the American Civil Liberties Union, 2009, p. 1).

Ubiquitous from birth to death, modern organizations perform powerful roles in human societies (Kassirer, 2001). Almost every stage of life occurs within an organizational context. Organizations are created by human beings, but organizations behave independent of human beings (Farazmand, 2002).

> Organizations even control us, dominate society, stifle development or progress, promote growth and change, alter our environmental conditions, and at the same time fulfill our human and societal needs. Their role is multidimensional and dual in nature: they can make possible the progress and fulfillment of human needs, but at the same time they can be a major obstacle to our achieving those same goals. They are a powerful instrument in governance and the promotion of democratic values, therefore enhancing human values. But, ironically, they may serve at the same time as a formidable instrument of repression. (Farazmand, 2002, p. xv)

Viewed in a different context, organizations are like people in many ways. They are born, develop and grow, develop relationships with others, marry or merge with other organizations, have offspring or subsidiaries, become overweight, slim down, move to a different community, and die or go bankrupt (Newman, 2002). Legally speaking, the law has aided the reification of organizations by ruling in 1884 that corporations, which are organizations, are persons with respect to the Fourteenth Amendment (*Butchers' Union Slaughter-House and Live-Stock Landing Company v. Crescent City Live-Stock Landing and Slaughter-House Company*, 1884), an amendment that was initially passed to help newly freed slaves. The Fourteenth Amendment says in part that the state cannot deprive any *person* of life, liberty, or property without due process of law. From 1890 to 1910, the U.S. Supreme Court decided 307 cases involving the Fourteenth Amendment, and 288 involved corporations and 19 involved African Americans (Achbar, Abbott, & Bakan, 2005). As a result, corporations grew in power and influence. For example, the McDonnell Douglas Corporation was a very large company that built aircraft and had an organizational structure that could sue or be sued (*McDonnell Douglas Corp v. Green*, 1973).

There are several types of both formal and informal organizations (Laubach, 2005). Both formal and informal organizations may be grouped into one of three types—nonprofit, corporate, or government (Moore, Sobieraj, Whitt, Mayorova, & Beaulieu, 2002). Formal organizations are large, secondary social collectives that follow structured practices, whereas informal organizations are those entities that do not follow structured practices. Normative organizations, such as political campaigns, religious groups, or Rotary clubs, are groups that individuals join generally without pay and voluntarily because they share the goals of the organizations. Coercive formal organizations, such as correctional or mental institutions, comprise people who do not volunteer to become members. Then, there are utilitarian organizations, which are those that people join for material benefits, such as a business venture or a **corporation** (Stolley, 2005). While some individuals see corporations as social institutions (Bakan, 2004), we see corporations as for-profit organizations because corporations do not by definition serve the public good as social institutions are supposed to do.

This chapter discusses bureaucracies and groups as well as group dynamics within organizations. Within the group context of organizations, we provide knowledge about work groups, group stages, group problem solving, gender differences within groups in organizations, and racial and gender factors affecting groups within organizations. Then, we discuss the growth of organizations to aid society, theories of educational organizations, and theories of social movement organizations. We discuss nonprofit organizations, voluntary organizations, and faith-based organizations. Last, we discuss the positive and negative economic and social forces of various organizations.

This chapter also illustrates the connection of organizations and corporations to world systems theory as discussed by Chase-Dunn (2001) in Chapter 1. Many of the world communities that have been exploited by organizations and corporations are located in the periphery. Another connection of world systems theory to organizations according to Chase-Dunn is that individuals within the core are more likely to belong to voluntary organizations than individuals not within the core.

KNOWLEDGE AND THEORIES ABOUT ORGANIZATIONS

Netting, Kettner, and McMurtry (2004) wrote a chapter for their book, *Social Work Macro Practice,* titled "Understanding Organizations." Distinguishing between descriptive approaches that analyze organizations and prescriptive approaches that state how to improve organizations, they described 16 theories, including complex systems theory, total quality management, managing diversity, in search of excellence, theory Z, organizational culture, power and politics, contingency theory, open systems, decision making, organizational goals, management by objectives, theory Y and X, human relations, scientific and universalistic management, and bureaucracy (Netting et al., 2004). We do not present 16 theories about organizations because doing so would be beyond the purpose of this text. Instead, we emphasize several theories that have been tested through research studies.

Bureaucracies

Max Weber has been acknowledged as one of the first persons to dissect organizations when he discussed bureaucracies (Stolley, 2005). Weber's analyses are still relevant today as contemporary observers discuss the inertia and problems of bureaucracies, such as the strong criticisms that the Federal Emergency Management Agency has received since 2005 for its response to the hurricanes that hit the Gulf Coast. **Bureaucracies**, as expanded from Weber and summarized by Stolley (2005, pp. 94–95), are characterized by

1. *Hierarchy*—A hierarchical structure exists with clear lines of authority. When depicted in organizational charts, this hierarchy takes a pyramid shape, with a smaller number of people at the top of the pyramid having authority over an increasingly larger number of people lower in the structure.

2. *Formal Rules and Regulations Governing the Organization*—Written rules and regulations govern administration and conduct. These rules and regulations ensure consistency, standardization, and that people within the bureaucracy do not make up rules as they go along.

3. *Written Documentation*—This documentation (the "files") encompasses the policies that are to be followed in the organization.

4. *Specialization*—A formal division of labor is set forth in bureaucracies, with positions organized on the basis of the duties assigned to each position. Every member of an organization has certain functions to perform, meaning that members may be required to be experts in their areas.

5. *Technical Knowledge*—Members of a bureaucracy should meet all the required qualifications to completely fulfill the duties of their position. By fitting skill sets to positions, rather than designing positions to fit the skills of individual workers, bureaucracies create a situation in which members who leave a position can be replaced by someone with the same qualifications and the organization can continue to operate.

6. *Impersonality*—Organizational members are required to follow procedures and deal with all clients on the basis of policy rather than on the basis of personal relationships or opinions.

7. *Career Employment*—Career advancement is through achievement-based promotion. Promotions should be determined by such prescribed factors as seniority, job performance, or increased training, not by factors such as being the supervisor's relative.

8. *Salaried Positions*—Compensation for work performed is assigned on the basis of the position. It is not determined by personal factors (for example, how physically attractive a worker is or how much the supervisor enjoys his or her jokes).

9. *Separation of Official and Private Income and Duties*—The office is separate from the sphere of private life. Official monies and property of the organization are not intermingled with members' private funds or interests.

Of course, Stolley's (2005) summary of bureaucracies reflects goals and preferences and does not reflect realities in all cases. Laws and lawsuits have been enacted and filed to address favoritism and discrimination in bureaucracies and organizations. Laws have been passed to prevent nepotism in which relatives are hired in public organizations, and some chief executive officers (CEOs) have been reprimanded or forced out of organizations for promoting women with whom they were personally involved. They have also been sued for not promoting individuals because those individuals refused to provide sexual favors. Moreover, CEOs have been fired and sometimes imprisoned for stealing company funds or commingling company funds with private funds.

Groups and Group Dynamics Within Organizations

Within organizations, there are formal groups and informal groups. Formal groups are those created by management, and informal groups are those formed from day-to-day work interactions. Hellriegel, Slocum, and Woodman (1992) depicted the most commonly observed groups in organizations. First, there are friendship groups that develop informally, principally to meet workers' personal needs for security, esteem, and belonging. Second, task groups are constructed by administrators to achieve goals important to the organization. The Boeing Company, one of the largest airplane manufacturers in the world with thousands of employees, created small teams of 8 to 10 workers to accomplish group tasks to build one of its most popular airplanes (Hellriegel et al., 1992).

Task groups are additionally categorized by the interdependencies among and between workers as they undertake the accomplishment of a goal or task. These task groups may be called counteracting, co-acting, or interacting. A counteracting task group involves a group where members, using negotiation and compromise, cooperate to solve a conflict within the organization. Typically, a union consisting of several members and management consisting of several members all together would be a counteracting group. A co-acting group exists when members perform their duties independently, relatively. As an example, social work professors in a large academic college interact interdependently when discussing required objectives in a research course, but each professor independently delivers the objectives in the classroom. An interacting group exists when a group is able to achieve its goal because everyone does his or her job. These are typically assembly line environments, such as those in which workers assemble automobiles. But other typical interacting groups are committees, task forces, project teams, boards, advisory councils, work crews, or review panels, where each member performs his or her defined role (Hellriegel et al., 1992).

Organizational Group Stages

Both George and Jones (1999) and Hellriegel et al. (1992) embraced the notion of the five-stage development sequence for an organizational group; however, the stages are applicable to groups outside of organizations. These five stages are forming, storming, norming, performing, and adjourning. Each stage is characterized by different task-oriented and social behaviors. Important too is the level of group maturity. A group can fail or dissolve during each stage or as it progresses from one stage to the next stage. Hellriegel et al. (1992, p. 315) stated that "pinpointing the developmental stage of a group at any specific time is difficult. Nevertheless, managers and members of teams must understand the developmental stages of a group because each stage can influence effectiveness." An examination of each stage will reveal the task-oriented and relations-oriented (social) behaviors found there. However, groups may not always progress in a timely manner at the conclusion or the finishing point of each stage. Pressures and demands from management could shorten, speed up, or slow the evolution of a group.

The Forming Stage: This stage is characterized by members focusing their behaviors on delineating goals and forming a consensus for how each member will carry out his or her tasks. Relations-oriented behaviors involve addressing members' feelings and the tendency of most members to look to one or two members to give them directions. In this stage, the group seeks to get acquainted and understand each member's roles and from where leadership will come. This stage is further characterized by members (a) keeping feelings to themselves until they process the situation, (b) acting more secure than they truly feel, (c) feeling confused and uncertain about what is demanded of them, (d) being nice and polite or at least not visibly hostile, and (e) attempting to compare the costs and benefits of being in the group.

The Storming Stage: This stage is characterized by emerging conflict over tasks, the priority of the goals, the responsibilities of each member, and the leader's direction and assistance in task management. An assortment of expressions of hostility and intense feelings emerge in these relations-oriented behaviors. Differences over goals and rivalry over leadership roles dominate this stage. As emotions arise and tension intensifies, some members may withdraw emotionally or isolate themselves. Withdrawal can lead to the quick failure of the group. However, a group does not have to fail at this point as a matter of course. A skillful leader can help the group correct itself. Rather than suppressing conflicts as they emerge, a leader should embrace the conflict and manage it, for suppressing it will create bitterness and resentment.

The Norming Stage: This stage is represented by task-oriented behaviors involving sharing information, embracing different opinions, and attempting to achieve positive consensus for the group's goal. Also in this stage, the group establishes rules. Social or relations-oriented behaviors center on empathy, concern, and positive expressions of feeling contributing to group cohesion. Cooperation within the group is emphasized, and a sense of collective responsibility for the group progresses.

The Performing Stage: In this stage, the group demonstrates efficiently and effectively how well it can perform group tasks. Individual members' roles are understood and accepted. Usually, the members know when they should help other members and when they should work independently. Some individual group members build on and learn from their group activities and experiential learning tasks. While these groups progress in their effectiveness and efficiency, other groups, such as those groups whose norms do not embrace efficiency and effectiveness, do just enough to ensure its survival. When a modestly sufficient quantity of performance exists, the causes of it are too much self-oriented behavior by group members, the creation of norms that impede task effectiveness and efficiency, weak group leadership, and other negative dynamics.

The Adjourning Stage: This stage is marked by the ending of task behaviors and disengagement from social or relations-oriented behaviors. Some groups, such as project teams, have a definite ending point. Some groups, however, may continue indefinitely. Adjourning for a long-term group is more subtle, such as when a key member leaves and another member is appointed. An example of such adjourning would be a leader or CEO of a corporation group who leaves. The group does not disband and continues, but the end of the tenure of a key member is a pseudo-end for the management group and the beginning of a new group. A similar process would take place for the boards of the National Association of Social Workers and the Council on Social Work Education.

The above discussions describe the stages of a group within organizations, but these stages do not specifically describe how problems are solved. The next section presents a problem-solving model that fits the five-stage development sequence for an organizational group.

General Group Problem-Solving Model

Synthesizing the broad group problem-solving literature and related literature, Fuller and Aldag (2001) proposed the General Group Problem-Solving Model. The aim of this comprehensive model is to provide guidance to researchers utilizing knowledge learned about group problem solving. Although it is partly intended for researchers, it also provides knowledge about what is known about groups. Fuller and Aldag (2001, pp. 10–14) presented a number of propositions, which relate to power and politics, group development and group type, and group knowledge.

Power and Politics Propositions

Proposition 1: Increases in leader power will result in enhanced likelihood of self-censorship and in the increased probability that the leader will be the source of the final solution.

Proposition 2: Organizational political norms will moderate the relationships of decision process characteristics to selected outcomes. For instance, in organizations that permit open political activity, decision process characteristics such as failure to reexamine selected and rejected alternatives will be positively associated with future use of the group and satisfaction with the group process. In organizations in which norms proscribe political activity, the opposite pattern of relationships will be evidenced.

Proposition 3: Member political motives will moderate the relationships between decision process characteristics and outcomes.

Proposition 4: Explicit problem definition, increased predecisional information search, and increased survey of objectives will reduce the incidence of political behavior.

Group Development and Group Type Propositions

Proposition 5: Stage of group development will moderate the relationship of leader impartiality to decision process characteristics. For instance, groups with a history of working together will exhibit a more positive constellation of decision process characteristics in the absence of leader impartiality than will ad hoc groups.

Proposition 6: Stage of group development will moderate the relationships of group cohesiveness to members' self-censorship and to perceived unanimity. For example, cohesiveness will have a more positive relationship to divergence of members' stated opinions in the mature stage of group development than in earlier stages.

Proposition 7: Group type will affect emergent group characteristics. For example, perceived unanimity will be lower in an advisory group than in a group given final decision-making responsibility.

Proposition 8: Group type will affect decision process characteristics. For example, an advisory group may give less attention to development of contingency plans and gathering of control-related information than would a group having the responsibility for implementing the decision.

Proposition 9: As probability of future group interaction increases, the degree of self-censorship and perceived unanimity will increase.

Group Knowledge Propositions

Proposition 10: Cohesiveness and member homogeneity will result in enhanced member satisfaction and increased probability of future use of the group.

Proposition 11: As leader impartiality increases, the emergence of a preferred alternative will occur later in the problem-solving process.

Proposition 12: The group decision rule will influence the degree to which decision process characteristics are oriented toward convergence. For example, there will be more pressure for convergence with a consensus decision rule than with a majority decision rule.

Proposition 13: As member-perceived unanimity increases, there will be less attention to reexamination of preferred and rejected alternatives, to development of contingency plans, and to gathering control-related information.

Proposition 14: When the leader's initially preferred solution is rejected by the group, such that the final solution is not the leader's preference, there will be reductions in the probability that the leader will adhere to the decision, the future motivation of the leader, and the probability of future use of the group by the leader.

Proposition 15: Solutions that were initially proposed by group members, rather than by the leader or a source external to the group, will be associated with greater member acceptance of the decision; with implementation success; with future motivation of the group; with member satisfaction with the group process; and with satisfaction with the decision.

Gender Differences Involving Group Dynamics Within Work Groups

Gender differences with respect to work group dynamics have been an interest of researchers. Some researchers have found that women, more than men, prefer equality in groups, and women tend to adapt to men's preferences at the beginning of a group (Berdahl & Anderson, 2005). Deducing hypotheses from the sociological, structural, and psychological literatures, Karakowsky, McBey, and Miller (2004) sought to provide knowledge about the influences of men and women exercising power in a work group and how that exercise of power affected perceptions of men's and women's competence. Power was operationalized as the amount of interruptive behaviors. Competence was operationalized by the ratings of expert judges and the ratings of group members. Their hypotheses were as follows:

Hypothesis 1: Men in numerical majority positions (in male-dominated groups) will engage in higher levels of interruption behavior compared with women in numerical majority positions (in female-dominated groups).

Hypothesis 2: Men in numerical minority positions (in female-dominated groups) will engage in lower levels of interruption behavior compared with men in numerical majority positions (in male-dominated groups).

Hypothesis 3: Women in numerical minority positions (in male-dominated groups) will engage in higher levels of interruption behavior compared with women in numerical majority positions (in female-dominated groups).

Hypothesis 4: Women will experience a greater decrement in interruption behavior compared with men when both targets shift to performing gender-incongruent tasks in female-dominated groups.

Hypothesis 5: Interruption behavior is negatively correlated with perceived leadership behavior for both men and women in a work group context.

Hypotheses 1–3 explored the importance of gender roles and proportional group makeup in influencing the display of power in team conversation. Hypothesis 1 was supported, meaning that men in male-dominated groups were significantly more likely to display power compared with women in female-dominated groups. Hypothesis 2 was partially supported as men in the majority exhibited more power (interruptive behavior) compared to same-gender counterparts in minority and numerically balanced positions. Also, partial support for Hypothesis 3 was found in that as women move from minority numerical to majority numerical positions, their interruptive behavior decreases. Hypothesis 4 was supported as women, compared to men, were more negatively impacted by being perceived as "out of their domain." Specifically, women demonstrated less powerful verbal behavior.

Last, Hypothesis 5 was supported. Interpreting the findings for Hypothesis 5, Karakowsky et al. (2004, p. 430) wrote that

> our study attempted to explore the consequences of power displays among group members. Our findings offered support for the assertion of Hypothesis 5, which predicted a negative relationship between interruption behavior and emergent leadership ratings. Among both men and women, our results suggested that interrupters are less likely to be viewed as emergent leaders in the group. This implies that the more a group member participates in group conversation via intrusive interruptions, the less likely the member will be viewed as exhibiting leaderlike qualities in the group's activities. Although interrupters may have gained dominance in the group discussion, this dominance was not viewed as leaderlike by colleagues nor by independent observers. This finding may seem somewhat paradoxical—interruptions are allegedly a form of power display, yet their ultimate effect is to reduce the member's leadership ranking in the group.

Racial and Gender Factors Affecting Group Dynamics

Several researchers reminded us that in the past, work groups tended to be almost entirely Caucasian and male. However, they repeated what demographers have observed, which is that the U.S. population is becoming less Caucasian and more diverse. Projections are that around 2040, Hawaii, California, New Mexico, and Texas will be more than 50% minority and New York, Maryland, and New Jersey will be close to 50% minority (Paletz, Peng, Erez, & Maslach, 2004). As the United States becomes more heterogeneous, work teams will mirror that heterogeneity and be less likely to be totally Caucasian and male. Important, then, is the type or amount of heterogeneity and its influence on individuals from different ethnic groups. The groups of interest were Caucasians, African Americans, Asians, and Latinos. The variables of interest were creativity, group enjoyment, and positive and negative emotions. Following a complex research design and analyses, these researchers presented an intricate representation of how ethnic makeup of groups affected creative performance and group enjoyment (Paletz et al., 2004). Among their findings were that teams composed mostly of ethnic minorities were more likely to enjoy working together and that such teams have more positive emotions and less negative emotions. Individuals reporting to be of mixed race and ethnicity, African Americans, and Latinos were less likely to report negative emotions on the whole than Asians and Caucasians. Teams composed mainly of ethnic minorities reported having a better time than teams composed mainly of Caucasians (Paletz et al., 2004).

Paletz et al. (2004, p. 152) concluded that

> these findings are important theoretically and practically. They provide evidence for the overall effects of ethnic composition regardless of individual race/ethnicity. Ethnic composition can truly be more than a sum of its individual members. Asians, non-Asian ethnic minorities, and Caucasians all enjoyed working in minority-dominated teams more. We suggest that this is because of the effects of group-level collectivism. Even Caucasians within teams of mostly Caucasians had less fun. All other things (like performance) being equal, it seems that groups dominated by minorities are more enjoyable for everyone.

Additionally, they concluded that non-Asian minorities were more influenced by ethnic context than Asians and Caucasians, meaning that, if practical, making interactive teams of mostly ethnic minorities can have social benefits without lowering task effectiveness (Paletz et al., 2004).

The Growth of Organizations to Aid Society

Throughout different societies over time, organizations emerged to take over various social functions, including but not limited to policing, education, national defense, agriculture, and economic production. For these organizations to come into existence, certain basic **environmental conditions** had to exist. One essential characteristic for organizational development is primary and secondary educated citizens. A second characteristic is urbanization, for urbanization produces elements conducive to organizational development, such as heterogeneity of lifestyle, frequency of interactions with strangers, and impersonal laws. A third characteristic is the existence of a money economy so that resources can flow easily to nurture the development of the organization. The fourth characteristic is organizational density, which means that the more organizations there are in existence, the easier it is for new ones to emerge as experienced personnel become available to lead them (Hall, 2002).

Beyond these basic environmental conditions are what Hall (2002) called environmental dimensions. These are technological, legal, political, economic, demographic, ecological, and cultural conditions. Technological conditions, such as the creation of research and development units to create current information for the organization, are important to many organizations. Even some small organizations will have research departments to provide research necessary for organizational functioning. Legal conditions could represent extreme positions on a continuum as well as the middle ground. Some informal organizations evade the law. Some organizations are deluged with local, state, and federal laws, requiring creation of a legal department. State and federal statutes such as the Americans with Disabilities Act impact organizations, and case decisions from the U.S. Supreme Court impact organizations regarding race and gender discrimination. Political dimensions force laws and policy changes. From time to time, organizations are under pressure to change or reform. Police organizations are necessary to uphold law and order, but some members may be charged with police brutality, such as in the demonstration by the Latino community in 2007 in which police officers overreacted, resulting in injuries to demonstrators and the demotion of police leadership overseeing officers dealing with demonstrators. School organizations are pressured to rid curriculum of sex education, while also coming under pressure now to include content on gay and lesbian contributions to society. The political process can directly affect some organizations as the executive director can be replaced by an elected official promising change. Economic conditions are important to organizations as budgets are prepared, defended, and appropriated. Universities, departments of corrections, and health departments, for instance, may cut some programs or staff because of decreased budgets from state legislatures. State organizations may be merged or eliminated for economic reasons. Demographic conditions are important because they let organizations know the number, age, sex, and social status of their clients or customers.

Census data give organizations some information, but migration patterns make census data collected every 10 years inadequate. Knowing current demographic information is important for employee hiring or marketing strategies. Ecological conditions reflect the physical location of organizations, where relationships may be developed with other organizations. An organization in an urban area is more likely to have contact with other organizations than one in a rural area. In addition, organizations in Washington, DC, such as trade organizations, benefit when they are located near each other and can bring pressure to bear on Congress. Cultural conditions are constantly changing. Values and norms evolve as society is faced with certain events. A current example is that there have been tremendous changes in values and norms in race, gender, and sexual orientation (Hall, 2002).

Theory of Educational Organizations

Meyer and Rowan (2007) described the structure of educational organizations and offered a theory that explains them. Relatively contemporary schools created education not for children or their families per se but for society. Beginning in the 19th century, developed societies assumed the central function of delineating and controlling the socialization of their nascent citizens. Governmental control of education increased during World War II, firmly establishing educational systems to integrate citizens into the economic, political, and status order of society. This integration is administered by a large public bureaucracy that mandates homogeneous standardization and authority over all local school systems. Further, school systems organize schooling on a great dimension, classifying students, certifying teachers, accrediting schools, and controlling the curriculum (Meyer & Rowan, 2007). The end result is the schooling rule—"education is a certified teacher teaching a standardized curricular topic to a registered student in an accredited school" (Meyer & Rowan, 2007, p. 79).

Increased corporate control of education has had significant effects for educational organizations. As young people or students are systematically sorted and placed on different levels of the social structure based on classified or certified educational criteria, the ritual classifications of education achieve statuses in the market of societal identity. Being an honor or advanced student is highly valued; taking a precollege or an advanced course is highly valued; becoming a master teacher is highly valued; and attending a magnet, private, or prep school is highly valued. As a consequence, there is the social expansion of education resulting in a change in social structure. The stratification of education creates a number of types that have educational meaning. Citizens below a high school education level are presumed to have very basic literacy or to have the ability only to read and write their names. Citizens with a high school education are presumed to have more skills, such as knowledge of world events, history, and the sciences. Citizens with a college education are presumed to know and have a significant amount of knowledge in a specified major. Citizens with graduate degrees are presumed to have a highly significant amount of knowledge and are eligible for various licenses, such as in medicine, law, social work, psychology, and other fields (Meyer & Rowan, 2007).

Theory of Social Movement Organizations

Social movement organizations develop in response to the desires of some individuals to oppose or effect social change (Edwards & McCarthy, 2004). Edwards and McCarthy (2004) proposed a theory to explain the survivability of social movement organizations. The theory posits that variables that explain the survivability of social movement organizations are social capital/social networks, patronage, organizational strategy, and the interaction of victim assistance emphasis and strong leadership ties. Social capital was defined as the networked access to resources found in specific sociopolitical contexts. Previous literature had revealed the connection between social capital and the effect on groups and organizations. This literature reported that there is strength in weak ties among organizational leaders. A broader range of nonduplicated weak ties leads to more access to information and other resources than strong ties among a small group of leaders. As an illustration, several people who are very good friends are likely to know many of the same people and seek the same resources. However, a small group of leaders who do not know each other well is likely to know a wider network of individuals and have a greater availability of resources. As elaborated by Edwards and McCarthy (2004, p. 625), social movement organizations "founded by individuals who already share strong social ties would be less widely to penetrate the broader structure of social relations in a community . . . [and these organizations with close friends among the leadership] can become a subsequent liability due to corresponding lack of wide social penetration that would aid in recruiting new members among diverse pools of potential adherents as well as appropriating social and other resources embedded in those diverse social infrastructures."

Another form of social capital is financial and in-kind assistance. This form of assistance may be startup grants or the giving of offices or buildings. Research has shown that the initial giving of resources increases the likelihood that further resources will be given later. However, just because an organization provides resources, there is no guarantee that the organization will survive. Organization strategy is a key factor in outcome or survivability. Social movement organization leaders decide organizational strategies that play a critical role in the life of the organization. Decisions can be made that either sustain or terminate support. Further, when leaders have had family or close friends injured or killed, their decisions are affected in ways that may lead to the survivability of the organization. The emphasis might be on victim assistance, including them (Edwards & McCarthy, 2004).

This theory was tested with leaders within Mothers Against Drunk Driving (MADD) chapters throughout the United States. The dependent variable was whether a MADD chapter that existed in 1985, when incidental data were collected, was still in existence in 1988. The researchers found that groups with initial access to financial or in-kind resources were more likely to have survived. Also, consistent with their theory, organizations with a greater amount of weak ties with large amounts of victim members were more likely to have survived. At the same time, MADD organizations were more likely to have survived when they relied on personal social networks to recruit new members and did not emphasize assistance to victims. Further, social movement organizations that grow from a preexisting organization are less likely to survive because the first group is likely to deplete resources. Hence, group leaders should think long and hard before initiating a social movement group from another group (Edwards & McCarthy, 2004).

Nonprofit Organizations

The history of nonprofit organizations has its beginning in British law and practice and in colonial practices in Boston and Philadelphia. Nonprofit organizations have evolved from colonial times to the present time, and the roles they play in society are different. To understand these roles, Hammack (2006) advocated a historical analysis involving legal and economic frameworks. For example, following the American Revolution, state governments and state courts took over from the British the issuance of nonprofit charters and the supervision of nonprofit organizations (Hammack, 2006). State courts issued rulings regarding the rights of women and minorities, such as the right of immigrants to associate and hold nonprofit offices; the legitimacy of bequests, especially to a nonprofit organization; tax exemption and the legal status and privileges of a benevolent nonprofit corporation; and charitable immunity. An economic framework illustrates how various sets of economic measures and variations relate to other sets of economic measures and variations. Hughes (2006) also touted the benefits of economic research to help nonprofit organizations make better decisions. Explaining the theory of consumer behavior, he wrote that "the theory may be adapted to suit the goal of welfare maximization [and] to maximize social welfare, the optimal level of service equates the marginal value to the marginal cost" (Hughes, 2006, p. 433). Related to social welfare, Passey and Lyons (2006) explained how nonprofit organizations helped in the development of social capital.

Nonprofit organizations, also called human service agencies (Hasenfeld, 1984), are an important part of social work and social welfare as they provide services to a vast number of needy clients, employ numerous professional social workers, and provide field placements for social work students. According to Lampkin and Boris, in 2002 there were about 1.6 million nonprofit organizations in the United States, and they employed about 11 million people. Of course, many of these organizations do not provide social services. Recently, nonprofit organizations that provide social welfare have had to demonstrate their effectiveness in providing services. Pressured by funders, more nonprofit organizations are utilizing performance or outcome measures to demonstrate their effectiveness. One study of nonprofit organizations in South Carolina found that about two thirds of them were utilizing performance measures, but their use of these measures did not increase funding (Zimmermann & Stevens, 2006).

The Response of Nonprofits to External Threats

Barman (2002) theorized what occurs when nonprofit organizations perceive that other organizations in their environment have created competition for them. According to Barman, in response to these perceived threats, nonprofit organizations engage in **differentiation**. As he explained,

> differentiation occurs when nonprofit organizations encounter competition within their environment. Facing a limited amount of resources, nonprofits will seek to increase their share of a crowded market. They will work to convince other actors that they, rather than their competitors, deserve resources. To that end, they will assert their uniqueness and superiority over rivals. In order to make this claim of difference, they will construct a hierarchical relationship between themselves and their competitors based on particular criteria. (Barman, 2002, p. 1192)

Barman (2002) refined his theory after he studied United Way, the largest fundraising organization in the United States, which raised $3.5 billion in 1999.

At one time, United Way was unchallenged in the field. But other nonprofit organizations began to emerge, presenting a challenge to United Way. In Barman's research, he learned that one United Way agency, which perceived competition from other nonprofit organizations, likened itself to donors as a mutual fund and likened a charitable gift to an investment. This United Way agency argued that it, rather than its competitors, provided the highest return on contributions because of its experience and the resources that it provided to people in need.

Hence, research has become an important activity in the field of nonprofit organizations. Unlike other organizations, nonprofit organizations that seek tax-exempt status must file a 990 form with the Internal Revenue Service (IRS) if they have more than $25,000 in gross receipts and are not religious organizations (Lampkin & Boris, 2002). Private foundations must file a type of 990 form, and most of this information is public, including revenues, expenses, net and total assets, balance sheets, program information, board members, the five highest employee salaries, and lobbying activities (Lampkin & Boris, 2002). For research purposes, the IRS is a major data source for nonprofit organizations. Data are placed by the IRS in three files—Business Master File (BMF), Return Transaction File (RTF), and Statistics of Income (SOI) (Lampkin & Boris, 2002). These three files provide source information for the National Center for Charitable Statistics, which has 125 variables, and its national nonprofit organization database, which has 400 variables (Lampkin & Boris, 2002).

IRS Conditions for Tax Exemption for Social Welfare Organizations

The IRS has established conditions for social welfare organizations to earn nontax status, like other organizations. To be tax exempt as a social welfare organization, an organization must not be organized for profit and must be operated exclusively to promote social welfare. To be operated exclusively to promote social welfare, an organization must operate primarily to further the common good and general welfare of the people of the community (such as by bringing about civic betterment and social improvements). An organization that restricts the use of its facilities to employees of selected corporations and their guests is primarily benefiting a private group rather than the community and, therefore, does not qualify for tax-exempted status. Similarly, an organization formed to represent member-tenants of an apartment complex does not qualify, since its activities benefit the member-tenants and not all tenants in the community, while an organization formed to promote the legal rights of all tenants in a particular community may qualify as a social welfare organization. An organization is not operated primarily for the promotion of social welfare if its primary activity is operating a social club for the benefit, pleasure, or recreation of its members or if it is carrying on a business with the general public in a manner similar to organizations operated for profit. A social welfare organization may lobby for legislation related to its purpose, but it may not engage in direct or indirect participation or intervention in political campaigns on behalf of or in opposition to any candidate for public office (Internal Revenue Service, 2009). From time to time, certain tax-exempt organizations will be reported to the IRS for engaging in politics.

Voluntary Organizations

When Republican Ronald Reagan won the U.S. presidency in the 1980 election and ushered in more conservative social policies, as well as with the election of another Republican president, George W. Bush, and his "compassionate conservatism," a policy position was enacted that government should do less for poor people and that the voluntary, nonprofit sector and organizations would meet people's needs as they have traditionally done. Referred to as *économie sociale* in the French lexicon and *Gemeinwirtschaft* in the German lexicon, voluntary organizations provide a major proportion of economic activities in developed democracies and are expected to deliver considerable social services to the public. In English-speaking countries, voluntary organizations are referred to by a number of names, including *charitable*, *philanthropic*, *third sector*, and especially *nonprofit* (Dollery & Wallis, 2003).

Economists have offered various theories to explain voluntary organizations and the people who govern them. Demand theories provide explanations for the origin of voluntary organizations and link them to market failures. Market failures occur when the market or systems of markets do not provide goods and services in an economic and optimal manner. Also, market failures occur when public agencies do not accomplish their stated objectives. Then, there are supply theories, which explain voluntary organizations as creations from social entrepreneurship. This social entrepreneurship involves explicit and implicit government subsidies, such as tax-exemption statuses, reduced postal rates, and lower unemployment taxes (Dollery & Wallis, 2003).

Why Do People Join Voluntary Organizations?

The United States has always ranked high in citizens' membership in voluntary organizations, and these organizations have been of research interest (Schofer and Fourcade-Gourinchas, 2001). Studying data from 32 countries, including the United States, and over 37,000 persons, Schofer and Fourcade-Gourinchas (2001) were interested in understanding voluntary association membership. Their three dependent variables were overall associational membership, old social movement membership, and new social movement membership. Their independent variables were individual-level variables (i.e., age, gender, education, marital status, religious belief, employment status, trust, and postmaterial values) and country-level variables (i.e., democracy, national economic development, statism, and corporateness). Their primary interests were statism and corporateness because these two concepts are grounded theoretically in the historical analysis of macro evolution societies. **Statism** is "a centralized and totally autonomous state apparatus at one end and a form of political power totally decentralized within an active and organized society at the other" (Schofer and Fourcade-Gourinchas, 2001, p. 811). **Corporateness** involves the extent to which society is organized around corporate lines or around collectives united by a particular economic project. Both variables were more important than individual-level variables in explaining membership in volunteer organizations.

Faith-Based Organizations

Religious institutions have had a long history of providing social services to the poor of their communities (Jeavons, 2003). For instance, the Children's Aid Society, which was founded by a Methodist minister in 1853, transported thousands of children from urban communities to the West (Bergner, 2006a). Further, many social service organizations have had religious ties, such as Catholic Charities, the Jewish Board of Family and Children's Services, and the YMCA (Oakley, 2003). Early faith-based organizations experienced a reduced role in providing social services as government expanded its role in attending to the broader needs of society with the creation of police departments, fire departments, departments to run prisons, departments to address family and children's needs, and departments to address social welfare (Chapman, 2003). Faith-based programs were further reduced as a result of the New Deal in the 1930s and the creation of what has often been called the welfare state. When the Republicans came into power with the election of Ronald Reagan, there was increased talk about reducing the size of government and letting local organizations, including faith-based organizations, do more in providing for the needs of poor people. In 1996, Congress passed the Personal Responsibility and Work Opportunity Reconciliation Act, and a part of it mandated "charitable choice," which meant that faith-based organizations were to be treated equally to other organizations in securing federal grants to provide social services to the poor (Kim, 2001). The belief of conservatives was that faith-based organizations would help decrease social problems, including drug use, teenage pregnancy, and welfare dependency (Chambré, 2001). Advocates also urged the expansion of faith-based organizations, insisting that "religious organizations provide more guidance, teach individual responsibility, and provide a framework for individual transformation that is absent in secularized human service programs" (Chambré, 2001, p. 436).

When President George W. Bush took office in 2001, he created the White House Office of Faith-Based and Community Initiatives. President Bush issued six executive orders related to faith-based initiatives from 2001 to 2006. His first executive order, issued on January 29, 2001, created centers for faith-based and community initiatives in five cabinet departments—Health and Human Services, Housing and Urban Development, Education, Labor, and Justice. This executive order charged each center to conduct

> a department-wide audit to identify all existing barriers to the participation of faith-based and other community organizations in the delivery of social services by the department, including but not limited to regulations, rules, orders, procurement, and other internal policies and practices, and outreach activities that either facially discriminate against or otherwise discourage or disadvantage the participation of faith-based and other community organizations in Federal programs. (Federal Register, 2001)

On July 25, 2006, the White House hosted a regional conference on faith-based and community initiatives in Austin, Texas. Over 1,000 persons attended this conference, which was geared toward those individuals new to the initiatives, those who had no history of applying for federal grants, and those who had applied unsuccessfully for grants. In effect, this conference was to help faith-based organizations be more competitive in securing grants for their programs. As proponents noted, faith-based community organizations were an integral part of the nation's social service network. Illustrating one example, the White House Office of Faith-Based and Community Initiatives (2006) observed that 1 out of every 6 child care centers is located within a religious institution and the largest chain of child care establishments is run by the Roman Catholic Church and the Southern Baptist Convention. Further, many faith-based organizations seek to assist returning prisoners as they integrate back into their communities.

Since its inception, the White House Office of Faith-Based Community Initiatives (reestablished by the Obama administration in February 2009 as the White House Office of Faith-Based and Neighborhood Partnerships) has encouraged faith-based organizations to apply for federal grants. President Bush allocated $15 billion for AIDS programs and reserved $200 million specifically for organizations that had no governmental grant experience, such as faith-based organizations. The federal government gave funds to a number of faith-based organizations with no experience working with individuals with AIDS, such as Samaritan's Purse, run by the Reverend Billy Graham's son; World Vision, a Christian organization; Catholic Relief Services; The HOPE Organization; and World Relief. President Bush stated that he embraced organizations that emphasized an ABC strategy—abstinence before marriage, being faithful to one partner, and condoms targeted for high-risk activity. However, programs that just pass out condoms are less likely to be funded, and some experienced programs working with HIV have had their funding eliminated for not embracing ABC (MSNBC.com, 2006).

A number of researchers and professionals have studied faith-based organizations, noting positive and negative factors (Chaves, 2001; Dewan, 2006; Monsma, 2003; Schwartz, 2003; Staral, 2004; Vanderwoerd, 2003). Even in the 1800s with the Children's Aid Society, there were praises for the organization for transplanting parentless children from cities to rural farms in the West, but there were criticisms that these children were mostly Catholics and were converted to Protestantism (Bergner, 2006a).

More recently, Pipes and Ebaugh (2002) studied the programs and operations of 14 faith-based coalitions that provided social services in Harris County (Houston), Texas. In the mid-1980s, Texas and especially Houston experienced a recession that was tied to the oil industry. About 200,000 jobs evaporated, and the unemployment rate was in double digits. At the same time, the Latino population in Texas increased by 60%, and many of these persons were poor and had come to Houston looking for work. Congregations throughout Harris County were showered with requests for assistance. Churches responded with the creation of a coalition so that resources could be stretched as much as possible in a coordinated effort among the churches. There were 14 faith-based coalitions consisting of 279 congregations. These coalitions provided food, clothing, and limited financial assistance for rent and utilities. Six members of the coalition expanded their services to include job posting, computer training, life skills training, English teaching, and citizenship training. Other members offered health care, shelter, child care, senior care, and specific services for elderly persons, such as recreation, house repairs, and transportation (Pipes & Ebaugh, 2002).

In another study exploring a faith-based organization, Wuthnow, Hackett, and Hsu (2004) were interested in comparing individuals who had received services from different social service agencies—a public welfare agency, a hospital, a congregation, a nonsectarian organization, and a faith-based organization. They had 37 independent variables to predict or explain their dependent variables. In terms of the faith-based organization, which was coded as 1 for yes and 0 for no, they found that it was associated with being African American, being Latino, having lower income, having more children, having more family problems, receiving more informal assistance, and attending church more often. They noted that their research supported the literature, which suggested that faith-based organizations have a significant role in social service delivery. Their research showed that the pressing needs that force individuals to go to public welfare agencies also force them to seek out faith-based organizations. Their research found that individuals' (i.e., those who had received services) level of trustworthiness and effectiveness was not significant for faith-based organizations.

Chikwendu (2004) discussed the work of faith-based organizations in Africa to provide anti-HIV/AIDS activities among African youth and women. Because Chikwendu was employed at New York University and discussed a faith-based program essentially based in the United States, we believe this discussion is relevant here and not in the international chapter presented later in the text. The U.S. Conference of Catholic Bishops stated that of all the continents, Africa has the highest growth of individuals converting to Christianity (Chikwendu, 2004). Among the 800 million people in Africa, more than 350 million are Christians, and more than 116 million are Catholics (Chikwendu, 2004). African Catholics make up 15% of the African population (Chikwendu, 2004). In 2001, there were more than 10,000 parishes and 75,000 mission stations in Africa (Chikwendu, 2004). Because of these numbers, the number of church-affiliated social institutions in Africa has increased, providing social services that include schools, hospitals, clinics, and agricultural cooperatives.

In addition, with some faith-based resources, combined with contributions from the United States and the United Nations, there has been an expansion of drug treatment for persons afflicted with HIV/AIDS. The African Forum of Faith-Based Organizations in Reproductive Health and HIV/AIDS is an alliance of faith-based organizations serving the area of sexual and reproductive health of Africans. According to Chikwendu (2004, p. 314):

It advocates for the recognition of women's and men's right to modern, safe, integrated and affordable sexual reproductive health services. Churches United in the Struggle against HIV/AIDS in Southern and Eastern Africa (CU-AHA) is a network formed in 2002 with five focal areas: theology and ethics of HIV/AIDS, the caring ministry; education and training; information and communication; and networking. CUAHA is targeting HIV/AIDS workers in Angola, Botswana, Ethiopia, Kenya, Malawi, Namibia, Rwanda, South Africa, Swaziland, Tanzania, Uganda and Zimbabwe. This organization develops materials on ethical and theological issues, shares the latest training methods and information, and ways of supporting not only HIV positive people, but also their caregivers. At their meeting in Dar-es-Salaam [Tanzania] in 2003 they addressed issues of stigma and discrimination against AIDS sufferers.

One area of conflict has been the church's position on the use of condoms, but the relaxation of that stance, along with the loosening of other restrictive positions, has led to more effective work with the HIV/AIDS-affected population (Chikwendu, 2004).

Concerns Regarding Faith-Based Organizations

As discussed by Chikwendu (2004), issues exist when faith-based organizations provide social services to persons in need. Other observers have noted similar issues with faith-based organizations. Because religious organizations do not have to report to the IRS and have seen increased federal funding for faith-based organizations to provide social services, research data are not available to the extent that they are for nonreligious organizations (DiMaggio, Weiss, & Clotfelter, 2002). Also, some faith-based organizations have imposed their religious beliefs on clients and expect anyone working for their organizations to advance that part of their mission. For example, Kaplan (2006) described controversies on some college campuses regarding religion, including issues related to social work. For her field placement, a student was assigned to a faith-based organization in Michigan. Her supervisors at the organization believed their faith to be an important part of counseling clients and expected students to initiate a discussion with clients regarding faith. This student had a different religious orientation and was not devout. According to her, she had no problem with discussing faith issues provided the client raised it first, but she did not feel comfortable raising those issues herself. Her field instructors had a problem with her reluctance, and her university was forced to intervene on her behalf (Kaplan, 2006).

ECONOMIC AND SOCIAL FORCES ON AND BY ORGANIZATIONS

Hall (2002) discussed the impact of the environment on organizations. Organizations vary in the degree to which they are affected by environmental pressures. Some organizations are stronger than others financially, and some might be stronger due to influential supporters. For instance, tobacco companies have attempted to overcome the burdens imposed on them by government and the courts. According to Hall (2002, p. 216), "contingency theory strongly suggests that there is no best way to cope with environmental pressures. The specific stance that an organization takes derives from choices that are made within it. This decision-making process is a political one in the sense that different options are supported by different factions within the decision-making structure." Roland (2006) discussed the political clout and political influence of Bechtel, one of the largest construction companies in the world. Bechtel has been accused of performing shoddy work on the "Big Dig" in Boston and has evaded responsibility for leaks and the fatal accident involving the collapse of a portion of the tunnel (Roland, 2006).

For sure, the nature of economic and social forces is far different for organizations than it is for families. Meyer and Rowan (2007) stated that schools and other organizations are vitally and intricately affected by their institutional environments. However, they were referring to environments surrounding and including comparisons between societies, other institutions, and internal components. Congress and state legislatures do not pass legislation that causes serious trouble for organizations, although organizations may complain that some governmental regulations do so. For instance, the car industries have complained that putting air bags in cars was too costly for them, but these costs were passed on to consumers, and these air bags have saved lives. To protect themselves many organizations and corporations hire lobbyists, and they have considerable influence in all levels of government. Other organizations are able to use governments to effect economic and social forces upon categories, families, and communities. Although a few of these organizational forces may be positive, most of these forces are quite negative.

Organizations' Involvement in Society's Issues

Organizations, as Farazmand (2002) stated, are involved in promoting or opposing social policies. Sometimes, their views are made known to state legislators and Congress or the president and governors. Organizations also attempt to influence the courts, especially state supreme courts or the U.S. Supreme Court, by filing amicus curiae (i.e., friend of the court) briefs. They are not direct parties in a case, but they can take sides by submitting legal briefs arguing for a particular outcome. For example, in *Hernandez v. Robles* (2005), the Supreme Court of New York decided whether gay and lesbian persons may get married in New York. A number of organizations, both small and large, including the National Association of Social Workers, filed briefs in the case (see Table 6.1). Observers believe that South Dakota passed a law banning

Table 6.1	List of Organizations Filing Amicus Curiae Briefs in *Hernandez v. Robles* (2005)

American Academy of Matrimonial Lawyers, New York Chapter
American Psychological Association
Asian American Legal Defense and Education Fund
Bronx Lesbian and Gay Health Resource Consortium
Capital District Gay and Lesbian Community Council
City Action Coalition
Empire State Pride Agenda
Family Pride Coalition (known as the Family Equality Council since 2007)
Family Research Council
Gay Alliance of the Genesee Valley
Gay and Lesbian Youth Services of Western New York
Gay Men of African Descent
Gay Men's Health Crisis
Human Rights Campaign
Human Rights Campaign Foundation
In Our Own Voices
Lesbian and Gay Family Building Project
Long Island Crisis Center
Long Island Gay and Lesbian Youth
Metropolitan Black Bar Association
National Asian Pacific American Legal Consortium (now known as the Asian American Justice Center)
National Association of Social Workers
National Association of Social Workers, New York City Chapter
National Black Justice Coalition

National Center for Lesbian Rights
National Employment Lawyers Association, New York
National Gay and Lesbian Task Force
National Organization for Women, New York State
New York Congregations and Clergy and Other New York Faith-Based Communities
New York County Lawyers' Association
New York Family Policy Council
New York State Catholic Conference
Pace Women's Justice Center
Parents, Families, and Friends of Lesbians and Gays
People for the American Way Foundation
Pride Center of Western New York
Professors of History and Family Law
Rainbow Heights Club
Sage Upstate
The Association of the Bar of the City of New York
The Institute for Human Identity
The Lesbian, Gay, Bisexual, and Transgender Law Association of Greater New York
The LOFT: The Lesbian and Gay Community Services Center
The New York City Gay and Lesbian Anti-Violence Project
Tompkins County Bar Association
United Families International
Vermont Freedom to Marry Task Force
Women's Bar Association of the State of New York

abortions in 2006 because of a belief that recent changes in composition of the U.S. Supreme Court may overturn *Roe v. Wade* (1973). When litigation over this South Dakota legislation commences and is heard by the U.S. Supreme Court, it is likely that a multitude of organizations will file amicus curiae briefs.

Positive Forces of Philanthropic Organizations

In the early 1990s, Warren E. Buffett, a wealthy American investor, and Bill Gates, the cofounder of Microsoft—two of the richest men in the United States—met at a social function and quickly became friends. Buffett encouraged Gates to read a copy of the World Bank's World Development Report. This report detailed the poverty in developing countries. Buffett, eschewing the belief that capitalism could cure poverty, stated that capitalism alone is incapable of addressing the root cause of poverty (Thomas, 2006). After discussing the issue with Buffett and reading this report, Bill Gates and his wife created the Bill and Melinda Gates Foundation, the largest foundation in the United States and the world, with assets of close to $30 billion (see Table 6.2). A major focus of this foundation is to address the human needs of poor individuals in developing countries, especially in the area of health needs and the curing of diseases. Immensely impressed with the Gates Foundation and its work, Buffett gave his stock in Berkshire Hathaway to the Gates Foundation in 2006. The value of Buffett's stock is estimated at more than $30 billion, increasing the wealth of the already significant Gates Foundation to close to $60 billion (McNeil & Lyman, 2006).

Table 6.2   Top 100 Foundations and Their Assets (2007)

Rank	Name (State)	Assets
1.	Bill and Melinda Gates Foundation (WA) (Before Buffet Gift)	$28,798,609,188
2.	The Ford Foundation (NY)	11,570,213,000
3.	J. Paul Getty Trust (CA)	9,642,414,092
4.	The Robert Wood Johnson Foundation (NJ)	8,991,086,132
5.	Lilly Endowment Inc. (IN)	8,585,049,346
6.	W. K. Kellogg Foundation (MI)	7,298,383,532
7.	The William and Flora Hewlett Foundation (CA)	6,525,004,389
8.	The David and Lucile Packard Foundation (CA)	5,328,293,452
9.	The Andrew W. Mellon Foundation (NY)	5,301,066,615
10.	Gordon and Betty Moore Foundation (CA)	5,042,534,007
11.	John D. and Catherine T. MacArthur Foundation (IL)	5,023,223,000

Rank	Name (State)	Assets
12.	The California Endowment (CA)	3,729,571,524
13.	The Starr Foundation (NY)	3,546,599,566
14.	The Annie E. Casey Foundation (MD)	3,295,299,665
15.	The Rockefeller Foundation (NY)	3,237,183,825
16.	The Kresge Foundation (MI)	2,752,257,750
17.	The Annenberg Foundation (PA)	2,603,501,021
18.	The Duke Endowment (NC)	2,542,619,779
19.	Charles Stewart Mott Foundation (MI)	2,527,897,211
20.	Carnegie Corporation of New York (NY)	2,244,208,247
21.	Casey Family Programs (WA)	2,184,894,330
22.	The McKnight Foundation (MN)	2,073,754,860
23.	Robert W. Woodruff Foundation (GA)	2,050,757,772
24.	The Harry and Jeanette Weinberg Foundation (MD)	2,027,561,526
25.	John S. and James L. Knight Foundation (FL)	1,939,340,905
26.	The New York Community Trust (NY)	1,810,817,540
27.	Ewing Marion Kauffman Foundation (MO)	1,774,756,631
28.	Richard King Mellon Foundation (PA)	1,742,201,835
29.	Doris Duke Charitable Foundation (NY)	1,693,460,630
30.	The Cleveland Foundation (OH)	1,632,621,913
31.	The James Irvine Foundation (CA)	1,541,924,918
32.	Alfred P. Sloan Foundation (NY)	1,505,602,994
33.	Houston Endowment (TX)	1,461,271,723
34.	The Wallace Foundation (NY)	1,364,654,036
35.	The Chicago Community Trust (IL)	1,324,379,128

(Continued)

Table 6.2 (Continued)

Rank	Name (State)	Assets
36.	The Brown Foundation (TX)	1,314,216,005
37.	W. M. Keck Foundation (CA)	1,307,546,774
38.	Tulsa Community Foundation (OK)	1,255,966,405
39.	Donald W. Reynolds Foundation (NV)	1,248,736,254
40.	Lumina Foundation for Education (IN)	1,196,062,690
41.	The William Penn Foundation (PA)	1,185,344,692
42.	The Michael and Susan Dell Foundation (TX)	1,178,008,895
43.	The Samuel Roberts Noble Foundation (OK)	1,161,500,185
44.	Marin Community Foundation (CA)	1,153,585,937
45.	Walton Family Foundation (AR)	1,129,770,302
46.	The Freeman Foundation (NY)	1,105,283,491
47.	The California Wellness Foundation (CA)	1,095,660,990
48.	The Moody Foundation (TX)	1,056,384,643
49.	Daniels Fund (CO)	1,040,647,749
50.	Kimbell Art Foundation (TX)	1,019,561,229
51.	Howard Heinz Endowment (PA)	933,443,085
52.	The Freedom Forum (VA)	924,229,500
53.	Greater Kansas City Community Foundation (MO)	895,377,250
54.	The Ahmanson Foundation (CA)	890,412,590
55.	The Joyce Foundation (IL)	859,149,036
56.	The Meadows Foundation (TX)	842,877,031
57.	Barr Foundation (MA)	838,237,131
58.	Horace W. Goldsmith Foundation (NY)	837,631,585

Rank	Name (State)	Assets
59.	Conrad N. Hilton Foundation (NV)	828,446,724
60.	The Columbus Foundation and Affiliated Organizations (OH)	809,783,848
61.	Weingart Foundation (CA)	795,207,659
62.	Longwood Foundation (DE)	785,221,853
63.	Hall Family Foundation (MO)	785,079,156
64.	The Henry Luce Foundation (NY)	780,692,462
65.	The Packard Humanities Institute (CA)	779,174,772
66.	Rockefeller Brothers Fund (NY)	773,436,060
67.	California Community Foundation (CA)	762,726,071
68.	Community Foundation Silicon Valley (CA)	760,821,244
69.	The San Francisco Foundation (CA)	757,717,972
70.	The J. E. and L. E. Mabee Foundation (OK)	750,335,362
71.	The Oregon Community Foundation (OR)	742,207,820
72.	Bush Foundation (MN)	732,455,635
73.	The Edna McConnell Clark Foundation (NY)	729,113,815
74.	M. J. Murdock Charitable Trust (WA)	708,881,176
75.	Boston Foundation (MA)	686,124,331
76.	Surdna Foundation (NY)	681,880,246
77.	The Lynde and Harry Bradley Foundation (WI)	665,329,753
78.	Fred C. and Katherine B. Andersen Foundation (MN)	662,906,121
79.	Marguerite Casey Foundation (WA)	651,864,991
80.	Wayne and Gladys Valley Foundation (CA)	648,163,609

(Continued)

Table 6.2 (Continued)

Rank	Name (State)	Assets
81.	Communities Foundation of Texas (TX)	647,469,000
82.	Hartford Foundation for Public Giving (CT)	646,120,566
83.	The AVI CHAI Foundation (NY)	644,925,391
84.	Burroughs Wellcome Fund (NC)	640,786,060
85.	The Commonwealth Fund (NY)	634,403,522
86.	William Randolph Hearst Foundation (NY)	619,868,118
87.	The Pittsburgh Foundation (PA)	617,284,142
88.	Peninsula Community Foundation (CA)	611,716,329
89.	The Robert A. Welch Foundation (TX)	611,141,615
90.	The John A. Hartford Foundation (NY)	597,722,183
91.	The Minneapolis Foundation (MN)	597,646,545
92.	The Saint Paul Foundation (MN)	594,648,660
93.	Jack Kent Cooke Foundation (VA)	592,886,751
94.	McCune Foundation (PA)	588,866,274
95.	J. Bulow Campbell Foundation (GA)	588,384,744
96.	George S. and Dolores Doré Eccles Foundation (UT)	564,534,643
97.	Broad Foundation (CA)	560,931,566
98.	Community Foundation for Greater Atlanta (GA)	560,410,937
99.	The Wells Fargo Foundation (CA)	556,683,066
100.	The Virginia G. Piper Charitable Trust (AZ)	552,859,276

Source: From the Foundation Center, http://fdncenter.org.

Buffett, as indicated above, does not believe that capitalism acting alone and without societal intervention can address the root cause of poverty. Certainly, not everyone holds this belief. Conservatives contend that rich people become rich by hard work and intelligence. For sure, Buffett and Gates are intelligent people and worked hard for their billions. But Buffett said something else that indicated why some rich people become rich. Specifically, a lot of wealth in this country is inherited wealth, and Buffett stated that he does not believe in dynastic wealth, which is why he left his children a smaller amount of his wealth. According to Buffett, many children who have inherited wealth are members of "the lucky sperm club" (Thomas, 2006, p. C1). Members of the lucky sperm club have not pulled themselves up by their bootstraps, and the difference between them and people steeped in poverty is biology and social environment.

Positive Forces of Peace and Social Justice of the Ford Foundation

The Ford Foundation is the second largest foundation in the United States with assets of $11.5 billion. This foundation provides grants domestically and internationally for a number of programs. One of its funding programs is called Peace and Social Justice. The creation of this specific funding program was based on the view that over the past 100 years, societies worldwide have created more wealth than in any previous century. However, these societies during that period have also shed more blood and created greater inequities than at any other time in recorded history. In effect, there is a positive relationship between wealth creation and human rights violations. The best chance for diminishing and alleviating these injustices and people's suffering is to have an engaged citizenry and governments that are committed to social justice. To this end, a movement is under way to strengthen the rule of law, create democratic and accountable governments, and fashion opportunities for citizens and society to flourish. The Peace and Social Justice division of the Ford Foundation strives to address the most pressing problems of developing societies, as well as the United States. Grants from the Peace and Social Justice division are awarded to organizations and agencies that lead efforts to build inclusive democracies; reduce government waste and corruption; safeguard the rights of women, refugees, and other vulnerable groups; and ensure reproductive freedom. For example, in 2005 Peace and Social Justice awarded $250,000 to a women's program in Russia to address its extremely high rate of domestic violence. In addition, Peace and Social Justice awarded grants to end racial discrimination, stop nuclear proliferation, slow the spread of HIV/AIDS, and resolve inequities in the international system (Ford Foundation, 2006).

The Ford Foundation's efforts to advance social justice and peace target four interrelated domains—governance, civil society, human rights, and sexuality and reproductive health. These four goals of the Ford Foundation's

Peace and Social Justice efforts mirror the goals of social work or a macro perspective of human behaviors in the social environment. Governance—although governments have very negative connotations in some developing societies and represent bureaucracy, tyranny, and corruption—is an essential institution to having safe, free, and prosperous societies. Governments can and do perform a critical role in mediating and fulfilling the different aspirations of their citizens. Citizen participation is vital to good governance not only at the local level but also at the international or global level. More and more, decisions impacting individuals, families, and communities are made in faraway capitals by international organizations such as the World Trade Organization (Ford Foundation, 2006).

Civil society is characterized by individuals coming together voluntarily to defend and promote their common good, which they have always done. Optimally, civil groups foster social cohesion and protect against the abuses of government and private businesses. However, civil groups encounter considerable opposition from governments and private businesses. The environments in which civil groups thrive in many societies are eroded by censorship, commercialization and consolidation of the news media, security concerns, and weakening rates of political participation. Many countries do not provide their citizens with rights of free speech and association. Even in the United States, increasing economic inequities among the poor and powerless and the rich and powerful means that mostly the rich and powerful voices will be heard and their organizations will flourish. Nevertheless, the voices of the less powerful groups have been heard as they have bought pressure to bear to prohibit land mines, advocate for debt relief for developing countries, and mitigate the excesses of globalization (Ford Foundation, 2006).

Human rights has as its goal the achievement of peace and social justice by the realization of rights that all human beings have by virtue of their humanity. Advocacy on behalf of human rights has been made since the end of World War II in the late 1940s. But it was the struggle against apartheid in South Africa that galvanized the human rights movement. When apartheid ended and the people elected a democratic government, they created a new constitution that many observers call the most progressive in the world. It strongly affirms such liberties as freedom of expression and association, which were long denied to South Africa's Black population. Moreover, it endorsed economic and social rights, including the rights to health, education, food, and housing. For sure, the goals have been achieved for economic reasons, but South Africa has a blueprint for the advancement of human rights (Ford Foundation, 2006).

Sexuality and reproductive rights help women be healthier and control their destinies. Equally, when women are free to choose the number and spacing of children, birthrates decline, which has implications for overpopulation of the Earth. In 1994, 179 countries represented at the International Conference on Population and Development endorsed a framework for protecting the reproductive health of individuals, but mostly women. However, many countries have not fulfilled their pledges. Achievement of their pledges serves a broader framework of gender equity and human rights (Ford Foundation, 2006).

Positive Forces of Organizations Helping Communities

In 1980, Local Initiatives Support Corporation (LISC) was created. Working through local community affiliates, LISC is a national organization with a community focus that helps neighborhoods build communities. It has 35 local offices and a national rural program involving 70 partnerships with rural agencies (Local Initiatives Support Corporation, 2005a, 2006). Since its inception, LISC has raised about $4.5 billion from the private sector and invested it to generate over $11 billion (Local Initiatives Support Corporation, 2006). Annually, LISC invests about $600 million in low-income neighborhoods and rural communities (Local Initiatives Support Corporation, 2006).

The Local Initiatives Support Corporation (2005a) reported four case studies that it said demonstrated its effectiveness. In 2001, LISC established its Affordable Housing Preservation Initiative, and this new program helped several struggling communities. Case 1 occurred in Boston's South End, which once was a struggling low-income community. It had been transformed to a diverse and vibrant neighborhood, with three South End buildings that housed 345 apartments being owned by a residents' association called Tenants Development Corporation. The rents for these units were kept low until market forces caused financial tensions (Local Initiatives Support Corporation, 2005a). Case 2 involved the East Hills neighborhood in Pittsburgh. This neighborhood had been characterized for years by its poverty, crime, and numerous abandoned buildings. Some of the buildings in this neighborhood were financed by the U.S. Department of Housing and Urban Development, and this source of funding was being threatened. Further, the surrounding area had run-down apartment buildings and an abandoned shopping center.

LISC, in partnership with the nonprofit Action Housing and the Telesis Corporation, worked with community leaders to restructure the financing and subsidies, renovate the building, and even generate interest in revitalizing the abandoned shopping center. With a $300,000 predevelopment loan and technical assistance with renewing and restructuring federal subsidies, LISC helped the community turn Second East Hills around. LISC's local investment and national technical help allowed the partners to win additional commitments from the Pennsylvania Housing Finance Agency and an allocation of Low-Income Housing Tax Credits, among other sources of new capital. The complex is now not only an attractive property but a strong, economically viable enterprise. Best of all, other buildings in the neighborhood are now under development. (Local Initiatives Support Corporation, 2005a, p. 9)

Case 3 occurred in Woodstock, Illinois—a rural community about 60 miles northwest of Chicago that was populated by many immigrants, senior citizens, and individuals with disabilities. When the owner of the Walden Oaks Apartments, a building that had 150 units, agreed to seek a buyer for his property, residents were threatened with loss of their low-income homes as pressures had been increasing on the amount of rent paid by residents. At the urging of the Hispanic Housing Development Corporation (HHDC), LISC helped HHDC buy Walden Oaks and preserved low-income houses in a rural area (Local Initiatives Support Corporation, 2005a). Case 4 involved two small rural towns in the Mississippi Delta where Catholic Charities owned three buildings that had 290 apartments where residents received federally subsidized assistance with their rents. The towns were Canton, Mississippi, which had a population of 13,000, and Leland, Mississippi, which had a population of 5,500. Overwhelmed by administrative requirements for renewing Section 8 housing assistance and required to set aside 20% of capital reserves for repairs, Catholic Charities sought the technical assistance of LISC. Using its national experts who were familiar with Section 8 housing requirements, LISC was able to help the small staff at Catholic Charities with its application and helped structure a financial plan by providing a loan, which was to be repaid from the rents paid by residents. Summing up the success of this collaboration, LISC stated that "the result is not only a better place to live for low-income rural families, but three more-attractive, stable buildings in Leland and Canton. These buildings, in fact, provide the only federally subsidized rental apartments in those towns—a resource for tenants and the wider community that would otherwise have been permanently lost" (Local Initiatives Support Corporation, 2005a, p. 11).

LISC stated that one of its partners, the Federal Reserve Bank of Richmond, commissioned a methodologically rigorous research study to document the success of a project in Richmond, Virginia. The study was conducted by Dr. John Accordino of the Virginia Commonwealth University, Dr. George Galster of Wayne State University, and Peter Tatian of the Urban Institute in Washington,

DC. Community leaders had envisioned stimulation of an economic ripple effect in Richmond, similar to a pebble being thrown into a pond. Called Neighborhoods in Bloom, the Richmond program guided public and nonprofit investments to specific communities, hoping to invite and maintain private investments in these communities. Starting in 1999, 80% of Richmond's federal housing money, about $6 million to $7 million, went into a 6- to 12-block area that made up seven Richmond neighborhoods (Local Initiatives Support Corporation, 2005b). These neighborhoods, due to crime and economic disinvestments, were some of the most depressed and blighted areas in the city of Richmond. Five years later, the program's effectiveness was studied by the research team identified above (Local Initiatives Support Corporation, 2005b). The results were called impressive. Among the findings:

1. Housing prices in targeted neighborhoods in Bloom areas (i.e., targeted areas) appreciated at a rate of 9.9% per year faster than the citywide average.

2. Prices in nontargeted blocks but within 5,000 feet of the impact areas increased annually at a rate of 5.3% faster than the citywide average. This suggests that the effects of neighborhoods in Bloom investments reach beyond the impact areas, although to a lesser degree.

3. The most significant home price impacts occurred after a threshold investment of $20,100 in the same block had been reached.

4. As investment in a given block increased beyond the level of this threshold, a significant boost in prices of initially 50% with continued 9.6% annual increases thereafter was experienced.

5. Even blocks in the target area that had no investment experienced substantial increases in value, suggesting a spillover effect in the entire target area.

In conclusion, LISC boasts that the increasing property values reflected in the study have hastened neighborhood change. As the gap between development costs and market values shrinks, private investments return to formerly isolated neighborhoods. This is the ripple effect. New and diverse families move in. Existing residents recommit themselves. There is a growing sense of possibility and hope—a shared vision, encompassing downtown development and community revitalization, that the city of Richmond can now offer a better quality of life to more of its citizens. (Local Initiatives Support Corporation, 2005b, p. 5)

Positive Forces of a Community Organization Changing Its Neighborhood

Organizations are more likely than an unconnected individual or small group to influence governmental officials. Speer et al. (2003) described how a huge organization was able to use its power to address a serious community problem. The organization was called the Camden Churches Organized for People (CCOP), consisting of over 1,000 individual members. Located in Camden, New Jersey, CCOP was concerned about the area's high crime rates and high concentration of poverty. CCOP suspected that much of the violent crimes in the city were related to vacant, dilapidated housing in poor areas. However, when CCOP met with the mayor of Camden, the mayor was totally unconvinced that there was a relationship between crime and vacant housing. The mayor also believed that housing and crime were two separate issues. CCOP fervently believed that "change comes about only through the exercise of power. For citizens and communities to exercise power, this model requires that citizens come together collectively through formal organizations; this perspective views voluntary, non-economic organizations successful only to the degree that they develop relationships among members within a community" (Speer et al., 2003, p. 399). To this end, CCOP met with the city attorney, members of the police department, members of the fire department, building inspectors, the state Department of Community Affairs, a state congressman's office, city council members, the state Department of Environmental Protection, the county prosecutor's office, the state Housing and Mortgage Finance Agency, county freeholders, local banks, state legislators, the Camden Redevelopment Agency, the local department of public works, the governor's office, the mayor, and the local community development corporation.

In addition, CCOP partnered with the Centre for Social and Community Development at Rutgers University (now known as the Center for Urban Policy Research) to conduct a study on the relationship between vacant housing and crime. CCOP was able to use its authority and influence to get data from the Camden Police Department, which the center could not acquire. A study indeed was able to demonstrate a relationship between vacant, dilapidated housing and crime. Among the findings were that the median proportion of vacant housing per city block in Camden was 10%; in blocks with greater than 10% vacant housing, drug arrests were 3.5 times more likely (Speer et al., 2003). Further, in city blocks with greater than 20% vacant housing, violent crimes were almost 7 times more likely than in blocks with less than 10% vacant housing (Speer et al., 2003).

Armed with these research findings, CCOP held a public meeting to present these findings to its members. The mayor was invited to come, and a press release was prepared so that the news media would cover this community forum. As easily understood maps and graphs were presented, no one could seriously deny that a problem existed, and commitments were made to address the problem. One of the outcomes of CCOP's strategy was that the Camden Fire Department inventoried all the vacant and dilapidated housing, which was identified as numbering over 3,300 in a city with a population of about 80,000 people. A patronage system existed in Camden. But with the spotlight put on this problem, a new competitive bidding system was implemented for demolition companies, cutting the price to demolish a single house from about $30,000 to about $8,000. Also, there was a significant reduction in landfill fees associated with materials from this demolished housing. Some houses were boarded up effectively to prevent individuals from using them to sell drugs. One year after CCOP's initiatives, drug crime dropped 31%, but vacant housing rose (Speer et al., 2003). The increase in vacant housing was due to a continuing pattern of individuals leaving the city (Speer et al., 2003).

Effective Advocacy Against Corporations

Some concerned citizens have organized against some corporations, and despite the power and influence of corporations, they can be made to adjust some of their behaviors. For instance, the town of Cochabamba, Bolivia, resisted and successfully fought Bechtel's ownership of the water with massive demonstrations, some of which became violent. Some of the tactics communities have used against corporations include direct action, boycotts, legal action, education, social investment, and legislation. Because corporations have charters granted to them, these charters can get taken away by government, although it is unlikely to occur. However, it can be done. A group of Californians asked their attorney general to revoke the charter of Union Oil Company (Unocal), accusing Unocal of engaging in corporate lawbreaking, causing the 1969 oil blowout in the Santa Barbara Channel and numerous other acts of pollution, committing hundreds of occupational safety and health violations, treating workers unjustly, committing human rights violations in Afghanistan and Burma, and usurping political power (Cray, 2002). The attorney general refused but stated that he indeed had the authority to revoke Unocal's charter. Further, some protests, originated on college campuses, can cause changes in corporate behaviors. Some colleges have removed Coke machines and held protests on their campuses due to the Coca-Cola

Company's exploitive behaviors in Colombia (Wolfson, 2006). Also, American advocates have brought attention to sweatshops in developing countries and the exploitation of workers. College students and professors helped dismantle apartheid in South Africa by pressing their colleges and universities to not invest in companies and corporations that did business in South Africa.

Negative Forces of Corporations

One type of organization is the corporation, which provides a number of high-paying jobs for some individuals. A corporation is an artificially created paper entity designed to generally do business. Born during the Industrial Revolution, corporations were considered a gift from the public to serve the public good, theoretically speaking. However, as described above, most corporations do not serve the public good. They are designed to create considerable wealth, but they sometimes do considerable harm. Corporations became more powerful as a result of the Fourteenth Amendment to the U.S. Constitution, which was developed to protect newly freed slaves from injustices by the states (Achbar et al., 2005). In one case, the U.S. Supreme Court ruled that corporations were persons within the meaning of the Fourteenth Amendment, which succinctly says that no person shall be deprived of life, liberty, or property without due process of law; nor shall one be denied equal protection of the law (*Butchers' Union Slaughter-House and Live-Stock Landing Company v. Crescent City Live-Stock Landing and Slaughter-House Company*, 1884).

The pursuit of profits often leads to exploitation and indifference to the health and safety of the public. The previous chapter discussed Fox's investigative reporters and their attempt to report the negative, harmful effects of a growth hormone the powerful Monsanto corporation gave to its milk cows. One powerful organization influenced another organization to the detriment of citizens. Further, numerous jobs have left America because the labor in developing countries is cheaper. For instance, a Liz Claiborne jacket that is sold in this country for $178 nets $0.74 for the woman who makes it (Achbar et al., 2005). A shirt that sells for $14.99 in America nets $0.03 for the woman who makes it (Achbar et al., 2005). Often, these women are laboring in sweatshop conditions.

A number of criminals in prisons are diagnosed as psychopaths, but one mental health professional, accepting that a corporation is a person, diagnosed corporations as psychopaths too. Corporations were found to be callous, unable to sustain relationships, possessing a reckless disregard for the safety of others, deceitful, repeatedly lying and conning others for profit, unable to experience guilt, and unwilling to conform to social norms with respect to lawful behaviors (Achbar et al., 2005). As one instance of deceitfulness, one corporation undertook a study of children's nagging. Parents were misled about the overall purpose of the study, which was not to help parents deal with their children's nagging but instead was to help children nag more and better so that their parents would be coerced into buying the corporations' products (Achbar et al., 2005). Moreover, these studies were conducted by psychologists who did not see anything unethical about what they were doing for the corporations (Achbar et al., 2005).

A commodity trade broker confessed that there is money to be made from devastations. The price of gold went up sharply after the terrorist attack on 9/11 (Achbar et al., 2005). Holders of gold saw their money doubled as a result of 9/11 (Achbar et al., 2005). When the United States went to war in Iraq in 1991, a barrel of oil went from $13 to $40 (Achbar et al., 2005). Some individuals working for major businesses were very excited when the drums were beating to attack Iraq a second time (Achbar et al., 2005). Months before the United States attacked Iraq a second time, reportedly because Iraq had links to terrorism and had weapons of mass destruction, Halliburton, a corporation in which Vice President Dick Cheney was an officer, signed contracts to provide services to soldiers and rebuild portions of Iraq. Although President Bush stated that going to war is a solemn decision because it means that many young soldiers will die, he was not speaking for the corporations and businesses that make money from war and specifically Iraq. Presently, oil is selling for over $70 a barrel with the threat that it could go to more than $100 a barrel, due in part to what is occurring in Iraq, and oil corporations are making exorbitant profits.

The government of the United States has been advocating for free trade among countries and for globalization. However, one of the factors behind this position is pressure from corporations. Some corporations in the United States have always done business with fascist countries, including Nazi Germany, and the U.S. military has been used to subjugate countries for the interests of American corporations. U.S. General Smedley Darlington Butler has stated that he had pacified/subjugated Mexico for the American oil interests, Haiti and Cuba for National Citibank, the Dominican Republic for sugar interests, Nicaragua for the Brown Brothers Brokerage House, Honduras for fruit interests, and China for Standard Oil. Reportedly, General Butler stated that he was tired of being a "gangster for capitalism" and disclosed that some of the leading corporations in the United States wanted to overthrow the U.S. government because of President Franklin Roosevelt's New Deal (Achbar et al., 2005).

Globalization is a current interest of American corporations because it is seen as a way of making more profits. Bolivia took a loan from the World Bank, and one of the conditions for the loan was that it must privatize everything. Bechtel, an American corporation, seized the water in Cochabamba, Bolivia, and even acquired ownership of the rainwater.

The Wal-Mart corporation is another example of the negative force a large organization can wield. Pressured by rising health care costs, Wal-Mart, the largest retailer in the world, discussed a confidential internal proposal that revealed that it could save $220 million to $670 million by 2011 by dissuading ill people from applying for employment at Wal-Mart and creating a strategy to get rid of ill employees. The strategy was to define all jobs as requiring physical activities, which would dissuade infirm individuals from applying. For those who applied and were interviewed, they would be asked specifically about doing physical aspects of the job. A negative response would provide legal justification not to hire the individual (Belkin, 2005). If an individual stated that he or she could do a physical activity, knowing he or she could not, then it would provide justification for later termination based on lying. If this strategy were employed successfully, workers would have little legal recourse as the law currently stands.

POSITIVE OR NEGATIVE ASPECTS OF ORGANIZATIONS DEPENDING ON ONE'S POLITICS

In 1983, a small number of pastors in Cincinnati, Ohio, calling themselves "prayer warriors," created a group known as Citizens for Community Values. Its initial goal was to fight pornography and strip clubs in the Cincinnati area. However, this small group has grown in 20 years to become a very powerful organization with considerable influence in the Ohio legislature and national governing bodies (i.e., Congress, the White House, and federal agencies, such as the Federal Communications Commission). It has formed a political action committee to financially support candidates running for office and hired two full-time lobbyists in Columbus, Ohio. Almost single-handedly, Citizens for Community Values persuaded the Ohio legislature to pass a gay marriage ban in 2004. It has been pressing hotels to cease showing pay-per-view pornography in rooms and has intervened in a sex education lawsuit in Kentucky. Their core issues are opposition to abortion and gay rights and the promotion of traditional marriage and school choice. A leader for Citizens for Community Values stated that he did not care if a person was running for dog catcher; the organization wanted to know where the candidate stood on the core issues supported by the organization. Citizens for Community Values sends questionnaires to candidates to learn their views on the core issues. Initially thought to be committed to legislation to force strip clubs to close at 11 p.m., an Ohio Republican state senator incurred the wrath of Citizens for Community Values for agreeing to a compromise in the legislature. As a result, the organization promised to oppose the senator when he came up for reelection. To support itself financially and promote its causes, the organization engages in fundraising, but it receives considerable donations from rich conservatives (Johnson, 2006). Republican U.S. Senator Mike DeWine also incurred the wrath of Citizens for Community Values when he did not actively support an amendment to the state constitution that would define marriage as a union between one man and one woman, and the organization let it be known that it would support his Republican challenger and would come to the polls as it did in 2004. Citizens for Community Values, with other like-minded groups, was instrumental in carrying Ohio for Bush in 2004 when the organization went to the polls in droves to ban gay marriage. Without their support, Bush would have lost Ohio to John Kerry (Donovan, Tolbert, Smith, & Parry, 2005). Seeing the consequences of angering Citizens for Community Values, Senator DeWine agreed to back a U.S. constitutional amendment in 2006 to ban gay marriage (Torry, 2006). John Green, a University of Akron political scientist with expertise in religion and politics, observed that organizations like Citizens for Community Values have evolved to become more like secular organizations in advocating for their goals (Johnson, 2006).

CONCLUSION

This chapter noted that organizations are instrumental to society, fulfilling human needs for various services such as health care, safety, transportation, and food supply. Corporations, which fill many of these needs, have been given the same rights as people under the Fourteenth Amendment to the U.S. Constitution. Like people, organizations and corporations are good and bad. Further, this chapter described the growth of organizations and the various types of organizations, focusing on those organizations relevant to social work and social welfare. These organizations include nonprofit and voluntary organizations. In addition, the chapter discussed faith-based organizations and their increasing role in providing social welfare services. A number of work groups within organizations were presented, including stages of work groups and dynamics within work groups. We then discussed the positive effects organizations can have, underlining the considerable funding that the Gates and Ford foundations are doing worldwide. At the same time, we noted the negative effects of organizations such as the American corporation that took control of the water supply, including rainwater, in Cochabamba, Bolivia. However, the people of Cochabamba fought back and regained their water, showing that powerful corporations can be forced to modify their dysfunctional behaviors.

Key Terms and Concepts

Bureaucracies

Corporateness

Differentiation

Environmental Conditions

Nonprofit Organizations

Statism

CHAPTER 7

U.S. Urban Communities and Human Behavior

INTRODUCTION

During the 2008 presidential campaign, CNN interviewed numerous persons to glean the pulse of individuals and communities regarding perceived important issues and problems for the candidates to address. One person, Joseph Hayden, did not like what he was hearing. He stated that CNN was only interested in what the middle class thought and it never really sought the opinions of people in the lower class. As a result, Hayden, along with some friends, created "Still Here" Harlem Productions. According to its mission statement, the goal of this company was to "cover every aspect of the community life of the marginalized and voiceless in Harlem." Hayden argued that "there's not enough air time for low-income communities and our issues and ideas." Consequently, Hayden and his friends created a Black CNN for the Harlem community (Grant, 2009).

The U.S. Census Bureau (2005) defines community as a place, but a community can be a psychological place or even a cyber-place. *The Social Work Dictionary* defines **community** as "a group of individuals or families that share certain values, services, institutions, interests, or geographic proximity" (Barker, 2003, p. 83). This definition embraces the perspective that a community can manifest itself physically, psychologically, and virtually. The most traditional perspective sees a community as a physical place where individuals live near each other and engage in various social networking functions. We know that some communities strive to provide a healthy and functional social environment for their residents, but some communities are severely burdened and crime-ridden and provide an unhealthy, dysfunctional, and very challenging environment for their residents. In 1906, Upton Sinclair wrote *The Jungle*, which novelized the scurrilous practices in the meat industry in Chicago that led to the creation of the Food and Drug Administration. One character, Jurgis Rudku, is a Lithuanian immigrant who works in the meatpacking industry but is still poor and unable to support his family. In the book, Sinclair discusses how the poor are exploited in the city. Robert Park (1915/1925) wrote a chapter titled "The City: Suggestions for the Investigation of Human Behavior in the Urban Environment." In this chapter, Park states that a large city, more than a small town, manifests all the human characteristics and traits that are normally hidden in rural towns. The city, according to Park, shows the extremes of good and evil in human nature. Since this early scholarly attention, we have always heard and read about the problems in urban centers and the inner cities, which are now often associated with places where Latinos and African Americans live. In this chapter, we describe urban communities, knowledge about them, social and economic activities that both help and hinder them, and negative and positive aspects of urban communities. We will discuss rural communities separately in the next chapter.

THEORIES AND KNOWLEDGE ABOUT URBAN COMMUNITIES

Community Theory

Many professionals have been reluctant to define community, contending that it is difficult to operationalize. However, Etzioni (1996) has disagreed, stating that though a chair is hard to define precisely, there is a consensus on what constitutes a chair. Community, according to a consensus of sociologists, is characterized by two qualities: (a) "a web of affect-laden relations among a group of individuals, relations that often crisscross and reinforce one another (rather than merely one-on-one relations or chains of individual relations)" and (b) "a commitment to a set of shared values, norms, and meanings, and a shared history and identity—in short, a shared culture" (Etzioni, 1996, p. 5). Etzioni adds a third characteristic that departs from his fellow sociologists and reflects a concept of high interest in social work. Particularly, Etzioni states that community involves a high level of responsiveness, which is society's response to the needs of its members. Etzioni calls the type of community that embraces these three characteristics an *authentic community*. Communities that lack responsiveness are *partial* or *distorted communities*.

Like other sociologists, Etzioni wanted to know how society could maintain both social order and personal autonomy, which are antagonistic to some point and must be kept in balance. Central to this issue is how society can protect individuals from one another, in cases of everything from civil war to violent crime. According to Etzioni (1996, p. 1), "simply seeking to prevent hostilities will not guarantee social justice to members of the society, other than indirectly, when it is argued that the absence of justice leads to violence." One key feature of social theory is its assertion that all social entities are impacted by **centrifugal and centripetal forces**. These centripetal and centrifugal forces pull a community in opposite directions. On one hand, centripetal forces pull toward increased levels of community service, regulation, and mobilization, which can serve the common good. On the other hand, centrifugal forces pull toward increased levels of differentiation, individualization, self-expression, and subgroup liberty, which can hinder efforts to maintain social order.

As Etzioni (1996, p. 10) stated,

even communities that are responsive and well-balanced will be particularistic, having identities that are separate and a sense of sociological boundary that distinguishes members from nonmembers. These features render even these communities potentially hostile, if not dangerous, to nonmembers. Communities can be exclusive—they can take positions against immigrants or persons of different economic, racial, or ethnic backgrounds, or sexual orientation; they can seek to break up societies in order to gain greater autonomy for their members (e.g. Quebec); they can engage in tribal warfare against other communities that were once members of their own society (Afghanistan, Bosnia, Sri Lanka, India, and the former U.S.S.R). . . . [To lessen these conflictual situations involves developing] layered loyalties in members of various communities. . . . To the extent that layered loyalties evolve, they discourage exclusivity and tribal wars.

Psychological Community

Some social scientists have examined and studied a psychological sense of community, which is defined as the degree to which individuals fit in and feel they share consequentially in a larger collectivity (Omoto & Malsch, 2005). This concept consists of individuals' perceptions of similarities with others in the community, acknowledged interdependence with others in the community, willingness to maintain that interdependence by giving to or doing what is expected of members in the community, and feelings that they are part of a larger reliable and secure structure (Omoto & Malsch, 2005). The concept of a psychological sense of community is important because it is related to other social issues, such as volunteerism and donating, and social problems, such as delinquency and crime. As an illustration, for a number of years, older Americans have lamented the loss of community among themselves. In the past individuals in communities would look after neighborhood children and monitor what the children were doing. Knowing that "Mrs. Jones" was watching them and would tell their parents if they misbehaved acted as a check on children. Many of these neighbors also had the authority to chastise and discipline neighborhood children. The belief now is that this sense of community has been lost.

Omoto and Malsch (2005) studied the impact of psychological sense of community, social support, and social identity on AIDS-related activism and civil participation. They found all three variables to be statistically significant with psychological sense of community and social support being the most important predictive variable. They concluded that

quality of life and the well-being of both communities and individuals may depend importantly on psychological sense of community and the connections that people share. Whereas some have decried the breakdown of social capital in contemporary society, along with decreases in its psychological concomitants, we feel optimistic that this apparent trend can be reversed. Specifically, based on our results, we suggest that one way to build social capital would be by intervening to increase people's sense of community. This suggestion derives from the reciprocal relationship between sense of community and behaviors indicative of social capital, as well as our findings that psychological sense of community predicts subsequent volunteerism and social action. (Omoto & Malsch, 2005, pp. 97–98)

Sex Market Theory

A **sex market** is a subsystem of a community in which individuals are mutually relevant to each other and for the most part share some common orientation by inspecting and assessing each other's strategies about sexual partnering. As a quick illustration, sex markets exist on university and college campuses where students, straight and gay, converge to meet individuals with whom they might become intimate. These places are keg parties and campus bars. There are three structural features of sex markets that are not mutually exclusive, but these markets have micro and macro factors. In essence, roles and positions, local brokers, and social and cultural embedment structure sex markets. Roles and positions determine how individuals develop and redevelop markets by their choices of partners, relationship types, and places to search. Local brokers involve the means by which individuals, networks, clubs, voluntary associations, formal organizations, and other social institutions facilitate partnering within and between sex markets. Social and cultural embedment of sex markets involves how sex markets are impinged upon by social networks, sexual cultures, and institutions (Ellingson, Laumann, Paik, & Mahay, 2004). Social institutions have always attempted to control sexual behaviors or sex markets. Social institutions impose considerable control over sexual behaviors by prohibiting specific practices and identities, providing penalties for choosing certain partners, and determining normative sexual practices. These social institutions include religion, medicine, education, law, and family (Ellingson, 2004), which we discussed in previous chapters.

Mahay and Laumann (2004) studied the sex markets in four Chicago neighborhoods, focusing on space, social networks, culture, and institutions. All these factors interacted to define the dynamics of a neighborhood sex market. The researchers surveyed individuals from these four neighborhoods, gathering data on the distance of sex partners, the type of place where individuals met their most recent sex partner, religious affiliation, church attendance, attitudes about sexual practices and partners, and where individuals go for health care (Mahay & Laumann, 2004). This survey involved mostly heterosexual sex markets, which exhibit different characteristics than homosexual sex markets.

A somewhat similar study was undertaken for homosexual sex markets in the same four Chicago neighborhoods. Comparisons were made between male same-sex markets (MSSMs) and female same-sex markets (FSSMs). Both MSSMs and FSSMs are mostly segregated by race, with women of color reporting discrimination when they enter sex markets within White neighborhoods. Further, minority women face stronger pressures from their communities to conform to traditional expectations of identity and behavior than minority men (Ellingson & Schroeder, 2004). According to Ellingson and Schroeder (2004, p. 115),

> Chicago's FSSMs differ significantly from its MSSMs in several ways. More prominent [from the perspective of FSSMs] is that they are organized in relational rather than transactional terms. While some informants discussed cruising and the search for casual partners among lesbians under thirty, this type of behavior was framed as the exception rather than the rule. Space is defined and used primarily to help women build relationships and communities, sometimes across racial and ethnic groups, and only secondarily to meet partners for causal sex. Unlike the MSSMs, the FSSMs are not centered geographically in a white, middleclass neighborhood; rather, they are scattered across several ethnically and economically diverse North Side neighborhoods and a few, largely African American South Side neighborhoods. They also lack the same institutional infrastructure (e.g., bars and cafes, bookstores, and social and health-care services) that is available in Shoreland. This is especially true in African American and Latino neighborhoods where, consequently, the markets tend to operate in private rather than public space.

Simply, this discussion about sex markets in Chicago is designed to illustrate numerous themes in the book and to comply with Council on Social Work Education mandates about a textbook on human behavior and the social environment from a macro perspective. This discussion is primarily to provide knowledge about a social institution (i.e., neighborhoods) based on empirical research about an underdiscussed minority group—White gays and lesbians and minority gays and lesbians. It reflects the conceptualization of systems theory that was discussed earlier in the textbook. Recall that a system can be a whole or a subsystem and these systems reflect social environments. The overall neighborhood is a system and a social environment, and so are the sex markets. Systems are connected, and a disturbance in one system will affect other systems. Neighborhoods and sex markets are impacted differentially. A case in point comes from African American lesbians who experience different pressures than African American gay males in their social environments.

The growth of personal computers and the expansion of the Internet has changed the sex marketplace. Yahoo, for instance, provides a service for individuals to post pictures, demographics, and personal requirements for relationships for those interested in meeting people and potentially entering into a relationship. Individuals may attempt to meet someone within their city, in nearby communities, nationally, or internationally. Some activities constitute criminal behaviors, as some individuals seek to link up with underage partners.

Since courts have increasingly recognized First Amendment rights since the 1970s, there has been a growth in "gentlemen's clubs" or "strip clubs" where men, and sometimes women, may go to see partially or completely nude dancers. These clubs may be viewed too as sex markets. For a few dollars, an individual may get a lap dance, where a woman dances topless for that individual in a semiprivate location in the bar and sits on his or her lap for part of the dance. In a manner, these dances represent simulated sex. Some communities have tried to force the closing of these clubs, stating that they cause crime in neighborhoods, cause property values to go down, and exploit women. But these arguments have failed legally as little or no research exists to support these suppositions. Communities have the right to restrict some activities, such as closing times and where these clubs may be located, but they cannot close them, and the courts have held many restrictions to be unconstitutional and a violation of free speech.

Undoubtedly, strip clubs or gentlemen's clubs constitute a sex market, where individuals engage in behaviors that are sexual in nature but usually not criminal. This legally protected simulated sex may have beneficial social effects, such as reducing the transmission of HIV and eliminating the occurrence of open prostitution in neighborhoods. Numerous poorer communities have complained about prostitution in their communities and used condoms found on the streets. Law enforcement spends a considerable amount of resources trying to control street prostitution, using resources and personnel to catch offenders and prosecuting them in courts. Of course, criminal activities may occur inside a strip club, too.

CRIME IN THE COMMUNITY AND COMMUNITY RESPONSES

Tim Hope (2000) edited a book on strategies of crime reduction, called *Perspectives on Crime Reduction*. Some of the book's chapters deal with strategies to activate the community. Seemingly grounded in routine activity theory, one strategy, community crime prevention, focuses on changing the behavior of potential victims (Lewis & Salem, 2000). As you will recall, according to routine activity theory, a predatory crime occurs when three variables interact: (a) motivated offenders, (b) the absence of capable guardians, and (c) suitable targets. People can be taught to make themselves less of a target. One study examined the effects of instituting foot patrols in communities. Although the study found that neighborhoods with foot patrols did not have lower crime rates than neighborhoods without foot patrols, there were other interesting findings. Neighborhoods with foot patrols had less fear and more positive attitudes about law enforcement, and officers on foot patrols had more positive attitudes about people in the neighborhoods than officers in patrol cars.

Sampson, Raudenbush, and Earls (2000) studied 343 neighborhood clusters in Chicago to ascertain the effects of the degree of collective efficacy on violent crimes in those neighborhoods. Using social disorganization theory, they hypothesized that **collective efficacy**, defined as the degree of social cohesion and the amount of willingness to work toward the social good, explained neighborhood crimes more than demographic factors. They found that three measures of neighborhood stratification—concentrated disadvantage, immigration concentration, and residential stability—were highly related to collective efficacy. In turn, collective efficacy was related to several measures of violence.

Sex Offenders

Under community pressures, legislatures have long enacted laws reputedly designed to protect communities. Some of the most prominent of these laws today are designed to protect communities and children from sex offenders. In Hamilton Township, New Jersey, Megan Kanka was sexually assaulted and killed, and as a result, legislators in New Jersey passed Megan's Law, which requires law enforcement officers to notify residents when sex offenders move into their neighborhoods (LaFond, 2005). Because of pressure from Congress and the threat of cuts in federal funding to states, all states have passed similar laws (LaFond, 2005). Some laws ban sex offenders from living within 1,000 feet of a school (Woods, 2006). Newark, Ohio, has such a law and has expanded it to include banning sex offenders from being within 1,000 feet of a licensed day care center, city park, playground, or swimming pool (Sheehan, 2006). A councilperson from Upper Arlington, Ohio, has determined to pass a law that would forbid sex offenders from working or living within city limits (Narciso, 2006). Georgia has passed what has been called the most restrictive law in the country, banning sex offenders from living near school bus stops and essentially forcing sex offenders to live in the woods in a rural county (Bluestein, 2006). Like Megan's Law, these banning laws have the effect of expanding nationally, and many persons declare that these laws are needed to protect children.

Moreover, some real estate developers in Texas have specified in their covenant agreements that sex offenders are not welcome (Koch, 2006). Housing covenant agreements have long been used to prevent minorities from moving into some communities. The courts have found these covenants to be illegal. However, when they apply to sex offenders, the law seems to suggest that these covenants are legal. The Texas developers stated that the restriction on sex offenders has helped sales tremendously. If a person buys a property and is later convicted of a sex offense, he or she will be fined $1,500 a day until he or she moves. As of 2006, 15 states have such laws on the books, and more states are predicted to follow (Koch, 2006). Critics of these laws contend that sex offenders have to live somewhere and these types of laws will drive them underground or force them not to register (Koch, 2006). LaFond (2005), who has written extensively on sex offenders, stated that these laws give communities a false sense of security as 80% of sex offenders know their victims.

Delinquency and Neighborhoods

In the 1930s, the Chicago Area Project, grounded in studies from 1929 to 1933 and sociological theories of delinquency, was created and implemented. It was based on the epidemiology of delinquency in city neighborhoods with high rates of delinquency and targeted these neighborhoods to reduce delinquency and to prevent youths from becoming delinquent. The developers realized that difficulty "rests on the fact that such programs, as efforts to intervene in the life of a person, a group, or a community, cannot by their very nature constitute more than a subsidiary element in changing the fundamental and sweeping forces which create the problems of groups and of persons or which shape human personality" (Kobrin, 1959/2000, p. 42). This sociological disorganization theory of delinquency and its prevention recognizes the processes by which individuals submit to the influences and control of social groups and imbibe their values. It also recognizes the processes affecting communal and collective action aimed at alleviating social problems. Essentially, people participate only in those activities in which they have a significant role. The organized activities of individuals anywhere serve institutions and organizations indigenous to their cultural practices and those social relationships characteristic of their social groups. Individuals will not devote their time to endeavors that benefit the social systems of groups with which they have no associations. In sum, the community needs to be involved in any program to reduce delinquency in its neighborhoods (Kobrin, 1959/2000).

Reflecting the themes of this book on macro human behavior and the social environment, Kobrin (1959/2000, p. 43) wrote that

> a final assumption necessary to the rationale of the Area Project program had to do with the social and institutional organization of the high delinquency rate neighborhood and with the related issue of capacity of residents of these areas to organize and administer local welfare programs. It was observed that despite the real disorder and confusion of the delinquency area, there existed a core of organized communal life centering mainly in religion, economic, and political activity. Because the function of the slum area is to house the flow of impoverished newcomers and to furnish a haven of residence for the multitudes who, for various reasons, live at the edge of respectability, the nucleus of institutional order actually present is sometimes difficult to discern. There seemed further to be strong evidence that the residents most active in these local institutions were, in terms of interest, motivation, and capacity, on their way up the social class ladder. With respect to these elements of the population it was assumed, therefore, that they represented forces of considerable strength for initiating delinquency prevention activities.

Kobrin (1959/2000) provided a qualitative analysis of the Chicago Area Project without any quantitative data. He argued that in the final analysis the Chicago Area Project rested its case on logical and analytic grounds because "progress in the solution of these problems comes only slowly, [and] permanent declines in delinquency are not expected even after years of effort" (Kobrin, 1959/2000, p. 47). Qualitatively, he viewed the achievements of the Chicago Area Project favorably in relation to the theory of delinquency causality within the social setting of neighborhoods with high rates of delinquency. Theoretically, delinquency is a manifestation of the local milieu in which (a) adults in neighborhoods do little or nothing publicly to marshal their resources for the welfare of adolescents residing in these neighborhoods, (b) the partial isolation of urban males becomes total isolation with complete loss of adult control, and (c) formal agencies performing correction and reformation do not seek the collaborative assistance of persons and groups influential in the neighborhoods. Kobrin identified the accomplishments of the program as the demonstrated capacity to create a delinquency prevention program in neighborhoods, the successful highlighting of the problem of the isolation of adolescent males, and the decreased bureaucracy of juvenile courts, school systems, police departments, probation and parole, training schools, and reformatories. Last, the Chicago Area Project learned that in local organizations there were persons capable of relating to delinquents, which made it easier for teachers, police, social workers, and court officials to work with these local persons so that they could "formulate and execute for the supervision of delinquent children jointly conceived plans designed to meet the specific problems and needs of the person" (Kobrin, 1959/2000, p. 48).

RETIREMENT COMMUNITIES FOR THE ELDERLY

Gist and Hetzel (2004) presented a portrait of the social and economic characteristics of all individuals aged 65 and over in the United States. In 2000, there were almost 35 million persons living in the United States who were 65 and over, about 20.5 million of whom were female and a little more than 14 million of whom were male (Gist & Hetzel, 2004). Of this nearly 35 millions persons, about 5.7% were living in group quarters (Gist & Hetzel, 2004). This means that about 2 million persons 65 and over lived in group quarters, primarily retirement centers and assisted living institutions.

As people are living longer and the elderly population is growing, the number of retirement homes and communities is growing as well. Among these communities, assisted living facilities are the least regulated facilities for elderly individuals (Eisler, 2005). Congress has not included assisted living facilities within federal fire safety laws and has left this issue to state legislatures. As a consequence, considerable variation exists throughout the nation, with many states having little regulation. As a result, assisted living facilities are frequent sources of fatal fires due to a lack of sprinklers and smoke detectors (Eisler, 2005). In 2003, a national conference was convened to discuss fatal fires in assisted living facilities, and the Tucson, Arizona, fire marshal stated that the conclusion from a panel discussion was that Congress and many states are reluctant to impose costly requirements on these facilities for fear of putting them out of business when the country needs more and more facilities for the growing elderly population (Eisler, 2005).

Gay and Lesbian Retirement Communities

No one knows for sure how many elderly persons are gay, lesbian, bisexual, or transsexual as there is no relevant question on the U.S. census questionnaire. According to the latest census, about 37 million persons are 65 and over, and about 79 million more individuals are approaching retirement age (Ritter, 2006). If we assume that the number of gays and lesbians among elderly individuals mirrors the number of gays and lesbians among the population at large, almost 3 million gays and lesbians are over 55 (Ritter, 2006). As gays and lesbians near retirement age, they have a strong desire for community, according to Gerontological Services, Inc., a market research firm. They strive for a community consisting of their families of choice rather than their biological families. Gays and lesbians nearing retirement are not comfortable with straight retirement centers and believe that the discrimination that exists in them increases the incidence of illness, depression, and substance abuse among elderly gays and lesbians (Ritter, 2006).

Some communities are soliciting gay, lesbian, and bisexual retirees. One such community is the Palms of Manasota, a community just north of Bradenton, Florida, which caters to retirees with high incomes. Some of the homes in the Palms sell for between $190,000 and close to $300,000. Residents indicate that they purchased homes at the Palms of Manasota because of the social comfort that the community offers. The social network is extensive, and there is a highly developed sense of community and perception of community as family. Some gays and lesbians fear straight retirement centers because they believe that they would be discriminated against. As such, they expect to feel isolated and believe their mental health would suffer. In a community of mostly gay and lesbian retirees, less isolation means a higher level of mental and spiritual health (Wilson, 2005).

Another retirement village, RainbowVision, has been developed and opened in Santa Fe, New Mexico (Ritter, 2006). It has 146 condominium and rental units that are built on 13 acres of land. RainbowVision is a retirement community strictly targeted toward gays and lesbians. It has a comprehensive social center where individuals can gather and has a floor that has been developed for the frail elderly who want to remain at RainbowVision.

THE AFRICAN AMERICAN COMMUNITY'S RESPONSE TO ITS HUMAN NEEDS

In 1999, the National Congress for Community Economic Development (NCCED) identified about 3,600 organizations committed to improving the economic health of poor and working-class communities (Daly, 1978). About 14% percent of these organizations were faith based (Daly, 1978). Daly (1978) traced the growth of community economic development in the 1990s carried out by African American churches. However, African American churches have long been involved in economic assistance dating back to 1899 as described by W. E. B. Du Bois, one of the founders of the National Association for the Advancement of Colored People (NAACP). The extent of African American churches' activities has been affected by various social movements—particularly the War on Poverty in the 1960s that was promoted by Democratic politicians and the conservatism of the Republican Party in the 1980s. Daly (1978) attributed the expansion of economic involvement in the African American community to a particular theory, as shown in Table 7.1.

Table 7.1   A Theory of Mobilization for African Americans

Shift in Political Opportunities	Community economic development, present in the 1960s, eroded (in the 1980s) as a result of changes in federal urban policies. Under the Reagan administration, the erosion of community economic development increased rapidly. Federal support to increase employment for the poor masses and housing development shrank to almost nothing. Also, social services for the urban poor were significantly reduced. African American churches shouldered a large share of the burden for caring for urban poor African Americans as they came to their churches seeking basic needs for food, clothing, shelter, health care, and job assistance.
A Sense of Grievance +	Just as African American churches were feeling the pressures of providing more for the basic needs of their communities because the federal government had retreated, a number of African American churches in the South suffered arson. In the days of the civil rights movement in the 1960s, a number of African American churches were set afire because they were the centers for launching and organizing voter registration and marches for civil rights for African Americans. As a result of this history, African American churches felt under siege again and had a heightened sense of grievance.
Moral Imperative and Resources =	The African American church has an immensely complex combination of historical traditions and institutions and does not lend itself easily to sociological study. Debate has occurred over whether the African American church is an instrument of resistance or protest or is an institution that the dominant culture uses to help African American people accommodate to the social order. To be sure, the African American church has regularly shown a moral imperative to confront the oppression and discrimination African American people encounter. Further, African American churches have had an effect in directing resources to the African American community. For example, an African American church in Oakland, California, was responsible for generating $20 million in construction in its neighborhood. In addition, some African American churches have purchased houses in their communities used by drug dealers, evicted them, and replaced them with socially responsible tenants.

(Continued)

Table 7.1	(Continued)
A Sense of Viability	According to Katherine Day (2001, p. 331), "the predominant strategy for developing a sense of viability remains exposure to successful cases studies, or models. A resulting taste of what is possible is the critical variable which can lead a community of faith from a heightened sense of grievance and imperative into action, rather than disillusionment, cynicism, rage, or despair." Essentially, an organization's capacity to show concrete examples and demonstrations of a can-do spirit establishes a sense of viability.
Social Action	Social action can be varied—in this case, the actions by the African American community in response to the election of President Ronald Reagan (i.e., providing more social services) or the rising rate of HIV and African American churches' response to it.

Note: A Sense of Grievance + Moral Imperative and Resources = A Sense of Viability. This then leads to social action.

Specifically, Daly (1990), in an updated paperback version of her book, recounted how a shift in politics affecting the African American community occurred under President Ronald Reagan. African American churches had to pick up more of the burden as more African Americans came to them to secure basics like food, clothing, shelter, health care, and job assistance. This led to a sense of grievance against the federal government. African American churches explored their moral imperative and marshaled their resources. A sense of viability was established when churches showed a can-do sprit. Social action, then, occurred.

In addition, the Balm in Gilead, taken from biblical sources and based in Richmond, Virginia, was one of the first faith-based programs to address HIV/AIDS in the African American community. It is dedicated to the empowerment of churches to address HIV in their community, seeking to mobilize the African American community through prayer, HIV prevention education, advocacy, and service. The aim is to utilize one of the primary social institutions in the African American community to reach out to individuals affected or potentially affected by this disease (Martin, Younge, & Smith, 2003).

Moreover, Tavis Smiley, an African American television professional, has long discussed issues affecting the African American community. Aligned with several African American professionals, Smiley (2006) has championed 10 principles, called covenants, which would improve conditions in the African American community (see Table 7.2). For each covenant, he lists several tasks that individuals and the community can do. Smiley requested that African

Table 7.2	The Covenants With Black America

Covenant 1. Health Care and Well-Being

Covenant 2. Establishing a Better System of Public Education

Covenant 3. Correcting the System of Unequal Justice

Covenant 4. Community-Centered Policing

Covenant 5. Ensuring Broad Access to Affordable Housing

Covenant 6. Claiming Our Democracy

Covenant 7. Strengthening Our Rural Roots

Covenant 8. Accessing Good Jobs, Wealth, and Economic Prosperity

Covenant 9. Ensuring Environmental Justice

Covenant 10. Closing the Racial Digital Divide

Source: From Smiley (2006), *The covenant with Black America.* Chicago: Third World Press.

American communities throughout the United States meet and debate the covenants and discussed what else such communities can do to advance the covenants and to determine their priorities. For example, members of the African American community in Columbus, Ohio, met to discuss the covenants, and the number-one covenant expressed passionately was Covenant 3—Correcting the System of Unequal Justice.

CYBER COMMUNITY

The advances of the modern computer age have created another type of community—the **cyber community**. Chat rooms where individuals may come together and discuss various social, political, and personal issues constitute communities. MSN Place or Windows Live Spaces, MySpace, Facebook, blogs, and other online communities make up a huge social network. Many of these Web site communities are broken down into groups that members may join. (See http://groups.myspace.com/index.cfm?fuseaction=groups.categories for a list of MySpace group categories and the number of groups in each category; as of August 2009, for example, there were 405,946 entertainment groups,

377,595 music groups, 208,417 school and alumni groups, and 92,049 fashion and style groups.) MySpace boasts of over 100 million members, and its owner stated that "he's particularly optimistic about the growth of social networks, like Fox's MySpace, which has come from nowhere to become the sixth most-visited website . . . [and] internet users spend more time at MySpace than at any other website. Social networking isn't a fad, but a real phenomenon. . . . It's not something that will go away" (Graham, 2006, p. 2B).

SOCIAL AND ECONOMIC FORCES ON AND BY URBAN COMMUNITIES

Economic and social forces can impact a community in positive and negative ways, and a community can also impact families and categories. At the urging of communities, states pass some laws, but these laws may be ineffective and counterproductive. For instance, the issue of unintended and uncontemplated effects of some laws purportedly designed to protect children has seldom been studied. Applauded by politicians behind a victim shaking hands with the governor, a new Wisconsin law allegedly provides community protection from juvenile sex offenders. Reportedly, this victim, 18 at the time the governor signed the new law in 2006, was assaulted at the age of 8 by a 14-year-old male, who was adjudicated as delinquent and sent to a treatment facility. Upon his release, he was subsequently charged and convicted of another sexual molestation and was given 25 years in prison. The first victim, upon learning of this new crime, began a campaign to advocate for a law for **community notification** of juvenile sex offenders, and this law was finally passed. Many persons said that this new Wisconsin law would protect the community from juvenile sex predators, but some states do not include juveniles in their laws regarding sex offenders. However, Congress may pass a similar law and force all states to implement community notification for juvenile sex offenders, or it may threaten states with a cutoff of all federal funds if they do not pass similar laws, as was the case with Megan's Law (Moore, 2006c).

However, there is another side of this coin. A 22-year-old female college student who was interested in majoring in social work in Michigan was rejected from field placements and was refused employment with a fast food restaurant because her name is on a registry for sex offenders. When she was 10 years old, she engaged in what she called "stupid child play" with two younger half-brothers. According to her, they all flashed each other and pretended to have sex although none of them removed their clothing. Because she was the oldest, she was charged with a sex crime and pled guilty at the age of 12. She was sent to a treatment facility for 18 months. But another part of her punishment was for her to be on a sex offender registry for 25 years, and she could not attend social functions where children were located, such as a school play or sporting events (Moore, 2006c).

While these laws have been hailed as protecting children, they may have other reciprocal effects. With the amount of sex shown on television and available through other media outlets, such as music videos, any child could copy or mimic sexual behaviors and suggestive sexual movements. Videos, such as those done by hip-hop artists, Madonna, and Britney Spears, have considerable sexual lyrics and sexual dances. In reality, a very large number of children could be branded as juvenile sex offenders and put on a sex offender registry, with consequences that last for years.

The Impact of Natural Disasters on a Community

In Chapter 3, we learned about social disorganization theory. What happened in Florida in 2004 in the wake of Hurricane Charley, which destroyed much of the city of Punta Gorda, may have provided evidence of social disorganization theory. Punta Gorda is in Charlotte County, Florida, and at the time of Charley had a population of 33,606, 95% of whom were White, according to the 2000 U.S. census. Normally, social disorganization theory is used to study poor urban communities and the stresses and instabilities in them. The results of socially disorganized communities are increased levels of crime and other social ills. Hurricane Charley forced numerous poor residents in Punta Gorda to live in trailers that were called "FEMA Village." About 1,200 people lived in 446 trailers that made up FEMA Village. According to one resident, there were lots of drugs and prostitution activities in FEMA Village, since the construction of which the sheriff's department had averaged seven calls a day. Residents reported a lot of domestic violence and troubles emanating from stress (Copeland & Cauchon, 2005). In August 2005, there were 257 calls to the sheriff's department (Kaufman, 2005). Bob Hebert, then director of recovery for Charlotte County, called FEMA Village a socioeconomic time bomb just waiting to blow up because so many different people were thrown together and living under a tremendous amount of stress (Kaufman, 2005).

Another social and economic impact of disasters like Hurricane Charley is that when disasters hit, many residents suffer economically, regardless of federal assistance. An insured apartment owner who rents units may take advantage of rebuilding to raise rents. As a result, a number of poor people cannot afford to rent in the areas where they lived before disasters struck

(Copeland & Cauchon, 2005; Kaufman, 2005). One woman, divorced since Hurricane Charley with a 2-year-old daughter and quartered at FEMA Village, stated that she had been looking for an apartment for her and her daughter but could not find anything that she could afford (Kaufman, 2005).

Social Disorganization Resulting From a Major Disaster in a Community

In 2005, Hurricane Katrina impacted the Gulf Coast in a very devastating manner, causing widespread destruction and the displacement of most of the population of New Orleans. Hurricane Katrina's unprecedented impact on New Orleans has spawned numerous professional papers and studies to learn the impact of such disasters on individuals and families. But a major disaster can have an effect on a community, too. Howard J. Osofsky, chairman of the psychiatry department at Louisiana State University, clarified the impact of the environment on the New Orleans community. After Hurricane Katrina, the suicide rate for the New Orleans community almost tripled (Saulny, 2006). Moreover, there was a very high rate of posttraumatic stress disorder diagnoses following Hurricane Katrina. According to Saulny (2006), Osofsky stated the trauma that affected New Orleans did not last for 24 hours and then dissipate. Instead, the trauma was still reemerging daily 10 months later. Contributing to the trauma that affected New Orleans was the fact that 10 months later the city still had considerable debris, block after block. This debris throughout the city served as a daily reminder of the destruction that hit the city. Osofsky declared that if he could do anything it would be "to have a quicker pace of recovery for the community. The mental health needs are related to this" (Saulny, 2006, p. A15). Apparently, Osofsky was indicating that the still visible destroyed environment negatively impacted the community. In addition, the generally depressed mood of the community was still negatively impacting others in the community 10 months later, forcing some to want to leave the city for a healthier environment (Saulny, 2006).

The Cost of Crimes to a Community

Crimes impact communities in many intricate ways. Budgets devoted to address crimes (i.e., law enforcement, courts, jails, prisons, parole, and probation) are high, siphoning money that could otherwise be used to address other social needs. For instance, Hughes (2006) reported that in 2003 communities and states spent $185 billion for police protection, corrections, and legal activities. In 1982, the amount spent was $36 billion, but it increased by

418% to the 2003 figure. As Hughes (2006, p. 1) noted, "compared to justice expenditure, State and local governments continued to spend almost 4 times as much on education, twice as much on public welfare, and roughly an equal amount on hospitals and health care." Several states spend more money on prisons and criminal justice than they spend on education. But criminal justice has other impacts on a community. For instance, Louisiana, which has a very large prison population that is vastly overcrowded, has synthesized its culture of incarceration with the local economy, and "local jail inmates are integrated into every aspect of economic and social life" (Nossiter, 2006, p. A13). This integration is accomplished by a system in which anyone in the community can request from the sheriff inmates to work at local businesses or repair community facilities. Jail inmates are even used at the main concession stands at local Little League and softball games, and these prisoners cook hamburgers for community gatherings (Nossiter, 2006). Of course, Louisiana is unique in this respect, and most states have not used inmates in this manner although it was quite common after slavery in the South to lease prisoners to farms and companies.

Immigration

Although America's purported motto is to "give us your poor and huddled masses yearning to breathe free," America has not always welcomed or embraced immigrants (Caldwell, 2006). Tensions have long existed over newly arrived immigrants, such as the Irish, Italians, and Jews. For years until 1965, federal laws established quotas for immigrants, and this quota system favored Europeans over immigrants from Asia, Latin America, and Africa (Barker, 2003). Presently, more immigrants from other countries have been permitted to come legally to the United States. Dalla and Baugher (2001) contend that rapid demogaphic change in a community leads to worsened racism and discrimination. Supporting Dalla and Baugher's thesis, an armed group of vigilantes, named after the Minutemen of the American Revolution, patrol some southwestern borders looking for Latinos from Mexico trying to enter the country illegally. In addition, major tension arose over a bill that was being considered by Congress in 2006 to charge all illegal immigrants in this country and anyone who hires and assists them with a felony. Even giving illegal immigrants food and water would be a felony (McFadden, 2006). This bill sparked massive demonstrations in numerous major American cities and divided the country (Swarns, 2006a). Much of the tension was directed at Latinos. Many Americans, according to several scientific polls, believe that illegal immigrants use more public services than they pay for in taxes (Connelly, 2006).

Estimates by the Pew Hispanic Center are that as of March 2006, about 11.5 million to 12 million Latino children and adults are in the United States illegally (Passel, 2006). Some of these individuals are from Mexico and some from Central America. About two thirds of them have been in the United States 10 years or less, and 40% of them have been in the United States 5 years or less (Passel, 2006). While the largest percentage of workers (24%) are employed in farming or agriculture, about 43% are employed in cleaning, construction, and food preparation (Passel, 2006). Further analyzing these data, Kochhar (2005) reported that these construction jobs are located in Atlanta (Georgia), Dallas (Texas), and Raleigh (North Carolina); the hospitality jobs (cleaning) are located in New York City; and the manufacturing jobs are located in Chicago. What these data and Kochhar say is that a sizeable group of unauthorized Latinos are in urban cities or communities. Their social and economic impact is qualitatively different from that of Latinos in rural communities working in agriculture or farming, which is discussed in the next chapter.

Kochhar (2005) asserts that unauthorized workers from Mexico are very valuable to the U.S. labor market numerically and economically. In about 2005, immigrants from Mexico totaled 3.5 million individuals and accounted for 20% of the Latino labor force in the United States. From 2000 to 2004, about 300,000 undocumented workers came from Mexico each year. This number represented not only a significant growth in the Latino labor force but also a significant part of the overall U.S. labor force. For the same years, 2000 to 2004, the Bureau of Labor Statistics reported that 1.2 million workers were added to the labor force each year. In simple terms, unauthorized Latinos from Mexico represented about 1 of every 4 new workers in America's labor force (Kochhar, 2005).

Demographers, newspapers, and reports have discussed the "Browning of America" and the growth of the Latino community in America. Currently, Latinos are the largest minority group in the United States, surpassing African Americans according to the 2000 census (Ramirez, 2004). These reports include Latinos in America both legally and illegally. Hence, the continued entrance of Latinos into this country likely is a major concern of White America. When deliberating the Border Protection, Antiterrorism, and Illegal Immigration Control Act, introduced in 2005 and debated in 2006, Congress considered whether Latinos who are in the country illegally should be granted amnesty and allowed to stay in America. Many members of Congress were opposed to amnesty, for Latinos are already a potentially potent political force and could get stronger if 3 million to 5 million more Latinos could vote. President Bush conducted a nationally televised speech on May 15, 2006, to encourage a compromise. Hence, the immigration bill in Congress has been labeled by some observers as racist in nature. Former President Jimmy Carter stated that the current immigration bill has overtones of racism, and

U.S. Senator Harry Reid commented that an addendum to the immigration bill requiring English to be the national language was racist and divisive ("Race Part of Debate on Borders," 2006).

Filling the void of inaction by the federal government, a number of states have proposed legislation targeting illegal immigration. As of April 2006, 43 state legislatures have proposed 461 bills addressing illegal immigration in at least one respect (Preston, 2006). Of these state legislatures, the Georgia legislature was the first to pass a comprehensive law to address immigration, which was signed into law on April 17, 2006. However, to ease passage of the bill, many provisions of this bill did not go into effect until 2007, 2008, and 2009. These delays were put into the law to address concerns of the business community, which wanted more time to present its concerns to Congress and to seek a federal law that would supersede Georgia's law (Lyman, 2006a). Among its many features, the Georgia law makes it a felony to engage in human trafficking for labor or sexual reasons and to hire someone without verifying that a potential employee is in the United States legally (Georgia Security and Immigration Compliance Act, 2006).

Even when foreigners come to the United States legally looking for employment, they may meet with some resistance. Highly skilled workers from developing countries are assisted with securing H-1B visas and should be eligible for green cards or permanent work permits. However, immigration authorities have been slow to act on a long backlog of applications. As a result, these highly skilled immigrants have created an organization called Immigration Voice. As noted by Caldwell (2006, p. 16), "When high-skilled immigrants who are already like us show themselves willing to become even more so, jumping every hoop to join us on a legal footing, it dissolves a lot of resistance. But it doesn't dissolve everything. It doesn't dissolve our sense that people like them are different and potentially even threatening." To support this conclusion, Caldwell (2006) pointed to the resistance by some segments of the United States to the immigration of Americans from one part of the United States to another part of the United States. For instance, North Carolina was very leery of Northerners moving to its areas, fearing a change in its political leaders. While many transplanted Northerners voted for Jesse Helms, a conservative darling, North Carolinians were not seeking more Northerners (Caldwell, 2006).

Community-Imposed Social Problems Related to Housing

In acts that exacerbated housing discrimination in cities, the U.S. government created the practice of redlining and forbidding the loaning of money for housing to members of minority communities in the 1930s

(Alexander, 2005a). In about 1930, all parts of the United States were color coded, and the different colors determined whether financial institutions should make loans in those areas and whether insurance companies should insure property. Green marked the most favorable areas, and red indicated the areas where loans should not be made or property should not be insured. Redlining comes from this process. Typically, the redlined areas were poor and minority areas. Later, the United States made redlining illegal, but many banks continued this practice (Alexander, 2005a). As a result, the U.S. government helped segregate communities and schools along racial lines. Communities, therefore, built housing projects for minorities in selected areas of cities. Later, it tried to stop communities from imposing racial discrimination in housing, perhaps due to the civil rights movement of the 1960s. For example, in 1981, the U.S. Justice Department, joined by the NAACP for Yonkers, New York, sued the City of Yonkers, the Yonkers Board of Education, and the Yonkers Community Development Agency for segregating housing and schools in Yonkers (*United States v. Yonkers Board of Education*, 1981). Following the taking of evidence, the U.S. District Court ruled against the defendant, and the district court ordered desegregation of the school system and housing. But the Yonkers government attempted to stonewall the district court, which imposed a fine against the city that doubled each day. The city relented and built housing for low-income African Americans and Latinos in White communities, which set up what has been called the Yonkers experiment (Santos, 2006).

Although the court order required Yonkers to desegregate its housing and schools, no rigorous studies have been conducted on the long-lasting effects of that court order (Santos, 2006). But anecdotal reports and interviews of Whites and African Americans suggest what has happened in the Yonkers community following the influx of minorities. Some African Americans, including a social worker, reported that they encountered cold stares and some racial epithets when they moved into the working-class community of Yonkers. Despite the unwelcome atmosphere for many minority residents, they felt that Yonkers was a better alternative than the violence-prone housing projects from which they came. Many Whites reported fearing that crime would increase and property values would go down when the housing integration occurred, but their fears were not realized (Santos, 2006).

However, Yonkers was not the only American city to be forced to undo its racial discrimination in housing projects. The same process has occurred in Chicago, where some public housing projects were destroyed and residents were helped to move to townhomes in other communities throughout the city.

The Intersection of Community, Organization, Group, and Social Institution

Rarely does an institution operate in isolation. It's important to examine institutions within the context of other institutions. A situation involving the Somali community in Columbus, Ohio, provides an example for us. Columbus is home to almost 45,000 Somalis (Williams, 2006), second only to Minneapolis, Minnesota, which has the largest Somali community in the United States. When Somalis began relocating to Columbus, they formed the Somali Community Association of Ohio and established bylaws for how it was to operate. The Columbus City Council has given the association money since its formation, and in 2006 it received almost $600,000, which it shared with the Somali Women and Children's Alliance (Williams, 2006). These funds were provided to the Somali organizations to pay for social services for the Somali refugees who had come to Columbus.

When a dispute arose in 2006 between a group of Somalis and the elected leader of the Somali Community Association of Ohio, the parties took their grievances to the Columbus City Council. The issue was that though the association bylaws require an election every 2 years, the elected leader of the association had not held elections since 2001. Somalis are not one monolithic community and represent different clans who have come to Columbus. They charged that they were being discriminated against by the current leader because they were of a different clan. In response, the elected president claimed that this group was attempting to destabilize the association and that a vote had been held to not have elections every 2 years so as to provide stability for the organization. Because the Columbus City Council held the purse strings, it promised to look into the election issue (Williams, 2006). Subsequently, elections were held according to the bylaws.

This example shows the interconnection of several institutions—a group (Somali Women and Children's Alliance), an organization (Somali Community Association of Ohio), a community (the Somali community), and a social institution consisting of a government that provides funding for social services (Columbus City Council). Further, another social institution—the legal system—could get involved if someone decides to sue. It would not make sense to look at this situation as just a community issue or an organization issue.

Community Interventions: Effective or Ineffective?

One focus of human behavior in the social environment is to achieve an understanding of how various systems interact to address a perceived problem and whether or not these interventions help alleviate the social problem. Here, we have one social institution, communities, pressuring other social institutions, law-enacting institutions, to address a problem. Typically, a number of people believe that the passage of a law solves problems, but that is not always the case. To ascertain whether a law has had a designed effect, we need a policy analysis, which is grounded in research. Among the issues in community notification are who gives it, how it is given, and what individuals do with the information once it is given. If a sex offender moves into a house, should everyone on that block be notified? What about the blocks in the front and back of the offender's house? Further, what do parents tell their children when they are told that a sex offender lives five houses from them? Are children molested near parks, schools, swimming pools, and libraries? A carefully conducted study could provide these answers.

Why are sex offenders banned within 1,000 feet of a school? What is so magical about 1,000 feet? Do we have knowledge from a study that children are more likely to be sexually molested when they live within 1,000 feet of an offender? Are children safer when they live 1,001 feet from sex offenders?

Some research has been conducted on child molestation, and all the studies show that children are more likely to be molested by a relative or close friend than by a stranger. The research on the effects of community notification has been scant, but some recent research on banning laws suggests that they do not protect children from sexual assaults. In a number of cases, child molesters have kidnapped children from their neighborhoods, which banning and communication laws are not designed to prevent.

With respect to the protective factors of community notification laws regarding child sex offenders, LaFond (2005) concluded that these laws provide a community with a sense of safety. However, these laws lead to the inaccurate dissemination of information, miss the target area, and provide a false sense of security (LaFond, 2005). For example, most children are molested by siblings, relatives, or close family friends, but the focus is often on the strangers. Thus states miss the target when they focus laws only on strangers. More important, there are no studies that support the contention that community notification laws protect children from sexual abuse (LaFond, 2005). Levenson and Cotter (2005) interviewed sex offenders in Florida, and these offenders reported that these laws were counterproductive and might trigger sex offenders to reoffend.

Cohen and Felson (1979) developed a theory of predatory crimes that can be used to explain sexual assaults, robberies, and burglaries and that may also explain why many of the laws intended to protect children from sexual assaults are not effective. They theorized that three variables must be present before a predatory crime can occur—the availability of suitable targets, the absence of capable guardians, and motivated offenders. It takes all three before a predatory crime can occur. For example, there is the very popular law that sex offenders cannot reside within 1,000 feet of a school, playground, day care center, and so on. The 1,000-foot boundary would only be rational and sound if research showed that most children are molested within 1,000 feet of a sex offender's home and these offenses drop precipitously after 1,000 feet. Cohen and Felson's theory says that 1,000 feet is irrelevant. A child could be molested at a rest area 2,000 miles from the sex offender's home if the sex offender is motivated, the child is a suitable target, and no capable guardians are around.

NEGATIVE ASPECTS OF URBAN COMMUNITIES

The Impact of Community Violence on Children

Garbarino and colleagues have consistently written about the impact of community violence on children (Garbarino & Kostelny, 1997; Garbarino, Kostelny, & Grady, 1995). Applying the concept of the war zone to urban American communities, they have referred to the "urban war zone" that exists in many urban communities (Garbarino, 1999). In one of his scholarly works from 1999, Garbarino used statistics from 1973 to 1993 to describe the socioeconomics and demographics of violence in the urban war zone, and observations of more current statistics confirm Garbarino's discussion. Snyder and Sickmund (2006) reported that from 1980 to 2002 about 2,000 juveniles annually were the victims of homicide. From birth to about 12 years old, girls and boys were equally likely to be homicide victims, but through the teen years, males were more likely to become victims (Snyder & Sickmund, 2006). African American juveniles were 16% of the juvenile population in 2002, but they were 47% of the homicide victims (Snyder & Sickmund, 2006). Supporting Garbarino's (1999) perspective, Snyder and Sickmund (2006) stated that of the three overall factors that researchers have studied (i.e., individual characteristics, family characteristics, and community characteristics), family and community rather than individual characteristics are the most important in explaining juvenile homicide victimizations (Snyder & Sickmund, 2006). Also supporting Garbarino's (1999) perspective, the Federal Interagency Forum on Family and Child Statistics (2009) reported that while one can view youth violence as an indication of young persons' inability to control and channel their behaviors into appropriate conduct, one can also view it as the failure of social institutions, families, peers, schools, and religious institutions to control youths in their neighborhoods. Interpreted in a different manner, it could be viewed as the inability of the community to restrain youth. The Federal Interagency Forum on Family and Child Statistics examined several indicators of children's well-being, including population and family characteristics, economic security indicators, health indicators, educational indicators, and behavior and social environment indicators. Within this last group, besides examining smoking, drug use, and suicide, one indicator was the rate of violent crimes (e.g., homicide, rape, aggravated assaults, and robbery) in 2003 for juvenile victims.

Lauritsen (2003) studied community disadvantage as a measure of economic and social factors and its impact on youth victimizations. She concluded that community factors are more important than individual factors and that, particularly, the more single-parent homes in a neighborhood, the more likely youths will be victimized. According to Lauritsen's (2003, p. 6) analysis and conclusions,

> one of the most important community predictors of youth risk for violence is the proportion of female-headed households with children. Results show that the other important correlates of risk (i.e., levels of poverty and race) are not statistically significant when family composition is taken into account. Moreover, the results show that the effect of the family composition coefficient does not change significantly once racial composition and poverty levels are included in the analysis. This evidence suggests that youth face a higher risk for victimization in disadvantaged areas because these places contain greater proportions of children living in single-parent families—not because they tend to be poorer or have larger percentages of racial and ethnic minorities.

Returning to Garbarino (1999), a risk model helps explain the impact of community violence on youth. First, an understanding of normal child development processes shows how war and communal violence eviscerate normal development. In addition to the psychological trauma on children, the loss of key familial and community relationships is equally damaging (Garbarino & Kostelny, 1996). Garbarino (1996) stated that children exposed to danger respond in one of two ways. First, they employ ideological interpretations that give meaning to hazardous events, which then give social structure and significance to those events. The result of this mode of responding is that mental health difficulties may be lessened. Second, they can respond without any ideological interpretations, causing them to exhibit hopelessness, despair, and self-destructive behaviors (e.g., within-group violence, depression, and self-hatred).

A study of the urban war zone suggests that risk accumulates and opportunities ameliorate. As negative or pathogenic pressures increase, so does the likelihood of children reaching their breaking point. On the other hand, the more positive or salutogenic influences, the greater the likelihood that children can bounce back and develop in a socially appropriate manner (Garbarino, 1999). The development model, germane mostly for understanding the impact of community violence on children, provides that children who are at greatest risk for community violence are those who live in the context of incremental risks. For example, communities with high numbers of socially marginal families, broken families, and drug-addicted parents present significant risks. Children have a lesser risk if they are exposed to an environment infused with strength (i.e., social support, caregivers who model social competence, and functional parents). Garbarino (1999) asserts that this model applies to genuine war zones and urban war zones. Garbarino et al. (1995) tested this model by comparing high-risk and low-risk communities for child maltreatment and found differences between the two. High-risk neighborhoods were more socially impoverished than low-risk neighborhoods. High-risk neighborhoods were less socially integrated, had less positive neighbors, and had more stress in families' everyday interactions. In sum, community violence and child maltreatment were positively related. Moreover, in the urban war zones, Garbarino (1999) found that community violence and its consequences can drive youth to groups that replace their families, such as gangs.

Census Counting Unfairness in Urban Communities

Census counting issues impact communities and families nationwide. Detainees in jails and inmates in prison are counted for census purposes where they are incarcerated. As such, they are included in population counts that are used to determine which communities receive grants and how much they receive. As an illustration, the city of Florence, Arizona, had a population of 5,224 but was able to raise its population to 17,054 by expanding its city limits to add 11,830 prisoners incarcerated in nearby prisons (Kulish, 1991). This maneuver helped Florence receive approximately $4 million worth of federal and state funds (Kulish, 1991). Stinebrickner-Kauffman (2004, p. 257) discussed extensively the legality of counting prisoners in census population bases but did not address the economic issues, "noting the impact that prisons have on the distribution of federal funds is certainly a worthwhile topic of study." Most prisoners come from urban communities, but they are incarcerated mostly in rural communities nationwide. This means that prisoners inflate the populations of rural communities, which permits these communities to get increased grants based on the population of an area. Rural communities in Texas and New York have received increased grants based on the prisoners in their counties. Thus, urban communities from where prisoners come can lose money. Moreover, this issue could potentially change the political landscape in state legislatures. Issues have been raised about the makeup of the New York Senate, which is affected by how prisoners from urban New York are counted (Roberts, 2006).

Another way in which criminal justice activities impact communities involves African American children in poor areas. From time to time, reports are aired about the lack of many African American men supporting their children financially. Pager (2003) has indirectly provided an explanation for this lack of support, although this was not her research focus. Research states that African American males have a higher probability of being involved in and under the control of social control agencies. Despite the impression given in the news media that most crimes are violent, most individuals regardless of race are arrested for property and drug crimes, not violent crimes. More Whites are involved in drugs and are arrested for drug activities than African Americans, but it is mostly African Americans who go to prison for drug possession. For instance, in 2004, 1,244,134 arrests were made for drug violations. Of this total, 66% involved Whites, and 32.7% involved African Americans (Federal Bureau of Investigation, 2006). Yet, in 2002, 57% of the persons incarcerated for drug offenses were African Americans, but just 23% were White (Harrison & Beck, 2004). These estimates and percentages have been stable for several years (P. M. Harrison, BJS Statistician, personal communication, March 29, 2005).

POSITIVE ASPECTS OF URBAN COMMUNITIES

While the community may in some ways impede the ability of individuals, families, and groups to meet their needs, in other ways it can help these same systems meet their needs. Communities respond, for instance, to the needs of their constituencies by creating and supporting food banks for poor families that do not have enough food. Often, these food pantries are supplied by other elements in the communities, such as major grocery stores and food plants. Many communities have health departments where poor residents may be treated and tested for venereal diseases or HIV. Most of all, communities provide emotional and social support for individuals and families. A strong example of such support was seen when New Orleans was evacuated due to

Hurricane Katrina. Although there were some exceptions, communities near and far took in evacuees from New Orleans. Glaser, Parker, and Li (2003) observed that some communities contain viable and meaningful social networks that contribute to the quality of life of residents within those communities. Further, change is possible within a community when the resources the community provides are combined with the efforts of committed individuals within the community. Their research shows that using relative deprivation as a framework helps

> for better understanding of the views of residents of an urban enclave, including the nature and relative strength of centripetal and centrifugal forces that define commitment to an urban place. Persons who perceive the enclave where they live to be a ghetto filled with crime and houses in disrepair, and at the same time view life outside in a more positive light, are expected to focus their efforts on escape and accordingly will be reluctant to invest their time, energy, and personal resources in support of community improvement. In contrast, persons who carry positive mental images of the urban place where they live, particularly those who are connected through the bonds of friendship, family, and community, are less likely to see the world outside their enclave as an attractive option, and as a result are expected to become willing contributors to community improvement. (Glaser et al., 2003, p. 527)

Their findings confirmed that residents' perceptions of community as their choice are important in making community development successful.

CONCLUSION

We began this chapter by discussing the different definitions of community, including the cyber community. We noted that urban communities' problems have been debated and discussed since 1906, when Upton Sinclair wrote his classic novel about the meat industry in Chicago. Sinclair's book also described the life of poor people in a major urban city, like Chicago. Presently, we are told about the inner city, which really has become a code word for a Black or Latino community. Then, we discussed the theories and knowledge about urban communities, beginning with a theory of the sex market and how individuals seek sex partners in an urban community. Because crime is a current concern of many Americans, we discussed the community efforts to address sex offenders, noting that many of these laws may be suspect and ineffective. We discussed issues involving delinquency in urban communities, drawing on a classic study. We presented for you a discussion about retirement communities and that some of these communities are being built primarily for retiring gays and lesbians where they feel that they are accepted and welcome. We discussed African Americans' response to their social needs. With the growth of the Internet, we discussed MySpace because it is a cyber community. In the latter section, we discussed how poor communities pay more for services than middle-class communities, and if these hidden taxes were eliminated, poor communities would have increased economic assistance without the help of government. We discussed immigration, a significant current issue. We described the impact of violence and disasters on communities. Finally, we pondered whether some communities' interventions were effective or ineffective.

Throughout this book, we attempt to show the relevance of world systems theory as a framework for understanding macro issues. In this chapter, we pointed to the discussion about the Somali community in Columbus, Ohio, an area with the second largest Somali community in the United States. We saw how newly arriving Somali immigrants have come to Columbus and entered a conflict with existing Somali residents. An organization with bylaws was created to meet the social and human needs of Somali immigrants, and funds were made available to the organization for these needs by the Columbus City Council. The bylaws called for elections every 2 years, but no election had been held in several years. Furthermore, showing that the Somali community is not a monolithic community, a newly arrived Somali immigrant group, which was of a different clan, accused the entrenched leadership of discrimination. The issue was presented to the Columbus City Council, as the holder of the purse strings, to fix. From a world systems perspective, we can see an international system intertwined with several other macro systems.

Key Terms and Concepts

Centrifugal and Centripetal Forces

Collective Efficacy

Community

Community Notification

Cyber Community

FEMA Village

Sex Market

CHAPTER 8

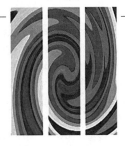

Rural Communities and Human Behavior

INTRODUCTION

Rural communities are often depicted by tranquil pictures of quaint small towns and Grant Wood's *American Gothic* painting of a farmer, a woman, and a pitchfork. In the Midwest and the Mid-Atlantic states, Amish communities, which have maintained the same lifestyles they exhibited in the 1700s when they came to America, are often used to typify rural American communities. Today, though, rural communities, for the most part, are characterized by poverty, overcrowded schoolrooms, substandard housing, and social upheaval (Dalla & Baugher, 2001; Wells, 2002). But some rural communities also incorporate ski slopes, retirement communities, mining towns, manufacturing, and farming communities (Flora, Flora, & Fey, 2004). Essentially, a rural community is not just a farming community as depicted by *American Gothic* or pictures of Amish life.

In the 1960s, President Lyndon B. Johnson used the White House and the "bully pulpit" to direct national attention to poverty and his War on Poverty (Dehaan & Deal, 2001). President Johnson also commissioned a group to study and report on rural poverty in the United States. In 1964, he created the Appalachian Regional Commission to stimulate economic growth. In 1967, the commission issued its report titled *The People Left Behind*. Almost a third of all individuals living in rural America were in poverty, according to *The People Left Behind* (Duncan, 1999). Changing the names and locations of participants in her study of rural America, Duncan (1999) reported that 50% of people in Blackwell, a mostly White Appalachian coal community, and 75% of the community in Dahlia, a mostly African American rural Mississippi Delta community, were in poverty.

Because of the high level of poverty, the federal government built roads and improved existing ones, and $14 billion was spent on public and social infrastructure to stimulate economic growth (Mencken & Tolbert, 2005). Further, school policy changes helped rural schools catch up with urban schools (Reeves & Bylund, 2005). Despite the high number of individuals in poverty in rural areas, the media tend to focus on urban poverty, and rural poverty receives a lesser amount of scholarly, political, and economic attention (Dehaan & Deal, 2001). The scant studies that have been conducted indicate that rural poverty is qualitatively different from urban poverty (Sherman, 2006). Some studies and books have been written about various rural issues, but they receive significantly less attention than urban problems.

Beaulieu (2004, pp. 1–2), a rural sociologist, stated that there are a number of challenges facing rural communities today:

1. A dramatic influx of new people with a diversity of cultures, languages, and values.

2. The out-migration of talented youth and adults who seek greater economic opportunities in larger populated areas.

3. The accelerated growth of service-sector jobs that are offering rural workers fewer opportunities to secure decent-paying jobs.

4. The stubborn persistence of poverty among rural women, children, and minorities.

5. The decaying state of roads, bridges, and other basic components of the community's infrastructure.

6. Rural individuals' declining capacity to afford or to have access to quality health care in close proximity to their places of residence.

7. The accelerated demands on rural schools to meet performance and accountability standards that are best suited or modeled for urban and suburban school systems.

8. The daily outflow of workers whose absence hinders their active engagement in the civic life of their communities.

9. Local governance structures that are struggling to keep pace with program management and fiscal responsibilities that were once the purview of federal and state agencies.

10. Urban areas that are encroaching on the rich natural resources of rural areas.

11. A technologically sophisticated world that has had a limited presence in the corridors of many rural areas.

THEORIES AND KNOWLEDGE ABOUT RURAL COMMUNITIES

The Amish Community: A Case Study

Although *American Gothic* is one of the most stereotypical depictions of rural life in America, a horse and buggy, still used by many Amish persons, provides a more realistic flashback of classic rural life in America. The Amish people are direct descendants of a religious order from 16th-century Europe, the Anabaptists. They rejected many of the reforms of Martin Luther and championed the separation of church and state in England. Early Amish fled to many other countries to escape religious persecution, and a sizeable group of them came to America in 1730 and settled in Lancaster County, Pennsylvania. They were attracted to this area because of William Penn, who advocated religious tolerance. However, some Amish settled in other states and countries, including parts of Canada. Presently, about 80% of the Amish living in the United States live in Pennsylvania, Ohio, and Indiana (Powell, n.d.).

What makes the Amish so unique is that they have retained many of their ways that they had in 1730 when they arrived in America. They eschew many modern technologies, including electricity, telephones, televisions, radios, tractors, and automobiles because they believe these technologies weaken the family and the community. The Amish still choose to use outhouses as toilets. In many rural areas, they can be seen traveling down roads and highways in a horse and buggy. They follow what is known as Ordnung, which consists of written and oral rules that govern their lives. Small variations may exist among communities, such as use of a telephone if it is not located in one's home or taking an airline flight, but the major rules are generally the same (Powell, n.d.).

The most important social institution in the Amish culture is the family, probably followed by the church. Divorce is not permitted, and no marriages outside the community are allowed. Males do the traditional farming chores, and females undertake household chores. As in rural life in America in the 1800s, Amish families are large, usually ranging from 7 to 10 children (Powell, n.d.). School for Amish children ends in the eighth grade, and secondary schooling is exempted for religious reasons. As the U.S. Supreme Court noted in 1972,

> the traditional way of life of the Amish is not merely a matter of personal preference, but one of deep religious conviction, shared by an organized group, and intimately related to daily living; the values and programs of the modern secondary school are in sharp conflict with the fundamental mode of life mandated by the Amish religion; secondary schooling, by exposing Amish children to worldly influences in terms of attitudes, goals, and values contrary to sincere religious beliefs, and by substantially interfering with the religious development of the Amish child and his integration into the way of life of the Amish faith community at the crucial adolescent state of development, contravenes the basic religious tenets and practice of the Amish faith, both as to the parent and the child; compulsory school attendance until the age of 16 for Amish children carries with it a very real threat of undermining the Amish community and religious practice as it currently exists; thus, enforcement of a state's requirement of compulsory formal education after the eighth grade would gravely endanger, if not destroy, the free exercise of Amish religious beliefs. (*Wisconsin v. Yoder*, 1972, p. 205)

Because of their very unique community (Galindo, 1994), the Amish have engendered some attention from researchers, both social (Buck, 1978; Kreps, Donnermeyer, Hurst, Blair, & Kreps, 1997; Randaxhe, 2002) and medical (Dorsten, Hotchkiss, & King, 1996; Hewner, 1997). For instance, because intermarriages are forbidden and the community is small, some married couples are related, producing children with some medical issues. Socially, researchers have been interested in the social life of the Amish and how they have resisted almost all modern technologies but have used some farming knowledge to produce better crops. However, the Amish community is not without some issues that contemporary society would call social problems. While about 80% of Amish children adhere to the Amish faith and culture, a few do not. Reiling (2002) studied deviance among Amish youth, for example.

Then, in 2006, the television show *20/20* broadcast a show on sexual abuse in the Amish community involving one young lady who stated that one of her eight brothers began abusing her when he was 12 and she was 6 years old. This abuse continued into her teens, and some of the other brothers also sexually abused her. Sociologically, an interesting facet of this situation was how the family and community handled this sexual abuse. Unlike some sexual assault victims in other societies, the Amish victim was not disbelieved when she told her mother. In fact, the brothers had confessed to the Amish elders what they had done. The elders serve as judge and jury, and the punishment for most transgressors is banishment from church activities for 6 weeks and restoration after the transgressors have shown true repentance. The community believes in public apologies, and when a transgressor has done so and shown true repentance, he or she is accepted back into the community. This occurs regardless of the seriousness of the transgressions. However, the legal system became involved in this situation, and one of the brothers was given a prison sentence (ABC News, 2006).

While some may find this sexual abuse horrible, the Amish community's handling of the situation reveals at the same time that the Amish community believes in restorative justice, which many social workers have adopted. Wrongdoers must stand before the congregation and confess their transgressions publicly in order to begin the process of forgiveness and return to the community. Understandably, child sexual abuse is very serious. Other deviant behaviors, such as alcohol use by Amish youth, are treated in the same way. Similar sentiments may be seen by the massacre in 2006 of several Amish schoolgirls in Pennsylvania and the Amish community's almost immediate forgiveness of the shooter (Hampson, 2006). In a way, the Amish practice true restorative justice, which many would argue is not seen in the American justice system (Alexander, 2006).

Characteristics of Populations in Rural Communities

Single Mothers and Poverty

A strong link exists between the type of family in which women and children live and their economic condition (Wells, 2002). Female-headed families are more likely to be associated with poverty. Snyder and McLaughlin (2004) compared family and household structures in nonmetro (rural) and metro (urban) areas for the decades of 1980, 1990, and 2000 (see Table 8.1). Examining census data, they found that in 1980, 20.2% of household and family structures were single-parent, 2.3% were nonfamily, and 77.3% were family. For 1990 and 2000, the percentage of single-parent households increased in nonmetro areas, although the United States saw increases in economic well-being for some individuals.

Table 8.1   Type of Rural Families in 1980, 1990, and 2000

	1980	1990	2000
Single-Parent	20.2%	23.9%	24.7%
Nonfamily	2.3%	2.7%	3.9%
Family	77.3%	73.8%	71.3%

Source: Adapted from Snyder and McLaughlin (2004), Female-Headed Families and Poverty in Rural America. *Rural Sociology, 69*(1), 127–149.

Using more sophisticated analysis, these researchers found that nonmetro female-headed families and subfamilies (i.e., a young mother and her child living with the mother's parent or parents) have characteristics that increase poverty risks. Rather than to individual-level characteristics, their poverty is attributed mainly to where they live or rather to living in a nonmetro context. In sum, "holding other characteristics constant, nonmetro female-headed families and subfamilies remain significantly and substantially more likely to be poor than their counterparts in other residential areas" (Snyder & McLaughlin, 2004, p. 146).

Providing related knowledge and noting that most research on public assistance involved women in metro or urban communities, Brown and Lichter (2004), analyzing data from the National Survey of Family Growth, were interested in single mothers, poverty, welfare, and livelihood strategies in nonmetro communities. They defined four family livelihood strategies: employment, cohabiting with a male partner, doubling up with at least one adult other than the male cohabitant, and food stamps and cash assistance. These researchers believed that food stamps and cash assistance were a livelihood strategy for single mothers, especially when parenting limited their involvement in paid employment, school, or vocational training. The dependent variable of interest was the family income-to-poverty ratio. As discussed in

Chapter 2, the Office of Management and Budget defines the family-to-income ratio as the ratio of income to the official poverty line (i.e., income/poverty threshold). If this ratio is 1.0 or below, the family is in poverty, and if this ratio is above 1.0, the family is not in poverty. As Table 8.2 shows, 39.4% of mothers in Brown and Lichter's study were not working, and 20.4% were living with a male. (Keep in mind that some of these variables do not add up to 100% because a woman could be employed full-time or part-time, cohabiting, and receiving food stamps.) About 47% received food stamps and 32.9% were on Aid to Families with Dependent Children (AFDC) before Congress terminated this program in favor of Temporary Assistance for Needy Families (TANF). Several other relevant variables are absent from the table. For instance, 70% of the mothers studied were White, and 21% were African American. About 73% were divorced or separated, and 27% were never married. As far as children, 46.5% had one child under 18 years of age, 35% had two children under 18 years of age, and 18.5% had three or more children under 18 years of age. Brown and Lichter conducted more in-depth analyses of their data, and they found that nonmetro and metro single mothers, despite different social

Table 8.2	Employment, Living Arrangement, and Government Assistance
	Nonmetro Mothers
Employment	
Full-Time	39.2%
Part-Time	21.4%
Not Working/Other	39.4%
Living Arrangement	
Cohabiting With Male Partner	20.4%
Doubling Up (Other Than Cohabiting Male)	31.4%
Government Assistance	
Food Stamp Receipt	47.4%
AFDC	32.9%

Source: Adapted from Brown and Lichter (2004), Poverty, Welfare, and the Livelihood Strategies of Nonmetropolitan Single Mothers. Rural Sociology, 69(2), 281–301.

circumstances and labor markets, were alike in their adoption of livelihood strategies. However, nonmetro single mothers had lower family income and more poverty than metro single mothers. Yet, nonmetro mothers were less likely than metro mothers to receive food stamps and public assistance.

Effects of Poverty on Families and Adolescents

Dehaan and Deal (2001) summarized the available literature to discuss the effects of poverty on family interaction, risk-taking behaviors, and psychological adjustment among rural children and adolescents. They reviewed previous studies dating back to a longitudinal study that began in 1929 and tracked families as the country experienced the Great Depression in the 1930s. Poverty increased inconsistent parental disciplinary strategies, and as a result, those in poverty had more behavioral problems with their children. Economic deprivation also led to more rejecting behaviors by fathers, which harmed their daughters' peer relationships but increased their sons' peer identification. Some of these studies focused on rural effects of poverty on families. These studies reported that economic deprivations were associated with more marital conflicts, emotional distress, disruptive parenting, antisocial behavior by boys, decreased psychological well-being in girls, and high stress for mothers. Risk-taking behaviors were defined as substance use and delinquent behavior. Studies have reported mixed results when comparing rural and urban substance abuse. One study indicated that the size of a rural community is a critical variable in that the larger the rural community, the more it is like urban communities with respect to substance use. Dehaan and Deal (2001) declared that rural delinquency has risen faster than urban delinquency, but the relationship between poverty and delinquent behavior is mediated by other variables, such as parental management or parental discipline and fathers' adjustments to economic hardships. Academic achievement among poor children has been studied, and some studies report differences between these children and middle- and upper-class children in reading and math. Poor children performed less well than middle- and upper-class youth. Poor children also had fewer educational aspirations than middle- and upper-class youth. Psychologically, poor children in rural areas report a high level of feelings of loneliness and depression. Some mental health professionals contend that loneliness and depression are higher in rural areas than in urban areas. Linked to these mental health problems is an increased risk for suicide (Dehaan & Deal, 2001).

TANF in Rural Communities

The 1996 Welfare Reform Act primarily targeted urban communities. Supporters of welfare reform believed that AFDC had a deleterious effect on the urban poor, particularly African Americans in urban cities. There is little or no evidence that thought was given to the impact of welfare reform on the rural poor. For instance, TANF, created from the 1996 welfare reform, required that recipients secure employment after temporarily receiving benefits; however, fewer jobs exist in rural areas. Also, the 1996 Welfare Reform Act relied on local charities to assist the poor, but far fewer resources of this type are available in rural areas than in urban areas. Several researchers studied rural communities in Mississippi, which has "a variety of rural communities endowed with different human, economic, and social resources" (Parisi, McLaughlin, Grice, Taquino, & Gill, 2003, p. 493). These researchers found considerable differences in TANF participation rates among nonmetro communities in rural Mississippi. Specifically, their research found differential treatment of African American communities in the Mississippi Delta. Further,

the variation in TANF participation rates across communities and the fact that community conditions are associated with participation rates indicate that communities differ in their ability to provide opportunities to reduce residents' TANF participation. Equally clear is that welfare reform that shifts responsibility for assisting TANF participants to successfully leave TANF to the local community has failed to consider the variability in community ability to meet this challenge. In many cases, poor economic conditions, low human capital, minority concentration, high inequality, and low civic engagement occur together, magnifying the disadvantages the poor experience in these communities. (Parisi et al., 2003, p. 508)

Special Elderly Populations in Rural Communities

Elderly Indigenous

Prior to 2000, the U.S. Census Bureau did a poor job of accurately counting indigenous people on reservations. Borrowing a strategy employed by settlement house workers, the U.S. Census Bureau for the 2000 census hired and trained indigenous workers to count the indigenous population. Due to their efforts and the addition of more categories for counting Native Americans, more than 4.1 million people identified themselves as Native American or part Native American, an increase from 2 million in 1990 (Barusch & TenBarge, 2003). About 50% of elderly indigenous people 55 and older lived in five states—Oklahoma, California, New Mexico, Arizona, and North Carolina— and they did not live on reservations. For elderly living on reservations, living conditions were meager. Of homes on reservations, 16%–21% had no electricity, refrigerators, or indoor toilets. In addition, transportation was difficult because of dirt roads that were made impassable when severe weather occurred (Barusch & TenBarge, 2003).

One of the recent changes in some indigenous communities is the growth of casinos on or near reservations. Not all indigenous people share in these casino revenues, but certain tribal members have shared in the profits, including some elderly Native Americans. Since the passage of the Indian Gaming Regulatory Act in 1988, 200 of the 556 federally recognized tribes have opened 310 gaming operations (Evans & Topoleski, 2002). Payments to the tribes were in excess of $350 million from about 1990 to 2000. Studying the social and economic impact of these casinos, Evans and Topoleski (2002) concluded that casinos have had positive and negative effects. Among the positives are higher employment; a higher number of younger indigenous people returning to the reservations, which has increased the populations; and a reduction in the working poor on reservations. The negative effects are more crimes and more bankruptcies (Evans & Topoleski, 2002).

Elderly African Americans

About 2.5 million African Americans in the United States are 65 and older, and among African Americans this age group is the most vulnerable. Their vulnerability stems from a shorter life span, more disabilities, and more chronic health problems than comparably aged Whites. Nonetheless, some professionals have found numerous encouraging findings, such as African American elderly seeing old age as a reward, having higher morale than comparable Whites of the same age, being more likely to remain in the family structure, having more religious beliefs, and being less likely to commit suicide than Whites (Rasheed & Rasheed, 2003). However, not all African American elderly are living an idyllic life. In rural communities, 50% of African American elderly live in poverty. Their social life is highlighted by trips to the general store, post office, and church. African American rural elderly have a cultural ethos and belief system that are characteristically found in rural African American communities. Religious faith, rather than traditional medicine or formal health care systems, is used to protect health. In addition, an important cultural belief is that to be able to walk and move about is an indication of adequate health.

Rasheed and Rasheed (2003, pp. 142–143) described the African American sense of community, which has aided African American elderly:

> Being a part of a unique community has long dominated the social consciousness of African Americans. This sense of "peoplehood" has emerged from a commonality of experience. These experiences result from a collective response to the forces of racism and oppression. Notwithstanding the debilitation impact of these forces, the African American community has contained a reservoir of strength and resources which often go untapped and/or unrecognized.

Elderly Latinos

The elderly Latino population in the United States is estimated to be about 2.5 million, and most of them reside in the southwestern border states near agricultural communities (Applewhite & Torres, 2003). Many live in poverty and thus face numerous problems, such as chronic diseases, limited access to services, inadequate housing, social and geographical isolation, and cultural and linguistic issues. Many elderly Latinos derive benefits from the cultural context of life in rural communities, buffering them from social, cultural, and economic pressures. Some elderly Latinos seek help from families, churches, friends, and associates in the community when they have significant health and social needs, but the majority of elderly Latinos seek help, when available, from agencies and service providers (Applewhite & Torres, 2003). Advocating for culturally competent practice, Applewhite and Torres (2003, p. 170) projected that "the population of elderly Latinos in rural areas will continue to grow in size and diversity based on shifts in rural to urban residence patterns. In addition a growing influx of new immigrant populations moving into rural areas will result in new challenges and issues related to health and social services, employment, and resource availability."

Rural Disabled Elders

DePoy and Gilson (2003, p. 180) synthesized rural, disability, and elderly to define "rural disabled elders" as "individuals who live outside of urban areas, who are advanced in age and experience, and whose explanations for an atypical nature are determined by at least one formal source to fit legitimate eligibility criteria for disability." In effect, the difference between rural elders and rural elders who are disabled is the presence or absence of a legitimate disabling feature. Based on this definition, rural elders with a disability constitute 23% of those who are 65 or older. As elderly individuals become older, they are likely to be grouped as a rural disabled elder.

Delinquency in Rural Communities

In Chapter 3, we discussed routine activity theory, which predicts that a predatory crime is more likely to occur when three variables are present: the availability of suitable targets, the absence of capable guardians, and motivated offenders. Spano and Nagy (2005) revised routine activity theory, adding the concept of social isolation to explain juvenile delinquency in a rural community. In their conceptualization, social isolation is not a macro social explanatory variable from urban sociology but is an individual characteristic. Social isolation can act in a rural area as either a risk or a protective factor in the occurrence of personal crime. As a risk factor, social isolation denotes extremely low degrees of social guardianship. Hence, social isolation from peers and adults intensifies the spatial estrangement of rural adolescents from capable guardians, such as watchful neighbors and law enforcement. Consequently, socially isolated rural adolescents are less likely to garner the attention of sympathetic bystanders who would help prevent violent offenses. As a protective factor, social isolation lessens the exposure to potential co-offenders and the influences of other deviant adolescents. Spano and Nagy tested their reconceptualization of routine activity theory among rural adolescents in Alabama and found support for their revised theory. As they concluded, "these findings suggest that social isolation should be integrated into the empirical and theoretical study of violent victimization as well as violence prevention initiatives. Since socially isolated rural youth are at increased risk for violent victimization, these communities need to broaden (and strengthen) social networks that act as a deterrent for potential offenders" (Spano & Nagy, 2005, pp. 432–433).

Professionals in Rural Communities

Mellow (2004) discussed the **Gemeinschaft-Gesellschaft gavotte** among professionals working in rural communities. *Gemeinschaft* refers to natural will, and *Gesellschaft* refers to rational will. A gavotte is a type of Baroque dance. Essentially, Mellow compared differences between urban and rural professionals and the dance performed by rural professionals. Four qualities differentiate professionals from nonprofessionals: (a) having an abstract specialized knowledge, (b) having autonomy, (c) having authority over clients and adjunct occupations, and (d) having norms of altruism and service. To this end, Mellow reviewed studies involving the work in rural areas performed by nurses, doctors, lawyers, mental health professionals, and social workers. With respect to mental health professionals and social workers, social workers must labor particularly diligently to gain the trust of rural residents before being able to provide services. This might mean frequenting places in the community (local cafés, churches, general stores, etc.) and might mean helping out in agricultural activities. This might mean that social workers might need to abandon what they were taught in schools of social work about not establishing dual relationships with clients. While engaging in sexual relationships would always be taboo, other dual relationships might be needed, such as socializing with clients. In a similar fashion, mental health professionals must be flexible regarding dual relationships, and also counseling sessions might focus less on individualistic counseling and be more sensitive to informal and community support in rural communities. Both social workers and mental health professionals practicing in rural communities need to be generalist in their orientation and not have primarily a specialized professional orientation (Mellow, 2004).

Rural Community Theories

Haves and Have-Nots

As we related earlier, Duncan (1999) performed a study of rural people living in "Blackwell," a coal community in rural Appalachia, and "Dahlia," a rural community in the Mississippi Delta. She also compared those two communities to a rural community in northern New England. According to Duncan, Blackwell and Dahlia were divided into two communities: "the haves" and "the have-nots." The haves engaged in practices to prevent the have-nots from elevating themselves socially, educationally, and financially. By contrast, the middle-class community in Northern New England had a more helpful attitude toward those in poverty who wanted to climb out of poverty. The isolation and poverty of individuals in Blackwell and Dahlia were fortified by the corrupt and undemocratic politics in these rural communities. Unchallenged and powerful, the haves create and maintain the vulnerability of rural poor people, and all decent-paying jobs go to the haves' friends, relatives, and supporters, making social changes almost impossible. The rural poor thus have a very difficult time developing the ambitions, skills, and habits to change their social situations. Reinforcing the poor's situation, they are stigmatized and blamed for their poverty, and many of them come to accept their status. Also, social institutions in these rural communities, such as churches, schools, and groups, segregated by race and social class, are weakened and ineffective in assisting poor rural residents. In both Blackwell and Dahlia, inequality corroded the social fabric, and the effects were that trust was shattered and social institutions were destabilized. Consequently, poor families had no chance to achieve the American Dream (Duncan, 1999).

Great Change Hypothesis

However, Krannich and Luloff (2002), testing the **Great Change hypothesis** as described in Chapter 3 and disputing portions of it, reported the results of a long-term study, which were not as bleak as what other rural researchers have found. During the 1940s, the U.S. Department of Agriculture funded and oversaw six studies of rural America, conducted in El Cerrito, New Mexico; Sublette, Kansas; Landaff, New Hampshire; the Old Order Amish community of Lancaster County, Pennsylvania; Irwin, Iowa; and Harmony, Georgia. Fifty years later, Krannich and Luloff summarized the knowledge learned from these six studies. They stated that when the six communities were first studied in the 1940s, these rural communities were already in the midst of change and upheaval. Migration and settlement patterns were under way as a result of urban industrial expansion and the initial impacts of the mechanization of farming. The Great Depression of the 1930s quickened the economic and demographic destabilization in most rural communities (Krannich & Luloff, 2002).

Krannich and Luloff (2002, pp. 172–173) stressed that

> the key finding that emerges from our restudy of these six communities, a half-century after the initial effort, revolves around the somewhat amazing persistence of localized social organization, community attachment and community action—regardless of the disparate and transformed settings characteristic of these places. In no case is there evidence that the social fabric of community collapsed in the face of population change, economic transitions or increased linkages to extra-local organizations and processes. Certainly, each community is dramatically different from what it was in 1940. All have witnessed the effects of declining local autonomy and increased vertical linkages to external organizations and authorities that accompanied the Great Change process outlined by Warren [1963].

Krannich and Luloff's (2002) reanalysis of the data further disclosed communities' persistence and vibrancy 50 years later. All the communities celebrated major events, such as Old Home Day in Landaff, the annual Limpia— a semifestival that consisted of clearing and repairing irrigation ditches—in El Cerrito, and the Centennial Celebration in Irwin. Further, evidence emerged of collective action in the community to address local needs and concerns. For example, Krannich and Luloff observed Irwin residents helping a family who lost their café, the Amish Community's traditional barn raising, Putnam County's creation of a Concerned Citizen Group to combat unfair tax assessment in Harmony, and Landaff's efforts to save a school. Considerable evidence was present in the reanalysis to convey that local residents had high levels of community attachment and identification. Moreover, in each community, there was evidence of a substantial commitment to preserving and celebrating cultural traditions and supporting local institutions (Krannich & Luloff, 2002).

Economic Development

Two researchers, conceptualizing several research questions from a theory of economic development in rural areas, posed whether there was an association between hazardous waste facilities and rural "**brain drain**" (i.e., the best and brightest leaving rural communities). Rural communities had been concerned about decreases in their populations and sought to increase economic development, hoping that new jobs would stem out-migration. So, some rural communities have sought and welcomed prisons, nuclear waste dumps, landfills, and power plants—almost anything that would produce jobs and spur more economic development. The impact of strategies to boost economic impact has been the subject of a variety of studies. These studies have produced mixed results. Hunter and Sutton (2004) did not formulate any hypotheses for testing, but they did pose research questions, aiming to clarify, if possible, the relationship between hazardous waste and rural brain drain. Their investigation was specific in that they were interested in the out-migration of educated individuals and not the overall population. After analyzing the data, they found that the presence of hazardous waste facilities had no effect on population loss. Rural communities lost population, but this loss occurred regardless of hazardous waste facilities. Next, these researchers asked whether the level of ruralness was a factor, which essentially meant that level of ruralness was a control variable (i.e., they examined the relationship again between presence or absence of hazardous waste facilities and brain drain for different levels of ruralness, but variables also can be controlled by some statistical techniques). They found that the level of ruralness was not significant, and it appeared that the presence of hazardous waste facilities only dampened, but did not reverse, population loss (Hunter & Sutton, 2004). Hunter and Sutton only posed the possibility that hazardous waste facilities might quicken the pace of more educated individuals leaving rural communities, regardless of job gains in the community and economic development. However, they found no evidence for this effect.

Nursing Theory

Drawing on a qualitative study in rural Montana 20 years earlier, Findholt (2006) discussed a nursing theory to explain the willingness of a rural community to participate in health development. Theoretical predictor variables were the community's social structure, physical setting, and cultural factors. The cultural factors were the priority given to health, perceived efficacy of collective action, and insider/outsider differentiation. The priority given to health means the significance consigned to health programs as compared to other programs at the community level, such as economic programs. The perceived efficacy of collective action means the community members sense that they could solve problems by working together. Insider/outsider differentiation is the extent to which community residents, as a group, accept and trust individuals based on their length of time in the community. Findholt studied many cultural efforts from this theory in a qualitative study and did not conclude them to be effective. She concluded that the culture of rural communities in Montana had changed over the 20-year period. This change was due to the loss of jobs in traditional rural industries, advances in telecommunications and transportation, and other major social changes.

Migration Behaviors

Immigration, especially as regards the Latino community, has become a hotly discussed issue. In 2005, a bill was introduced in Congress to criminalize illegal immigration, and the public has been intensely interested in this issue (Connelly, 2006). Another way to view immigration is that it is a form of migration, and African Americans' migration to the North from the South has long been studied. Now, some researchers, such as Falk, Hunt, and Hunt (2004) and Price-Spratlen (1998), have investigated the migration of African Americans back to the South, and often African Americans are returning to the rural South. Drawing on Lee's (1966) theory of migration, which we learned about in Chapter 3, Falk et al. (2004) investigated the streams of migration for African Americans who had returned to the South. They found that as a result of African Americans leaving the North, African Americans are becoming less Northern and less urban. The return migration of African Americans indicates that they are becoming more rural when they return South. Guided by one of Lee's (1966) hypotheses, Falk et al. (2004) found that African Americans returning to the South, compared to African Americans who have always lived in the South, are younger and more likely to be male. African American migrants are more educated and more likely to be in the labor force than African Americans who left the South or African Americans who have always lived in the South (Falk et al., 2004). The latter finding seems to contradict Lee's (1966) theory in part.

Community Attachment and Well-Being

Social scientists have long been interested in the study of community attachment, which encompasses generally one's emotional and sentimental bond with a particular community. Believing that community attachment consisted of broader dimensions, Brehm, Eisenhauer, and Krannich (2004) included physical environmental factors, or what they called amenity variables, in addition to social environmental factors. These were such factors as climate, geography, topography, water, clean air, and forests. They employed factor analysis to identify those dimensions that pertained to the social environment and those that pertained to the physical environment. Factor analysis is a statistical procedure that permits the identification of specific subcomponents of a concept. Based on their analyses, they had four variables to measure the social dimension of attachment: the number of friends close by, the strength of family ties in the area, the local culture and tradition, and the degree of opportunities to be involved in community projects and activities. Natural environment dimensions were captured by three variables: natural landscape or views, presence of wildlife, and opportunities for recreation. They were interested in well-being, and it involved the social, cultural, and physical needs of individuals, institutions, and communities. These two dimensions—social attachment and natural environment—were conceptualized as representative of individuals' well-being.

Their first analysis was to learn the variables that predicted or explained social attachment, and the significant predictors were religion, length of residence, perceptions of the importance of involvement in community decisions, amount of interest in knowing what happens in the community, and social involvement. Using the same predictor variables as were used to predict social attachment, only one variable was significant in predicting natural environment attachment, and this was the degree of importance of freedom to express opinions about community affairs. These researchers concluded that their theory of community attachment was validated by their research and their "findings have significance for community development efforts that seek to enhance attachment, particularly in rapidly growing, high natural amenity rural communities" (Brehm et al., 2004, p. 422).

SOCIAL AND ECONOMIC FORCES ON AND BY RURAL COMMUNITIES

Some rural communities actively recruit retirees because they benefit from the strong economic impact retirees bring with them. In 2000, Floridians age 50 and over spent $135 billion, which was nearly $13 billion more than what younger residents spent (Jones, 2005). Every month, the largest influx of income in Smith County, Texas—amounting to nearly $30 million—comes from Social Security checks (Jones, 2005). As a result, a lot of rural communities are recruiting individuals nearing retirement in order to boost their economies. The relationship is mutually accommodating—rural communities get the economic benefits, and retirees get communities that are supposedly safe and have a good quality of life (Jones, 2005). But only a relatively small number of rural communities benefit from retirees.

Mencken and Tolbert (2005) studied the effects of federal public investment on measures of economic development, consisting of poverty, median family income, and income inequality. Examining data from the 1980s and the 1990s, they found that per capita federal public investment was an important variable in explaining economic development or poverty, median family income, and income inequality. In a similar vein, another study of rural families' well-being found that families residing in areas with high growth in amenities and recreation tend to have higher family incomes than rural families living in economically stagnant areas (Hunter, Boardman, & Onge, 2005). This relationship held regardless of family size or sex, race, or age of the family head (Hunter et al., 2005). Further, socioeconomically disadvantaged long-term residents, specifically female-headed families and less educated family heads of the household, were financially better off in amenity growth counties compared to their counterparts in counties without such amenity growth (Hunter et al., 2005).

In 2005, the U.S. Department of Commerce created the Strengthening America's Communities Advisory Committee, whose charge was to advise the U.S. Secretary of Commerce on policies, principles, and guidelines to help communities deal with how globalization had changed the world economy.

Among its expert witnesses was Brian Dabson, associate director of the Rural Policy Research Institute at the University of Missouri, who gave the committee recommendations for strengthening both rural and urban communities. The committee believed that globalization has changed the world and that in the 21st century, American communities will develop economic strength by interacting regionally. Entrepreneurship and innovation are the new locomotive that will produce job creation, productivity, growth, economic prosperity, and healthy communities. One of the key recommendations of the committee was that federal economic and development funding be targeted to communities of the greatest need, which were determined to be rural communities (U.S. Secretary of Commerce, 2005).

Earlier in this chapter, we discussed the building of toxic waste dumps and nuclear plants in rural areas. Having lost textile plants and jobs, Gaffney, South Carolina, population 13,000, actively sought the building of a nuclear power plant in its town. Despite the nuclear accidents at Three Mile Island and Chernobyl, people's memories of these events had faded, and many citizens of Gaffney stated that they had no fear of having a nuclear power plant in their backyard. Energy companies had been targeting rural communities that had lost jobs and their tax bases, knowing these communities were eager to attract new businesses. Duke Power, the builder of the nuclear plant, planned to create 1,500 jobs to build the nuclear power facility and would employ about 1,000 individuals to operate the plant. To ensure that the area would have qualified workers, Gaffney officials promised to create new science, math, and engineering courses in the local schools (Lyman, 2006b), showing the linkages between education, one social institution, and an organization.

Prejudice and Bias in Rural Communities: Three Case Studies

Prejudice and bias can be found in all walks of life and in every community (Hansen & Hansen, 2003). Researchers have long noted that while rural areas are often portrayed as idyllic, neighborly environments, rural communities have long been noted for their conservatism, which is more than what one will find in urban communities. Years ago, researchers conducted a classic study to test which areas were more conservative. A researcher left stamped, addressed envelopes in obvious places to see if these letters when found would be put in a mailbox. Some of the letters appeared to be intended to be sent to a communist organization or an organization such as the National Association for the Advancement of Colored People. These researchers found that rural residents were less likely to mail these letters. Subsequent elections have shown that rural areas are more conservative than their urban or suburban counterparts. Also, while suburban residents may mount legal or political challenges to projects or individuals they deem undesirable, rural residents have historically been more willing to use violence to prevent change in their social environments.

African Americans and Sundown Towns

Loewen (2005) has written an important work explaining why a large number of small communities, mainly outside of the Deep South, are all White. In 2001, a White store clerk confirmed to Loewen that the city name Anna, Illinois, stands for "Ain't No Niggers Allowed" and that the city had been all White since 1909, when African Americans were driven out. Loewen called Anna a "**sundown town**," which warned African Americans not to let the sun set on them when they were still in town. Through his research, Loewen claimed that thousands of small towns in the West, the Midwest, and the North were sundown towns. He asserted that there were 194 sundown towns in Illinois and 9 sundown towns in Wisconsin. Nevada also had some sundown towns that targeted primarily Latinos. Generally, these communities became sundown towns after a racial incident (e.g., an African American man allegedly attacking a White woman), and then the entire African American community would be driven out of town by violence. These towns then would be kept all White by the posting of signs warning African Americans not to be in town after dark, and later these towns and small communities would enact policies preventing African Americans from moving there. When his book was published in 2005, Loewen contended that there were still sundown towns in the United States. He also charged that numerous historians and social scientists, while comfortable writing about the lynching of African Americans, purposely avoided writing about sundown towns, how they got that way, and the current practices to maintain them (Loewen, 2005). Loewen, a sociologist by training, stated that he was the first person to study and publish on what he called a very shameful period in American history.

According to Loewen (2005), sundown towns grew from 1890 to 1940 and reflected a period when race relations became systematically worse in the United States following the Civil War and the very short-lived Reconstruction period. Most towns were not sundown towns during slavery, the Civil War, or the Reconstruction period. After slavery, African Americans dispersed throughout the United States looking for a better life. For instance, early census data showed that African Americans were in every county in Montana and in the Upper Peninsula of Michigan. But around 1890 this began to change. By the 1930s, 11 Montana counties had no African Americans. Also, in the Upper Peninsula of Michigan, the White population grew by 75%, but there was a decrease in the population of African Americans. Only 331 African Americans were in the Upper Peninsula of Michigan, and 180 of them were inmates at a Michigan prison in that area. This pattern was duplicated in a number of small communities nationwide. Loewen's contention is that African Americans did not just decide to move, but they were driven out and a wall of silence emerged to not talk about it. He called it the ethnic cleansing of African Americans (Loewen, 2005).

Charged with dredging up the past needlessly and unjustifiably, Loewen (2005) explained why this issue is important and the social impact on communities, racism, and African Americans. First, this history is worth knowing because it happened and because not being able to live where one wants to live is a violation of human rights. Also, these communities had considerable help through governments, pillars of the communities, and law enforcement on some occasions. Second, the U.S. government and local governments embraced White supremacy and had a hand in helping maintain sundown communities. For instance, it was the U.S. government that created the practice of **"redlining"** (i.e., color coding communities in which red designates areas where banks should not make loans) and supported banks and insurance companies in maintaining sundown towns and communities. If historical societies, chambers of commerce, and public relations offices want to keep something hidden, then whatever it is, it is worth knowing. Third, although Loewen was not equating the two situations, he referenced what Nazi Germany had done to the Jews. There was an effort first to drive them out of their homes, neighborhoods, and towns. Loewen (2005, p. 21) observed that "beginning in 1938, Germany's 'Final Solution' made communities free of Jews in a much more vicious way than anything the United States ever achieved. Still, it is sobering to realize that many jurisdictions in America had accomplished by 1934–36 what Nazis in those years could only envy." Fourth, sundown towns help perpetuate current racism. Many Whites never had any experiences with African Americans and often see them in stereotypical ways. When Whites live in sundown communities, go to sundown schools, and work in sundown jobs, it is easier for them to oppress and discriminate against African Americans and fault African Americans for not advancing like other ethnic groups. As stated by Loewen (2005, p. 17), "as soon as we realize that the problem in America is White supremacy, rather than black existence, or black inferiority, then it becomes clear that sundown towns and suburbs are an intensification of the problem, not a solution to it. So long as racial inequality is encoded in the most basic single fact in our society—where one can live—the United States will face continuing racial tension, if not overt conflict."

A Retreat for Lesbians and Gays in Mississippi

In 1993, a group of women who portrayed themselves as radical lesbian feminists from Hattiesburg, Mississippi, purchased a hog farm in Ovett, Mississippi, a town with a population of about 200 people. They purchased this land with the intent to convert it to a retreat for oppressed groups, but mostly for lesbians, and it was to be called Camp Sister Spirit. When word spread that an outside group of lesbians had come to the community to create a retreat, the community mobilized itself to prevent the women from opening this retreat. Additionally, verbal threats were telephoned to the women, who were told that they would be killed and the Ku Klux Klan would burn a cross on their property. Used as a hunting lodge after the hog farm went out of business, the women's property was showered on occasions with gunshots fired by nearby hunters (Greene, 2003).

Greene (2003), employing Mary Daly's (1978) sado-ritual syndrome, studied the behaviors of both the women of Camp Sister Spirit and the community of Ovett. The **sado-ritual syndrome** consists of seven observable characteristics or patterns:

1. The sado-ritual syndrome begins with an obsession with purity.

2. There is a total erasure of responsibility for the atrocities performed through such rituals.

3. Ritual practices have an inherent tendency to catch on and spread.

4. Women are used as scapegoats and token torturers.

5. The syndrome includes a compulsive orderliness, obsessive repetitiveness, and fixation upon minute detail, which divert attention from the horror.

6. Behavior which at other times and places is unacceptable becomes acceptable and even normative as a consequence of conditioning through the ritual.

7. There is a legitimation of the rituals by the rituals of objective scholarship despite appearances of disapproval. (Daly, 1978, pp. 131–133)

This syndrome was applied to wide-ranging rituals directed at women and furthered by religious, cultural, and institutional influences, such as witch burning, genital mutilation in Africa, Indian suttee, Chinese foot-binding, and American gynecology. More current practices would include honor killings in Arab countries and woman burning in India. However, sado-ritual syndrome can be applied not only to wide-ranging oppressive practices against women but also to "the patriarchal struggle to keep women oppressed [which] repeats these patterns in the smaller, often isolated battles lived out each day in real time by real women" (Greene, 2003, p. 87). The events that occurred in Ovett, Mississippi, were not ritualistic in a pure sense like African genital circumcision and the traditional Chinese practice of binding women's feet, which has not been done since the early 20th century. Therefore, Greene did not use the sado-ritual syndrome as if the actions against the women were purely ritualistic, but the syndrome provides a unique framework for analyzing the politics of the events.

Pattern 1 Analysis: The sado-ritual syndrome begins with an obsession with purity. Greene (2003) found direct and indirect references to purity in the dispute regarding Camp Sister Spirit. Opponents of the camp frequently voiced that the Ovett community had a right to keep out "undesirable," "immoral," and "abominable" influences. Further, community meetings ignored the social services that were planned for traumatized women and focused exclusively on the issue of homosexuality, showing at one point a film of individuals opining their views that homosexuality is a sin and an affront to God. A sign near the women's property stated that no men were allowed on the property, and this sign was stated as evidence of depraved activities occurring on the property. Ovett was portrayed as a community close to becoming a siege community where more and more homosexuals would come and attempt to seduce the young girls and women of Ovett into becoming lesbians. Opponents of the camp contended that Ovett's purity as a rural community, imbued with family values, was being threatened by Camp Sister Spirit.

Pattern 2 Analysis: There is a total erasure of responsibility for the atrocities performed through such rituals. To erase the responsibility of the patriarchal society, proponents of patriarchy direct women to perform the rituals or blame the victims. Critics of the women of Camp Sister Spirit accused these women of moving to Ovett in order to incite the community and thereby attract national publicity for the gay community and the gay agenda. Op-ed pieces in the Hattiesburg newspaper leveled these charges in several articles, pointing out the number of interviews women from the camp granted to television stations and their appearance on *Oprah*. The newspapers portrayed residents of the community as innocent victims of the gay agenda. In a sense, the Ovett community's actions could be seen as self-defense. Further, many of the charges and threats allegedly made to the women were fabricated by them to make the community appear to be prejudiced and bigoted. For example, the women called the sheriff to report that someone had put a dead puppy in their mailbox. However, some residents of Ovett circulated a story that the women killed the puppy and put it in their mailbox and then called the sheriff.

Pattern 3 Analysis: Ritual practices have an inherent tendency to catch on and spread. Greene (2003) noted that the patriarchal elite have a tendency to cause the spreading of ritualistic practices, and she observed some of this in the dispute, although the character of it was different from that of other applications. When the dispute became public, the harassment increased. Intoxicated men would come on the property and shout hatred of gay people. Reportedly, a school bus stopped in front of the property, and the children all began to shout, "Faggots!" While both sides used the media, Greene wrote that women of Camp Sister Spirit used it as a defensive measure and Ovett community spokesmen used it as an offensive weapon. According to Greene, the Ovett community sought state and national help to stop the construction of the camp, and some conservative religious organizations offered their support. At the same time, the women of Camp Sister Spirit reached out for help from national gay rights organizations.

Pattern 4 Analysis: Women are used as scapegoats or token torturers. Greene (2003) observed that while most of the visible opponents of the camp were men, women also denounced the camp in op-ed pieces and on television. These women denounced feminism and lesbians and stated that they were concerned about their daughters. Speaking in religious tones and reflecting patriarchy, the women stated the role of men and women in the Bible and that the man was the head of the household. Thus, lesbians and feminists were anti-God. One woman in an op-ed piece suggested the sending of several "Steel Magnolias" to take on the lesbians at their retreat. In addition, critics used these women as scapegoats as was routinely done with other minorities. These same critics blamed minorities and the liberal government for the fact that almost every White male in the community could not find a job or was having a difficult time economically. Similarly, many residents of Ovett blamed the women of Camp Sister Spirit for the moral decline of American society.

Pattern 5 Analysis: The syndrome includes compulsive orderliness, obsessive repetitiveness, and fixation upon minute detail, which divert attention from the horror. Greene (2003) stated that the real issue in this dispute was whether women could build a retreat for other women on private property. However, this issue was bogged down and lost in the hysteria about lesbians and feminists. Both sides had used military terms against the other. The dispute became "a war," and sides were "under attack" and "under siege." Opponents of Camp Sister Spirit were called "terrorists." In this charged and countercharged environment, the real issue was lost. Normally, people can do whatever they want on their property in a rural area, and restrictions do not exist like one would find in a community suburb or a condominium complex where bylaws prevent owners from doing whatever they want. However, it seemed implausible that in a rural community where an owner had purchased land, the owners could not construct living quarters for a retreat. A retreat for women wanting to get away from urbanization would be no different from White males buying land for hunting retreats and cabins for hunting or wilderness camps that have been constructed for emotionally disturbed adolescents. However, this simple question of women's ownership rights was obscured in the debate.

Pattern 6 Analysis: Behavior that at other times and places is unacceptable becomes acceptable and even normative as a consequence of conditioning through the ritual. Greene (2003) found that the climate of the community was very intolerant as demonstrated by the schoolchildren, supported by the bus driver, shouting, "Faggots!" to the women of Camp Sister Spirit. One male stated that the hatred of homosexuals was so strong in the county that he could kill two homosexuals and get away with it, but he was convicted and jailed for this threat. Greene, however, noted the silence of gays and lesbians in the area as supportive of this proposition. Many gays and lesbians near Camp Sister Spirit were too afraid to publicly support the camp, and some were angry with the women of Camp Sister Spirit for purchasing this land and inciting the people. Hence, while nearby gays and lesbians were against homophobia, they were silenced by the rituals occurring in the area.

Pattern 7 Analysis: There is a legitimation of the rituals of objective scholarship despite appearances of disapproval. Greene (2003) analyzed the coverage of the dispute by the media and a professor of communication at a university. Community readers portrayed the paper as unbiased and just reporting news, but this was not the case with the Hattiesburg newspaper. A scholarly content analysis detailed this newspaper's clear bias against the women. For instance, most discussions about the camp included a discussion of the women's sexuality, and "feminism" was used interchangeably with "lesbianism." Another nearby newspaper, the *Laurel Leader-Call,* was clearly in support of opposition to the camp and instigated individuals to oppose the camp and the women associated with it.

In conclusion, Greene (2003) stated that her analyses of the conflict in Ovett revealed that this issue was more about women's rights than it was about lesbians' rights in particular. She stated also that her analyses showed how "a hostile, homophobic atmosphere of public opinion can influence social and political action in a community" (Greene, 2003, p. 103).

Latino Immigrants

As stated in the introduction, one of the problems facing rural communities is social upheaval, but there is some degree of dispute on the issue. This social upheaval is mostly due to the relocation of immigrants and migrant workers into rural communities. Dalla and Baugher (2001) described dramatic changes in the rural Midwest, in a 10-state region, which occurred as immigrants and migrant workers came to rural communities looking for employment in the meatpacking industry and agricultural fields. Based in the Midwest, three meatpacking corporations (Iowa Beef Processing, which was acquired by Tyson Foods in 2001; Cargill's Excel Corporation; and ConAgra's Monfort Inc.) slaughter and package 80% of the beef cattle in the United States and supply a very high percentage of meats sold in most supermarkets. These companies also handle a very large portion of the pork industry. To help process these animals for human consumption, immigrants from Asia and Mexico have been recruited to rural Midwestern communities. One rural community, for instance, went from 2% immigrant population to 20% in a very short period (Dalla & Baugher, 2001).

The growth of the food processing corporations and the recruitment of immigrants have altered communities and affected the social, physical, and economic well-being of individuals, families, and communities. Some immigrants feel that they are not welcome and have been subjected to discrimination, while some long-term residents resent the changes to their communities and believe that immigrants cost the communities money in terms of public assistance and crime. As a result, anti-immigrant flyers have been circulated in some communities that are tainted by hatred and racism (Dalla & Baugher, 2001). Further, the Ku Klux Klan has entered some communities hoping to exploit these tensions. In Worthington, Minnesota, 30% of the population of 11,000 residents are immigrants, and many work at Swift & Company, which employs 2,300 workers. Both the mayor and the hospital administrator want to see immigrants stay in the community, but some long-term residents do not. The mayor wrote to the governor seeking help for immigrants with procuring identity cards, such as Social Security cards and birth certificates. Instead, the governor asked for a study of the number of immigrants in Minnesota. When he was informed that there were 85,000 illegal immigrants in Minnesota, costing the state $188 million a year, he advocated for the enforcement of immigration laws, tough penalties for possessing a false identification card, and fining employers who knowingly hired illegal immigrants. In sum, the governor was advocating for means for making illegal immigrants feel unwelcome in Minnesota and coercing them to leave (Keen, 2006).

In an in-depth ethnographic study, Chávez (2005) interviewed Latinos and Whites in an anonymous rural California community to learn how each group constructs, maintains, and contests community and to discuss how social class and ethnicity affect their construction. Whites in this rural community viewed Latinos as disengaged from the community, but Chávez contended that Latinos had formed **communities of need** as a vehicle for securing the same social, cultural, and economic support that was denied them by Whites who controlled the community resources. Previous research on rural communities focused on interaction and place, but Chávez (2005, p. 315) integrated those two concepts with ethnicity and class to understand "how subaltern interactions challenge the dominant agrarian view of community in rural places." Fallaciously called Yodoy, California, this small rural community has always demonstrated Latinos' collective actions to improve their socioeconomic status as they live their daily lives. In the 1930s, Latinos in the community formed the *Comité de Campesinos*. This committee helped immigrants access housing, health care, and employment. It also offered assistance in mitigating the abuse of Latino workers. Many people also participated in other activities promoting the Latino culture, including school activities, church, and community. When a Latino school won a state education award, it was ignored and dismissed by Whites because the school embraced bilingual education. Whites were also resentful when they saw the Mexican flag flying in Latino communities and at Latino events and saw these behaviors as treasonous to the United States and their rural community.

Whites who had been residents of the community for years held an idealized agrarian culture and promoted a sense of homogeneity and cohesiveness among Whites before Latinos flooded the community. Whites accused Latinos of not wanting to participate in the community fully and demonstrate their embrace of the American culture. According to Chávez (2005, p. 332),

In Yodoy, Mexicans were actively engaged in crafting both formal and informal communities of need. They were involved in voluntary associations, the school, the Catholic Church, Parent Teacher Club, the park, and the Comité. Involvement in these activities helped Mexicans develop their own sense of community which has often mobilized around ethnic pride. However, their efforts were often dismissed because community continues to be anchored in agrarian ideals—namely, the privileging of family farm life in which social relations among townspeople were defined by longevity, homogeneity, and proximity. Additionally, white residents' control of community-based resources allowed them to officially ascribe themselves the label of "neighborly," "caring," and "actively engaged citizens." In contrast, Mexicans were categorized as "uncaring citizens" who did not strive to develop trust, cooperation, and mutual respect necessary for the reproduction of community ties because of their lack of involvement in mainstream organizations and social groups dominated by long-term white residents. Additionally, white residents' control of local recourses, such as the publication of the local history book and annual dinner, helped to effectively erase Mexicans from the history of the town despite the fact that they were now demographically the majority in most of California's rural landscape.

As Chávez (2005, p. 315) determined, "immigrant members defined community participation based not only on collective involvement in formal organizations, but also on the daily routines of survival and the maintenance and preservation of cultural practices in an environment in which immigrants were seen as second-class citizens."

Conducting qualitative research involving Whites and Latinos similar to Chávez (2005) but examining differences in the language the two groups used, Sizemore (2004) found a similar pattern in a rural southern Illinois community. In 1980, persons of Spanish origin made up 0.4% of the population, but in 2000, persons of Spanish origin constituted 13% of the population. Whites in Appleton, a pseudonym, acknowledged that Latinos suffered discrimination and experienced inequality, but compensation for Latinos was unfair to Whites. As told to Sizemore (2004, p. 544), "Appleton's Anglo residents asserted that they were not 'racist,' but rather, they merely insisted on 'fair' rules of the game and that they were capable of handling the Hispanic 'problem' in their own way, without the intrusion of outsiders." Sizemore characterized Whites as exhibiting an ethnocentric and paternalistic attitude toward Latinos, and these two patterns were couched in dualistic language. According to Sizemore (2004, p. 546), for White Appleton insiders, problems associated with ethnic inclusion were linguistically evaded in one of two ways, each of which was arguably a tactic to avoid claims of discriminatory treatment. Insiders talked as if (1) the town's ethnic affairs were "fine" and therefore should be left alone, and (2) when there were problems, they stemmed from outsiders pushing for unwarranted ethnic entitlements. Insiders wanted to be left alone to deal with the community's ethnic transition as they saw fit, using disclaimers effectively by asserting, "We treat Hispanics well, but it's those 'outsiders who cause trouble.'" Outsiders simultaneously perceived little interest among whites in the community for the welfare of Hispanics, arguing that the town "plodded along," "didn't care about Hispanics," and that "more needed to be done for them." The language used to describe interethnic relations smacked of paternalism because when all the "niceties" were boiled away, both insiders and outsiders regarded Hispanics as needing care: for insiders, Hispanics were cared for adequately and should be free from further intervention; for outsiders, Hispanics were cared for poorly, needing more assistance as they settled. Both groups were keenly aware of how to discuss race relations; no informants wanted to convey a lack of understanding what they knew was a sensitive issue, and they worked hard to avoid "racist," "bigoted," or "paternalist" labels. Ultimately, Hispanics were caught in the middle of a linguistic dual between insiders and outsiders that effectively stifled their voice by stripping them ideologically from the decision-making processes associated with integration. (Sizemore, 2004, p. 546)

NEGATIVE ASPECTS OF RURAL COMMUNITIES

As stated, rural communities have more poverty than urban communities, and their high poverty worsens their other problems. For instance, extensive and comprehensive resources are not likely to be found in most rural communities. As an example, medical specialists are not likely to be found in most rural communities, and thus when patients in these areas have serious medical injuries, they are likely to be transported to urban hospitals. In addition, other social services may be more difficult to secure in rural communities, such as shelters for battered women. Further, in some rural communities, the educational systems lack resources. Texas and Ohio, for instance, have not solved their funding for school systems, and often it is the rural schools that suffer. The Supreme Courts in both states have ruled that these states' funding of school systems violates their respective constitutions. Due to inadequate funding, rural schools in Ohio must ration chalk and toilet paper.

POSITIVE ASPECTS OF RURAL COMMUNITIES

Despite the issues that rural communities have, they also have qualities that attract some individuals. For instance, many African Americans are returning to the South and are relocating in rural areas. These rural areas are also attracting retirees. Rural communities offer a more relaxed living style with less traffic and often less crime than is found in urban communities. The Amish community, as well as other persons, believes that rural life promotes family and community values. If one is looking for a less corrosive environment in which to rear a family, a rural community may be a better option than a large urban area.

CONCLUSION

We began this chapter by discussing the apparent neglect of rural communities. Some social policies in the past have been specifically targeted at urban communities where the new media are primarily located. Rural communities have a high amount of poverty, and efforts to address this poverty were not implemented until the 1960s. We discussed a number of characteristics of rural communities, including single mothers in poverty and the effects of poverty on families and adolescents. We highlighted TANF issues in rural communities. We discussed elderly persons including Native Americans, African Americans, Latinos, and disabled elderly persons. This chapter also included some discussions about delinquency in rural communities as well as differences in how professionals, including social workers, interact in a rural community. A number of theoretical discussions were included to help us understand rural communities better. We noted that some rural communities benefit from retirees as some retirees have a strong economic impact on communities. Then, we ended this chapter with a discussion about prejudice in rural communities toward African Americans, lesbians, and Latino immigrants.

In terms of world systems, an understanding was provided by an examination of Duncan's (1999) research on the haves and have-nots, which correlate with the core and periphery zones. Migration has been part of the world systems theory since the 1500s, and it is replicated in the current debate regarding Latino immigration to the United States. As stated earlier, world systems theory has been adapted to include sex and racial bias. We saw proof of such linkages with the discussions about the retreat in Mississippi for lesbians and the ethnic cleansing of African Americans from some communities in the early 1900s.

Key Terms and Concepts

Brain Drain

Comité de Campesinos

Communities of Need

Gemeinschaft-Gesellschaft Gavotte

Great Change Hypothesis

Redlining

Sado-Ritual Syndrome

Sundown Towns

CHAPTER 9

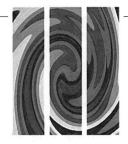

International Communities and Human Behaviors

IINTRODUCTION

A chapter on international communities is difficult to write because no chapter—and no book—can capture all the countries, islands, and territories of the world and then discuss human behaviors in all these environments. The United Nations reports that it has 191 member countries but concedes that there are additional countries that are not members (United Nations, 2006). Scholarly literature on developing countries, particularly Africa, is sparse. According to Dodoo and Beisel, in 2005 the American Sociological Association had two subsections that provided avenues for sociologists who researched Asian/Asian American and Latino populations. Although there were sections within the sociological academy, such as subsections on racial and ethnic minorities, there was nothing on Africa (Dodoo & Beisel, 2005). Further, the two flagship journals in sociology, *American Sociological Review* and the *American Journal of Sociology,* had published three articles on Africa in the prior 15 years, two of which were written by the same author (Dodoo & Beisel, 2005). In Western social work journals, there are a few articles on Africa but nothing close to what is published yearly on other countries. African countries, more than other poor countries, are besieged by what some observers call the triple threat—weakened capacity of stabilized governments, HIV/AIDS, and **food insecurity**, providing significant problems for scholars to research and publish academic articles and books.

ABC News evening anchor Charles Gibson created a stir when he criticized NBC news anchor Brian Williams for going to Africa. A magazine story quoted Gibson as saying, "Now he's [Brian Williams is] in Africa. I don't know why you do that. Why the hell do you go to Africa?" (Bauder, 2006, p. C6). Though Gibson denied that he meant to suggest that Africa was not important for the news media (Bauder, 2006), many feel the episode is yet another example of how journalists generally disregard Africa.

The United Nations, Human Rights Watch, and Amnesty International frequently report on glaring and troublesome **human rights** violations and thus unmet human needs. Both Amnesty International (2005a) and Human Rights Watch (2005a) have documented human rights violations such as the forced eviction of entire communities representing millions of people. In addition, Amnesty International (2000) has documented sex trafficking of women from Russia to Israel. This chapter relies heavily on these reports to convey to you theories and knowledge about families, categories, and communities and how economic and social forces impact these systems around the world. For the most part, this chapter focuses on developing countries as these countries have the greatest human needs.

THEORIES AND KNOWLEDGE ABOUT
SELECTED INTERNATIONAL COMMUNITIES

Poverty and Its Effects

Poverty is a worldwide problem (Chetwynd, Chetwynd, & Spector, 2003). Of people in Nicaragua, 45% live on less than $1 a day, and 80% live on less than $2 a day (Global Partnerships, 2009); in El Salvador, 31% of people live on less than $1 a day, and 58% live on less than $2 a day (Global Partnerships, 2009); of Hondurans, 24% live on less than $1 a day, and 44% live on less than $2 a day (Global Partnerships, 2009); and a full 60% of people in Malawi survive on a dollar a day or less (Wines, 2005a). International organizations have also documented significant levels of poverty in Eastern European and Asian countries, including Albania, Armenia, Azerbaijan, Belarus, Bosnia-Herzegovina, Bulgaria, Croatia, Estonia, Georgia, Hungary, Kazakhstan, Kosovo, Kyrgyz Republic, Latvia, Macedonia, Moldova, Poland, Romania, Russia, Slovak Republic, Serbia and Montenegro, Tajikistan, Turkey, Ukraine, and Uzbekistan (World Bank Group, 2005).

Most professionals agree that poverty is worst on the continent of Africa and that the Western world has played a major role in keeping Africa in poverty. According to Sachs (2005, p. 189),

> little surpasses the western world in the cruelty and depredations that it has long imposed on Africa. Three centuries of slave trade, from around 1500 to 1800s, were followed by a century of brutal colonial rule. Far from lifting Africa economically, the colonial era left Africa bereft of educated citizens and leaders, basic infrastructure, and public health facilities. The borders of the newly independent states followed the arbitrary lines of the former empires, dividing ethnic groups, ecosystems, watersheds, and resource deposits in arbitrary ways.

During the Cold War, emerging African leaders espoused nationalism and sought assistance from the Soviet Union in renegotiating treaties and contracts that tapped Africa's minerals and energy deposits for the benefit of the West. The United States and European countries sought to prevent such activities. The Central Intelligence Agency (CIA) and Belgian agents assassinated the prime minister of the Congo, Patrice Lumumba, and installed a puppet leader who deferred to the West. Throughout Africa, heads of state who preached socialism or self-determination for their countries engendered the wrath of the West, and the West provided military and economic support for any opposition leaders dedicated to the overthrow of the governments of African countries that did not subjugate themselves to the West and Europe. Almost every African political crisis has the fingerprints of the United States behind it (Sachs, 2005).

While the United States was long willing to destabilize Africa, it rejected long-term development in Africa. In the 1960s, the U.S. government rejected a Marshall type of plan for Africa as it had done for Europe and Japan following World War II. Africa's poverty stems mainly from its historical exploitation, interference, and neglect. Critics state that Africa's poverty is caused by its incompetent and corrupt governments, but numerous countries have corrupt governments without the poverty that Africa has (Sachs, 2005), such as many Eastern European countries including Bosnia, Slovakia, and Poland (World Bank, 2009). As Sachs (2005, p. 208) emphasizes, "the combination of Africa's adverse geography and its extreme poverty creates the worst poverty trap in the world."

Poverty is correlated with and exacerbates other human problems, such as health (Becker, 1995), famine, food shortages, and malnutrition. The following sections discuss the linkages of poverty to other human needs.

Food Insecurity and Famine

A corollary of extreme poverty is the need for food. Of course, some countries may have a sudden need for food due to a natural disaster or diseases that have crippled crops (World Food Programme, 2005b), but some countries regularly need food, indicating that poverty is the cause. Thus, the amount of food aid delivered to countries is a marker for poverty. According to the World Food Programme (2005b), the leading threat to health since humankind first appeared on Earth that still exists today is hunger and hunger-related diseases. In 2004, more people died because they were hungry and malnourished than all the people who died from AIDS, malaria, and tuberculosis combined (World Food Programme, 2005b). One out of eight people worldwide does not get enough to eat to stay healthy, and most of these individuals are children (World Food Programme, 2005b). The World Food Programme (2005b) provided food assistance to 80 countries in 2004, representing 113 million persons. African countries received 57% of the food aid, Asia received 26%, the Middle East and North Africa received 15%, and Latin America received 3%.

Illustrative of the dynamics of food problems in Africa, the population of Malawi, a country on Africa's east coast, has a population of about 12 million, and more than one third were need of food in 2005 (Wines, 2005a). A similar hunger problem exists in Zimbabwe, Zambia, Mozambique, Lesotho, and

Swaziland. Although prolonged drought in these countries contributes to the hunger problem, the primary cause is poverty. For example, corn, the main staple in these countries, is grown there and in other African countries. When crops are damaged by drought, African countries turn to the market to buy sufficient crops to carry them through it. These countries may also be affected by what is occurring in the world. As stated in Chapter 1, when Hurricane Katrina closed the New Orleans port, Japan purchased corn from South Africa. Not only did this purchase reduce the amount of corn available to Africans, but the price rose too high for poor African countries to buy it (Wines, 2005a).

The United Nations estimated in 2002 that about 15 million Africans who lived within the horn of Africa were at risk for **famine** (Somerville, 2002). Long periods of drought were the immediate cause, but there were other causes. For example, most African countries cannot produce the amount of food they need for survival and must rely on relatively expensive imports. Foreign food may be available, but African countries cannot afford to buy it. Thus, poverty is a significant factor in the cause of famine in Africa. A Nobel Prize–winning economist, Amartya Sen, attributed the chief cause of famine to poverty rather than African countries not being able to produce enough food. Other factors contributing to famine in Africa are armed conflict, corruption and mismanagement of food supplies, environmental degradation, and African trade policies (Somerville, 2002).

Jenkins and Scanlan (2001) conducted an empirical study of food security, which is connected to the issue of famine, in less developed countries from 1970 to 1990. Food security was operationalized by the amount of food supply and the child hunger rate, which served as the dependent variables. The explanatory or independent variables were the degree of modernization, the amount of economic dependency, the extent of urban bias, the amount of neo-Malthusian pressures (i.e., overcultivation, excessive fertilizer use, deforestation, desert formation, and soil degradation caused by high fertility and population growth), and the degree of militarism (i.e., arms import, ethnic violence, genocide, and civil wars). Their findings led to a number of conclusions. Specifically, they stated that genocide/politicide, civil wars, arms imports, and discriminatory treatment of ethnic minorities were significantly causal for child hunger. To reduce child hunger rates, developing countries needed to increase their political democratization. Thus, developed countries, in order to help developing countries, needed to monitor human rights, impede internal violent conflict, and prevent arms shipments. Jenkins and Scanlan concluded that food surplus does not prevent hunger in developing countries and that hunger is a political problem that requires political solutions.

Civil Wars

In 1983, several International Symposium of Children and War–commissioned studies found that 5% of all casualties of World War I, 50% of all casualties of World War II, and 80% of all casualties of the Vietnam War were civilians. In current conflicts, over 90% of casualties are civilians, and characteristically, these casualties come from the poorest regions of countries. Clearly, terror is used to exert social control by upsetting the foundations of grassroots social, economic, and cultural relations. Terrorists' goal is often to affect the population, not to capture territory. Central is the employment of psychological warfare to subdue a population, and "atrocity, including public execution, disappearances, torture and sexual violation, is the norm" (Summerfield, 1995, p. 17). Further, terrorists target persons who are engaged in work that reflects shared values, such as religious leaders, teachers, and community leaders. These tactics and strategies, employed in areas with subsistence economies, can be devastating. For instance, in Cambodia in the 1970s, the Khmer Rouge targeted educated people for extermination, including medically trained individuals. This carnage resulted in the decimation of the heath care system and deepened poverty in Cambodia (Dugger, 2006). Since the 1980s, this pattern of civil conflict and war has been seen in Mozambique, Angola, Sudan, Somalia, El Salvador, Guatemala, Nicaragua, Peru, Afghanistan, Iraq, Indonesia, the Philippines, Sri Lanka, territories occupied by Israel, and the former Yugoslavia (Summerfield, 1995).

In earlier wars, the victims tended to be mostly soldiers, but war casualties today, especially in developing countries, tend to be women and children. Spurred by ethnic and religious conflict, national liberation, counterinsurgency, and guerrilla warfare, wars destroy a country's infrastructure and lead to deforestation, landlessness, drought, and famine. Further, research reveals that large numbers of children in war-torn countries have witnessed very destructive violence, and some children have been taken from their families and forced to fight as child soldiers. The violent environments in which many children live indicate a need for interventions to prevent or ameliorate the negative psychosocial effects of violence and war-related trauma on children. However, programs to address the psychosocial effects of violence on children in war-torn countries are relatively scarce, and scant attention is given to this issue in relief and development programs (Boothby, 1996). For instance, in 2009, child psychologists in Gaza and Israel stated that as a result of the bombs and shellings on Gaza some children will never recover mentally. Dr. Iyad Sarraj referenced a boy he treated 5 years ago, who during the night was a secondary casualty for a house next door where Israel believed Hamas fighters were. The boy felt something wet on his arm. It was his sister's flesh. According to Dr. Sarraj, "He realised it was the flesh of his sister who was blown into pieces. He was in such a state. He couldn't eat or smell meat for three years after that. I am sure he will suffer some kind of long-term psychological impact" (Sharp, 2009, ¶ 6). Continuing, Dr. Sarraj stated that "these children need help more than anyone. They look frightened, horrified, bewildered. They need a lot of attention but they can't receive it because their families are so terrified" (Sharp, 2009, ¶ 9). The Women's Commission for Refugee Women and Children (2008) noted that youth living in camps for over 20 years near the Thailand/Burma border lacked education and training. It follows then that individuals in these camps who were likely forced to flee their homes initially due to civil or military conduct have not received mental health intervention. The behaviors described here give rise to crimes against humanity and constitute human rights violations.

Human Rights Violations and Crimes Against Humanity

In 1864, the Geneva Convention was established to protect prisoners captured during wartime (Rubin, 2006). After the Civil War, the warden of the infamous Andersonville prison camp for Union soldiers, Henry Wirz, was hanged in 1865 for what were essentially crimes against humanity, although that term likely was not used then. The warden was responsible for atrocious living conditions that led to the deaths of thousands of Union soldiers and the arbitrary hangings and executions of prisoners for violating the camp's rules and regulations. Wirz was the only person to be executed after the Civil War for his behaviors during the war (Stewart, 2005). During serious conflicts between humans, there has long been a practice of holding some individuals responsible for extreme behaviors that occur even during war. For instance, after World War II, numerous Nazi leaders were sent to prison in the Soviet Union, and some Nazi leaders and officers were hanged not only for how brutal they were to Soviet soldiers and civilians but also for their behaviors in the death of millions during the Holocaust.

Following World War II, international criminal law was invoked to try Germans at Nuremberg and Japanese in Tokyo for crimes against humanity. From the 1940s to the early 1990s, no international criminal court was used. In 1993, the United Nations created the International Criminal Tribunal for the former Yugoslavia. Also, the International Criminal Tribunals were created for Rwanda, Sierra Leone, East Timor, and Cambodia for crimes against humanity and genocide (Hagan & Levi, 2005). Some countries have adopted laws that give them jurisdiction over crimes against humanity that occur in other countries. Italy created such a court called the Rome International Criminal Court that has jurisdiction over the most serious crimes of concern to the international community, including (a) the crime of genocide, (b) crimes against humanity, (c) war crimes (see Appendix B), and (d) the crime of aggression (see Appendix B) (Rome Statute of the International Criminal Court, 1999). Below are definitions of genocide and crimes against humanity.

Genocide means any of the following acts committed with intent to destroy, in whole or in part, a national, ethnical, racial, or religious group: (a) killing members of the group, (b) causing serious bodily or mental harm to members of the group, (c) deliberately inflicting on the group conditions of life calculated to bring about its physical destruction in whole or in part, (d) imposing measures intended to prevent births within the group, and (e) forcibly transferring children of the group to another group.

Crimes against humanity are defined as any of the following acts when committed as part of a widespread or systematic attack directed against any civilian population, with knowledge of the attack: (a) murder; (b) extermination; (c) enslavement; (d) deportation or forcible transfer of population; (e) imprisonment or other severe deprivation of physical liberty in violation of fundamental rules of international law; (f) torture; (g) rape, sexual slavery, enforced prostitution, forced pregnancy, enforced sterilization, or any other form of sexual violence of comparable gravity; (h) persecution against any identifiable group or collectivity on political, racial, national, ethnic, cultural, religious, or other grounds that are universally recognized as impermissible under international law, in connection with any act referred to in this paragraph or any crime within the jurisdiction of the Court; (i) enforced disappearance of persons; (j) the crime of apartheid; and (k) other inhumane acts of a similar character intentionally causing great suffering or serious injury to body or to mental or physical health.

Some International Examples of Human Rights Violations and Crimes Against Humanity

Bhutan

Bhutan is a small country just above eastern India to the east of Nepal. In the early 1990s, the Bhutan government refused to recognize the claims of Nepali-speaking Bhutanese or made it extremely difficult to prove citizenship. The Bhutan government's position is that these people were voluntary migrants or forfeited their citizenship when they fled the country. The Bhutan government targeted more than 100,000 Nepalese people, forcing them to leave their homes and to flee from violence (Human Rights Watch, 2003). These Bhutanese were forced to live in seven refugee camps located in Nepal.

The Nepalese government and the Office of the United Nations High Commissioner for Refugees (UNHCR) jointly administered the seven refugee camps. According to Human Rights Watch (2003, p. 8),

> Bhutanese women who are living as refugees in Nepal, many for more than a decade, confront not only the hardship of life in refugee camps, but also the injustice of gender-based violence and discrimination. Refugee women and girls have reported rape, sexual assault, polygamy, trafficking, domestic violence, and child marriage in the camps. Women suffering domestic violence are unable to obtain safety or their full share of humanitarian aid because of discriminatory refugee registration procedures and inadequate protection measures. The registration system also prevents married refugee women from applying for repatriation or rations independently and prohibits them from registering children not fathered by a refugee.

Although UNHCR and the Nepalese government were supposed to be helping refugees, their policies have in effect increased the hardships for women. Refugee women indicated to Human Rights Watch activists that their burdens were made more difficult because of the camps' use of unfair registration procedures and ration distribution policies. Camps issued ration cards in the name of the male in the household. If a woman was separated from her husband, she could not access the ration cards or get a ration card in her name. Basic humanitarian items, such as soap, blankets, and stoves, were withheld from noncardholders. Some women were able to get humanitarian items by making informal arrangements with the camps' overseers, either for sexual favors or relying on overseers' compassion. Further, these women could not get their own housing when they were separated from their husbands and had to rely on living with relatives in already cramped quarters (Human Rights Watch, 2003).

Sierra Leone

On September 20, 2005, Richard Dicker, director of international justice programs for Human Rights Watch, wrote a letter addressed to members of the Group of Interested States for the Special Court for Sierra Leone, which was created by the United Nations and the government of Sierra Leone. The letter pleaded with members to financially support a tribunal to address serious crimes committed during the Sierra Leone civil conflict. During the civil war, which lasted 11 years, extreme brutality and crimes occurred. These consisted of widespread amputations, rapes, abductions, murders, and the mass displacement of Sierra Leone citizens (Dicker, 2005). Rebels from the Revolutionary United Front and the Armed Forces Revolutionary Council, who were fighting the government of Sierra Leone, committed the majority of these crimes. However, government forces also committed crimes. Most victims were civilians. Estimates were that tens of thousands of people were killed and countless more were attacked. More than 25% of the population was forced to leave the country (Human Rights Watch, 2004a).

Uganda

In 1986, a Ugandan rebel group fighting the government seized power. Defeated soldiers from the government retreated to their birthplace in northern Uganda and formed the Lord's Resistance Army (LRA) to continue their fight with the new government, which then became the Uganda People's Defense Forces (UPDF). One of the ethnic groups in northern Uganda, the Acholi, and its spiritual leader, Alice Lakwena, created the Holy Spirit Movement and fought the government forces. When the Holy Spirit Movement was defeated by the UPDF, it was blended into the LRA. After 16 years of fighting, the Ugandan government announced "Operation Iron Fist," which was designed to flush the LRA from northern Uganda, where the government believed the LRA was hiding among the people and receiving aid and support. The government's goal was to drain the area as one might drain a pond—with the communities being the sea and the rebels being the fish. As a result, close to 2 million people were forced to leave their homes and live in refugee camps. Because of the longevity of this conflict, one human rights investigator called it the greatest humanitarian tragedy in the world. This civil war destroyed the economy of northern Uganda and exacerbated the impoverishment of the people of the region (Human Rights Watch, 2005e).

Refugees in the camps suffered in a variety of ways. First, the conditions of the camps ranged from poor to appalling. In addition, there was little hope for work, education, health care, or the likelihood of returning to their homes. Refugees were forced by severe need to leave the camps to farm, get water, and gather firewood. Members of the LRA killed people who were thought to be aiding the government, mutilated some people, abducted children to serve in the army, and raped women. The government failed utterly in fulfilling its duty to protect the people in the camps. Instead, government troops committed atrocities against this refugee population, including indiscriminate killings and rapes of women in the camps. Some women and girls were abducted from the camps and taken to military leaders, where they were assigned to military leaders for sexual purposes. Children abducted into the army were required to kill civilians as a demonstration of their commitment to the cause. Although many abducted persons escaped from their captives, many persons did not and stayed with the LRA for years. UNICEF has estimated that about 20,000 children have been abducted in the 19 years of conflict. According to one observer, the abductees "remain psychologically and often psychically scarred by the treatment they suffered and were forced to inflict—as are those who, although not abducted, witnessed killings, rapes and other violence by both sides" (Human Rights Watch, 2005e, p. 13).

Extensive human rights abuses on both sides in the conflict forced this displacement. Based on international humanitarian law (the laws of war), the civil war in northern Uganda was considered a noninternational (internal) armed conflict. Thus, it is governed by Article 3 common to the four Geneva Conventions of 1949, the Second Additional Protocol of 1977 to the Geneva Conventions, and normal international law. Pertinent to both sides, international humanitarian law proscribes indiscriminate or direct assaults against civilians and civilian property and mandates the humane treatment of all combatants captured in battle. In addition, the Ugandan government was obligated to adhere to regional human rights laws, such as the International Covenant on Civil and Political Rights and the African Charter on Human and Peoples' Rights (Human Rights Watch, 2005e).

Chad

In 2005, a Belgian judge issued an international arrest warrant for the former dictator of Chad, Hissène Habré, who was living in exile in Senegal. Habré had ruled Chad with U.S. and French support from 1982 to 1990. During that time, the Reagan administration viewed Chad as a counter to the leader of Libya, Muammar Qaddafi. So, the United States supported Habré's takeover of Chad and provided critical training and financial backing. During this time, Habré was committing crimes against various ethnic groups in his country, including the Sara, the Hadjerai, and the Zaghawa. According to a 1992 Truth Commission report, the Habré government committed more than 40,000 murders and numerous imprisonments and torture of believed dissenters (Human Rights Watch, 2005d).

Darfur

The conflict in Darfur, a Western area of the Sudan, became bloody in 2003, but the likely root of the conflict probably goes back years. The Sudan is composed of two major groups: Arabs who head the government—many of whom live the life of nomads—and Africans who are mostly farmers but some of whom oppose the government and are considered rebels. A central source of current conflict is the camel. Many nomads prize the camel as essential to their way of life. Camels provide transportation, meat, and milk. Moreover, they are used as a means of currency, for they provide dowries to the families of their future wives. When camels, as well as goats and cows, encroached on Africans' farming fields, major trouble occurred. When Arabs and Africans were more friendly, they engaged in trade—meat and milk for vegetables and farming crops. Now that conflict has occurred, trading has ceased, and trade routes have been blocked by the African rebels. Moreover, African rebels have been raiding nomads' camels, causing the camels' owners considerable stress. The nomads believe that a nomad who sees his camel being stolen must attempt to retrieve the animal even if he might lose his life. A decision to do nothing incurs the wrath of others in the community, and a wife would be justified in leaving her husband if he failed to attempt to retrieve a stolen camel. The government has armed nomads who have formed militia groups so that they can fight the rebels, and some of them go out on raids, earning them the name of Janjaweed—a robber who appears on horseback or camelback. Those nomads who are armed to protect their herds resent the lack of help from the international community as they see most aid going to farming communities. While some organizations are attempting to help the nomads, Africans' problems are much more severe because genocide is occurring (Lacey, 2005).

A number of countries in the international community have declared that genocide has occurred in Darfur. In September 2004, the Parliament of the European Union, by an overwhelming vote of 566 to 6, concluded that the conduct of the Sudan government was tantamount to genocide. Former Secretary of State Colin Powell and German Defense Minister Peter Struck stated similar views in September 2004, as the U.S. Congress affirmed unanimously that genocide was occurring in the Sudan. Several influential nongovernment agencies, including the U.S. Holocaust Memorial Museum, the U.S. Committee for Refugees, Physicians for Human Rights, Africa Action, Genocide Watch, and the Campaign to Prevent Genocide, have concluded that genocide is occurring in Darfur. Despite these universal declarations that genocide is occurring, neither the United Nations nor the countries declaring the conflict to be genocide have taken any action to stop it. The strategy from the international communities was to tell the Sudan government in Khartoum to disarm the Janjaweed. Further, the international communities relied on a vastly unmanned African Union to protect the African people of Darfur, but it could not protect itself from the Janjaweed and thus could not protect refugees. Moreover, attacks on aid workers disrupted the delivery of humanitarian aid to approximately 3.5 million people in refugee camps (Reeves, 2005).

Nicholas Kristof, a reporter for *The New York Times* who has visited Darfur and spoken to refugees and aid workers, has written numerous columns detailing the genocide and rapes that were occurring there (Kristof, 2005a, 2005b, 2005c) and criticizing the United States and the United Nations for not stopping it. According to Kristof, since 2003 the international community has treated the genocide as tolerable because the numbers were not great enough at that point (Kristof, 2005a). Kristof has recounted the history of the U.S. complacency toward genocide. In 1915, Woodrow Wilson looked askance at the Armenian genocide. Aware that Jews and others were being slaughtered in death camps in Germany, President Roosevelt vetoed the bombing of the rail tracks leading to those camps. President Clinton, who has apologized to the Rwandan people, did nothing when the Tutsis were being slaughtered by the Hutus. President Bush followed a similar pattern by his nonaction in Darfur (Kristof, 2005b). Kristof (2005b) listed a number of steps that could stop the genocide in Darfur. Although the federal government has declared that genocide is occurring in Sudan and Darfur, it has cut funds for paying the outmanned and understaffed African Union that is designated as the vanguard in stopping the Janjaweed and protecting African refugees. Kristof said that the president should quickly find the $50 million that was cut—a very paltry sum considering what was spent domestically and internationally and considering the gravity of the problem. Last, there were reports that China was underwriting the genocide in Sudan (Kristof, 2005c), but the United States appeared to be reluctant to criticize China due to its current and future economic relationships.

Rwanda

In April 1994, a genocide occurred in Rwanda. Estimates were that more than 800,000 Tutsis and moderate Hutus were killed by more militant Hutus in a mere 100 days. This slaughter constituted roughly 8,000 killings a day. The Interahamwe, a so-called civil defense group of young men who were committed to the Rwandan government, was responsible for many of these killings. The Interahamwe went door to door, searching for Tutsis and moderate Hutus to kill. Members also set up roadblocks and killed anyone who did not have proper papers identifying him- or herself as a Hutu. The

United Nations had some peacekeepers and troops in Rwanda, but they were primarily charged with helping the White people leave the country when the killings began. The slaughter ended only when the Rwandan Patriotic Front, a military group opposed to the government, gained a strategic advantage that forced the governmental leaders to go into exile (Temple-Raston, 2005).

Men, women, and children were summarily killed, and many women were raped first and then killed. Some persons speculated that nearly every woman and adolescent girl who survived the genocide was raped, resulting in many of them becoming pregnant. These children were known by several names, such as the *enfants non désirés* (unwanted children), *enfants mauvais souvenir* (children of bad memories), children of hate, or little Interahamwe. The women and girls who were raped and permitted to live were told that they were being allowed to live so that they would "die of sadness" (Temple-Raston, 2005). Simply, these women were depressed for having these children and were shunned in the community.

Bosnia

The Republic of Bosnia-Herzegovina consisted of Serbs, Croats, and Muslims. After Josip Tito, the country's leader, died in the 1980s, Slobodan Milosevic, a Serb, came to power. Milosevic stoked conflict between the Serbs and Muslims, reminding Serbs of atrocities against them years before. The Serbs attacked the Croats and later the Muslims. Systematically, the Serbs shot and killed Croats and Muslims and buried them in mass graves. When the conflict was over, over 200,000 Croats and Muslims had been killed (United Human Rights Council, 2009).

In the town of Srebrenica, the Serbs rounded up numerous men and boys over 13 years of age and killed them, burying them in mass graves. First, the Serbs shelled the town and had Serbian snipers shoot the Muslims inhabiting the town. The Serbs systematically raped and impregnated women and girls in an attempt to destroy the Muslim culture. From 1992 to 1995, a physician treated refugees, people who had relatives killed, and people who had witnessed the horrors of genocide in Bosnia. Observing daily bombings, murders, and the loss of loved ones placed extreme stress on all individuals. Children who were separated from their parents and forced to live with strangers for security reasons were subjected to a "sudden change in life style and anticipation of an uncertain future [which] exerted a profound effect in their psychological functioning" (Vrtikapa & Anisfeld, 2003, p. 163). Children of Bosnia reacted to their traumatic experiences in a variety of ways. Some children reacted immediately to their trauma, but other children went weeks, months, and years before displaying dysfunctional behaviors. Preschool children regressed markedly in their development. Older children had vague physical complaints. These older children, in addition, had a tendency to restlessness, saw no need to do school homework, questioned authority, and used drugs and alcohol. Many of the children had nightmares and flashbacks of seeing dead people. A 7-year-old girl had become terrified of sudden noises. For a significant period of time, the sight of meat made her nauseous, though she ate meat prior to the start of the genocide. The girl's 15-year-old brother, who along with his sister had left his family when the killings started, did not have contact with their parents for 3 years. He resented the life he was forced to undertake—assuming the role of a parent for his sister. Although he said he was thankful for his parents wanting him and his sister to be safe, he also resented them for what had occurred. When he had an opportunity to speak with his family by telephone 3 years later, he refused to do so (Vrtikapa & Anisfeld, 2003).

Human Rights and Cultural Clashes

In some countries, cultural practices collide with human rights and are difficult to erase. In November 2005, a comprehensive protocol on women's rights went into effect in 15 African countries as part of an endorsement of human rights. These countries passed laws protecting women, but these laws were seldom enforced, and in rural communities, the **"living law of custom"** prevails. Essentially, local custom laws prevail over laws passed by government. Since 1965, female circumcision has been against the law in Guinea, punishable by life imprisonment and death, but no one has ever been prosecuted for the crime, although about 99% of girls have been circumcised (LaFraniere, 2005). Proponents of the laws blame the legal inaction on men, but some women are also opposed to changes in customs. In Uganda, where 17% of the women are Muslim, Muslim women protested proposed legislation that barred polygamy, female circumcision, minimum ages of 18 for women to marry, and equal rights in marriage and divorces. In South Africa, Zulu leaders resisted attempts to outlaw virgin testing. Both Zulu men and women stated that such a ban was an attack on ancient tribal culture and family values, stating that virgin testing was an umbilical cord between modern Zulus and their ancestors. Another leader stated that virgin testing was one way to protect African values against the decaying effects of Western civilization. One Zulu tester, Nomagugu Ngobese, stated that she has recognized victims of sexual assaults through testing and that women's advocates in Africa and the West were devaluing their customs. The testing ceremony takes on a religious aspect with prayers to ancestors, bathing in a moonlit river, and the slaughter of a goat (LaFraniere, 2005). A compromise law was passed, which bans virgin testing for girls 16 and over without their consent, but community pressures persuade some families to have their daughters tested (LaFraniere, 2005).

Connection of Crimes Against Humanity to Social Work

Unknowingly drawing parallels to social work and human behavior in the social environment, An-Na 'im (2001, p. 87) declared that "human rights, in a generic sense, can be seen as a framework for an adequate response to the profound social concerns of persons and their communities. This primarily procedural sense of human rights is about creating and maintaining 'the space' for individuals and groups to achieve justice, personal security and well-being, general political stability and economic development, and so forth." Within sociology, human rights are not one of the areas that are typically investigated by sociologists. But there are areas of sociology that represent human rights. Freedom from discrimination, which is an overarching human rights tenet, embraces such fields in sociology as citizenship, national identity, education, stratification and mobility, and health policy. Freedom of speech and association, both human rights, are germane to political participation and labor. Race, sexuality, gender, and children's issues are major focuses of human rights scholars. The association between civil society and the state concerns the international expression and national implementation of human rights in all societies and concerns sociology. Human rights interests are also important to intervening fairly to rival demands for economic and social justice, identity, and communal independence globally. These concerns coincide with sociology over globalization and postcolonial power relations, social movement, development, accountability of transnational corporations for labor relations involving indigenous people, and respect and appreciation for the environment (An-Na 'im, 2001). An-Na 'im is a sociologist, but what he wrote exemplifies the social work principles discussed in Chapter 1.

GLOBAL CIVIL SOCIETY AND INTERNATIONAL HUMAN RIGHTS COLLABORATION

Drawing on social movement literature and world society theory, Tsutsui and Wotipka (2004) sought to provide a macrosociological explanation for the proliferation of the international human rights movement by studying human rights international nongovernmental organizations (HRINGOs). They considered individuals' involvement in HRINGOs as participation in the international human rights movement. Historically, after World War II, political leaders among the allies stressed that human rights should be a foundation for the new world order after the defeat of Nazi Germany and Japan. Their views and philosophy were included within the Charter of the United Nations in 1945 and the Universal Declaration of Human Rights in 1948. However, the advancement of human rights internationally was slowed considerably due to a power struggle between the United States and Russia, oppression in the colonies controlled by the West and the East, and racism within the countries of the West and the East (Tsutsui & Wotipka, 2004). As interest in human rights waned in the West, nongovernment activists and "Third World" countries, inspired by their yearning to eradicate Western colonialism and to establish a goal for racial equality in the postcolonialism era, picked up the human rights banner. Their activism led to an increased focus on human rights within the United Nations' agenda. Their efforts led to the creation of the International Convention on the Elimination of All Forms of Racial Discrimination in 1965 by the United Nations. But after many of these developed countries criticized developing countries for domestic human rights violations within their countries, these developing governments' enthusiasm for human rights began to wane again in the 1970s. However, nongovernment human rights activists and organizations began to proliferate and strengthen their involvement in organizations such as Amnesty International and Human Rights Watch. Many of the human rights reports produced by Amnesty International and Human Rights Watch, such as those in the next section, were investigated and written by members in developing countries (Tsutsui & Wotipka, 2004).

Tsutsui and Wotipka (2004) found that international variables explained the amount of variation within countries for citizen participation in international human rights activities. These variables were more important than domestic variables, except for domestic political opportunities. In the earlier period (i.e., prior to 1965), endogenous variables, rights, had a very significant positive effect on human rights memberships, but in the later period (i.e., after 1965), exogenous variables, consisting of memberships in international government organizations and international human inflows, had a strong, positive effect on membership in HRINGOs. Simply put, developed, democratic countries led the increase in HRINGOs after World War II, but countries with linkages to global civil societies, although they had weak economies and nondemocratic governments, led the surge in memberships in HRINGOs in later years. The results of Tsutsui and Wotipka's study had implications for international social movements, revealing that networking by individuals in democratic countries with individuals in developing countries can increase activism in these developing countries.

Domestic Violence in Russia

After the breakup of the former Soviet Union and the transition to the new Russia, information and knowledge increased internationally about social problems occurring in this country. Under the old Soviet Union, the image presented to the world was that family and society were ideal under socialism and communism, and negative reports were nonexistent in the state-controlled Soviet news media. However, after the breakup of the Soviet Union and the transition that occurred in its government, reports emerged, for instance, of the prevalence of domestic violence. Zakirova (2005), former director of the state-run Family Centre in the town of Ufa in the Bashkortostan Republic, provided some comparisons of domestic violence involving homicide between Russia and the United States. According to her, in 2000, the United States had about 1,300 homicides that could be classified as resulting from domestic relationships, but for the same year, there were about 15,000 similar homicides in Russia (Zakirova, 2005), although the United States has double the population of Russia (FitzGerald, 2006). The rates of women killed in the United States due to domestic violence were 5 per million women, compared to 100 per million in Russia (Zakirova, 2005). By all measures, woman killing is much higher in Russia than in the United States.

Zakirova (2005), who also holds a doctoral degree, studied the causes of domestic violence in Russia. She stated that domestic violence got worse after the breakup of the Soviet Union and attributed this social problem to an increase in alcohol use, which was high under the former Soviet Union but rose even higher after the breakup of the country. According to Zakirova (2005, p. 77), "Russia occupies a 'leading place' among developed countries of the world in alcohol consumption and the Bashkortostan Republic not only has the highest level of drinking but is also one of the leading Russian regions for mass production of alcoholic products." Under the former Soviet Union, women worked outside the home, but after the breakup of the Soviet Union, most women did not work outside the home. Consequently, women became more economically dependent on men, making it more difficult for them to leave an abusive relationship (Zakirova, 2005). Another factor in preventing women from leaving an abusive relationship was the lack of housing. Even if a woman was able to obtain a divorce without being killed, she was forced to stay in the same apartment with the divorced husband as housing is a very scarce resource in Russia (FitzGerald, 2006; Zakirova, 2005). Besides the human rights violations that occur in Russia involving domestic violence, there are negative effects on children who witness this violence, leading to what Zakirova (2005, p. 82) called social orphanhood or a "sharp increase in child and teenager drug addiction, prostitution and crime." Juvenile delinquents later become organized criminals, and "domestic violence is a major cause of social orphanhood" (Zakirova, 2005, p. 82).

Because of the severity of domestic violence in Russia, in 2005, the Ford Foundation awarded a grant for $250,000 to evaluate the impact of domestic violence in Russia, develop new strategies, and test a new model of intervention. This grant was awarded to the National Center for the Prevention of Violence, which is called ANNA and is located in Russia. In 2006, ANNA hosted Russia's first international conference on domestic violence (FitzGerald, 2006). Although Russia has its own culture, it relies heavily on the network of services for battered women in the United States. Thus, it is using the courts to change Russian laws, creating shelters for battered women, advertising in the media that domestic violence is wrong, and using some social workers who have desks in police stations (FitzGerald, 2006; Zakirova, 2005).

Human Sex Trafficking

The CBS program *48 Hours* learned that sex trafficking was a billion-dollar business in Europe and that it was possible to buy a woman or young girl as a sex slave. Thus, the program sent a reporter undercover with a hidden camera to Bucharest, Romania. The *48 Hours* reporter was directed to a woman and informed her that he wanted to buy a woman and take her back to the United States. She assured him that the girl would have papers that would get her into the United States. The reporter approached another seller, a woman and her business partner husband, who promised to sell the reporter a young blond woman. A young blond woman was brought to him, and she was made to undress to show that her body was not damaged. The reporter and the traffickers agreed to a price of $1,000, with the deal being consummated the following day. The following day, the traffickers wanted $2,000, but they compromised on $1,800. The woman then was taken to a shelter that served women who had been victimized by sex traffickers (Leung, 2005).

Although sex trafficking has received publicity that suggests that these types of activities are occurring mostly in developing countries, that is not the case. The U.S. State Department estimated that about 50,000 women and young girls from foreign countries are bought to the United States each year to work in the sex industry (Amnesty International, 2000). Further, the International

Organization for Migration has estimated that about 500,000 women and girls are trafficked in Western Europe alone (Amnesty International, 2000). Trafficking of women has been primarily from South to North but is increasing from North to South. The trafficking of women has been reported from Latin America to Southern Europe and the Middle East, from Southeast Asia to the Middle East and Central and Northern Europe, from South America to North America and Europe, from Eastern Europe to Western Europe, and from the former Soviet Union to Israel (Amnesty International, 2000).

International to the United States

Landesman (2004), an investigative reporter for *The New York Times*, undertook a 3-month investigation in the sex trafficking industries. He learned that one of the byproducts of the collapse of the Soviet Union and the emergence of democracy was extreme poverty. Young women were promised jobs in the United States or France, but these jobs were nonexistent. Talent agents, purporting to be looking for models and actresses to send to Hollywood, California, searched for attractive women. These women were funneled through Mexico for training and indoctrination to the United States as sex slaves. In addition, young women and children from Mexico were kidnapped and forced into the sex industry. These women and girls were not prostitutes per se because they did not earn any money themselves and were often sold to pimps and organized criminal groups. Estimates were that between 30,000 and 50,000 girls and women in the United States were virtually slaves (Landesman, 2004).

A house in Plainfield, New Jersey, kept several girls between the ages of 14 and 17 who were rarely seen in the neighborhood. On some occasions, they would be allowed to go to a nearby store for candy. Sex houses have been found in New York, Atlanta, Detroit, San Diego, and numerous other American cities. These young girls and women, who often do not speak English, are beaten and psychologically destroyed. Their lives and those of their families are threatened if they try to leave. Some Mexican sex traffickers have used the Internet to solicit bids for selling women and have shown videos of young girls being sexually molested to entice customers. Because of corruption by some Mexican law enforcement officers, little has been done on the Mexican side of the border. A Mexican law enforcement agent stated that 10 high-ranking Mexican officials received $200,000 a week to split up in return for protecting the sex industry there (Landesman, 2004).

Congress passed the PROTECT Act of 2003, which penalizes individuals who come to or leave the United States for the purpose of having sex with children. This law was used to convict a Canadian who brought a young woman to Vermont, apparently drugged her, and photographed himself performing sex acts on her. Four years later the tape was discovered in Canada, and an investigation revealed that it was shot in Vermont. The man pled guilty to transporting a minor in foreign commerce for the purpose of engaging in illegal sexual activity and to sexual exploitation of a child (*United States v. Alan Simmons*, 2003). Congress established minimum standards that foreign countries must accept to avoid sanctions by the United States. These foreign countries (a) should prohibit severe forms of trafficking in persons and punish acts of such trafficking; (b) should—for the knowing commission of any act of sex trafficking involving force, fraud, or coercion; in which the victim of sex trafficking is a child incapable of giving meaningful consent; or which includes rape or kidnapping or causes a death—prescribe punishment commensurate with that for grave crimes, such as forcible sexual assault; (c) should, for the knowing commission of any act of a severe form of trafficking in persons, prescribe punishment that is sufficiently stringent to deter and that adequately reflects the heinous nature of the offense; and (d) should make serious and sustained efforts to eliminate severe forms of trafficking in persons (22 U.S.C.S. § 7106, 2005).

Last, Congress mandated that the secretary of state issue an annual report to the appropriate subcommittee by June 1 of each year naming (a) any foreign country that failed to achieve the minimum standards for the elimination of trafficking, (b) any foreign countries to which the minimum standards for the elimination of trafficking are applicable and whose governments do not yet fully comply with such standards but are making significant efforts to bring themselves into compliance, and (c) any foreign countries to which the minimum standards for the elimination of trafficking are applicable and whose governments do not fully comply with such standards and are not making significant efforts to bring themselves into compliance (22 U.S.C.S. § 7107, 2005).

Terrorism

Sociologists have begun to undertake studies of terrorism since the attacks on New York City and Washington, DC, on September 11, 2001. Terrorism occurs in a number of countries, but the United States is primarily concerned with terrorism from Islamic groups that target Americans' interests. Turner (2005, p. 297) makes some key observations about sociologists' current interest in Islam:

Islam has been placed firmly on the agenda of modern sociology of religion by the crisis in international relations and the clash of civilizations. Political Islam is the consequence of the social frustrations resulting from the economic crises of the global neoliberal experiments of the 1970s and 1980s. The demographic revolution produced large cohorts of young Muslims, who, while often well educated to college level, could not find economic opportunities to satisfy the social aspirations that had been inflamed by the rise of nationalist governments in the period of de-colonization. Broadly speaking, we can identify four periods of Islamic political actions in response to the social and cultural crises that were associated with foreign domination and civil struggles. These religious movements that have critically attacked contemporary political and military weakness appeal to the early community of the Prophet as a model of social order, and hence they have been labeled "fundamentalist." In the nineteenth century, these reformist movements which were hostile to both traditional folk religion and the external Western threat included Wahhabism in Arabia, the Mahdi in the Sudan, the Sanusis in North Africa, and the Islamic reform movements of Egypt. The second wave of activism came in the 1940s with the growth of the Muslim Brotherhood in Egypt, and the third movement began in the aftermath of the Arab defeat in the 1967 war with Israel. It reached a crescendo with the Iranian Revolution in 1978–9 and the Russian incursion into Afghanistan. The contemporary wave of resistance commenced with the Gulf War in 1990, when the presence of American troops on Saudi Arabian soil created the groundwork for the formation of Al-Qaeda networks.

In 2003, the U.S. Department of State issued an advisory caution to Americans warning them not to travel to Zanzibar. This advisory warning was based on reports that extremist Muslims were recruiting youths in Zanzibar to fight in Iraq and Afghanistan and because the persons who bombed the U.S. embassies in Nairobi, Kenya, and Dar es Salaam, Tanzania, in 1998 had come from Zanzibar. Brents and Mshigeni (2004) conducted 40 in-depth interviews with members of the two largest youth political movements in Zanzibar. They traced the racial history of Zanzibar and colonialism, which helped explain current political views. Zanzibar is made of three racial groups—the Shirazi who are descendants of the intermarriages between Africans and Arabs dating back to the 7th century, Arabs from Oman, and Africans from the mainland.

In the late 1800s, colonial powers divided up Africa, and Zanzibar was a British protectorate. During World War II, the British exacerbated racial divisions in Zanzibar by instituting a food rationing system in which Europeans received food first, Asians (e.g., Indians, Pakistanis, Goans, and Arabs) were second, and Africans were last. This discrimination, combined with other discriminatory behaviors, created resentment and alliances to counter colonial rule and Christianity in the region. Youth groups had mobilized in response to their perceived beliefs of the religious oppression of Arabs by Africans. One group leader reported that he and his followers love and adore Osama bin Laden, who is viewed very positively because he is helping advance their social movement. Osama bin Laden is "fighting against cultural domination and exploitation by western powers and he is representing Islamic people who are oppressed and impoverished by the world system" (Brents & Mshigeni, 2004, p. 68). The goal of many of the youth organizations is to free Tanzanian society from the dictatorship of Christianity. These youths do not see themselves as terrorists and believe that to achieve their goals of freeing the people from the government, they must use violence because the government has given them no other alternative (Brents & Mshigeni, 2004).

However, sociologists have criticized the political definitions of terrorism and have discussed it from a sociological perspective—void of the emotions and outrage stemming from the 9/11 attacks. Sociologists have studied social movements, and violent conflict and terrorism fall within these areas. Brents and Mshigeni (2004) emphasize three points about terrorism. First, terrorists are rational individuals. Second, terrorism constitutes one form of activism to achieve political objectives. Third, terrorism is relational, and its emergence and trajectory must be comprehended in relation to other groups and in reaction to beliefs about perceived dangers. Boyns and Ballard (2004, p. 22) went further and provided a testable theory to explain terrorism:

> Terrorism is most unlikely when two groups, or societies, have relatively equal levels of power and prestige. It is more likely to occur when one group becomes more powerful than another and an imbalance of power exists. For example, when one group violates the negative prestige of another less powerful group, this is one indicator of potential for terrorism actions. As a matter of course, this violation should result in the loss of power and prestige in the less dominating group and a shift in the power balance that results in an increase in the potential for terrorism.

Extending this theory further, Boyns and Ballard (2004) offered six propositions or variables to explain terrorism, and these consist of Counter Hegemony (CH), Resource Mobilization (RM), Counter Institutionalization (CI), Power Prestige (PP), Ritualization (R), and Solidarity (S). Put into a regression equation, it is represented by the following:

$$T \text{ (Terrorism)} \approx f \text{ (CH + RM + CI + PP + R + S)}.$$

This equation is simpler than it may appear. Suppose you work at a very large child welfare agency, employing about 500 social workers. Each social worker has a salary, which would be the dependent variable. However, you and your coworkers make different salaries because some of you have considerable years of experience, while others have only a few years or months on the job. Also, differences exist in the amount of education, ranging from a bachelor's degree to 2 years post-master's. What if you wanted to predict or explain each caseworker's salary knowing only his or her amount of education, years of experience, race, and gender? You would collect the data for each variable and set up an equation similar to the equation above. You would be able to determine how important each variable is and to say that each year of education was worth $1,487, each year of experience was worth $1,875, an employee's gender was associated with a $500 difference, and being White was worth $100. After conducting the research, you could request any employee's sex, race, years of experience, and amount of education and predict that employee's salary. The equation cited above does something similar. It predicts whether a country is more likely to have terrorism based on knowledge of the variables on the right side of the equation.

Globalization

In Chapter 3, we presented a discussion by Chase-Dunn (2001) in which he argued that globalization is not a new phenomenon and has existed since early civilization. With him, the main difference is that technology (i.e., airplanes, shipping lines, and communications) has made it possible to engage in economic activities farther away and much faster. Other social scientists have offered similar observations that individuals have been traveling to other countries to trade and exploit economic opportunities for centuries (Bamodu, 2006; Blau & Moncada, 2006). Other social scientists have argued that *globalization* is a term that has replaced other terms, such as *postmodernity* (Perry & Maurer, 2003). Dine (2006), a human rights activist, stated that the proliferation of international companies is another means of oppressing the poor. Bamodu (2006) conceded that the practice of international trading is centuries old. Globalization, in his view, is different because of the speed of transactions across borders. Another distinctive feature is the amount of diversity among individuals engaged in globalization.

Proponents of globalization argue that it is good for growth, and growth is good for the poor (Bamodu, 2006). In a similar vein, former President Ronald Regan stated that "a rising tide lifts all boats," but someone remarked that if one does not have a boat, he or she would drown. Extending this logic, critics of globalization contend that the claimed benefits to the poor are a myth, and globalization is a further and more advanced illustration of Western imperialism (Bamodu, 2006). Globalization has been linked to more social problems (Navarro, 2002), such as prostitution and sex slavery (Sanchez, 2003) and forced immigration (Sadowski-Smith, 2002). Blau and Moncada (2006) added to this discussion how a form of globalization was devastating to Mexico. The United States forced Mexico to import the United States' subsidized genetically modified (GM) corn and have the government of Mexico encourage *campesinos* (farmers) to go to work in American factories that had been built and relocated in Mexico. Simply, *campesinos* would not need to farm because the United States would supply them with corn, a major Mexican staple. Looking for cheaper labor still, many American companies relocated their factories to China. The price of the GM corn rose, and the living standard of rural Mexicans was substantially lowered. Moreover, the GM corn does not produce seeds, which required already poor farmers to buy them.

As stated by Blau and Moncada (2006, p. 91):

> The cumulative effects of U.S. policies in Mexico were devastating: unemployment, higher food costs, and dependence in high-priced seeds. Additionally, having created economic havoc in Mexico, the United States increasingly implements a schizophrenic migration policy—both encouraging migration and militarizing the border with Mexico. More generally, it is becoming increasingly evident that the worldwide liberalizing economy is creating massive social upheavals and economic destitution. To survive the onslaught, many children and women have no choice but to become virtual slaves in the sex trade, the healthiest of poor families must migrate, and many turn to terrorism against the West as ways of defending their own societies against the massive social and cultural destruction that is caused by the marketization of entire societies and social relations within them.

Others have discussed different theories of globalization. For instance, Sadowski-Smith (2002) has theorized about the effects of globalization on the U.S./Mexican border. Central to globalization is the view that there should be minimal state intervention into the operations of private corporations. To help free private corporations from controls by nation-states, global institutions, such as the World Trade Organization, the International Monetary Fund, and the World Bank, have helped influence and coerce developing countries' policies. Examining Mexico, Sadowski-Smith found that corporate profits increased under globalization, and the seeds of a rising middle class in Mexico were planted. The North American Free Trade Agreement (NAFTA), a product of globalization involving the United States, Canada, and Mexico, has caused and aggravated social problems in Mexico. As stated by Sadowski-Smith (2002, p. 5),

> in the absence of enforceable labor, human rights, and environmental protections, NAFTA has contributed to a rise in environmental pollution, accelerated de-industrialization and job loss in the United States and Canada, and promoted a sharp drop in Canadian currency. The agreement has also set the context for the emergence of far inferior working conditions in the assembly factories of Mexican border towns, which in turn, has evolved into transit points for a growing number of northbound immigrants. Market-driven processes of globalization as inscribed in NAFTA have thus not simply worked around and weakened national borders, but they have also helped to strengthen structural inequalities between the three participating countries and among various segments of their populations.

ECONOMIC AND SOCIAL FORCES ON AND BY INTERNATIONAL COMMUNITIES

Social Institutions That Empower Citizens in South Africa

In South Africa, researchers studied the dynamics of civil society, social capital, and voluntary organization participation among Black South Africans after the end of apartheid. Viewed as critical to the maintenance of democracy, civil society represents the institution that serves as an intermediary between citizens and the state. Social capital represents the total efforts of citizens to sustain the network of voluntary associations within a society. Social capital that accrues from participation in voluntary associations is used to bargain and negotiate with the government for the benefit of citizens. Next to social capital in importance are social trust, the flow of information, and the norms and sanctions necessary to keep the network viable (Klandermans, Roefs, & Olivier, 2005).

Civil society associations are carried out by organizations. Thus, civil society associations' focus is on civil society organizations. Civil society organizations represent the instruments for political participation. They involve the public in the political decision-making processes through organizational behaviors, consisting of providing information, involving members, and coordinating activities. Further, civil society organizations watch politicians and their political decisions and pressure politicians to act in accordance with the organizations' wishes. Civil society organizations create feelings of belonging and connectedness. Based on this definition and explanation, civil society organizations include labor unions, consumer organizations, professional associations, commercial associations, nongovernmental organizations, social movement organizations, cultural and religious organizations, ethnic and communal organizations, and civil organizations consisting of community, neighborhood, and tenant organizations (Klandermans et al., 2005).

Klandermans et al. (2005) were interested in learning what makes individuals contribute to the social capital that is generated in their civil society organizations. Almost 60% of the South African population was energetically engaged after the end of apartheid in at least one civil society organization, with at least half of citizens involved in one particular civil society organization, which was the church. The other half were engaged in two or more civil society organizations. Participation in political parties had the most influence on trust in government and involvement in politics with participation in church organizations having the least influence on trust in government and involvement in politics. Among Black, Asian, White, and Coloured [sic] South Africans, Blacks, participating in two or more civil society organizations, were more likely engaged in civil society organizations. Specifically, 25% to 40% of Blacks were engaged in a civil society organization other than churches. Further, participation in civil society organizations had a major effect on people's favorable assessment of government and on their interest and involvement in politics. South Africans who participated energetically in civil society organizations had a higher level of trust in government than those who did not. In addition, they were more likely to be involved in politics, to vote, and to engage in collective action (Klandermans et al., 2005).

Health Care in Developing Countries

A number of organizations and countries have attempted to improve heath care in developing countries. Among these are Health Net International, which is based in the Netherlands; Save the Children Australia; and the World Bank, with support from Great Britain and the United States. Nonprofit groups that contracted with the government of Cambodia provide a successful model for improving health care. This model was developed after an experiment using random assignments to nonprofit health care programs, and government-run programs revealed that nonprofit programs provided the best services according to a survey from 1997 to 2003. Nonprofit-run programs were able to circumvent government bureaucracy and corruption and provide health care services to poor people in an efficient manner using very basic hospitals and clinics. Because of the success of the Cambodia program, similar programs have been implemented in Afghanistan, the Congo, Bangladesh, Bolivia, and Guatemala (Dugger, 2006).

HIV/AIDS in Developing Countries

The World Health Organization (WHO) and the Joint United Nations Programme on HIV/AIDS (UNAIDS) estimated that 36 million to 44 million people would be living with HIV by the end of 2004, and by 2005 about 30 million people had died of AIDS (U.S. Agency for International Development, 2005). Yearly, 5 million persons are infected with HIV, and more than 3 million die of AIDS (United States Agency for International Development, 2005). Daily, about 14,000 individuals are infected with HIV, and 95% of these individuals live in developing countries (U.S. Agency for International Development, 2005). However, AVERT, an international AIDS charity, provided lower estimates for the end of 2007 based on the estimates by UNAIDS/WHO in July 2008. It reported a range of 30.3 million–36.1 million individuals with AIDS by the end of 2007 (AVERT, 2008).

HIV in Vietnam

In many parts of Vietnam, intravenous drug addiction is a serious social problem, but it has been ignored by the country's communist government (Mydans, 2006). As a result, HIV infection has grown tremendously, inflicting over 250,000 with only about 10% of this group receiving proper treatment (Mydans, 2006). Being HIV positive carries a significant social stigma in Vietnam, and discrimination is rapid as individuals with the disease are fired from their jobs with no legal rights to regain their employment. Because of these problems, one woman who is HIV positive formed a support group for women who are infected, which they call Haiphong Red Flamboyant. They provide critical support for each other and care for each other as members become ill and die. They also volunteer to help other individuals with AIDS. For example, some prisoners with AIDS are transferred to a hospital where they receive very little care. Chained to their beds, these prisoners are forced to lie in filth, and it is the women from Haiphong Red Flamboyant who care for them. The support group is considered a model program and has been expanded in Haiphong and provided governmental and international support to expand to other cities in Vietnam (Mydans, 2006).

Amnesty Practices and Laws

Certainly, this book is about macro issues, but we believe it is necessary to discuss **amnesty** practices and laws because they involve and reflect not only individuals but also categories. For example, U.S. federal law provides that asylum may be granted if a person can show past or future persecution on account of race, religion, nationality, membership in a particular group, or holding a particular political opinion (8 U.S.C. § 1101). However, some individuals are barred from receiving asylum. These include anyone who has firmly resettled in another country before coming to the United States, has ordered or participated in the persecution of others on account of the five protected classes above, was convicted of a serious crime or committed a serious nonpolitical crime outside the United States, posed a danger to the security of the United States, was involved in a terrorist group, or has engaged in terrorist behavior (U.S. Department of Justice, 2005).

In 2001, the immigration court system handled about 271,000 cases involving individuals seeking asylum (U.S. Department of Justice, 2002). In 2005 the immigration courts received 50,753 applications, initially granted 10,164, and conditionally granted 1,573 (Executive Office for Immigration Review, 2006). The courts denied 19,166, and another 29,698 were abandoned, were withdrawn, or had some other undefined outcome (Executive Office for Immigration Review, 2006). These individuals came from 206 countries and territories throughout the world. The top five countries with the most individuals seeking asylum were China (7,540 applications, 1,442 initially denied), Haiti (4,550 applications, 653 initially denied), Colombia (3,888 applications, 1,150 initially denied), El Salvador (3,630 applications, 64 initially denied), and Guatemala (3,366 applications, 140 initially denied) (Executive Office for Immigration Review, 2006). The Transactional Records Access Clearinghouse at Syracuse University conducted a study of 297,240 immigration cases from 1994 to 2005 and found wide disparities in treatment (Swarns, 2006b). The study reported that more than 80% of asylum seekers from Haiti and El Salvador were denied asylum, but fewer than 30% from Afghanistan and Myanmar, formerly Burma, were denied (Swarns, 2006b). Another study by the U.S. Commission on International Religious Freedom found that 80% of Cubans were granted asylum, but only 10% of Haitians and 5% of El Salvadorans were granted asylum (Swarns, 2006b).

A few cases show issues presented in asylum cases. As an illustration, a young woman from China applied for asylum in the United States, contending that if she were returned to China she would be forced into marriage. The primary issue for the immigration judge was whether a forced marriage would constitute one of the five requirements for asylum (persecution for race, religion, a particular social group, sex, or political opinion). The young woman argued unsuccessfully before the immigration judge that forced marriage would constitute a particular social group. However, the Second Circuit Court of Appeals agreed with her, noting that a particular social group is broad enough to include forced marriage. Submitted in her defense was a U.S. State Department report that detailed the social pressures in many rural areas resulting from the low number of females in Chinese society and the competition for wives and prostitutes. As a result, the poverty in rural areas and demand for females forced some families to sell their daughters into arranged marriages. The Second Circuit Court of Appeals reasoned that persecution on account of a particular social group means persecution that is directed toward an individual who is a member of a group of individuals who share a common, immutable characteristic. This characteristic may be innate, such as sex, color, kinship ties, or some unique circumstances (*Gao v. Gonzales*, 2006).

However, a young woman from Togo was denied asylum based on her contention that she would be forced to be circumcised. In this case, the immigration judge found the young woman not to be credible. She claimed that forced circumcision was a cultural practice in her country, but she had five sisters who were not circumcised because her father refused to OK the procedures; however, her father had since died. After her father died, she claimed that the custom was for her relatives to expel her mother and her out of the village, and she did not know where her mother was. Fearing her relatives would find her and force her to undergo the circumcision, she left Togo and claimed to have met two strangers in Germany, one of whom permitted her to live with him for 2 months and the other of whom helped her acquire a false passport to come to the United States. Finding this story incredible, the immigration judge rejected the petition for asylum (*In re of Fauziya Kasinga*, 1995).

The Impact of Globalization

Sumner (2005, p. 30) studied 20 years of interdisciplinary research on globalization and concluded that "the evidence clearly indicates that corporate globalization has had devastating consequences for rural communities . . . around the world." Corporate globalization does not discriminate between rural and urban areas, but the impact is particularly grave for rural areas because they are more vulnerable. If one were studying Japan, India, or Great Britain, one would observe the same impact for all rural areas. Particularly, Sumner's study focused on the economic, social, environmental, gendered, and cultural effects of corporate globalization on rural communities worldwide. After reviewing the literature on globalization, Sumner turned her focus to the impact of globalization on Canada.

Economic

The economic impact of globalization has deleterious effects on rural communities' way of life. Values typically found in rural communities, such as cooperation, loyalty, sharing, mutual obligation, trust, and solidarity, are significantly weakened or eradicated when the forces of globalization are unleashed in rural communities. These effects are inevitable as a result of the dynamics of capitalism, which seeks profits and then investment opportunities to further increase profits. Taken as a whole, the dynamics of capital underlying the economic impacts of corporate globalization impinge on rural communities as a result of an interrelating milieu involving agro-industrialization, poverty and debt creation, restructuring, deregulation, privatization, changes in employment/unemployment patterns, and commodification/consumption.

Agro-industrialization. Small and medium-sized farms have had a difficult time surviving due to the pressures from globalization. These pressures stem from the transition from agriculture to agribusiness. Agribusiness, also known as the industrialization of agriculture, consists of enormous chemical and biological treatments of the land, monoculturing, habitat destruction, factory farming, and centralized corporate ownership based in areas far from rural communities. Moreover, international trade agreements encourage food production for export rather than for local consumption by individuals in rural communities. In Latin America, agribusiness produces fresh fruits and vegetables for export, causing and exacerbating hunger and poverty where the fruits and vegetables are grown.

Poverty and Debt Creation. In rural communities, poverty and debt are inextricably linked. To understand this linkage, a definition of poverty used by Duncan (1996) is needed, which is the lack of resources needed to permit participation in the activities, customs, and diets usually endorsed by society. Debt creation makes poverty worse and increases the gap between rich and poor. Regardless of whether it is individual or government indebtedness or a developed or developing country's indebtedness, all debts help keep money moving toward the wealthiest. In developed countries, the national debt was designed and constructed to limit social spending and provide impetus for the private sector to grab and profit from public services. For instance, under the Reagan administration, there was a strong push to shift control of public services, such as the U.S. mail, prisons, and social welfare, to the public sector. In a similar vein, indebtedness in developing countries was championed as a means of furthering development. But when countries were unable to pay their debts and needed help, the World Bank and the International Monetary Fund mandated free trade, foreign investments, and ownership of national resources as a condition for debt restructuring. Some countries, such as Kenya, spend more money on the interest from their debts than on the social welfare needs of their citizens. In Canada, debt restructuring contributed to more bankruptcies, unemployment, and homelessness.

Restructuring. Restructuring is a euphemism for explaining changes in the economy. Additional names for restructuring are downsizing, transition from factory jobs to public service jobs, and going south of the border for competitive labor. Besides being a natural phenomenon, restructuring is a misnomer and really is a process of capital reorganization. The interests of capital are central, and the general interests of the public are insignificant. As a consequence, "restructuring has had a devastating impact on the economics of rural areas, especially those communities that depend on manufacturing. Demanded in the name of economic efficiency, restructuring creates cascading repercussions" (Sumner, 2005, p. 38). In the Western Australian Wheat Belt, for example, employment declined by 30% due to rural restructuring and its impact on the employment structure in this rural area. Similarly, restructuring has had a negative impact in Canada, splitting the economy into good and bad jobs with most of the bad jobs in rural areas.

Deregulation. Capital craves freedom from governmental regulations. Fundamentally, deregulation requires the elimination or significant reduction of all constraints and easy participation of investors in foreign markets. An example of such a policy is the North American Free Trade Agreement, which is a form of deregulation and the unrestricted access of capital into foreign countries. On one hand, it may seem beneficial to all, but the stronger countries have an advantage, and some areas suffer. In several countries, NAFTA conferences incur violent protests by grassroots organizations. Sumner (2005, pp. 39–40) declared that

> New Zealand provides a classic study of deregulation. In that country, deregulation included two kinds of reforms: macroeconomic reforms, such as the floating of the exchange rate and removal of import licenses; and sectoral reforms, including deregulation of the agricultural sector. This

deregulation dismantled the structure of subsidies, tax and other fiscal incentives, and the price controls that had been built up to protect farmers. Although initially welcomed by farmers, agricultural deregulation was shortly followed by falling world commodity prices, worsening terms of trade, and rising interest rates and inflation, all of which meant that farmers were faced with dramatically reduced incomes and land values on one hand, and rising debts on the other. At the community level, deregulation had a number of impacts in New Zealand. It resulted in the acceleration of the centralization of services in larger centres, which directly affects rural community members' access to those services.

Privatization. Corporate globalization has an economic impact on the privatization of the public sector so as to generate more markets for private investments and profit expansion. A phrase has been developed for this goal— *neologism of privatization*, which is defined as the process of managing private-sector growth by using public-sector money. Although privatization champions espouse numerous reasons for putting service industries in private hands, such as more efficiency and better services provided to the public, these claims are false (Sumner, 2005). The sole reason for privatization is to put more wealth in private hands. Addressing social inequalities becomes a nonissue, but it might be possible when some industries are in public hands. In 1933, Congress created the Tennessee Valley Authority (TVA), which had as its mission the creation of power, navigation, flood control, reforestation, and erosion control. If the TVA had not been created and if power generation was totally in the hands of private investors, then many rural areas would not have been provided with electricity, for example. Providing electricity to poor rural communities would not have been economically viable.

Changes in Employment/Unemployment Patterns. Changes in employment and unemployment patterns have occurred because of the economic impact of corporate globalization. These changes involve a quest to find indentured, child, slave, and sweatshop laborers. As competition heats up the global market, the number of full-time jobs decreases. Corporate globalization has led to a quest to find the cheapest labor possible that pays the lowest wages and has the least protections for workers. There has been an increase in service jobs at the expense of manufacturing jobs. These service jobs are more likely to be found in urban areas, not in rural communities. Although the wages for service jobs may be low, a little pay is better than no pay. Rural communities do not benefit from the service jobs that have been declared the fruits of a changing economy.

Commodification/Consumption. Commodification is the practice of transforming objects into trade items. After this transformation has occurred, consumers are created. Creating consumers means convincing individuals to purchase what a seller has. Sumner (2005) has argued that rurality has been commodified, creating consumers who either shop at small heritage shopping centers or move to rural communities to experience idyllic living. But rural communities do not benefit from these shopping centers, and rural living is adversely affected (Sumner, 2005).

However, there is a better example of the principle of commodification/consumption to help us understand this concept. Several years ago, the PBS program *Frontline* presented a show on diamonds and how they were made valuable and highly desired. At one time, diamonds and rocks were about the same in terms of value, and rocks may have had more value than diamonds. Diamonds could be picked up off the ground and found in caves just like rocks. In the 1920s or 1930s, a marketing campaign was put into place to turn diamonds into a valuable commodity and to make people desire them and buy them. Representatives for the diamond industry went to Hollywood and asked the most beautiful and respected actresses to wear diamond necklaces in public, and they had commercials made that declared that "Diamonds Are a Girl's Best Friend" and "Diamonds Are Forever." The latter phrase targeted married women, suggesting that a diamond was a representation of everlasting love. As a result, diamonds became more valuable. The diamond industry promoted the ideas that the bigger the diamond in a wedding ring, the more prestige associated with the union, and the larger the diamond necklace, the more significant the relationship or marriage. On Valentine's Day, a number of commercials promote diamond buying. This is also an example of how consumers are created.

This principle of commodification/comsumption occurs in a number of settings, and sometimes poor people are targeted. For instance, cocaine is too expensive for poor people to buy. So, a less expensive form, "crack," was created so that poor people could afford to buy it, and then "crack" was marketed to the poor.

Social

Corporate globalization affects the social lives of individuals in rural communities. Major social changes in rural centers of agriculture, mining, fishing, and forestry have precipitated reciprocal effects in the communities involving decreased access to quality education, health care, and social institutions and unsettling effects of migration to and from rural areas. Further, the stresses and pressures placed on rural communities affect the mental health of the community, and adequate mental health services do not exist to meet the needs of these communities. As Sumner (2005, pp. 49–50) stressed,

> the changes brought on by rural restructuring have also affected the viability of local social institutions, such as churches, sport clubs, and social centres. For example, by 1994 in Western Australia, the majority of rural settlements that were not the administrative headquarters of local shires had not only collapsed commercially but also failed to retrain any viable social institutions, which are so important to the survival of rural communities. Social unraveling was evident in Canada, where . . . sharp increases in domestic violence and in alcohol and drug abuse, and less community involvement in three mining communities hard hit by rural restructuring [were observed].

Environmental

The environment has suffered tremendously as the result of the economic policies of corporate globalization. As a result of economic policies, forests have been overlogged, agricultural lands have been overcropped, wetlands have been overdrained, seas have been overfished, and "just about the whole terrestrial and marine environment [has been] overpolluted with chemical and radioactive poisons" (Sumner, 2005, p. 51). A U.S. waste management company paid a consulting firm to describe communities that would be least resistant to "locally undesirable land use." Put another way, the consulting firm was paid to describe communities that would not likely vehemently protest if a toxic waste dump were put in their communities. The consulting firm's report stated that the best communities would be rural, poor, not well educated, politically conservative, and easily subdued with promises of economic benefits to the community.

Gendered

Corporate globalization has had damaging effects for women throughout the world. At the Fourth World Conference on Women in 1995, delegates concluded that the increasing feminization of poverty worldwide has its roots in the pursuits of market economies. The feminization of poverty is manifested by women's invisibility in global production and their consignment to informal sectors, shadow industries, and housework. Another manifestation of the feminization of poverty is that the market economy has produced many low-paying jobs that are disproportionately performed by women, visible minorities, and immigrants. In Africa, governments have been forced to abandon or lessen their responsibilities for health care, education, public transportation, and other basic needs, and the burden of meeting these needs, especially the securing of food, has largely shifted to women. In Bangladesh, women, because they are believed to be more submissive and less likely to cause trouble, constitute the primary workforce to produce goods for exportation.

Cultural

Corporate globalization supplants countries' cultural legacies from one end of the globe to the other. For their substitutions, globalization proponents imposed a culture upon the masses in which indigenous individuals view themselves as consumers. Also, in rural towns, main streets have been a significant part of the cultures of rural communities, but as residents are taught to be consumers, many come to see travel to the nearby malls as being as important as watching television. In many countries, corporate globalization has changed rural communities' customs. As an illustration, in Europe, rural communities have evolved to be "progressively less self-sufficient and self-contained, and even more open to wider forces—economic, social, political—shaping European life and indeed global development" (Sumner, 2005, p. 57).

The Iraq Wars

A critical aspect of human behavior and the social environment is to elucidate the social and economic forces on and by systems. Here, we discuss the two Iraq wars as they represent conflicts that expose economic, social, and political forces at work. At one time, when Iraq was at war with Iran, the former dictator of Iraq, Saddam Hussein, was an ally of the United States. At that time the United States saw Iran as a foe as it had replaced its leader, who had been a friend of the United States. The United States assisted Saddam Hussein and Iraq militarily to help defeat Iran. At some point, the United States saw Saddam Hussein as an enemy especially when Iraq invaded Kuwait. Kuwait, Iraq believed, was part of Iraq but was partitioned from Iraq years ago by the British. To help galvanize support for the first Iraq war, representatives of Kuwait told lies to Congress and the American people. Specifically, a Kuwaiti woman testified before Congress that the Iraqis had taken incubation equipment for babies and left the babies without critical equipment. The Kuwaiti government hired a number of lobbyists to help convince Americans to go to war with Iraq over Kuwait. The United States created a coalition and drove the Iraqis out of Kuwait. Later, the United States accused Saddam Hussein and Iraq of having weapons of mass destruction, and the U.S. State Department and secretary of state convinced Congress and the American people that Saddam Hussein had to be driven from power. Principally, the U.S. military defeated the Iraqi army, and the new Iraqi government tried, convicted, and executed Saddam Hussein for ordering the execution of over 100 men and boys following a failed assassination attempt. He was executed for crimes against humanity, which were the deaths of 148 Shias. Yet, a number of dictators and leaders have killed far more people than Saddam Hussein, but there has not been any talk of executing them.

One question the Iraq wars, especially the last one, raise is whether these wars were waged for economic and political reasons rather than to protect the United States from terrorism. Iraq has almost as much oil as Saudi Arabia. Saudi Arabia is and has been very friendly to the United States, and the United States needs Saudi Arabia's oil. Toppling Saddam Hussein and facilitating the installment of a new government friendly to the United States would mean that Americans would have access to another major oil-producing country. Chase-Dunn (2001) and Hall (2002) would say that the second Iraq war is a classic example of world systems theory. As Hall stated, early capitalists were always seeking raw materials, labor, and markets, causing them to engage in colonization of many areas of the world. In the process of engaging in these behaviors, social inequality was created. According to Farley (2005), social inequality occurs when there is ethnocentrism, competition for resources, and unequal power.

Negative Aspects of Life in Developing Countries

We have presented a lot about poverty, famine, hunger, civil strife, genocide, and crimes against humanity. These are all negative aspects of many countries. The incidence of HIV is exceedingly high in a number of developing countries, and poverty exacerbates this disease and its spread. Child mortality rates are also exceedingly high. Because these issues were explored early in the chapter, they will not be repeated here. However, we will say that there are a plethora of negative aspects for individuals living in developing countries.

POSITIVE ASPECTS OF LIFE IN DEVELOPING COUNTRIES

While poor countries have a number of issues, there are some positive developments occurring in many international communities. We discuss the abject poverty that exists, but one intervention that has been developed is **microcredit,** which is aimed at assisting poor women. Also, some communities have successfully resisted the exploitation of their communities by business interests.

Microcredit for Poor People

In 1974, Muhammad Yunus, a Bangladeshi economist teaching at Chittagong University, took his students on a field trip to a nearby poor village. During this visit, they heard the story of a woman who made bamboo stools, and she described how she borrowed money to purchase bamboo and the interest that she paid on these loans. As a result of somewhat exorbitant interest payments, her profit margin was one penny. Dr. Yunus realized that if this woman was able to borrow at a much lower rate, she would be able to raise her profits and lift herself above the subsistence level, which she never could do by borrowing money at a high interest rate. Yunus loaned her a small amount, and she was able to repay him while increasing her income severalfold. From this experience, Yunus came up with the idea of microcredit as a means of helping poor people and later developed the Grameen Bank, which provides unsecured loans to poor people. Grameen has 1,084 branches in Bangladesh and has spread to more than 58 countries. About 94% of borrowers are women, and 98% of the loans are repaid. For his invention of microcredit, Muhammad Yunus was awarded the Nobel Peace Prize in 2006 (Yunus Centre, 2007).

In 2006, the international community held a microcredit summit campaign conference to discuss the extent to which it had progressed toward the goal to reach 100 million of the poorest clients. At the end of 2005, 3,133 microcredit institutions reported that they had served 113,261,390 clients (Daley-Harris, 2007). However, only 81,949,036 of these clients were the poorest of the poor, thus falling almost 19 million short (Daley-Harris, 2007). On the positive side, 84% of the nearly 82 million poor were women (Daley-Harris, 2007).

> While not a panacea, microcredit is one of the most powerful tools to address global poverty, and it does so in a way that builds self-esteem in the individual and self-sufficiency in the institution providing the financial services. It works in synergy with other development interventions, such as those that promote health, nutrition, democracy, and education and offers a hand up, not a hand out. Microcredit is an intervention capable of producing a quadruple bottom line. When executed effectively, it can 1)

relieve suffering, 2) bring dignity, 3) become sustainable, and 4) inspire supporters. (Daley-Harris, 2007, p. 1)

Further, Daley-Harris stated that microcredit is an important tool in helping achieve the Millennium Development Goals and a just world.

Lending strong support for microcredit and economic investment in women, Faiola (2008) described the economic and political aftermath of the genocide in Rwanda. Women emerged as Rwanda's most potent economic force. Rwanda "has become perhaps the world's leading example of how empowering women can fundamentally transform post conflict economies and fight the cycle of poverty" (Faiola, 2008, p. A01). Following the genocide, women, who then outnumbered men, were forced to take over farms and became principal farmers. With help from some international organizations, they were able to improve the yield of coffee. Women were more willing than men to reinvest profits in the family, renovate the home, improve nutrition, spend money on their children's education, and increase savings. Women made up the majority of borrowers from microcredit organizations, but men made up 80% of the defaulters (Faiola, 2008). Many men would borrow money and spend it on liquor and women, forcing them to default on loans. One woman, knowing that many people in her village did not have a cell phone, took out a microloan to purchase a cell phone. She then rented the cell phone to her neighbors and repaid her loan within a year. In 2008, women made up 41% of Rwandan businesses (Faiola, 2008). As women gained economic power, they also gained political power. In 2008 women made up 48% of parliament seats in Rwanda, and they held 36% of cabinet positions in President Paul Kagame's administration (Faiola, 2008).

A Successful Intervention to Prevent the Appropriation of a Water Supply

Many corporations are mighty and difficult to change, but they can be persuaded to change some of their practices. The people of Cochabamba, Bolivia, demonstrated this in their fight with Bechtel, an American corporation that seized the water in Cochabamba and even acquired ownership of the rainwater. The people were able to force Bechtel to relinquish its control of the water supply. Also, individuals have taken direct action against the World Bank and the International Monetary Fund in an effort to get them to modify their policies with respect to developing countries. We noted too that American students and professors were helpful in bringing an end to apartheid in South Africa by pressing their colleges and universities not to invest in corporations that do business there. Further, in 2006 solicitations were sent via e-mail for individuals to join in sending 1 million letters to the White House in support of ending the genocide in Darfur.

Efforts to Combat Discrimination

In Hungary, the legal and political systems are being used to combat discrimination and oppression. For instance, Roma, or Gypsies in Hungary, have borrowed strategies used by African Americans to secure their civil rights. Hungary has enacted antidiscrimination laws and wants to impress Western Europe with its sincerity in treating all its citizens civilly. Taking advantage of this propitious period, the Roma have sued the school system, coffee shops, nightclubs, hospitals, and other companies for refusing to hire or serve Roma people. Eventually, the European Roma Rights Centre was able to secure a decision banning discrimination in the school system—a decision that was called the Romas' *Brown v. Board of Education.* Also, a Roma police officer founded the Roma Police Association, which was patterned after the National Black Police Association in 1972 to help Black officers fight racist police practices and foster a more positive relationship with the Black community (Pohl, 2006).

India has emerged as a budding economic power in the world. However, about 327 million people, representing about 30% of the population, live on less than a dollar a day (Moritsugu, 2006). Poverty does not occur because some individuals choose to be poor. India has retained a 2,000-year tradition of dividing its people into castes. The highest caste is for priests and warriors, the middle caste is for laborers, and the lowest caste is for the untouchables, or Dalits. People in the two lower castes make up about two thirds of the population. Rigid enforcement of the caste system tends to occur more often in rural communities, where individuals are punished for behaving in a way deemed inappropriate to their caste. In one rural community, a woman believed to be an untouchable was stripped naked and paraded through the community, and teachers in a rural community refused to eat desserts from a colleague who was born into the lowest caste. The government, to help people in the lowest castes, implemented a quota system in which untouchables received 22.5% of the government jobs and the backward caste, which was a step up from the untouchables, received 27% of the government jobs (Moritsugu, 2006). In addition, a quota system has been implemented for college admissions. Both policies have engendered considerable criticism among individuals in the highest caste (Moritsugu, 2006).

International Criminal Court: Punishing Leaders for Crimes Against Humanity

During serious conflicts between humans, there has long been a practice of holding some individuals responsible for extreme behaviors that occur even during war. As stated earlier in the chapter, during the U.S. Civil War, the warden of the infamous Andersonville prison camp for Union soldiers, Henry Wirz, was hanged following the war essentially for crimes against humanity. The warden was responsible for atrocious living conditions that led to the deaths of thousands of Union soldiers and the arbitrary hangings and executions of prisoners for violating the camp's rules and regulations. In 1865, Wirz was the only person to be executed after the Civil War for his behaviors during the war (Stewart, 2005). But he was not the only person to be punished for inhumane treatment during wartime.

At the prompting of the United Nations, the Rome Statute created the International Criminal Court in 1998 and held its first session in 2003. The International Criminal Court had two essential goals: (a) to prevent crimes against humanity, genocide, and war crimes and (b) to punish those responsible for crimes against humanity, genocide, and war crimes (Rubin, 2006). A case may be brought to the International Criminal Court by any of three methods. First, a particular country may make a referral. For example, Uganda asked the International Criminal Court to investigate the conduct of the Lord's Resistance Army, an opposition group, for possible criminal prosecution. Second, the prosecutor for the International Criminal Court may initiate an investigation after learning of credible evidence that crimes against humanity are being or have been carried out. Third, the Security Council for the United Nations may refer a case to the International Criminal Court (Rubin, 2006).

Essentially, based on deterrence theory, the International Criminal Court serves to prevent crimes against humanity by putting leaders on notice that they could go to prison or be executed for ordering, encouraging, or abetting extreme behaviors against citizens, dissidents, or neighbors. About 120 countries voted to endorse the Rome Statute and 21 countries abstained, but

7 countries—Iraq, Israel, Libya, China, Qatar, Yemen, and the United States—voted against it (Rubin, 2006). Allegedly, the Rome Statute was viewed as a tool for weak countries, and President George W. Bush signed into law the American Service-Members' Protection Act, which authorized the American military to free or liberate any American in custody of the International Criminal Court. Some have called this law the Hague Invasion Act, because the International Criminal Court is based in The Hague, the Netherlands, and gives the American armed forces legal authority to retrieve Americans held for trial (Rubin, 2006). Seemingly, the Hague Invasion Act was passed due to criticisms of American leaders and the CIA for their behaviors in developing countries. A Turkish daily newspaper accused the CIA of crimes against humanity (Red Orbit, 2005), and international critics have called President Bush a war criminal and claimed he and his administration committed crimes against humanity.

Nonetheless, the International Criminal Court has prosecuted officials from Uganda, Bosnia, and Rwanda. Slobodan Milosevic, former president of Yugoslavia, was arrested and jailed, but he died in jail before he could be put on trial by the International Criminal Court (Rosenthal, 2006). Another person held responsible for atrocities during the Bosnian-Serbian conflict was General Zdravko Tolimir, who was accused of helping kill over 7,000 Bosnian Muslims in Srebrenica in 1995 and was captured in 2007 for trial in the The Hague ("No. 3 Balkan War-Crimes Suspect Captured," 2007). Also, Charles Taylor, former president of Liberia, has been arrested and charged with war crimes and crimes against humanity for backing rebels who killed over 50,000 people and maimed thousands (Hoge, 2006). On June 20, 2006, Taylor was transported to jail in the Netherlands to await trial before the Special Court for Sierra Leone (Simons, 2006). Held responsible for leading the genocide of the Tutsis in Rwanda, Georges Rutaganda, leader of the Interahamwe, was convicted and sentenced to life imprisonment. Moreover, General Augustin Bizimungu, who was in charge of the Hutu army in Rwanda, was captured in Angola in 2002 and brought before the UN International Criminal Tribunal for Rwanda. For the first time in international law, Serbs in Bosnia and Hutus in Rwanda were tried for rape as a crime against humanity. The systematic rape of women in an attempt to destroy a culture has been defined as a crime against humanity. Currently, the prosecutor for the International Criminal Court is building a case against some officials in the Sudan for the genocide and rapes that have occurred in Darfur (Rubin, 2006).

HUMAN NEEDS AND HUMAN RIGHTS
IN DEVELOPING COUNTRIES IN THE
INTERNATIONAL COMMUNITY: A SYNTHESIS

In Chapter 1, students learned about world systems theory, and in this final chapter, Chapter 9, students learned about a number of human needs and human rights in mostly developing and poor countries. This concluding section seeks to illuminate their connections. Most Americans accept that Native Americans were gravely exploited and nearly exterminated by early colonists and White Western expansionists in the 1800s. But these practices had a long history. World systems theorists explained the concept of incorporation, which is the process of a core society including a periphery society within its economic activities. In the wake of incorporation, a number of human needs and conflicts or human rights violations emerge or become exacerbated. World systems theorists have documented what happened to Native Americans as they were incorporated. Shannon (1992) and Hall (2002) documented the decimation of Native Americans as they were incorporated into the American economic system. Other scholars have documented the frequent violations of treaties and the wanton killings of Native Americans. One controversial disagreement among some scholars is whether or not the U.S. Army put smallpox virus in blankets and gave them to one Native American tribe to kill them off; some scholars insist that these practices occurred. As Farley (2005) repeated, ethnic inequality occurs when there is (a) ethnocentrism, (b) competition for scarce resources, and (c) unequal power.

To various degrees the same had occurred long prior to the 1800s throughout the world and subsequent to the 1800s throughout the world by different core states, such as the United States, Great Britain, Spain, and France. Spain traveled the Americas and had a major, negative influence in South America and Mexico. While some individuals may take for granted that people in Mexico and South America speak Spanish, these people were not speaking Spanish before Spain came into their regions. Spain changed the language and the religion in these countries. Spain influenced Cuba and Puerto Rico, and the United States fought Spain in the early 1900s and took control of Puerto Rico and Guantánamo Bay in Cuba, which the United States has control of today (Parillo, 2009). France once had portions of Louisiana and influenced the region as well as parts of Canada. Probably, Great Britain has had the most influence on various regions of the world, including Hong Kong, Ireland, China, Kenya, and India. Although many colonies received their independence from Great Britain and some of the other colonizers, these periphery countries were left with many more social problems and human needs than before they were colonized.

One British practice, though there are many others by other nations, typifies the dynamics of world systems theory and its fallout. As discussed in the section on terrorism, the British implemented a food rationing system during World War II. White Europeans received food first; Asians, consisting of Indians, Pakistanis, Goans, and Arabs, received food second; and Africans were last. This could be understood as the societies in the core being first, those in the semiperiphery being second, and those in the periphery being last. This unequal treatment inflamed people in the African country of Tanzania. As a result, many Tanzanian youths see Osama bin Laden as a hero for attempting to end Western influence in the region and freeing their country from the world systems. Currently, Tanzania is viewed as a terrorist region, where Al-Qaeda bombed the U.S. embassy in 1998. This bombing and other activities caused tourism to decrease, exacerbating the plight of the poor and working poor.

As another example, when the British took control of Kenya, they brought workers from India to help build the railroads. The Indians stayed in Kenya, and many prospered financially to the point that they hold most of the wealth in Kenya. Social relations between Indians and Kenyans are not good as many Kenyans resent the treatment of them by Indians. During a visit to Kenya in 2003, the author learned of this resentment by talking to some Kenyans, noting the businesses that Indians owned; seeing some of their houses behind gated, armed guards; and observing the interactions between Kenyans and Indians. Their interactions were reminiscent of how Whites in America interacted with African Americans from the end of slavery to the 1950s or just before the civil rights movement. Early in this textbook, we identified the focus as the impact of macro social institutions (i.e., families, education, religion, the media, the law, and medicine), organizations, and communities on human needs in the social environment. This chapter has shown that the lack of strong social institutions such as education, medicine, and law impact negatively human needs and human rights in the many international communities.

CONCLUSION

Initially, we acknowledged that this was a difficult chapter to write for the reason that the international community is very vast. Another issue is that little scholarly research exists for many international communities. Two sociologists criticized the lack of sociological interest in Africa while noting that other communities are studied. They noted as well that the two flagship journals in sociology have published only a couple of articles on Africa. As a result, we relied heavily on reports from Human Rights Watch, Amnesty International, and the United Nations. From the latter, we provided some statistics on poverty in poor countries, which is worse than poverty in the United States. Extreme or abject poverty means that many people live on less than a dollar or two a day. When this poverty exists, it intersects with other issues to exacerbate human problems. For instance, famine and food shortages are caused mostly by poverty as some countries simply cannot afford to buy food when there is a shortage or crop failures. Civil wars, too, make life difficult for people. Some civil wars lead to genocide and human rights violations. We provided some discussions of the countries where human rights violations have occurred. This chapter discussed the vastly serious problem of domestic violence in Russia, to which the Ford Foundation has given funds to educate the Russian people and provide intervention programs. We discussed the human sex trafficking that affects many countries, including the United States. Additionally, we provided a theory of terrorism that indicates which countries are likely to have terrorists. Finally, we discussed one Canadian researcher's work on globalization and its numerous negative effects, economically and socially.

Key Terms and Concepts

Amnesty	Food Insecurity
Crimes Against Humanity	Genocide
Enfants Mauvais Souvenir	Human Rights
Enfants Non Désirés	Living Law of Custom
Famine	Microcredit

Appendix A

United Nations Millennium Goals to End Poverty

Scope of Millennium Development Goals and Targets
Goal 1. Eradicate extreme poverty and hunger
Target 1. Reduce by half the proportion of people living on less than a dollar a day
Target 2. Reduce by half the proportion of people who suffer from hunger
Goal 2. Achieve universal primary education
Target 3. Ensure that all boys and girls complete a full course of primary schooling
Goal 3. Promote gender equality and empower women
Target 4. Eliminate gender disparity in primary and secondary education preferably by 2005 and at all levels by 2015
Goal 4. Reduce child mortality
Target 5. Reduce by two thirds the mortality rate among children under 5
Goal 5. Improve maternal health

Scope of Millennium Development Goals and Targets
Target 6. Reduce by three quarters the maternal mortality ratio
Goal 6. Combat HIV/AIDS, malaria and other diseases
Target 7. Halt and begin to reverse the spread of HIV/AIDS
Target 8. Halt and begin to reverse the incidence of malaria and other major diseases
Goal 7. Ensure environmental sustainability
Target 9. Integrate the principles of sustainable development into country policies and programs; reverse loss of environmental resources
Target 10. Reduce by half the proportion of people without sustainable access to safe drinking water
Target 11. Achieve significant improvement in lives of at least 100 million slum dwellers, by 2020
Goal 8. Develop a global partnership for development
Target 12. Develop further an open trading and financial system that is rule-based, predictable, and nondiscriminatory. Includes a commitment to good governance, development, and poverty reduction—nationally and internationally
Target 13. Address the least developed countries' special needs. This includes tariff- and quota-free access for their exports; enhanced debt relief for heavily indebted poor countries; cancellation of official bilateral debt; and more generous official development assistance for countries committed to poverty reduction
Target 14. Address the special needs of landlocked and small island developing states
Target 15. Deal comprehensively with developing countries' debt problems through national and international measures to make debt sustainable in the long term
Target 16. In cooperation with the developing countries, develop decent and productive work for youth
Target 17. In cooperation with pharmaceutical companies, provide access to affordable essential drugs in developing countries
Target 18. In cooperation with the private sector, make available the benefits of new technologies—especially information and communications technologies

Appendix B

United Nations Definitions Involving Crimes Against Humanity

War crimes means (a) grave breaches of the Geneva Conventions of August 12, 1949, namely, any of the following acts against persons or property protected under the provisions of the relevant Geneva Convention: (i) willful killing; (ii) torture or inhuman treatment, including biological experiments; (iii) willfully causing great suffering or serious injury to body or health; (iv) extensive destruction and appropriation of property, not justified by military necessity and carried out unlawfully and wantonly; (v) compelling a prisoner of war or another protected person to serve in the forces of a hostile power; (vi) willfully depriving a prisoner of war or another protected person of the rights of fair and regular trial; (vii) unlawful deportation or transfer or unlawful confinement; or (viii) taking of hostages; and (b) other serious violations of the laws and customs applicable in international armed conflict, within the established framework of international law, namely, any of the following acts: (i) intentionally directing attacks against the civilian population as such or against individual civilians not taking direct part in hostilities; (ii) intentionally directing attacks against civilian objects—that is, objects that are not military objectives; (iii) intentionally directing attacks against personnel, installations, material, units, or vehicles involved in a humanitarian assistance or peacekeeping mission in accordance with the Charter of the United Nations, as long as they are entitled to the protection given to civilians or civilian objects under the international law of armed conflict; (iv) intentionally launching an attack in the knowledge that such attack will cause incidental loss of life or injury to civilians or damage to civilian objects or widespread, long-term, and severe damage to the natural environment, which would be clearly excessive in relation to the concrete and direct overall military advantage anticipated; (v) attacking or bombarding, by whatever means, towns, villages, dwellings, or buildings that are undefended and that are not military objectives; (vi) killing or wounding a combatant who, having laid down his arms or having no longer means of defense, has surrendered at discretion; (vii) making improper use of a flag of truce, of the flag or of the military insignia and uniform of the enemy or of the United Nations, or of the distinctive emblems of the Geneva Conventions, resulting in death or serious personal injury; (viii) the transfer, directly or indirectly, by the occupying power of parts of its own civilian population into the territory it occupies or the deportation or transfer of all or parts of the population of the occupied territory within or outside this territory; (ix) intentionally directing attacks against buildings dedicated to religion, education, art, science, or charitable purposes; historic monuments; or hospitals and places where the sick and wounded are collected, provided they are not military objectives; (x) subjecting persons who are in the power of an adverse party to physical mutilation or to medical or scientific experiments of any kind, which are neither justified by the medical, dental, or hospital treatment of the person concerned nor carried out in his or her interest and which cause death to or seriously endanger the health of such person or persons; (xi) killing or wounding treacherously individuals belonging to the hostile nation or army; (xii) declaring that no quarter will be given; (xiii) destroying or seizing the enemy's property unless such destruction or seizure be imperatively demanded by the necessities of war; (xiv) declaring abolished, suspended, or inadmissible in a court of law the rights and actions of the nationals of the hostile party; (xv) compelling the nationals of the hostile party to take part in the operations of war directed against their own country, even if they were in the belligerent's service before the commencement of the war; (xvi) pillaging a town or place, even when taken by assault; (xvii) employing poison or poisoned weapons; (xviii) employing asphyxiating, poisonous, or other gases and all analogous liquids, materials, or devices; (xix) employing bullets that expand or flatten easily in the human body, such as bullets with a hard envelope that does not entirely cover the core or is pierced with incisions; (xx) employing weapons, projectiles, and material and methods of warfare that are of a nature to cause superfluous injury or unnecessary suffering or that are inherently indiscriminate in violation of the international law of armed conflict, provided that such weapons, projectiles, and material and methods of warfare are the subject of a comprehensive prohibition and are included in an annex to this statute, by an amendment in accordance with the relevant provisions set forth in articles 121 and 123; (xxi) committing outrages upon personal dignity, in particular humiliating and degrading treatment; (xxii) committing rape; sexual slavery; enforced prostitution; forced pregnancy, as defined in article 7, paragraph 2 (f); enforced sterilization; or any other form of sexual violence also constituting a grave breach of the Geneva Conventions; (xxiii) utilizing the presence of a civilian or another protected person to render certain points, areas, or military forces immune from military operations; (xxiv) intentionally directing attacks against buildings, material, medical units and transport, and personnel using the distinctive emblems of the Geneva Conventions in conformity with international law; (xxv) intentionally using starvation of civilians as a method of warfare by depriving them of objects indispensable to their survival, including willfully impeding relief supplies as provided for under the Geneva Conventions; or (xxvi) conscripting or enlisting children under the age of 15 years into the national armed forces or using them to participate actively in hostilities.

Crime of aggression is determined by articles 121 and 123 (future amendments as adopted by the United Nations) that define the crime and set out the conditions under which the court shall exercise jurisdiction with respect to this crime. Such a provision shall be consistent with the relevant provisions of the Charter of the United Nations.

References

Abbott, A. A. (1995). Substance abuse and the feminist practice. In N. Van Den Bergh (Ed.), *Feminist practice in the 21st century* (pp. 258–277). Washington, DC: NASW Press.

ABC News. (2006, August 29). Sexual abuse in the Amish community: Woman endured childhood of repeated rape by her brothers. Retrieved May 20, 2007, from http://abcnews.go.com/print?id=2365919.

Abueg, F. R., & Chun, K. M. (2001). Traumatization stress among Asians and Asian Americans. In A. J. Marsella, M. J. Friedman, E. T. Gerrity, & R. M. Scurfield (Eds.), *Ethnocultural aspects of posttraumatic stress disorder: Issues, research, and clinical applications* (pp. 285–299). Washington, DC: American Psychological Association.

Achbar, M., Abbott, J., & Bakan, J. (2005). The corporation [Television Program, Sundance]. Shown on December 29, 2005, based on Balkan, J. (2004). *The corporation: The pathological pursuit of profit and power.* New York: Free Press.

ACLU. (2006). Loving v. City of Black Jack. Retrieved June 8, 2008, from http://www.aclu-em.org/legal/legaldocket/currentcases/lovingvcityofblackjack.htm.

Adams, J. S. (1965). Inequality in social exchange. *Advances in Experimental Social Psychology, 2,* 267–299.

Adams, M. S. (1996). Labeling and differential association: Towards a general social learning theory crime and deviance. *American Journal of Criminal Justice, 20*(2), 147–164.

Aguayo, T. (2006, May 19). Youth who killed at 12 gets 30 years for violating probation. *The New York Times.* Retrieved July 25, 2009, from http://query.nytimes.com/gst/fullpage.html?res=9C07E3D7123EF93AA25756C0A9609C8B63.

Akers, R. L. (1973). *Deviant behavior: A social learning approach* (1st ed.). Belmont, CA: Wadsworth.

Akers, R. L. (1985). *Deviant behavior: A social learning approach* (3rd ed.). Belmont, CA: Wadsworth.

Akers, R. L. (1998). *Social learning and social structure: A general theory of crime and deviance.* Boston: Northeastern University Press.

Akers, R. L., Krohn, M. D., Lanza-Kaduce, L., & Radosevich, M. (1979). Social learning and deviant behavior: A specific test of a general theory. *American Sociological Review, 44,* 636–655.

Akers, R. L., La Greca, A. J., Cochran, J., & Sellers, C. (1989). Social learning theory and alcohol behavior among the elderly. *The Sociological Quarterly, 30*(4), 625–638.

Akers, R. L., & Lee, G. (1996). A longitudinal test of social learning theory: Adolescent smoking. *Journal of Drug Issues, 26*(2), 317–343.

Albrecht, G. L. (2005). The sociology of health and illness. In C. Calhoun, C. Rojek, & B. Turner (Eds.), *The Sage handbook of sociology* (pp. 267–283). Thousand Oaks, CA: Sage.

Alexander, R., Jr. (2003). *Understanding legal concepts that influence social welfare policy and practice.* Belmont, CA: Brooks/Cole.

Alexander, R., Jr. (2005a). *Racism, African Americans, and social justice.* Lanham, MD: Rowman & Littlefield.

Alexander, R., Jr. (2005b). The relationship of prisoners, poverty measures, and social welfare allocations in Ohio. *Journal of Policy Practice, 4*(2), 69–82.

Alexander, R., Jr. (2006). Restorative justice: Misused and misapplied. *Journal of Policy Practice, 5*(1), 67–81.

Alexander, R., Jr., & Gyamerah, J. (1997). Differential punishing of African Americans and Whites who possess drugs: A just policy or a continuation of the past? *Journal of Black Studies, 28*(1), 97–111.

Allen, B. (1996). *Rape warfare: The hidden genocide in Bosnia-Herzegovina and Croatia.* Minneapolis: University of Minnesota Press.

Allen, I. M. (2001). PTSD among African Americans. In A. J. Marsella, M. J. Friedman, E. T. Gerrity, & R. M. Scurfield (Eds.), *Ethnocultural aspects of posttraumatic stress disorder: Issues, research, and clinical applications* (pp. 209–238). Washington, DC: American Psychological Association.

Altman, L. (2006, May 26). Chimp virus is linked to H.I.V. *The New York Times,* p. A3.

American Civil Liberties Union of Tennessee v. Darnell, 2006 Tenn. LEXIS 610 (2006).

American Psychiatric Association. (2000). *Diagnostic and statistical manual of mental disorders* (Text rev.). Arlington, VA: Author.

Americans United for Separation of Church and State v. Prison Fellowship Ministries, 295 F. Supp. 2d 805 (2005).

Amnesty International. (2000). *Israel: Human rights abuses of women trafficked from countries of the former Soviet Union into Israel's sex industry.* New York: Author.

Amnesty International. (2005a, October 3). *Africa: Forced evictions are a human rights scandal* [Public Statement]. Retrieved October 5, 2005, from http://www.amnesty.org/en/library/info/AFR01/003/2005.

Amnesty International. (2006). *Report 2005: United States of America.* New York: Author.

Andersen v. King County, 2006 Wash. LEXIS 598 (2006).

Anderson, B. (1991). *Imagined communities.* New York: Verso.

Anderson, E. N., & Chase-Dunn, C. (2005). The rise and fall of great powers. In C. Chase-Dunn & E. N. Anderson (Eds.), *The historical evolution of world-systems* (pp. 1–19). New York: Palgrave-Macmillan.

Andreae, D. (1996). Systems theory and social work practice. In F. J. Turner (Ed.), *Social work treatment: Interlocking theoretical perspectives* (4th ed., pp. 601–616). New York: Free Press.

An-Na 'im, A. A. (2001). Human rights. In J. R. Blau (Ed.), *The Blackwell companion to sociology* (pp. 86–99). Malden, MA: Blackwell.

Appalachian Regional Commission. (1967). *The people left behind*. Washington, DC: Author.

Appleby, J. (2007, January 29). People left holding bag when policies revoked. *USA Today*, pp. 1A, 2A.

Applewhite, S. L., & Torres, C. (2003). Rural Latino elders. In S. S. Butler & L. W. Kaye (Eds.), *Gerontological social work in small towns and rural communities* (pp. 151–174). New York: The Haworth Press.

Apuzzo, M. (2006, November 15). Federal judge decries disparity in cocaine sentencing. *Columbus Dispatch*, p. A7.

Archibold, R. C., & Goodnough, A. (2008, November 5). California voters ban gay marriage. *The New York Times*. Retrieved July 25, 2009, from http://www.nytimes.com/2008/11/06/us/politics/06ballot.html.

Arizona Criminal Justice Commission. (2004). *Arizona auto theft study*. Phoenix, AZ: Author.

Armas, G. C. (2009, April 21). Study paints picture of collegiate mental health. Retrieved May 9, 2009, from http://www.ajc.com/health/content/health/stories/2009/04/21/college_mental_health_study.html.

Associated Press. (2005, September 23). Despair, depression, set in a month after storm: Survivors of Hurricane Katrina coping with emotional wreckage. Retrieved September 23, 2005, from http://www.msnbc.msn.com/id/9450526/print/1/displaymode/1098/.

Atkins v. Virgina, 536 U.S. 304 (2002).

AVERT. (2008). Worldwide HIV & AIDS statistics. Retrieved January 25, 2009, from http://www.avert.org/worldstats.htm.

Babiak, P., & Hare, R. D. (2006). *Snakes in suits: When psychopaths go to work*. New York: Regan Books.

Bailey, K. D. (2001). Systems theory. In J. H. Turner (Ed.), *Handbook of sociological theory* (pp. 379–401). New York: Kluwer Academic/Plenum Publishers.

Bakan, J. (2004). *The corporation: The pathological pursuit of profit and power*. New York: Free Press.

Baker, R. (1999). Minority distrust of medicine: A historical perspective. *The Mount Sinai Journal of Medicine, 66*(4), 212–222.

Ballantine, J. H. (2001). *The sociology of education: A systematic analysis* (5th ed.). Upper Saddle River, NJ: Prentice Hall.

Bamodu, G. (2006). Managing globalisation: UK initiatives and a Nigerian perspective. In J. Dine & A. Fagan (Eds.), *Human rights and capitalism: A multidisciplinary perspective on globalisation* (pp. 145–168). Cheltenham, United Kingdom: Edward Elgar.

Bandura, A. (1977). *Social learning theory*. Englewood Cliffs, NJ: Prentice Hall.

Banerjee, N. (2005, December 30). Church to church, teenagers seek faith that fits. *The New York Times*, pp. A1, A14.

Bankruptcy Services, LLC. (2005). Docket # 677, letters to Honorable Allan L. Gropper dated 9/22/2005 to 9/29/2005. Retrieved November 28, 2005, from http://www.bsillc.com/.

Barbaro, M. (2006, January 13). Maryland sets a health cost for Wal-Mart. *The New York Times*. Retrieved July 10, 2008, from http://www.nytimes.com/2006/01/13/business/13walmart.html?_r=1&oref=slogin.

Barbaro, M. (2007, January 18). Appeals court rules for Wal-Mart in Maryland health care case. *The New York Times.* Retrieved July 10, 2008, from http://www.nytimes.com/2007/01/18/business/18walmart.html.

Barber, J. S., & Axinn, W. G. (2004). New ideas and fertility limitation: The role of mass media. *Journal of Marriage and Family, 66,* 1180–1200.

Barker, R. L. (2003). *The social work dictionary* (5th ed.). Washington, DC: NASW Press.

Barman, E. A. (2002). Asserting difference: The strategic response of nonprofit organizations to competition. *Social Forces, 80*(4), 1191–1222.

Bartlett, J. (2004). Making a difference after all: The relationship between media and strategic public relations. *Australian Journal of Communication, 31*(1), 75–87.

Barusch, A., & TenBarge, C. (2003). Indigenous elders in rural America. In S. S. Butler & L. W. Kaye (Eds.), *Gerontological social work in small towns and rural communities* (pp. 121–136). New York: The Haworth Press.

Baskerville, S. (2004). Child support and the marriage question. *Society, 41*(6), 17–24.

Bauder, D. (2006, June 3). Quote wasn't meant as slam of Africa, Gibson says. *Columbus Dispatch,* p. C6.

BBC News. (2005, January 7). *Timeline: Asian tsunami disaster.* Retrieved May 23, 2005, from http://news.bbc.co.uk/2/hi/asia-pacific/4154791.stm.

Beard v. Banks, U.S. S. Ct. Briefs LEXIS 238 (2006).

Beaulieu, L. J. (2004). Breaking walls, building bridges: Expanding the presence and relevance of rural sociology. *Rural Sociology, 70*(1), 1–27.

Beck, A. J., & Maruschak, L. M. (2001). *Mental health treatment in state prisons, 2000.* Washington, DC: Bureau of Justice Statistics.

Becker, D. (1995). The deficiency of the concept of posttraumatic stress disorder when dealing with victims of human rights violations. In R. J. Kleber, C. R. Figley, & B. P. R. Gersons (Eds.), *Beyond trauma: Cultural and societal dynamics* (pp. 99–110). New York: Plenum Press.

Belkin, L. (2005, December 17). When a worker's health crisis deteriorates into a job crisis. *The New York Times,* pp. A1, A16.

Belluck, P., & Reuthling, G. (2006, July 15). In Nebraska and Tennessee, more setbacks to gay rights. *The New York Times,* p. A8.

Berdahl, J. L., & Anderson, C. (2005). Men, women, and leadership centralization in groups over time. *Group Dynamics: Theory Research Practice, 9*(1), 45–57.

Bergesen, A., & Bartely, T. (2000). World-system and ecosystem. In T. Hall (ed.), *A world-system reader: New perspectives on gender, urbanism, culture, indigenous peoples, and ecology* (pp. 307–322). Lanham, MD: Rowman & Littlefield.

Bergner, D. (2006a, January 29). The call. *The New York Times Magazine,* p. 40.

Bergner, D. (2006b, July 23). The case of Marie and her sons. *The New York Times Magazine,* pp. 28, 53.

Berliner, L. (1996). Community notification of sex offenders: A new tool or a false promise. *Journal of Interpersonal Violence, 11*(2), 294–295.

Best, C. L., & Ribbe, D. P. (1995). Accidental injury: Approaches to assessment and treatment. Helping victims of military trauma. In J. R. Freedy & S. E. Hobfoll (Eds.), *Traumatic stress: From theory to practice* (pp. 315–337). New York: Plenum Press.

Biddle, B. J. (1979). *Role theory: Expectations, identities, and behavior.* New York: Academic Press.

Bills, D. B. (2004). *The sociology of education and work*. Malden, MA: Blackwell.

Birnbaum, J. H. (2005, February 6). Chamber of commerce a key player in driving agenda of Bush and largest corporations. *The Washington Post*, p. A1.

Black, D. (1976). *The behavior of law*. New York: Academic Press.

Blau, J., & Moncada, A. (2006). *Justice in the United States: Human rights and the U.S. constitution*. Lanham, MD: Rowman & Littlefield.

Blau, P. M. (1964). *Exchange and power in social life*. New York: John Wiley & Sons.

Bluestein, G. (2006, June 24). Sex criminals find few options: Georgia law puts much of state off limits. *Columbus Dispatch*, p. A5.

Boothby, N. (1996). Mobilizing communities to meet the psychosocial needs of children in war and refugee crises. In R. J. Apfel & B. Simon (Eds.), *Minefields in their hearts: The mental health of children in war and communal violence* (pp. 149–164). New Haven, CT: Yale University Press.

Boss, P. (2004). Ambiguous loss research, theory, and practice: Reflections after 9/11. *Journal of Marriage and Family, 66*, 551–566.

Boyd v. Coughlin, 914 F. Supp. 828 (N.D.NY. 1996).

Boyns, D., & Ballard, J. D. (2004). Developing a sociological theory for the empirical understanding of terrorism. *The American Sociologist, 35*(2), 5–25.

Bradley, G. V. (2005, April 13). Capitol Hill hearing testimony. Marriage Protection Initiative and Judicial Activism, Committee on Senate Judiciary Subcommittee on Constitution, Civil Rights and Property Rights.

Brehm, J. M., Eisenhauer, B. W., & Krannich, R. S. (2004). Dimensions of community attachment and their relationship to well-being in the amenity-rich rural West. *Rural Sociology, 69*(3), 405–429.

Brents, B. G., & Mshigeni, D. S. (2004). Terrorism in context: Race, religion, party, and violent conflict in Zanzibar. *The American Sociologist, 35*(2), 60–74.

Bridger, J. C., Luloff, A. E., & Krannich, R. S. (2002). Community change and community theory. In A. E. Luloff & R. S. Krannich (Eds.), *Persistence and change in rural communities: A 50-year follow-up to six classic studies* (pp. 9–21). New York: CABI Publishing.

Britt, C. L., & Gottfredson, M. R. (Eds.). (2003). *Control theories of crime and delinquency*. New Brunswick, NJ: Transaction.

Brooks, C. (2002). Religious influence and the politics of family decline concern: Trends, sources, and U.S. political behavior. *American Sociological Review, 67*, 191–211.

Brown, J. B., & Lichter, D. T. (2004). Poverty, welfare, and the livelihood strategies of nonmetropolitan single mothers. *Rural Sociology, 69*(2), 281–301.

Brown v. Board of Education of Topeka, 347 U.S. 483 (1954).

Browne, C. H. (1967). The correspondents' war: Journalists in the Spanish-American war. New York: Scribner.

Bryant, K. M., & Miller, J. M. (1997). Routine activity and labor market segmentation: An empirical test of a revised approach. *American Journal of Criminal Justice, 22*(1), 71–100.

Buck, R. C. (1978). Boundary maintenance revisited: Tourist experience in an old order Amish community. *Rural Sociology, 43*(2), 221–234.

Bureau of Justice Statistics. (2005a). *Criminal victimization in the United States, 2003 statistical tables*. Washington, DC: Author.

Bureau of Justice Statistics. (2005b). *Victim characteristics.* Washington, DC: Author.

Bureau of Justice Statistics. (2005c). *Violent victimization rates by gender, 1973–2004.* Washington, DC: Author.

Burgess, R. L., & Akers, R. L. (1966). A differential association-reinforcement theory of criminal behavior. *Social Problems, 14*(2), 128–147.

Burton, D. L., Miller, D. L., & Shill, C. T. (2002). A social learning theory comparison of the sexual victimization of adolescent sexual offenders and nonsexual offending male delinquents. *Child Abuse and Neglect, 26*(9), 893–907.

Butchers' Union Slaughter-House and Live-Stock Landing Company v. Crescent City Live-Stock Landing and Slaughter-House Company, 111 U.S. 746 (1884).

Butler, A. C. (2005). Gender differences in the prevalence of same-sex partnering: 1988–2002. *Social Forces, 84*(1), 421–449.

Caldwell, C. (2006, May 7). The other immigration. *The New York Times Magazine,* pp. 15–16.

California Department of Corrections and Rehabilitation. (2007). *Budget overview.* Retrieved August 3, 2009, from http://www.cdcr.ca.gov/Budget/Budget_Overview.html.

Capece, M., & Lanza-Kaduce, L. (2003). Substance use among college students: An examination of Akers' social structure-social learning theory. *Southern Sociological Society, 051.*

Caputo, R. K. (2001). The intergenerational transmission of grandmother-grandchild co-residency. *Journal of Sociology & Social Welfare, 28*(1), 79–86.

Carlson, E. B., & Ruzek, J. (2005). *PTSD and the family.* National Center for PTSD. Retrieved October 21, 2005, from http://www.ncptsd.va.gov/facts/specific/fs_family.html and August 3, 2009, from http://www.ptsduk.co.uk/article_ncpfact_family.html.

Carmona, R. H. (2005). Improving Americans' health literacy. *Journal of the American Dietetic Association, 105,* 1345.

Carnegie Endowment. (2007). *Globalization101.org.* Retrieved November 9, 2007, from http://www.globalization101.org/What_is_Globalization.html.

Casillas, O. (2009, May 10). One family, after all. *Chicago Tribune.* Retrieved May 10, 2009, from http://www.chicagotribune.com/news/local/chi-foster-moms-10-bdmay10,0,738308.story?page=1.

Center for Media and Democracy. (2006). How PR sold the war in the Persian Gulf. Retrieved August 7, 2006, from http://www.prwatch.org/books/tsigfy10.html.

Centers for Disease Control and Prevention. (2008). *Recent trends in infant mortality in the United States.* Retrieved July 24, 2009, from http://www.cdc.gov/nchs/data/databriefs/db09.htm.

Centers for Disease Control and Prevention and the Merck Company Foundation. (2007). *The state of aging and health in America 2007.* Whitehouse Station, NJ: The Merck Company Foundation.

Central Intelligence Agency. (2008). *World factbook.* Retrieved July 24, 2009, from https://www.cia.gov/library/publications/the-world-factbook/rankorder/2127rank.html.

Chambré, S. M. (2001). The changing nature of "faith" in faith-based organizations: Secularization and ecumenicism in four AIDS organizations in New York City. *Social Service Review, 75*(3), 435–455.

Chapman, C. D. (2003, April). Case study: A faith-based organization's collaborative effort with the public. *Southern Sociological Society.*

Chappell, A. T., & Piquero, A. R. (2004). Applying social learning theory to police misconduct. *Deviant Behavior, 25*(2), 89–108.

Chappell, P., & Peix, C. (Directors). (2004). *The origin of AIDS* [Television Program]. Shown on December 6, 2005.

Chase-Dunn, C. (2001). World-systems theorizing. In J. H. Turner (Ed.), *Handbook of sociological theory* (pp. 589–612). New York: Kluwer Academic/Plenum Publishers.

Chase-Dunn, C., & Ford, M. (1999). Foreword. In P. N. Kardulias (Ed.), *World systems theory in practice: Leadership, production, and exchange* (pp. xi–xiii). Lanham, MD: Rowman & Littlefield.

Chaves, M. (2001). Religious congregations and welfare reform. *Society, 38*(2), 21–27.

Chávez, S. (2005). Community, ethnicity, and class in a changing rural California town. *Rural Sociology, 70*(3), 314–335.

Chetwynd, E., Chetwynd, F., & Spector, B. (2003). *Corruption and poverty: A review of recent literature, a final report.* Washington, DC: Management Systems International.

Chew, S. C. (2005). From Harappa to Mesopotamia and Egypt to Mycenae: Dark ages, political-economic declines, and environmental/climatic changes 2200 B.C.–700 B.C. In C. Chase-Dunn & E. N. Anderson (Eds.), *The historical evolution of world-systems* (pp. 52–74). New York: Palgrave-Macmillan.

Chikwendu, E. (2004). Faith-based organizations in anti-HIV/AIDS work among African youth and women. *Dialectical Anthropology, 28,* 307–327.

Christensen, R. (2002). *Value of benefits constant in a changing world: Findings from the 2001 EBRI/MGA value of benefits survey.* Washington, DC: Employee Benefit Research Institute.

Citizens for Equal Protection v. Bruning, 2006 U.S. App. LEXIS 17723 (2006).

CNN. (2007, June 28). Paris Hilton on *Larry King Live.* Retrieved July 8, 2008, from http://www.cnn.com/2007/SHOWBIZ/TV/06/27/king.hilton.transcript/index.html.

Cohen, A. W. (2003). The racketeer's progress: Commerce, crime, and the law in Chicago, 1900–1940. *Journal of Urban History, 29*(5), 575–596.

Cohen, L. E., & Felson, M. (1979). Social change and crime rate trends: A routine activity approach. *American Sociological Review, 44,* 588–608.

Conarton, S., & Silverman, L. K. (1988). Feminine development through the life cycle. In M. A. Dutton-Douglas & L. E. Walker (Eds.), *Feminist psychotherapies: Integration of therapeutic and feminist systems* (pp. 37–67). Norwood, NJ: Ablex.

Connelly, M. (2006, April 14). In polls, illegal immigrants are called burden. *The New York Times,* p. A16.

Connolly, C. (2002). The voice of the petitioner: The experiences of gay and lesbian parents in successful second-parent adoption proceedings. *Law & Society Review, 36*(2), 325–346.

Copeland, L., & Cauchon, D. (2005, October 20). "FEMA Village" wary of Wilma, still weary from Charley. *USA Today.* Retrieved August 2, 2009, from http://www.usatoday.com/news/nation/2005-10-20-fema-village_x.htm.

Crawford, A. J. (2006, January 4). Code blue for health care. *The Arizona Republic,* pp. A1, A12.

Cray, C. (2002, October 1). Chartering a new course: Revoking corporations' right to exist. *Multinational Monitor, 23*(10), p. 1.

CSWE. (2005). *Katherine A. Kendall institute for international social work education.* Alexandria, VA: Author.

Currie, E., & Skolnick, J. H. (1988). *America's problems: Social issues and public policy* (2nd ed.). Glenview, IL: Scott, Foresman and Company.

Daley-Harris, S. (2007). *State of the microcredit summit campaign report 2006.* Washington, DC: Microcredit Summit Campaign.

Dalla, R., & Baugher, S. L. (2001). Immigration and the rural Midwest. In R. M. Moore III (Ed.), *The hidden America: Social problems in rural America for the twenty-first century* (pp. 219–233). Cranbury, NJ: Associated University Presses.

Daly, M. (1978). *Gyn/ecology: The metaethics of radical feminism* (Hardback ed.). Boston: Beacon Press.

Daly, M. (1990). *Gyn/ecology: The metaethics of radical feminism* (Paperback ed.). Boston: Beacon Press.

Darnell v. Thermafiber, 417 F.3d 657 (7th Cir. 2005).

Day, K. (2001). The renaissance of community economic development among African-American churches in the 1990s. In R. K. Fenn (Ed.), *The Blackwell companion to sociology of religion* (pp. 321–335). Malden, MA: Blackwell.

Dehaan, L., & Deal, J. (2001). Effects of economic hardship on rural children and adolescents. In R. M. Moore III (Ed.), *The hidden America: Social problems in rural America for the twenty-first century* (pp. 42–56). Cranbury, NJ: Associated University Presses.

DePoy, E., & Gilson, S. F. (2003). Rural disabled elders. In S. S. Butler & L. W. Kaye (Eds.), *Gerontological social work in small towns and rural communities* (pp. 175–190). New York: The Haworth Press.

Derolph v. State of Ohio, 780 N.E. 2d 529 (Ohio 2002).

Derolph v. State of Ohio, 754 N.E. 2d 1184 (Ohio 2001).

Dewan, S. (2006, May 14). Call them "refugees," if it gets the job done. *The New York Times*, p. B14.

DeYoung, M. (1989). The world according to NAMBLA: Accounting for deviance. *Journal of Sociology and Social Welfare, 16*, 111–126.

Dicker, R. (2005, September 20). *Letter to interested states on funding for the special court for Sierra Leone.* Retrieved October 5, 2005, from http://www.hrw.org/english/docs/2005/09/20/siera11777.htm.

DiMaggio, P. J., Weiss, J. A., & Clotfelter, C. T. (2002). Data to support scholarship on nonprofit organizations. *American Behavioral Scientist, 45*(10), 1474–1492.

Dine, J. (2006). Using companies to oppress the poor. In J. Dine & A. Fagan (Eds.), *Human rights and capitalism: A multidisciplinary perspective on globalisation* (pp. 48–79). Cheltenham, United Kingdom: Edward Elgar.

Dodoo, F. N., & Beisel, N. (2005). Africa in American sociology: Invisibility, opportunity and obligation. *Social Forces, 84*(1), 595–600.

Dollery, B. E., & Wallis, J. L. (2003). *The political economy of the voluntary sector: A reappraisal of the comparative institutional advantage of voluntary organizations.* Northampton, MA: Edward Elgar.

Donovan, T., Tolbert, C., Smith, D. A., & Parry, J. (2005). Did gay marriage elect George W. Bush? Paper presented at the State Politics Conference, May 14–15, East Lansing, MI.

Dorsten, L. E., Hotchkiss, L., & King, T. M. (1996). Consanguineous marriage and early childhood mortality in an Amish settlement [Book Review]. *Sociological Focus, 29*(2), 179–185.

Doulin, T. (2006, April 20). Ohioans head for exit: Pace of departures faster than a decade ago. *Columbus Dispatch*, p. A1.

Downey, D. B., & Ainsworth-Darnell, J. W. (2002). The search for oppositional culture among Black students. *American Sociological Review, 67,* 156–164.

Downs, C. A., & James, S. E. (2006). Gay, lesbian, and bisexual foster parents: Strengths and challenges for the child welfare system. *Child Welfare Journal, 85*(2), 281–298.

Dozier, R., & Schwartz, P. (2001). Intimate relationships. In J. R. Blau (Ed.), *The Blackwell companion to sociology* (pp. 114–127). Malden, MA: Blackwell.

Dugger, C. W. (2006, January 8). A cure that really works: Cambodia tries the nonprofit path to health care. *The New York Times,* p. A8.

Dunaway, W. A. (2000). Women at risk: Capitalist incorporation and community transformation on the Cherokee frontier. In T. D. Hall (Ed.), *A world-systems reader* (pp. 195–210). Lanham, MD: Rowman & Littlefield.

Duncan, C. M. (1996). Understanding persistent poverty: Social class context in rural communities. *Rural Sociology, 59*(3), 103–124.

Duncan, C. M. (1999). *Worlds apart: Why poverty persists in rural America.* New Haven, CT: Yale University Press.

Durkheim, E. (1956). *Education and sociology* (S. D. Fox, Trans.). Glencoe, IL: Free Press.

Dutton-Douglas, M. A., & Walker, L. E. A. (1988). Introduction to feminist therapies. In M. A. Dutton-Douglas & L. E. Walker (Eds.), *Feminist psychotherapies: Integration of therapeutic and feminist systems* (pp. 3–11). Norwood, NJ: Ablex.

Early, A., & Ludwig, K. (2003). The destabilization of attachment processes in children and adolescents: Clinical materials from the Oklahoma city bombing. In J. A. Cancelmo, I. Tylim, J. Hoffenberg, & H. Myers (Eds.), *Terrorism and the psychoanalytic space: International perspectives from Ground Zero* (pp. 138–145). New York: Pace University Press.

Edwards, B., & McCarthy, J. D. (2004). Strategy matters: The contingent value of social capital in the survival of local social movement organizations. *Social Forces, 83*(2), 621–651.

EEOC v. Wal-Mart Stores, Inc., No. 04-cv-0076 (W.D. Mo. 2007).

Eisen, M., Zellman, G. L., McAlister, A. L. (1992). A health belief model-social learning theory approach to adolescents' fertility control: Findings from a controlled field trial. *Health Education Quarterly, 19*(2), 249–262.

Eisler, P. (2005, December 16). Thousands of facilities go without oversight. *USA Today,* p. 13A.

Elias, M. (2005, September 28). Storms' collateral damage: Danger signs' point to stress disorders after disasters. *USA Today,* p. 10D.

Ellingson, S. (2004). Constructing causal stories and moral boundaries: Institutional approaches to sexual problems. In E. O. Laumann, S. Ellingson, J. Mahay, A. Paik, & Y. Youm (Eds.), *The sexual organization of the city* (pp. 283–308). Chicago: The University of Chicago Press.

Ellingson, S., & Schroeder, K. (2004). Race and the construction of same-sex markets in four Chicago neighborhoods. In E. O. Laumann, S. Ellingson, J. Mahay, A. Paik, & Y. Youm (Eds.), *The sexual organization of the city* (pp. 93–123). Chicago: The University of Chicago Press.

Ellingson, S., Laumann, E. O., Paik, A., & Mahay, J. (2004). The theory of sex markets. In E. O. Laumann, S. Ellingson, J. Mahay, A. Paik, & Y. Youm (Eds.), *The sexual organization of the city* (pp. 3–38). Chicago: The University of Chicago Press.

Emerson, R. M. (1962). Power-dependence relations. *American Sociological Review, 27,* 31–41.

Employee Benefit Research Institute. (2003). *EBRI research highlight: Health benefits.* Washington, DC: Author.

Epstein, J. L., & Sanders, M. G. (2000). Connecting home, school, and community: New directions for social research. In M. T. Hallinan (Ed.), *Handbook of the sociology of education* (pp. 285–306). New York: Kluwer Academic/Plenum Publishers.

Erikson, E. H. (1980). *Identity and the life cycle.* New York: Norton.

Escobar-Chaves, S. L., Tortolero, S. R., Markham, C. M., Low, B. J., Eitel, P., & Thickstun, P. (2005). Impact of the media on adolescent sexual attitudes and behaviors. *Pediatrics, 116,* 303–326.

Etzioni, A. (1996). The responsive community: A communitarian perspective. *American Sociological Review, 61*(1), 1–11.

Evans, W. N., & Topoleski, J. H. (2002). *The social and economic impact of Native American casinos.* National Bureau of Economic Research, Working Paper No. 9198.

Everson v. Board of Education, 330 U.S. 1 (1947).

Executive Office for Immigration Review. (2006). *FY 2005 asylum statistics.* Washington, DC: U.S. Department of Justice.

Faiola, A. (2008, May 16). Women rise in Rwanda's economic revival. *The Washington Post,* p. A01.

Falk, W. W., Hunt, L. L., & Hunt. M. O. (2004). Return migrations of African Americans to the South: Reclaiming a land of promise, going home, or both. *Rural Sociology, 69*(4), 490–509.

Falsetti, S. A., & Resnick, H. S. (1995). Helping the victims of violent crimes. Helping victims of military trauma. In J. R. Freedy & S. E. Hobfoll (Eds.), *Traumatic stress: From theory to practice* (pp. 263–285). New York: Plenum Press.

Farazmand, A. (2002). Introduction: The multifaceted nature of modern organizations. In A. Farazmand (Ed.), *Modern organizations: Theory and practice* (2nd ed., pp. xv–xxix). Westport, CT: Praeger.

Farkas, G., Lleras, C., & Maczuga, S. (2002). Does oppositional culture exist in minority and poverty peer groups? *American Sociological Review, 67,* 148–155.

Farley, J. F. (2005). *Majority-minority relations* (5th ed.). Englewood Cliffs, NJ: Prentice Hall.

Federal Bureau of Investigation. (2006). *Crime in the United States 2004.* Retrieved August 2, 2009, from http://www.fbi.gov/ucr/cius_04/.

Federal Interagency Forum on Family and Child Statistics. (2009). *America's children: Key national indicators of well-being 2009.* Retrieved July 30, 2009, from http://www.childstats.gov/index.asp.

Federal Register. (2001). *Executive order 13198: Agency responsibilities with respect to faith-based and community initiatives.* Retrieved July 26, 2009, from http://www.access.gpo.gov/su_docs/aces/fr-cont.html.

Fellner, J. (2006). *Cruel and degrading in Connecticut prisons.* New York: Human Rights Watch.

Fellowes, M. (2006). *From poverty, opportunity: Putting the market to work for lower income families.* Washington, DC: The Brookings Institution.

Felson, M. (1987). Routine activities and crime prevention in the developing metropolis. *Criminology, 25*(4), 911–932.

FEMA. (2008). *Grand Forks 1997 flood recovery: Facts and statistics.* Retrieved July 24, 2009, from http://www.fema.gov/hazard/archive/grandforks/statistics.shtm.

Ferree, M. M., Gamson, W. A., Gerhards, J., & Rucht, D. (2002). *Shaping abortion discourse: Democracy, and the public sphere in Germany and the United States.* Cambridge, United Kingdom: Cambridge University Press.

Festinger, L. (1968). A theory of social comparison processes. In H. H. Hyman & E. Singer (Eds.), *Readings in reference group theory and research* (pp. 123–146). New York: Free Press.

Fields, J. (2003). *Children's living arrangements and characteristics: March 2002.* Washington, DC: U.S. Census Bureau.

Figley, C. R., & Kleber, R. J. (1995). Beyond the "victim": Secondary traumatic stress. In R. J. Kleber, C. R. Figley, & B. P. R. Gersons (Eds.), *Beyond trauma: Cultural and societal dynamics* (pp. 75–98). New York: Plenum Press.

Findholt, N. (2006). The culture of rural communities: An examination of rural nursing concepts at the community level. In H. J. Lee & C. A. Winters (Eds.), *Rural nursing: Concepts, theory, and practice* (2nd ed., pp. 301–310). New York: Springer Publishing Company.

Finstuen v. Edmondson, 2006 U.S. Dist. LEXIS 32122 (W.D. Okla. 2006).

FitzGerald, N. (2006, June 14). Center helps free battered women: Campaign works to change attitudes in Russia. *USA Today,* p. 7A.

Flora, C. B., Flora, J. L., & Fey, S. (2004). *Rural communities: Legacy and change* (2nd ed.). Boulder, CO: Westview.

Flounders, S., & Langley, D. (2004). *Tsunami—134,000 dead: The role of U.S. criminal negligence on a global scale: Casualties of a policy of war, negligence, and corporate greed.* New York: International Action Center.

Ford Foundation. (2006). *Peace & social justice.* Retrieved August 2, 2009, from http://www.fordfound.org/pdfs/impact/program_psj.pdf.

Ford, J. (2005). *Managing stress and recovering from trauma: Facts and resources for veterans and families.* National Center for PTSD. Retrieved August 2, 2009, from http://www.ptsd.va.gov/public/pages/managing-stress-facts.asp.

Fornek, S. (2007, September 9). Stanley Ann Dunham: Most generous spirit. *Chicago Sun-Times.* Retrieved January 26, 2009, from http://www.suntimes.com/news/politics/obama/familytree/545458,BSX-News-wotreeff09.stng.

Fox News. (2008, March 14). Obama's pastor's sermon: "God damn America." Retrieved July 5, 2008, from http://elections.foxnews.com/2008/03/14/obamas-spiritual-adviser-questioned-us-role-in-spread-of-hiv-sept-11-attacks/.

Fraser, M. W., Hawkins, J. D., & Howard, M. O. (1988). Parent training for delinquency prevention. *Child and Youth Services, 11,* 93–125.

Frasier, P. Y., Belton, L., Hooten, E., Campbell, M. K., DeVellis, B., & Benedict, S., et al. (2004). Disaster down east: Using participatory action research to explore intimate partner violence in Eastern North Carolina. *Health Education & Behavior, 31*(4), 69S–84S.

Friesen, K. (2007). The effects of the Madrid and London subway bombings on Europe's view of terrorism. *Review Digest: Human Rights & the War on Terror—2007 Supplement.* Retrieved July 24, 2009, from http://www.du.edu/korbel/hrhw/digest/terror/europe_2007.pdf.

Fronczek, P. (2005). *Income, earnings, and poverty from the 2004 American community survey.* Washington, DC: U.S. Census Bureau.

Frostin, P. (2006). *Workers' health insurance: Trends, issues, and options to expand coverage.* Washington, DC: Employee Benefit Research Institute.

Fuller, S. R., & Aldag, R. J. (2001). The GGPS model: Broadening the perspective on group problem solving. In M. E. Turner (Ed.), *Groups at work: Theory and research* (pp. 3–24). Mahwah, NJ: Lawrence Erlbaum Associates.

Gadon, K. D., Sprafkin, J., & Ficarrotto, T. J. (1987). Effects of viewing aggression-laden cartoons on preschool-aged emotionally disturbed children. *Child Psychiatry & Human Development, 17,* 257–274.

Gaines v. Relf, 53 U.S. 472 (1852).

Galindo, R. (1994). Amish newsletters in the budget: A genre study of written communication. *Language in Society, 23*(1), 77–105.

Gamson, W. A. (2004). On a sociology of the media. *Political Communication, 21,* 305–307.

Gao v. Gonzales, 440 F.3d 62 (2nd Cir. 2006).

Garbarino, J. (1995). Growing up in a socially toxic environment: Life for children and families in the 1990s. In G. B. Melton (Ed.), *The individual, the family, and social good: Personal fulfillment in times of change* (pp. 1–20). Lincoln: University of Nebraska Press.

Garbarino, J. (1996). Youth in dangerous environments: Coping with the consequences. In K. Kurrelmann & S. F. Hamilton (Eds.), *Social problems and social contexts in adolescence: Perspectives across boundaries* (pp. 269–290). Hawthorne, NY: Aldine de Gruyter.

Garbarino, J. (1999). The effects of community violence on children. In L. Balter & C. S. Tamis-LeMonda (Eds.), *Child psychology: A handbook of contemporary issues* (pp. 412–425). Philadelphia: Psychology Press.

Garbarino, J., & Abramowitz, R. H. (1992). The family as a social system. In J. Garbarino (Ed.), *Children and families in the social environment* (2nd ed.). New York: Aldine de Gruyter.

Garbarino, J., & Kostelny, K. (1996). What do we need to know to understand children in war and community violence. In R. J. Apfel & B. Simon (Eds.), *Minefields in their hearts: The mental health of children in war and communal violence* (pp. 33–51). New Haven, CT: Yale University Press.

Garbarino, J., & Kostelny, K. (1997). Coping with the consequences of community violence. In A. P. Goldstein & J. C. Conoley (Eds.), *School violence intervention: A practical handbook* (pp. 366–387). New York: The Guilford Press.

Garbarino, J., Kostelny, K., & Grady, J. (1995). Children in dangerous environments: Child maltreatment in the context of community violence. In D. Cicchetti & S. L. Toth (Eds.), *Child abuse, child development and social policy* (pp. 167–189). Norwood, NJ: Ablex Publishing.

George, J. M., & Jones, G. R. (1999). *Understanding and managing organizational behavior* (2nd ed.). Reading, MA: Addison-Wesley.

Georgia Security and Immigration Compliance Act. (2006). Ga. ALS 457; 2006 Ga. Laws 457; 2006 Ga. Act 457; 2005 Ga. SB 529.

Gideon v. Wainwright, 372 U.S. 335 (1963).

Gil, D. G. 2004, Perspectives on social justice. *Reflections,* Fall 32–39.

Gilgoff, D. (2009, March 31). Exclusive: Former NFL coach Tony Dungy invited to join White House Faith Council. *U.S. News & World Report.* Retrieved July 25, 2009, from http://www.usnews.com/blogs/god-and-country/2009/03/31/exclusive-former-nfl-coach-tony-dungy-invited-to-join-white-house-faith-council.html.

Gist, Y. J., & Hetzel, L. L. (2004). *We the people: Aging in the United States.* Washington, DC: U.S. Census Bureau.

Glaser, M. A., Parker, L. E., & Li, H. (2003). Community of choice or ghetto of last resort: Community development and the viability of an African American community. *Review of Policy Research, 20*(3), 525–548.

Glenn, N. D. (2004). The struggle for same-sex marriage. *Society, 41*(6), 25–28.

Global Partnerships. (2009). *Progress report 2008.* Retrieved August 3, 2009, from http://www.globalpartnerships.org/sections/newsinfo/documents/GPARFY08.pdf.

Golombok, S. (1999). New family forms: Children raised in solo mother families, lesbian mother families, and in families created by assisted reproduction. In L. Balter & C. S. Tamis-LeMonda (Eds.), *Child psychology: A handbook of contemporary issues* (pp. 429–446). Philadelphia: Psychology Press.

Gonzales v. Oregon, 2006 U.S. LEXIS 767 (2006).

Goodman, A. (2008, January 28). *Suspects planned suicide attacks.* CNN.com/Europe. Retrieved July 24, 2009, from http://edition.cnn.com/2008/WORLD/europe/01/23/spain.suspects/.

Goodridge v. Department of Public Health, 798 N.E. 2d 941 (Mass. 2003).

Gore, A. (2004). The politics of fear. *Social Research, 71*(4), 779–798.

Graham, J. (2006). Google promises all searchers stay private. *USA Today,* p. 2B.

Grant, J. (2009, May 17). A newsroom to cover the disenfranchised voices in Harlem. *The New York Times.* Retrieved May 27, 2009, from http://www.nytimes.com/2009/05/18/nyregion/18harlem.html?_r=1&ref=smallbusiness.

Greene, J., Pranis, K., & Ziedenberg, J. (2006). *Disparity by design: How drug-free zone laws impact racial disparity—and fail to protect you.* Washington, DC: Justice Policy Institute.

Greene, K. (2003). Fear and loathing in Mississippi: The attack on camp sister spirit. *Journal of Lesbian Studies, 7*(2), 85–106.

Gross, J. (2006, January 3). Seeking doctors' advice in adoption from afar. *The New York Times,* pp. A1, A12.

Hagan, J., & Levi, R. (2005). Crimes of war and force of law. *Social Forces, 83*(4), 1499–1534.

HajYahia, M. M., & Dawud-Noursi, S. (1998). Predicting the use of different conflict tactics among Arab siblings in Israel: A study based on social learning theory. *Journal of Family Violence, 13*(1), 81–103.

Hall, R. H. (2001). *Organizations: Structures, processes, and outcome* (8th ed.). Upper Saddle River, NJ: Prentice Hall.

Hall, T. D. (1999). World-systems and evolution: An appraisal. In P. N. Kardulias (Ed.), *World systems theory in practice: Leadership, production, and exchange* (pp. 1–23). Lanham, MD: Rowman & Littlefield.

Halsell, G. (1993). Women's bodies a battlefield in war for "Greater Serbia." *Washington Report on Middle East Affairs, 11*(9). Retrieved August 2, 2009, from http://www.wrmea.com/backissues/0493/9304008.htm.

Hammack, D. C. (2006). Historical research for the nonprofit sector. *Nonprofit Management & Leadership, 16*(4), 451–466.

Hampson, R. (2006, October 5). Amish community unites to mourn slain schoolgirls. *USA Today.* Retrieved August 2, 2009, from http://www.usatoday.com/news/nation/2006-10-04-amish-shooting_x.htm.

Hansen, G. L., & Hansen, E. K. (2003). Talking out of the closet: Discussing homosexuality in a rural community [Abstract]. *Southern Sociological Society.*

Hanson, R. F., Kilpatrick, D. G., Falsetti, S. A., & Resnick, H. S. (1995). In J. R. Freedy & S. E. Hobfoll (Eds.), *Traumatic stress: From theory to practice* (pp. 129–161). New York: Plenum Press.

Harper v. Occidental Petroleum Services et al., 111 f.3d 131 (6th Cir. 1997).

Harrison, P. M., & Beck, A. J. (2004). *Prisoners in 2003.* Washington, DC: Bureau of Justice Statistics.

Hasenfeld, Y. (1984). Analyzing the human service agency. In F. M. Cox, J. L. Erlich, J. Rothman, & J. E. Thompson (Eds.), *Tactics and techniques of community practice* (2nd ed., pp. 14–26). Itasca, IL: Peacock.

Hawkins, D. N., & Booth, A. (2005). Unhappily ever after: Effects of long-term, low quality marriages on well-being. *Social Forces, 84*(1), 451–471.

Hays, T. (2005, October 16). Terror hoaxes, false alarms vex authorities after 9/11. *Columbus Dispatch,* p. A6.

Hearn, G. (1979). General systems theory and social work. In F. J. Turner (Ed.), *Social work treatment: Interlocking theoretical approaches* (2nd ed., pp. 333–359). New York: Free Press.

Hellriegel, D., Slocum, J. W., Jr., & Woodman, R. W. (1992). *Organizational behavior* (6th ed.). St. Paul, MN: West.

Helvering v. Davis, 301 U.S. 619 (1937).

Henderson, N. (2005, October 1). Katrina contributes to drop in spending. *The Washington Post,* p. A01.

Henggeler, S. W., Halliday-Boykins, C. A., Cunningham, P. B., Shapiro, S. B., & Chapman, J. E. (2006). Juvenile drug court: Enhancing outcomes by integrating evidence-based treatments. *Journal of Consulting & Clinical Psychology, 74*(1), 42–54.

Herman, D. B., Aaron, B. P., & Susser, E. S. (2003). An agenda for public mental health in a time of terror. In S. W. Coates, J. L. Rosenthal, & D. S. Schechter (Eds.), *September 11: Trauma and human bonds* (pp. 239–253). Hillsdale, NJ: The Analytic Press.

Hernandez v. Robles, 2006 N.Y. LEXIS 1836; 2006 N.Y. slip op at 5239 (2006).

Hernandez v. Robles, 2005 N.Y. App. Div. LEXIS 13892 (2005).

Heuveline, P., & Timberlake, J. M. (2004). The role of cohabitation in family formation: The United States in comparative perspective. *Journal of Marriage and Family, 66,* 1214–1230.

Hewner, S. J. (1997). Biocultural approaches to health and mortality in an old order Amish community. *Collegium Antropologicum, 21*(1), 67–82.

Hicks, D. J. (1971). Girls' attitudes toward modeled behavior and the content of imitative private play. *Child Development, 42,* 139–147.

Hilgard, E. R., Atkinson, R. L., & Atkinson, R. C. (1979). *Introduction to psychology* (7th ed.). New York: Harcourt Brace Jovanovich.

Hill v. State of Florida, 688 So. 2d 901 (1997).

Hipp, J. R., Bauer, D. J., Curran, P. J., & Bollen, K. A. (2004). Crimes of opportunity or crimes of emotion? Testing two explanations of seasonal change in crime. *Social Forces, 82*(4), 1333–1372.

Hodgens v. General Dynamics Corporation, 144 F.3d 151 (1st Cir. 1998).

Hoge, C. W., Castro, C. A., Messer, S. C., McGurk, D., Cotting, D. I., & Koffman, R. L. (2004). Combat duty in Iraq and Afghanistan, mental health problems, and barriers to care. *New England Journal of Medicine, 351,* 13–22.

Hoge, W. (2006, April 1). Britain backs request to move Liberian's trial to the Hague. *The New York Times*, p. A8.

Hollingshead, A., & Redlich, F. C. (1958). *Social class and mental illness: A community study*. New York: Wiley.

Holman, E. A., Silver, R. C., Poulin, M., Andersen, J., Gil-Rivas, V., & McIntosh, D. N. (2008). Terrorism, acute stress, and cardiovascular health: A 3-year national study following the September 11th attacks. *Archives of General Psychiatry, 65*(1), 73–80.

Hope, T. (2000). *Perspectives on crime reduction*. Ashgate, VT: Ashgate Publishing Company.

Hough, R. L., Canino, G. J., Abueg, F. R., & Gusman, F. D. (2001). PTSD and related stress disorders among Hispanics. In A. J. Marsella, M. J. Friedman, E. T. Gerrity, & R. M. Scurfield (Eds.), *Ethnocultural aspects of posttraumatic stress disorder: Issues, research, and clinical applications* (pp. 301–338). Washington, DC: American Psychological Association.

Hughes, K. A. (2006). *Justice expenditure and employment in the United States, 2003*. Washington, DC: Bureau of Justice Statistics.

Hughes, P. (2006). The economics of nonprofit organizations. *Nonprofit Management & Leadership, 16*(4), 429–450.

Human Development Report 2005. (2006). *Violent conflict*. New York: United Nations.

Human Rights Watch. (1999a, July 7). *Annan must reject amnesty for Sierra Leone crimes*. Retrieved August 3, 2009, from http://www.hrw.org/en/news/1999/07/07/annan-must-reject-amnesty-sierra-leone-crimes.

Human Rights Watch. (1999b). *Famine in Sudan, 1998: The human rights causes*. New York: Author.

Human Rights Watch. (1999c, April). *Human rights violations in the United States: Red onion state prison: Super-maximum security confinement in Virginia*. New York: Author.

Human Rights Watch. (1999d). *Leave none to tell the story: Genocide in Rwanda*. New York: Author.

Human Rights Watch. (2002a). *Hopes betrayed: Trafficking of women and girls to post-conflict Bosnia and Herzegovina for forced prostitution*. New York: Author.

Human Rights Watch. (2002b). *World report: United States*. New York: Author.

Human Rights Watch. (2003). *Trapped by inequality: Bhutanese refugee women in Nepal*. New York: Author.

Human Rights Watch. (2004a). *Bringing justice: The special court for Sierra Leone: Accomplishments, shortcomings, and needed support*. New York: Author.

Human Rights Watch. (2004b). *The rest of their lives: Life without parole for child offenders in the United States*. New York: Author.

Human Rights Watch. (2005a). *Clear the filth: Mass evictions and demolitions in Zimbabwe*. New York: Author.

Human Rights Watch. (2005c). Social and psychological results of sexual violence. Retrieved October 12, 2005, from http://hrw.org/backgrounder/africa/darfur0505/4.htm.

Human Rights Watch. (2005d). *The case against Hissène Habré, an "African Pinochet."* New York: Author.

Human Rights Watch. (2005e). *Uprooted and forgotten: Impunity and human rights abuses in Northern Uganda*. New York: Author.

Human Rights Watch. (2006a). *U.N. challenges U.S. Rights Record: Human rights committee criticizes U.S. practices*. New York: Author.

Human Rights Watch. (2006b, October 11). *U.S. attack dogs used against prisoners: Worst offenders are state prisons in Connecticut and Iowa.* New York: Author.

Human Rights Watch and the American Civil Liberties Union. (2009). *A violent education.* New York: Authors.

Hunter, L. M., Boardman, J. D., & Onge, J. M. S. (2005). The association between natural amenities, rural population growth, and long term residents' economic well-being. *Rural Sociology, 70*(4), 452–469.

Hunter, L. M., & Sutton, J. (2004). Examining the association between hazardous waste facilities and rural "brain drain." *Rural Sociology, 69*(2), 197–212.

Hyman, H. H., & Singer, E. (1968). Introduction. In H. H. Hyman & E. Singer (Eds.), *Readings in reference group theory and research* (pp. 3–21). New York: Free Press.

In re Marriage Cases, 2008 Cal. LEXIS 5247 (2008).

In re UAL Corp. 2005 U.S. App. LEXIS 23542 (7th Cir., 2005).

In re Fauziya Kasinga, Office of the Immigration Judge, File Number A 73 476 695 (1995).

Innes, S. (2006, January 2). Same-sex couples leaving state because of rules on adoption. *The Arizona Republic,* p. B3.

Institute for the Study of Diplomacy. (2005). *The 1998 terrorist bombings of U.S. embassies in Kenya and Tanzania: Failures of intelligence or of policy priorities?* Washington, DC: Edmund A. Walsh School of Foreign Service, Georgetown University.

Internal Revenue Service. (2009). *The restriction of political campaign intervention by section 501(c)(3) tax-exempt organizations.* Retrieved July 26, 2009, from http://www.irs.gov/charities/charitable/article/0,,id=163395,00.html.

Jacobs, J. W. (2004). *All you need is love and other lies about marriage: How to save your marriage before it's too late.* New York: Three Rivers Press.

Jacobs, T. (2007, December 7). AMBER alerts largely ineffective, study shows. Retrieved July 8, 2008, from http://www.miller-mccune.com/article/108.

James, D. (Producer & Director). (2005, December 26). *Slavery and the making of America* [Television broadcast]. New York: Public Broadcasting Service.

Jan, S. (2005, October 10). Rescuers comb quake rubble. *Columbus Dispatch,* p. A1.

Jeavons, T. H. (2003). The vitality and independence of religious organizations. *Society, 40*(2), 27–36.

Jehovah's Witnesses. (2005, December 22). Pandemics—what the future holds. *Awake* (pp. 10–11). Brooklyn, NY: Author.

Jenkins, J. C., & Scanlan, S. J. (2001). Food security in less developed countries, 1970 to 1990. *American Sociological Review, 66*(5), 718–744.

Jenkins, P. (1992). *Intimate enemies: Moral panics in contemporary Great Britain.* New York: Aldine de Gruyter.

Jensen, G. (2000). Prohibition, alcohol, and murder. *Homicide Studies, 4*(1), 18–36.

Joffe, H. (1992). Blame and AIDS among South African blacks and whites. International Conference on AIDS (Abstract No. PoD 5544). Retrieved July 6, 2008, from http://gateway.nlm.nih.gov/MeetingAbstracts/ma?f=102200747.html.

Johnson, A. (2006, March 30). Cincinnati religious group wields clout. *Columbus Dispatch,* pp. A1, A4.

Johnson, K. (2002). Politics of international and domestic adoption in China. *Law & Society Review, 36*(2), 379–396.

Johnson, M. M., & Rhoades, R. (2005). *Human behavior and the larger social environment: A new synthesis*. Boston: Allyn and Bacon.

Johnson, R. E., Selenta, C., & Lord, R. G. (2006). When organizational justice and the self-concept meet: Consequences for the organization and its members. *Organizational Behavior and Human Decision Processes, 99,* 175–201.

Jones, C. (2005, December 30). Retirees find that rural life suits them: Communities, baby boomers enjoy mutually beneficial relationships. *USA Today,* p. 4A.

Jones, E. F., Forrest, J. D., Goldman, N., Henshaw, S. K., Lincoln, R., Rosoff, J. I., et al. (1991). Teenage pregnancy in developed countries. In J. H. Skolnick & E. Currie (Eds.), *Crisis in American institutions* (pp. 277–294). New York: Harper Collins.

Kaplan, M. L. (2006, July/August). Getting religion in the public research university. *Academe,* 41–45.

Karakowsky, L., McBey, K., & Miller, D. L. (2004). Gender, perceived competence, and power displays: Examining verbal interruptions in a group context. *Small Group Research, 35*(4), 407–439.

Kardulias, P. N. (1999). Conclusion. In P. N. Kardulias (Ed.), *World systems theory in practice: Leadership, production, and exchange* (pp. 309–313). Lanham, MD: Rowman & Littlefield.

Kassirer, J. P. (2001). Mergers and acquisitions—who benefits? Who loses? In C. Harrington & C. L. Estes (Eds.), *Health policy: Crisis and reform in the U.S. health care delivery system* (3rd ed., pp. 132–135). Sudbury, MA: Jones & Bartlett.

Kaufman, M. (2005, September 17). FEMA's city of anxiety in Florida. *The Washington Post,* p. A01.

Kaufman, M., & Stein, R. (2006, January 10). Record share of economy is spent on health care. *The Washington Post,* p. A1.

Keen, J. (2006, March 23). Some uneasy as illegals change face of Minn. town: Use of false IDs stirs debate over immigrants. *USA Today,* p. 5A.

Kelley, D. S. (1994). Family victimization: An application of lifestyle and routine activity theory. *Dissertation Abstracts International, A: The Humanities and Social Sciences, 54*(7), 2745-A.

Kerr v. Farrey, 95 F.3d 472 (7th Cir. 1996).

Kim, S. (2001). Faith-based service delivery: A case study at ground zero. *Journal of City and State Public Affairs, 2*(1), 41–52.

Kimbrough v. United States, 128 S. Ct. 558 (2007).

Kitzmiller v. Dover Area School District, 2005 U.S. Dist. LEXIS 33647 (2005).

Klandermans, B., Roefs, M., & Olivier, J. (2005). Social capital in democratic transition: Civil society in South Africa. In A. M. Omoto (Ed.), *Processes of community change and social action* (pp. 127–148). Mahwah, NJ: Lawrence Erlbaum Associates.

Kleinfield, N. R. (2006a). Diabetes and its awful toll quietly emerge as a crisis. *The New York Times,* pp. A1, A18, A19.

Kleinfield, N. R. (2006b). Living at an epicenter of diabetes, defiance and despair. *The New York Times,* pp. A1, A20, A21.

Kobrin, S. (2000). The Chicago area project: A 25-year assessment. In T. Hope (Ed.), *Perspectives on crime reduction* (pp. 42–49). Hants, England: Ashgate. (Reprinted from *Annals of the American Academy of Political and Social Science, 322,* 19–29, 1959)

Koch, W. (2006, June 16). Developments bar sex offenders: Restriction boosts sales, but some predict problems. *USA Today*, p. 3A.

Kochhar, R. (2005). *The economic transition to America*. Washington, DC: Pew Hispanic Center.

Konty, M., Duell, B., & Joireman, J. (2004). Scared selfish: A culture of fear's values in the age of terrorism. *The American Sociologist, 35*(2), 93–109.

Kornfeld, E. L. (1995). The development of treatment approaches for victims of human rights violations in Chile. In R. J. Kleber, C. R. Figley, & B. P. R. Gersons (Eds.), *Beyond trauma: Cultural and societal dynamics* (pp. 115–131). New York: Plenum Press.

Krannich, R. S., & Luloff, A. E. (2002). A 50-year perspective on persistence and change: Lessons from the rural studies communities. In A. E. Luloff & R. S. Krannich (Eds.), *Persistence and change in rural communities: A 50-year follow-up to six classic studies* (pp. 171–177). New York: CABI Publishing.

Kreps, G. M., Donnermeyer, J. F., Hurst, C., Blair, R., & Kreps, M. (1997). The impact of tourism on the Amish subculture: A case study. *Community Development Journal, 32*(4), 354–367.

Kristof, N. D. (2005a, November 29). How much genocide in Darfur can be tolerated. *Columbus Dispatch*, p. A9.

Kristof, N. D. (2005b, November 22). Sudan's department of gang rape. *The New York Times*, p. A27.

Kristof, N. D. (2005c, November 29). What's to be done about Darfur? Plenty. *The New York Times*, p. A31.

Krohn, M. D. (1999). Social learning theory: The continuing development of a perspective. *Theoretical Criminology, 3*(4), 462–476.

Kuhn v. Thompson, 304 F. Supp. 1212 (M.D. Ala. 2004).

Kulish, N. (1991, August 9). Crime pays: Since census counts convicts, some towns can't get enough—federal and state funds tied to total population help Florence, Ariz. *The Wall Street Journal*, p. A1.

L.A. putting homeless issues on back burner to tackle crime. (2006, March 19). *Columbus Dispatch*, p. A6.

Lacey, M. (2005, December 5). Leading player in Darfur's drama: The hapless camel. *The New York Times*, p. A4.

LaFond, J. Q. (2005). *Preventing sexual violence: How society should cope with sex offenders*. Washington, DC: American Psychological Association.

LaFraniere, S. (2005, December 30). Women's rights laws and African custom clash. *The New York Times*, p. A1.

Lampkin, L. M., & Boris, E. T. (2002). Nonprofit organization data: What we have and what we need. *American Behavioral Scientist, 45*(11), 1675–1715.

Landesman, P. (2004, January 25). The girls next door. *The New York Times Magazine*, pp. 30–39, 66–67, 72, 75.

Lareau, A. (2002). Invisible inequality: Social class and childrearing in Black families and White families. *American Sociological Review, 67*, 747–776.

Laubach, M. (2005). Consent, informal organization and job rewards: A mixed methods analysis. *Social Forces, 83*(4), 1535–1566.

Lauritsen, J. L. (2003). *How families and communities influence youth victimization*. Washington, DC: U.S. Department of Justice, Office of Justice Programs, Office of Juvenile Justice and Delinquency Prevention.

Lawrence v. Texas, 539 U.S. 558 (2003).

Leary, J. D. (2005). *Post traumatic slave syndrome: America's legacy of enduring injury and healing.* Milwaukie, OR: Uptone Press.

Lee, E. S. (1966). A theory of migration. *Demography, 3,* 46–57.

Leung, R. (2005, February 23). Rescued from sex slavery. *48 Hours,* CBS News. Retrieved August 2, 2009, from http://www.cbsnews.com/stories/2005/02/23/48hours/main675913.shtml?tag=contentMain;contentBody.

Levenson, J. S., & Cotter, L. P. (2005). The impact of sex offender residence restrictions: 1,000 feet from danger or one step from absurd. *International Journal of Offender Therapy and Comparative Criminology, 49*(2), 169–178.

Levey, N. N. (2008, September 4). Obama courts female voters with family stories. *Los Angeles Times,* p. A22.

Lewis, D. A., & Salem, G. (2000). Community crime prevention: An analysis of a developing strategy. In T. Hope (Ed.), *Perspectives on crime reduction* (pp. 91–107). Ashgate, VT: Ashgate Publishing Company.

Lind, A. (2004). Legislating the family: Heterosexist bias in social welfare policy frameworks. *Journal of Sociology and Social Welfare, 31*(4), 21–35.

Liptak, A. (2006, August 5). Parental rights upheld for lesbian ex-partner. *The New York Times,* p. A10.

Litz, B. (2005). *A brief primer on the mental health impact of the wars in Afghanistan and Iraq.* White River Junction, VT: National Center for PTSD.

Local Initiatives Support Corporation. (2005a). *Preserving America's affordable housing: Retooling a 20th century asset for 21st century needs.* New York: Author.

Local Initiatives Support Corporation. (2005b). *The ripple effect: Economic impacts of targeted community investments.* New York: Author.

Local Initiatives Support Corporation. (2006). *Helping neighbors build communities.* New York: Author.

Lockyer v. City and County of San Francisco, 33 Cal. 4th 1055, 95 P.3d 459 (2004).

Loewen, J. W. (2005). *Sundown towns: A hidden dimension of American racism.* New York: New Press.

Lord, A., & Barnes, C. (1996). Family liaisons work with adolescents in a sex offender treatment programme. *Journal of Sexual Aggression, 2,* 112–121.

Loving v. Virginia, 388 U.S. 1 (1967).

Lyman, R. (2006a, May 12). As Congress dithers, Georgia tackles immigration. *The New York Times,* p. A17.

Lyman, R. (2006b, April 10). Town sees nuclear plans as a boon, not a threat. *The New York Times,* p. A14.

Lynch, J. M. (2004). The identity transformation of biological parents in lesbian/gay stepfamilies. *Journal of Homosexuality, 47*(2), 91–107.

Lynch, J. P. (1987). Routine activity and victimization at work. *Journal of Quantitative Criminology, 3*(4), 283–300.

Macgillivray, I. K. (2004). *Sexual orientation and school policy: A practical guide for teachers, administrators, and community activists.* Lanham, MD: Rowman & Littlefield.

MacKinnon, K. (2004). The family in Hollywood melodrama: Actual or ideal. *Journal of Gender Studies, 13*(1), 29–36.

Mahay, J., & Laumann, E. O. (2004). Neighborhoods as sex markets. In E. O. Laumann, S. Ellingson, J. Mahay, A. Paik, & Y. Youm (Eds.), *The sexual organization of the city* (pp. 69–92). Chicago: The University of Chicago Press.

Malkin, M. (2008, September 5). Why Obama's "community organizer" days are a joke. *Real Clear Politics*. Retrieved January 27, 2009, from http://www.realclear politics.com/articles/2008/09/why_obamas_community_organizer.html.

Marech, R. (2004, April 6). The battle over same-sex marriage: Gays find marriage a mixed bag, license doesn't guarantee benefits granted. *San Francisco Chronicle*. Retrieved January 14, 2006, from http://sfgate.com/cgi-bin/article.cgi?f=/c/a/2004/04/06/BAGBG610IJ1.DTL.

Marrett, C. B. (1990). The changing composition of schools: Implications for school organization. In M. T. Hallinen, D. M. Klein, & J. Glass (Eds.), *Change in societal institutions* (pp. 71–90). New York: Plenum Press.

Martin, P. P., Younge, S., & Smith, A. (2003). Searching for the balm in Gilead: The HIV/AIDS epidemic and the African American church. *African American Research Perspectives, 9*(1), 70–78.

Maslow, A. (1962). *Towards a psychology of being*. Princeton, NJ: D. van Nostrand.

Massey, J. L., Krohn, M., & Bonati, L. (1989). Property crime and the routine activities of individuals. *Journal of Research in Crime and Delinquency, 26*(4), 378–400.

Mayfield, N. (2003, March 18). U.S. executes Gulf War veteran. *Common Dreams News Center*. Retrieved August 2, 2009, from http://www.commondreams.org/headlines03/0318-09.htm.

Maynard v. Hill, 125 U.S. 190 (1888).

McCrea, R., Shyy, T., Western, J., & Stimson, R. J. (2005). Fear of crime in Brisbane: Individual, social and neigbourhood factors in perspective. *Journal of Sociology, 41*(1), 7–27.

McDonald, I. (2004). For better or for worse? The civil partnership bill [HL] 2004. *Journal of Social Welfare and Family Law, 26*(3), 313–324.

McDonnell Douglas Corp. v. Green, 411 U. S. 792 (1973).

McFadden, R. D. (2006, April 10). Protests staged for immigrants across the U.S. *The New York Times*, pp. A1, A20.

McFarlane, A. C. (1995). Helping the victims of disasters: Helping victims of military trauma. In J. R. Freedy & S. E. Hobfoll (Eds.), *Traumatic stress: From theory to practice* (pp. 287–314). New York: Plenum Press.

McIntosh, W. A. (1996). *Sociologies of food and nutrition*. New York: Plenum Press.

McIntyre, G. L. (2003). Differential reinforcement, drinking, and readiness to change: An application of social learning. *Dissertation Abstracts International, A: The Humanities and Social Sciences, 63*(10), 3744-A.

McNeil, D. G., Jr., & Lyman, R. (2006, June 27). Buffett's billions will aid fight against disease. *The New York Times*, pp. A1, C4.

"Medicine." (1996). In *Webster's New World College Dictionary* (3rd ed., p. 842). New York: Simon & Schuster.

Mellow, M. (2004). The work of rural professionals: Doing the Gemeinschaft-Gesellschaft gavotte. *Rural Sociology, 70*(1), 50–69.

Melton, G. B. (1995). Introduction: Personal satisfaction and the welfare of families, communities, and society. In G. B. Melton (Ed.), *The individual, the family, and social good: Personal fulfillment in times of change.* (pp. ix–xxvii). Lincoln: University of Nebraska Press.

Mencken, F. C., & Tolbert, C. M., II. (2005). Federal public investment spending and economic development in Appalachia. *Rural Sociology, 70*(4), 514–539.

Meyer, J. W., & Rowan, B. (2007). The structure of educational organizations. In J. H. Ballantine & J. Z. Spade (Eds.), *Schools and society: A sociological approach to education* (pp. 77–87). Belmont, CA: Wadsworth.

Michael J. v. Los Angeles County Department of Adoptions, 201 Cal. App. 3d 859, 247 Cal. Rptr. 504 (1988).

Michaels, K. W., & Green, R. H. (1979). A child welfare agency project: Therapy for families of status offenders. *Child Welfare, 58,* 216–220.

Mihalic, S. W., & Elliott, D. (1997). A social learning theory model of marital violence. *Journal of Family Violence, 12*(1), 21–47.

Miller, J. G. (1955). Toward a general theory of the behavioral sciences. *American Psychologist, 10,* 513–531.

Miller-Jenkins v. Miller-Jenkins, 2006 VT 78; 2006 Vt. LEXIS 159 (2006).

Miranda v. Arizona, 384 U.S. 436 (1966).

Moberg, D. (2007, April 3). Obama's community roots. *The Nation.* Retrieved January 27, 2009, from http://www.thenation.com/doc/20070416/moberg.

Monsma, S. V. (2003). Nonprofit and faith-based welfare-to-work programs. *Society, 40*(2), 13–18.

Montet, V. (2009, January 19). Fairy godfather invites disadvantaged to inaugural ball. *France 24.* Retrieved January 29, 2009, from http://www.france24.com/en/20090119-fairy-godfather-invites-disadvantaged-inaugural-ball.

Mooney, L. A., Knox, D., & Schacht, C. (2002). *Understanding social problems* (3rd ed.). Belmont, CA: Wadsworth.

Moore v. City of East Cleveland, 431 U.S. 494 (1977).

Moore, G., Sobieraj, S., Whitt, J. A., Mayorova, O., & Beaulieu, D. (2002). Elite interlocks in three U.S. sectors: Nonprofit, corporate, and government. *Social Science Quarterly, 83*(3), 726–744.

Moore, M. T. (2006a, May 18). ACLU to sue after community rejects unmarried pair. *USA Today,* p. 3A.

Moore, M. T. (2006c, July 11). Sex crimes break the lock on juvenile records: Some states list minors in their registries; Federal law may follow suit. *USA Today,* p. 5A.

Moritsugu, K. (2006, May 8). India struggles with discrimination: Push to set quotas for "untouchables" faces opposition. *USA Today,* p. 10A.

MSNBC.com. (2006, January 30). Religious groups getting AIDS funds: Bush administration earmarked $200 million for less-experienced groups. Retrieved January 30, 2006, from http://www.msnbc.msn.com/id/10789265/print/1/display mode/1098/.

Mullen, M. R., Beller, E., Remsa, J., & Cooper, D. (2001). The effects of international trade on economic growth and meeting basic human needs. *Journal of Global Marketing, 15*(1), 31–55.

Murder trial thrusts juror into rare bond with strangers. (2006, March 4). *Columbus Dispatch,* p. E1.

Muse, C. E. (2003). A difference in care? Implications for homosexual adoption policies based on a meta-analysis of the literature regarding homosexual parenting. *Southern Sociological Society.*

Mustaine, E. E., & Tewksbury, R. (1997). Obstacles in the assessment of routine activity theory. *Social Pathology, 3*(3), 177–194.

Mustaine, E. E., & Tewksbury, R. (1998). Predicting risks of larceny theft victimization: A routine activity analysis using refined lifestyles measures. *Criminology, 36*(4), 829–857.

Mydans, S. (2006, May 28). Shunned, women with HIV join forces in Vietnam. *The New York Times,* p. B3.

Najam, A. (2006, October 7). Earthquake numbers: A year later. *All Things Pakistan.* Retrieved July 24, 2009, from http://pakistaniat.com/2006/10/07/pakistan-earthquake-reconstruction-numbers/.

Narciso, D. (2006, July 13). Councilman pushing for total ban on sex offenders. *Columbus Dispatch,* p. D6.

National Center for Health Statistics. (2006). *Health, United States, 2006.* Hyattsville, MD: U.S. Department of Health and Human Services.

National Center for PTSD. (2005). *War-zone-related stress reactions: What families need to know.* Retrieved October 21, 2005, from http://www.ptsd.va.gov/public/pages/warzone-stress-reactions-family.asp.

National Institute of Justice. (2005). *Evaluation of OJJDP's commercial sexual exploitation of children demonstration program in Atlanta/Fulton County.* Washington, DC: Author.

National Public Radio. (2008, July 5). *Black Americans and medicine* [Radio program]. Washington, DC: Author.

National Veterans Foundation. (2005). *Facts about veterans.* Retrieved October 21, 2005, from http://www.nvf.org.

Navarro, S. A. (2002). Las voces de esperanza/voices of hope: La Mujer Obrera, transnationalism, and NAFTA-displaced women workers in the U.S.-Mexico borderlands. In C. Sadowski-Smith (Ed.), *Globalization on the line: Culture, capital, and citizenship at U.S. borders* (pp. 183–200). New York: Palgrave.

Navasky, M., & O'Connor, K. (2005, May 10). *The new asylums* [Video]. Boston: WGBH Educational Foundation.

Neeley v. West Orange-Cove Consolidated Independent School District, 49 Tex. Sup. J. 119 (2005).

Nes, J. A., & Iadicola, P. (1989). Toward a definition of feminist social work: A comparison of liberal, radical, and socialist models. *Social Work, 34,* 12–21.

Netting, F. E., Kettner, P. M., & McMurtry, S. L. (2004). *Social work macro practice* (3rd ed.). Boston: Allyn and Bacon.

New Strategist. (2005). *American attitudes: What Americans think about the issues that shape their lives* (4th ed.). Ithaca, NY: New Strategist Publications.

Newman, D. M. (2002). *Sociology: Exploring the architecture of everyday life* (4th ed.). Thousand Oaks, CA: Pine Forge Press.

No. 3 Balkan war-crimes suspect captured. (2007, June 1). *USA Today,* p. 8A.

Nordwall v. Sears Roebuck, 46 Fed. Appx. 364 (7th Cir. 2002).

Nossiter, A. (2006, July 5). With jobs to do, Louisiana parish turns to inmates. *The New York Times,* pp. A1, A13.

O'Connor v. California, 855 F. Supp. 303 (C.D. Cal. 1994).

Oakley, D. A. (2003). Fallacies of the American welfare state: The enduring response of community and faith-based organizations. Homeless shelters and relief services in

New York City during the 1920s and 1990s. *Dissertation Abstracts International, A: The Humanities and Social Sciences, 64*(3), 1099-A.

Obama, B. (1990). Why organize? Problems and promise in the inner city. In P. Knoepfle (Ed.), *After Alinsky: Community organizing in Illinois* (pp. 35–40). Springfield: University of Illinois Press.

Ohio Department of Rehabilitation and Correction. (2004). DRC current FY 2005 direct institution budget/inmate costs. Retrieved January 12, 2006, from http://www.drc.state.oh.us/web/Reports/costperinmate/July%202004.pdf.

Olujic, M. B. (1995). Women, rape, and war: The continued trauma of refugees and displaced persons in Croatia. *Anthropology of East Europe Review, 13*(1). Retrieved August 3, 2009, from http://condor.depaul.edu/~rrotenbe/aeer/aeer13_1/Olujic.html.

Omoto, A. M., & Malsch, A. M. (2005). Psychological sense of community: Conceptual issues and connections to volunteerism-related activism. In A. M. Omoto (Ed.), *Processes of community change and social action* (pp. 83–103). Mahwah, NJ: Lawrence Erlbaum Associates.

Ortiz, A. T., & Briggs, L. (2003). The culture of poverty, crack babies, and welfare cheats: The making of the "healthy white baby crisis." *Social Text, 21*(3), 39–57.

Page, J. (2004). Eliminating the enemy: The import of denying prisoners access to higher education in Clinton's America. *Punishment & Society, 6*(4), 357–378.

Pager, D. (2003). The mark of a criminal record. *American Journal of Sociology, 108*, 937–975.

Paletz, S. B., Peng, K., Erez, M., & Maslach, C. (2004). Ethnic composition and its differential impact on group processes in diverse teams. *Small Group Research, 35*(2), 128–157.

Pallas, A. M. (2000). The effects of schooling on individual lives. In M. T. Hallinan (Ed.), *Handbook of the sociology of education* (pp. 499–525). New York: Kluwer Academic/Plenum Publishers.

Parillo, V. N. (2009). *Strangers to these shores* (9th ed.). Boston: Pearson.

Parisi, D., McLaughlin, D. K., Grice, S. M., Taquino, M., & Gill, D. A. (2003). TANF participation rates: Do community conditions matter? *Rural Sociology, 68*(4), 491–512.

Park, R. E. (1915/1925). The city: Suggestions for the investigation of human behavior in the urban environment. In R. E. Park, E. W. Burgess, & R. D. Mckenzie (Eds.), *The city* (pp. 1–46). Chicago: University of Chicago Press.

Parkman, A. M. (1995). The deterioration of the family: A law and economic perspective. In G. B. Melton (Ed.), *The individual, the family, and social good: Personal fulfillment in times of change* (pp. 21–52). Lincoln: University of Nebraska Press.

Passel, J. S. (2006). *The size and characteristics of the unauthorized migrant population in the U.S.* Washington, DC: Pew Hispanic Center.

Passey, A., & Lyons, M. (2006). Nonprofits and social capital: Measurement through organizational surveys. *Nonprofit Management & Leadership, 16*(4), 481–495.

Patel, R., & Delwiche, A. (2002). The profits of famine: Southern Africa's long decade of hunger. *Backgrounder, 8*(4). Retrieved August 2, 2009, from http://www.foodfirst.org/en/node/51.

Patten, W. (2004). U.S.: Efforts to combat human trafficking and slavery. Testimony before the Senate Committee on the Judiciary on July 15, 2004. Retrieved October 5, 2005, from http://hrw.org/english/docs/2004/07/15/usdom9075.htm.

PBS. (2008). *People & events: The Northern migration of sharecroppers in the 1920s.* Retrieved July 24, 2009, from http://www.pbs.org/wgbh/amex/flood/peopleevents/ e_sharecroppers.html.

Pear, R. (2007, March 5). Without health benefits, a good life turns fragile. *The New York Times,* p. A1, A7.

Perdue v. O'Kelley, 2006 Ga. LEXIS 465 (2006).

Perry, R. W., & Maurer, B. (2003). Globalization and governmentality: An introduction. In R. W. Perry & B. Maurer (Eds.), *Globalization under construction* (pp. ix–xxi). Minneapolis: University of Minnesota Press.

Peters, J. D. (2001). Media and communications. In J. R. Blau (Ed.), *The Blackwell companion to sociology* (pp. 16–29). Malden, MA: Blackwell.

Pfefferbaum, B. J., Devoe, E. R., Stuber, J., Schiff, M., Klein, T. P., & Fairbrother, G. (2005). Psychological impact of terrorism on children and families in the United States. *Journal of Aggression, Maltreatment & Trauma, 9*(3), 305–317.

Pipes, P. F., & Ebaugh, H. R. (2002). Faith-based coalitions, social services, and government funding. *Sociology of Religion, 63*(1), 49–68.

Pivar, I. (2005). *Talking with children about going to war.* Retrieved August 2, 2009, from http://www.ptsd.va.gov/public/pages/talking-to-children-about-war.asp.

Plessy v. Ferguson, 163 U.S. 537 (1896).

Pohl, O. (2006, May 7). Gypsies gain a legal tool in rights fight. *The New York Times International,* p. B6.

Portelli, C. J. (2004). Economic analysis of same-sex marriage. *Journal of Homosexuality, 47*(1), 95–109.

Powell, A. (n.d.). *Amish 101—Amish beliefs, culture & lifestyle.* Retrieved May 20, 2007, from http://pittsburgh.about.com/cs/pennsylvania/a/amish.htm.

Powell, B. A. (2003). "The wrong direction": Health policy expert Helen Halpin decries Bush's Medicare proposal. Web feature, UC Berkeley News. Retrieved January 9, 2006, from http://www.berkeley.edu/news/media/releases/2003/03/07_medicare.shtml.

Prentky, R. A. (1996). Community notification and constructive risk reduction. *Journal of Interpersonal Violence, 11*(2), 295–298.

Preston, J. (2006, May 9). State proposals on illegal immigration largely falters. *The New York Times,* p. A17.

Price-Spratlen, T. (1998). Between depression and prosperity? Changes in the community context of historical African-American migration. *Social Forces, 77*(5), 515–540.

Qian, Z., Lichter, D. T., & Mellott, L. M. (2005). Out-of-wedlock childbearing, marital prospects and mate selection. *Social Forces, 84*(1), 473–491.

Race part of debate on borders. (2006, June 6). *Columbus Dispatch,* p. A11.

Raeburn, P. (2006, May 28). Home remedy. *The New York Times Magazine,* p. 22.

Ramer, H. (2006, January 4). In health care, young adults slipping through the cracks. *Houston Chronicle,* p. D2.

Ramirez, R. R. (2004). *We the people: Hispanics in the United States.* Washington, DC: U.S. Census Bureau.

Randaxhe, F. (2002). Times facing each other: Slow time vs fast time in the old order Amish community. *Annales, 57*(2), 251–274.

Rasheed, M. N., & Rasheed, J. M. (2003). Rural African American older adults and the Black helping tradition. In S. S. Butler & L. W. Kaye (Eds.), *Gerontological social work in small towns and rural communities* (pp. 137–150). New York: The Haworth Press.

Red Orbit. (2005, November 4). Turkish daily news accused CIA of crimes against humanity. Retrieved January 25, 2009, from http://www.redorbit.com/news/international/294917/Turkish_daily_accuses_cia_of_crimes_against_humanity/.

Redlich, A. D. (2001). Community notification: Perceptions of its effectiveness in preventing child sexual abuse. *Journal of Child Sexual Abuse, 10*(3), 91–116.

Reeves, E. (2005, October 9). Khartoum solution for Darfur: Preserving the genocidal status quo. *Sudan Tribune.* Retrieved October 10, 2005, from http://www.sudantribune.com/article.php3?id_article=12002.

Reeves, E. B., & Bylund, R. A. (2005). Are rural schools inferior to urban schools? A multilevel analysis of school accountability trends in Kentucky. *Rural Sociology, 70*(3), 360–386.

Reiling, D. M. (2002). The "simmie" side of life: Old order Amish youths' affective response to culturally prescribed deviance. *Youth and Society, 34*(2), 146–171.

Retailer Industry Leaders Association v. Fielder, 2006 U.S. Dist. LEXIS 49037 (2006).

Ribando, C. M. (2007). *Gangs in Central America.* Washington, DC: Congressional Research Service.

Richman, K. D. (2005). (When) are rights wrong? Rights discourses and indeterminacy in gay and lesbian parents' custody cases. *Law & Social Inquiry, 30*(1), 137–176.

Rimm, D. C., & Masters, J. C. (1979). *Behavior therapy: Techniques and empirical findings* (2nd ed.). New York: Academic Press.

Ritter, J. (2006, July 3). Gay seniors settle into a niche: Housing caters to overlooked market. *USA Today,* pp. 1D, 2D.

Robbins, S. P., & Alexander, R., Jr. (1985). Indian delinquency on urban and rural reservations. *Free Inquiry in Creative Sociology, 13*(2), 179–182.

Roberts, S. (2006, May 13). Courts ask if residency follows New York inmates up the river. *The New York Times,* p. A15.

Robertson suggests God smote Sharon. (2006, January 5). CNN. Retrieved August 2, 2009, from http://www.democraticunderground.com/discuss/duboard.php?az=view_all&address=132x2351842.

Robin, R. W., Chester, B., & Goldman, D. (2001). Cumulative trauma and PTSD in American Indian communities. In A. J. Marsella, M. J. Friedman, E. T. Gerrity, & R. M. Scurfield (Eds.), *Ethnocultural aspects of posttraumatic stress disorder: Issues, research, and clinical applications* (pp. 239–253). Washington, DC: American Psychological Association.

Robinson, S. L. (2004). *Hidden toll of the war in Iraq.* Washington, DC: Center for American Progress.

Roe v. Wade, 410 U.S. 113 (1973).

Roland, C. (2006, July 24). Probes may test Bechtel's clout: Responsibility on bolts at issue. *Boston Globe.* Retrieved December 24, 2008, from http://www.boston.com/news/traffic/bigdig/articles/2006/07/24/probes_may_test_bechtels_clout.

Rome Statute of the International Criminal Court. (1999). Retrieved August 2, 2009, from http://www.un.org/icc/romestat.htm.

Roper v. Simmons, 543 U.S. 551 (2005).

Rosenthal, E. (2006, June 5). Report details stormy relationship between Milosevic and court-appointed medical team. *The New York Times,* p. A10.

Rosewater, L. B. (1990). Diversifying feminist theory and practice: Broadening the concept of victimization. *Women & Therapy, 9*(1), 299–311.

Rössel, J., & Collins, R. (2001). Conflict theory and interaction rituals: The microfoundations of conflict theory. In J. H. Turner (Ed.), *Handbook of sociological theory* (pp. 509–531). New York: Kluwer Academic/Plenum Publishers.

Rotter, J. B. (1975). Some problems and misconceptions related to the construct of internal versus external control of reinforcement. *Journal of Consulting and Clinical Psychology, 43,* 56–67.

Rubin, E. (2006, April 2). If not peace, then justice. *The New York Times Magazine,* pp. 43–49, 66, 74–76.

Rubington, E., & Weinberg, M. S. (Eds.). (1995). *The study of social problems: Seven perspectives* (5th ed.). New York: Oxford University Press.

Ruggles, S., & Brower, S. (2003). Measurement of household and family composition in the United States, 1850–2000. *Population and Development Review, 29*(1), 73–101.

Ryan, K. (2009, July 16). Mixed flood recovery. *The Jamestown Sun.* Retrieved July 24, 2009, from http://www.jamestownsun.com/event/article/id/89348/.

Sachs, J. D. (2005). *The end of poverty: Economic possibilities for our time.* New York: The Penguin Press.

Sadowski-Smith, C. (2002). Border studies, diaspora, and theories of globalization. In C. Sadowski-Smith (Ed.), *Globalization and the line: Culture, capital, citizenship at U.S. borders* (pp. 1–27). New York: Palgrave.

Sampson, R. J., & Groves, W. B. (1989). Community structure and crime: Testing social-disorganization theory. *American Journal of Sociology, 94,* 774–802.

Sampson, R. J., Raudenbush, S. W., & Earls, F. (2000). Neighborhoods and violent crime: A multilevel study of collective efficacy. In T. Hope (Ed.), *Perspectives on crime reduction.* (pp. 127–133). Ashgate, VT: Ashgate Publishing Company.

Sanchez, L. (2003). Sex and space in the global city. In R. W. Perry & B. Maurer (Eds.), *Globalization under construction: Governmentality, law, and identity* (pp. 239–271). Minneapolis: University of Minnesota Press.

Santos, F. (2006, May 28). Mixed success in Yonkers. *The New York Times.* Retrieved July 31, 2009, from http://www.nytimes.com/2006/05/28/nyregion/28yonkers.html.

Santos, T. S. (1971). The structure of dependence. In K. T. Fann and D. C. Hodges (Eds.), *Readings in U.S. imperialism* (p. 226). Boston: Porter Sargent.

Saulny, S. (2006, June 21). A legacy of the storm: Depression and suicide. *The New York Times,* pp. A1, A15.

Saunders, J. M. (1991). Relating social structural abstractions to sociological research. *Teaching Sociology, 19,* 270–271.

Scarpino v. Grosshiem, 852 F. Supp. 798 (S.D. Iowa 1994).

Scarpitti, F. R., Anderson, M. L., & O' Toole, L. L. (1997). *Social problems* (3rd ed.). New York: Longman.

Schofer, E., & Fourcade-Gourinchas, M. (2001). The structural contexts of civic engagement: Voluntary association membership in comparative perspective. *American Sociological Review, 66,* 806–828.

School's pornography assignment prompts parental outcry. (2006, January 15). *Columbus Dispatch,* p. C7.

Schorn, D. (2006, April 16). *China: Too many men.* Retrieved August 2, 2009, from http://www.cbsnews.com/stories/2006/04/13/60minutes/main1496589.shtml?tag=contentMain;contentBody.

Schultz, D. (1976). *Theories of personality.* Monterey, CA: Brooks/Cole.

Schuster, C., & Petosa, R. (1993). Using social learning theory to assess the exercise related health education needs of post-retirement adults. *International Quarterly of Community Health Education, 14*(2), 191–205.

Schwartz, A. (2003). Stable vision: Charitable choice and the routinization of charisma. *Social Work & Christianity, 30*(1), 52–63.

Severson, K. (2008, December 23). Is a new food policy on Obama's list? *The New York Times.* Retrieved January 26, 2009, from http://www.nytimes.com/2008/12/24/dining/24food.html.

Sewpaul, V., & Jones, D. (2004). *Global standards for the education and training of the social work profession.* Retrieved August 3, 2009, from http://www.crin.org/docs/global%20standards%20for%20the%20edu.%20and%20training%20of%20social%20work%20profession.pdf.

Shannon, T. R. (1992). *An introduction to the world-system perspective* (2nd ed.). Boulder, CO: Westview Press.

Shapiro, E. (1999). *Cost of crime: A review of the research studies.* St. Paul: Research Department, Minnesota House of Representatives.

Sharp, H. (2009, January 7). Children hit hard as Gaza toll rises. Retrieved January 24, 2009, from http://news.bbc.co.uk/2/hi/middle_east/7814490.stm.

Sheehan, T. (2006, January 18). Newark reins in sex offenders: Housing limits extended to pools, park. *Columbus Dispatch,* pp. B1, B2.

Sherman, J. (2006). Coping with rural poverty: Economic survival and moral capital in rural America. *Social Forces, 85*(2), 891–913.

Sherman, M., & Feller, B. (2009, May 2). Speculation rampant about court vacancy. *Columbus Dispatch,* p. A3.

Simmons, T., & Dye, J. L. (2003). *Grandparents living with grandchildren: 2000.* Washington, DC: U.S. Census Bureau.

Simons, J. S., Gaher, R. M., Jacobs, G. A., Meyer, D., & Johnson-Jimenez, E. (2005). Association between alcohol use and PTSD symptoms among American Red Cross disaster relief workers responding to the 9/11/2001 attacks. *The American Journal of Drug and Alcohol Abuse, 31,* 285–304.

Simons, M. (2006, June 21). Former Liberian president in The Hague for trial. *The New York Times,* p. A6.

Sims, B., & Johnston, E. (2004). Examining public opinion about crime and justice: A statewide study. *Criminal Justice Policy Review, 15*(3), 270–293.

Sinclair, U. (1906). *The jungle.* New York: Doubleday.

Singer, S. D., & Hensley, C. (2004). Applying social learning theory to childhood and adolescent firesetting: Can it lead to serial murder? *International Journal of Offender Therapy and Comparative Criminology, 48*(4), 461–476.

Sizemore, D. S. (2004). Ethnic inclusion and exclusion: Managing the language of Hispanic integration in a rural community. *Journal of Contemporary Ethnography, 33*(5), 534–570.

Skinner, W. F., & Fream, A. M. (1997). A social learning theory analysis of computer crime among college students. *Journal of Research in Crime and Delinquency, 34*(4), 495–518.

Skinner, W. R. (2003). Social learning theory and gambling: Will Akers make book? *Southern Sociological Society, 051.*

Smiley, T. (Ed.). (2006). *The covenant with Black America.* Chicago: Third World Press.

Smith, C., & Woodberry, R. D. (2001). Sociology of religion. In J. R. Blau (Ed.), *The Blackwell companion to sociology* (pp. 100–113). Malden, MA: Blackwell.

Snyder, A. R., & McLaughlin, D. K. (2004). Female-headed families and poverty in rural America. *Rural Sociology, 69*(1), 127–149.

Snyder, H. N., & Sickmund, M. (2006). *Juvenile offenders and victims: 2006 national report.* Washington, DC: U.S. Department of Justice, Office of Justice Programs, Office of Juvenile Justice and Delinquency Prevention.

Solomon, S. D. (2003). Introduction. In B. L. Green, M. J. Friedman, J. T. V. M. de Jong, S. D. Soloman, T. M. Keane, J. A. Fairbank, et al. (Eds.), *Trauma interventions in war and peace: Prevention, practice and policy* (pp. 3–15). New York: Kluwer Academic/Plenum Publishers.

Solomon, S. D., Bravo, M., Rubio-Stipec, M., & Canino, G. (1993). Effect of family role on response to disaster. *Journal of Traumatic Stress, 6*(2), 255–269.

Solomon, Z., & Shalev, A. Y. (1995). Helping victims of military trauma. In J. R. Freedy & S. E. Hobfoll (Eds.), *Traumatic stress: From theory to practice* (pp. 241–261). New York: Plenum Press.

Somerville, K. (2002, November 12). Why famine stalks Africa. BBC News. Retrieved August 2, 2009, from http://news.bbc.co.uk/2/hi/Africa/2449527.stm.

Sontag, D., & Alvarez, L. (2008, January 13). Across America, deadly echoes of foreign battles. *The New York Times.* Retrieved July 24, 2009, from http://www.nytimes.com/2008/01/13/us/13vets.html.

Spano, R., & Nagy, S. (2005). Social guardianship and social isolation: An application and extension of lifestyle/routine activities theory to rural adolescents. *Rural Sociology, 70*(3), 414–437.

Speer, P. W., Ontkush, M., Schmitt, B., Jackson, C., Rengert, K. M., & Peterson, N. A. (2003). The intentional exercise of power: Community organizing in Camden, New Jersey. *Journal of Community & Applied Social Psychology, 13,* 399–408.

Stacey, J. (1993). Untangling feminist theory. In D. Richardson & V. Robinson (Eds.), *Introducing women's studies* (pp. 49–73). Basingstoke, United Kingdom: Macmillan.

Staral, J. M. (2004). Seeking justice: Faith-based community organizing—not faith-based initiatives. *Humanity and Society, 28*(2), 151–159.

Steen, J. A., & Mathiesen, S. (2005). Human rights education: Is social work behind the curve? *Journal of Teaching in Social Work, 25*(3/4), 143–156.

Stevenson, R. W. (2003, December 18). The struggle for Iraq: White House memo: Remember "weapons of mass destruction"? For Bush, they are a nonissue. *The New York Times.* Retrieved June 8, 2008, from http://query.nytimes.com/gst/fullpage.html?res=9C0DEFDC163FF93BA25751C1A9659C8B63.

Stewart, R. W. (2005). *American military history, Volume 1: The United States Army, and the forging of a nation, 1775–1917.* Washington, DC: Center of Military History, U.S. Army.

Stinebrickner-Kauffman, T. (2004). Counting matters: Prison inmates, population bases, and "one person, one vote." *Virginia Journal of Social Policy and Law, 11,* 229–305.

Stoller, E. P., & Gibson, R. C. (2001). The diversity of American families. In M. L. Anderson & P. H. Collins (Eds.), *Race, class, and gender* (4th ed., pp. 289–296). Belmont, CA: Wadsworth.

Stolley, K. S. (2005). *The basics of sociology.* Westport, CT: Greenwood Press.

Stuart, R. B., & Jacobson, B. (1986). Principles of divorce mediation: A social learning theory approach. *Mediation Quarterly, 14,* 71–85.

Summerfield, D. (1995). Addressing human response to war and atrocity: Major challenges in research and practices and the limitations of western psychiatric models. In R. J. Kleber, C. R. Figley, & B. P. R. Gersons (Eds.), *Beyond trauma: Cultural and societal dynamics* (pp. 17–29). New York: Plenum Press.

Sumner, J. (2005). *Sustainability and the civil commons: Rural communities in the age of globalization.* Toronto, Canada: University of Toronto.

Sunkel, O. (1969). National development policy and external dependence in Latin America. *The Journal of Development Studies, 6*(1), 23–48.

Supremely Liberal. (2009, May 5). *The Pueblo Chieftain* [Editorial]. Retrieved July 26, 2009, from http://www.chieftain.com/articles/2009/05/05/editorial/doc49ff9e06ae6b8157025097.txt.

Sutherland, E. H. (1939). *Principles of criminology.* New York: J. P. Lippincott Co.

Sutphen, R. D., Thyer, B. A., & Kurtz, P. D. (1995). Multisystemic treatment of high-risk juvenile offenders. *International Journal of Offender Therapy and Comparative Criminology, 39,* 327–334.

Swarns, R. L. (2006a, April 11). Growing effort to influence U.S. policy. *The New York Times National,* pp. A1, A17.

Swarns, R. L. (2006b, July 31). Study finds disparities in judges' asylum rulings. *The New York Times,* p. A15.

Szabo, L. (2006, January 16). Humanitarian tragedies the world has forgotten: Aid group list underreported global crisis. *USA Today,* p. 7D.

Tavernise, S. (2006, August 6). Charity wins deep loyalty for Hezbollah. *The New York Times.* Retrieved August 3, 2009, from http://www.nytimes.com/2006/08/06/world/middleeast/06tyre.html.

Temple-Raston, D. (2005). *Justice on the grass: Three Rwandan journalists, their trial for war crimes, and a nation's quest for redemption.* New York: Free Press.

Tewksbury, R., & Mustaine, E. E. (2003). College students' lifestyles and self-protective behaviors: Further considerations of the guardianship concept in routine activity theory. *Criminal Justice and Behavior, 30*(3), 302–327.

Texas Department of Criminal Justice. (2008). *Total operating budget for fiscal year 2009.* Retrieved August 3, 2009, from http://www.tdcj.state.tx.us/finance/budget/Operating%20Budget%20for%20FY%202009.pdf.

The Stafford Foundation. (2009, January 31). About us. Retrieved January 31, 2009, from http://www.thestaffordfoundation.org/about-us.

Thomas, L., Jr. (2006, June 27). A bequest between friends. *The New York Times,* pp. C1, C4.

Thomas, S. B. (2000). The legacy of Tuskegee: African Americans and AIDS. Retrieved July 5, 2008, from http://www.thebody.com/content/art30946.html.

Thompson, M. P., Norris, F. H., & Hanacek, B. (1993). Age differences in the psychological consequences of Hurricane Hugo. *Psychology and Aging, 8*(4), 606–616.

Thyer, B. A., & Myers, L. L. (1998). Social learning theory: An empirically based approach to understanding human behavior in the social environment. *Journal of Human Behavior in the Social Environment, 1*(1), 33–52.

Thyer, B. A., & Wodarski, J. S. (1990). Social learning theory: Toward a comprehensive conceptual framework for social work education. *Social Service Review, 64*(1), 144–152.

Tischler, C. A. (1996). A test of routine activity theory and disaggregated homicide. *Dissertation Abstracts International, A: The Humanities and Social Sciences, 56*(8), 3323-A.

Title 22 U.S.C.S. § 7101.

Title 22 U.S.C.S. § 7106.

Title 22 U.S.C.S. § 7107.

Title 29 U.S.C.A. § 1101.

Title 29 U.S.C.S. § 2601.

Title 42 U.S.C.S. § 15001.

Title 8 U.S.C. § 1101.

Tittle, C. R. (2004). Social learning theory and the explanation of crime: A guide for the new century. *Contemporary Sociology: A Journal of Reviews, 33*(6), 716–717.

Tontodonato, P., & Crew, B. K. (1992). Dating violence, social learning theory, and gender: A multivariate analysis. *Violence and Victims, 7*(1), 3–14.

Torry, J. (2006, March 31). DeWine wants to ban gay unions. *Columbus Dispatch,* pp. A1, A5.

Tryon, A. S., & Keane, S. P. (1986). Promoting imitative play through generalized observational learning in autistic-like children. *Journal of Abnormal Child Psychology, 14,* 537–549.

Tsutsui, K., & Wotipka, C. M. (2004). Global civil society and the international human rights movement: Citizen participation in Human Rights International Nongovernmental Organizations. *Social Forces, 83*(20), 587–620.

Tulloch, M. I. (2004). Parental fear of crime: A discursive analysis. *Journal of Sociology, 40*(4), 362–377.

Turner, B. (2005b). The sociology of religion. In C. Calhoun, C. Rojek, & B. Turner (Eds.), *The Sage handbook of sociology* (pp. 284–301). Thousand Oaks, CA: Sage.

United Human Rights Council. (2009). Bosnia genocide—1992–1995—200,000 deaths. Retrieved January 24, 2009, from http://www.unitedhumanrights.org/Genocide/bosnia_genocide.htm.

United Nations. (1948). *The universal declaration of human rights.* Retrieved July 30, 2009, from http://www.un.org/en/documents/udhr/.

United Nations. (2005). *The millennium development goals report 2005.* New York: Author.

United Nations. (2006). *Public inquiries unit.* Retrieved March 26, 2006, from http://www.un.org/geninfo/faq/faq/faq.html.

United Nations Development Programme. (2005). *Human development report 2005.* New York: Author.

United States v. Alan Simmons, 343 F.3d 72 (2003).

United States v. Yonkers Board of Education, 518 F. Supp 191 (S.D.N.Y. 1981).

U.S. Agency for International Development. (2005). *HIV/AIDS estimates and projections 2005–2010.* New York: Author.

U.S. Census Bureau. (2003). *Current population survey, March 2002.* Washington, DC: Author.

U.S. Census Bureau. (2004). *Current population survey (CPS): Definitions and explanations.* Washington, DC: Author.

U.S. Census Bureau. (2005). *American factfinder.* Retrieved October 6, 2005, from http://factfinder.census.gov.

U.S. Department of Justice. (2002). *Fact sheet: Board of immigration appeals: Final rule.* Washington, DC: Author.

U.S. Department of Justice. (2005). *Asylum protection in the United States.* Washington, DC: Author.

U.S. Department of Justice. (2009). *Confronting human trafficking at home and abroad.* Washington, DC: Author.

U.S. Department of Labor. (2005). *Social workers.* Retrieved November 24, 2005, from http://www.bls.gov/oco/ocos060.htm.

U.S. Department of State. (2001). *Patterns of global terrorism.* Retrieved August 2, 2009, from http://www.state.gov/s/ct/rls/pgtrpt/.

U.S. Department of Veterans Affairs. (2008). *National Center for PTSD home.* Washington, DC: Author.

U.S. Secretary of Commerce. (2005). *Report of the Strengthening America's Communities Advisory Committee.* Washington, DC: Author.

Urbina, I. (2006a). In the treatment of diabetes, success often does not pay. *The New York Times,* pp. A1, A26, A27.

Urbina, I. (2006b, July 23). With parents absent, trying to keep child care in the family. *The New York Times,* p. B13.

Vanderwoerd, J. R. (2003). Secular and religious tensions in government-funded faith-based social services organizations. *Dissertation Abstracts International, A: The Humanities and Social Sciences, 64*(3), 1099-A–1100-A.

Vesti, P.,&Kastrup,M. (1995). Treatment of torture survivors: Psychosocial and somatic aspects. Helping victims of military trauma. In J. R. Freedy & S. E. Hobfoll (Eds.), *Traumatic stress: From theory to practice* (pp. 339–363). New York: Plenum Press.

Vrtikapa, V., & Anisfeld, L. (2003). Instances of genocide in the modern world: The Bosnian and the Jewish Holocausts. In J. A. Cancelmos, I. Tylim, J. Hoffenberg, & H. Myers (Eds.), *Terrorism and the psychoanalytic space: International perspectives from ground zero* (pp. 163–165). New York: Pace University Press.

Walker, D. M. (2006). *Hurricane Katrina: GAO's preliminary observations regarding preparedness, response, and recovery.* Washington, DC: Government Accounting Office.

Wallace, B. C. (1995). Women and minorities in treatment. In A. M. Washton (Ed.), *Psychotherapy and substance abuse: A practitioner's handbook* (pp. 480–492). New York: The Guilford Press.

Wal-Mart to Pay $300,000 to Rejected Job Applicant With Disability. (2007). Minority Jobs.net. Retrieved July 10, 2008, from http://www.minorityjobs.net/article/1120/WalMart-To-Pay-300000-To-Rejected-Job-Applicant-With-Disability-Medical-Discrimination.html.

Walt, C. D., Proctor, B. D., & Lee, C. H. (2005). *Income, poverty, and health insurance coverage in the United States: 2004.* Washington, DC: U.S. Census Bureau.

Walters, B. (2004, December 20). Gay scientists shifting blame for AIDS to Africa—UWI lecturer. *Jamaica Observer.* Retrieved July 6, 2008, from http://www.jamaicaobserver.com/news/html/20041219T230000-0500_71724_OBS_GAY_SCIENTISTS_SHIFTING_BLAME_FOR_AIDS_TO_AFRICA__UWI_LECTURER.

Wardle, L. (2005, April 13). *Capitol Hill hearing testimony.* Marriage Protection Initiative and Judicial Activism, Committee on Senate Judiciary Subcommittee on Constitution, Civil Rights and Property Rights.

Warner v. Orange County Dept. of Probation, 870 F. Supp. 69 (S.D.N.Y. 1994).

Warren, R. L. (1970). Toward a non-utopian normative model of the community. *American Sociological Review, 35*(2), 219–228.

Washington, H. (2007). *Medical apartheid: The dark history of medical experimentation on Black Americans from colonial times to the present.* New York: Doubleday.

Watchtower Bible & Tract Society. (2002). *Our whole association of Brothers* [Videotape]. Brooklyn, NY: Author.

Wax, E. (2004, June 30). We want to make a light baby: Arab militiamen in Sudan said to use rape as weapon of ethnic cleansing. *The Washington Post,* p. A01.

Weathers, F. W., Litz, B. T., & Keane, T. M. (1995). Military trauma. In J. R. Freedy & S. E. Hobfoll (Eds.), *Traumatic stress: From theory to practice* (pp. 103–128). New York: Plenum Press.

Wells, B. (2002). Women's voices: Explaining poverty and plenty in a rural community. *Rural Sociology, 67*(2), 234–254.

Whealin, J., & Pivar, I. (2005). *Coping when a family member has been called to war.* National Center for PTSD. Retrieved August 2, 2009, from http://www .westga.edu/~gadmh/Military/fs%203%20military/Coping%20When%20a%20 Family%20Member%20Has%20Been%20Called%20to%20War.pdf.

White House Office of Faith-Based and Community Initiatives. (2006). Retrieved July 29, 2006, from http://www.whitehouse.gov/government/fbci/.

Wikipedia Encyclopedia. (2005). *2004 Madrid train bombings.* Retrieved October 17, 2005, from http://en.wikipedia.org/wiki/11_March_2004_Madrid_attacks.

Wilkerson, R. A. (2002). Written testimony on the criminal justice system and mentally ill offenders. Submitted to the U.S. Senate Judiciary Committee hearing on June 11, 2002.

Williams, S. (2006, June 23). City commission to look into complaints by Somali men. *Columbus Dispatch,* p. E5.

Wilson, C. (2005, November 20). Gay retirement communities are growing in popularity. *The New York Times.* Retrieved August 3, 2009, from http://www.nytimes.com/ 2005/11/20/realestate/20nation.html.

Wines, M. (2005a, November 2). Drought deepens poverty, starving more Africans. *The New York Times,* pp. A1, A8.

Wisconsin v. Yoder, 406 U.S. 205 (1972).

Wolf, B. D. (2006, July 26). Blackwell fights for freedom. *Columbus Dispatch,* p. D1.

Wolfson, R. (2006, April 24). Students protest Coca-Cola: ASUCLA board of directors hears both sides of dispute over alleged human rights violations. *Daily Bruin,* p. 1.

Women's Commission for Refugee Women & Children. (2008). *Living in limbo: Burma's youth in Thailand see few opportunities to use education and vocational skills.* New York: Author.

Woods, J. (2006, June 22). 2 sex offenders told to move. *Columbus Dispatch,* p. D1.

Word of Faith Fellowship, Inc. v. Rutherford County Department of Social Services, 329 F. Supp. 2d 675 (W.D.N.C. 2004).

World Bank. (2005). *Poverty: At a glance.* Retrieved October 5, 2005, from http://web .worldbank.org.

World Bank. (2009). Anti-corruption. Retrieved January 31, 2009, from http://web.worldbank.org/WBSITE/EXTERNAL/NEWS/0,,contentMDK:20040961~ menuPK:34480~pagePK:36694~piPK:116742~theSitePK:4607,00.html.

World Bank Group. (2005). PovertyNet: Europe & Central Asia. Retrieved November 7, 2005, from http://web.worldbank.org/WBSITE/EXTERNAL/COUNTRIES/ ECAEXT/EXTECAREGTOPPOVRED/0,,menuPK:904738~pagePK:34004175~ piPK:34004435~theSitePK:904723,00.html.

World Food Programme. (2005a). *Annual report 2004*. New York: United Nations.

World Food Programme. (2005b). *The WFP mission statement*. Retrieved November 7, 2005, from http://www.wfp.org.

World Health Organization. (2002). *First needs assessment situation report*. Retrieved August 3, 2009, from http://www.who.int/mediacentre/factsheets/fs090/en/.

Wuthnow, R., Hackett, C., & Hsu, B. Y. (2004). The effectiveness and trustworthiness of faith-based and other service organizations: A study of recipients' perceptions. *Journal for the Scientific Study of Religion, 43*(1), 1–17.

York, B. (2008, September 8). What did Obama do as a community organizer? And is it really a qualification to be president? *National Review Online*. Retrieved January 27, 2009, from http://article.nationalreview.com/?q=OWMxNGUxZWJjYzg1 NjA0MTlmZDZmMjUwZGU3ZjAwNmU=.

Young, B. H., Ford, J. D., Ruzek, J. I., Friedman, M. J., & Gusman, F. D. (2000). *Disaster mental health services: A guidebook for clinicians and administrators*. White River Junction, VT: National Center for Post-Traumatic Stress Disorder.

Yunus Centre. (2007). *Welcome*. Retrieved July 29, 2009, from http://muham madyunus.org.

Zakirova, V. (2005). War against the family: Domestic violence and human rights in Russia: A view from the Bashkortostan Republic. *Current Sociology, 53*(1), 75–91.

Zastrow, C., & Kirst-Ashman, K. K. (2001). *Understanding human behavior and the social environment* (5th ed.). Belmont, CA: Brooks/Cole.

Zeigler, C., Jr. (2007). Dungy proudly announces opposition to gay marriage. *Outsports*. Retrieved July 25, 2009, from http://www.outsports.com/nfl/2007/ 0321dungy.htm.

Zimmermann, J. M., & Stevens, B. W. (2006). The use of performance measurement in South Carolina nonprofits. *Nonprofit Management & Leadership, 16*(3), 315–327.

Zoroya, G. (2005, October 18). 1 in 4 Iraq vets ailing on return. *USA Today*. Retrieved July 24, 2009, from http://www.usatoday.com/news/world/iraq/2005-10-18-troops-side_x.htm.

Zussman, R. (1990). Medicine, the medical professional, and the welfare state. In M. T. Hallinan, D. M. Klein, & J. Glass (Eds.), *Change in societal institutions* (pp. 195–210). New York: Plenum.

Index

Note: In page references, f indicates figures and t indicates tables.

About the Author

Rudolph Alexander, Jr., is a full professor in the College of Social Work at The Ohio State University. He began his academic career as a criminal justice major, receiving an associate's degree in criminal justice from Armstrong State College and a bachelor's degree in criminology and corrections from Sam Houston State University. His advisor at Sam Houston State University held a DSW, and she recommended graduate studies in social work. Hence, he received an MSW from the University of Houston and later a PhD in social work from the University of Minnesota.

His scholarly work consists of about 60 articles in peer-reviewed social work and criminal justice journals. His primary focus has been the influence of law in shaping social work and criminal justice policies. In 2008, Dr. Alexander was invited to participate in a symposium at the University of Oxford in Oxford, England, where he presented a paper titled "Race, Ethnicity, and Immigration in the United States: Theoretical Perspectives." This presentation was revised into an article and accepted for publication in a University of Oxford journal, *Forum on Public Policy*. He was invited back to the University of Oxford in 2009 for a conference on social justice. Dr. Alexander has published five books, including *Counseling, Treatment, and Intervention Methods With Juvenile and Adult Offenders* (2000), *Race and Justice* (2000), *Understanding Legal Concepts That Influence Social Welfare Policy and Practice* (2002), *To Ascend Into the Shining World Again* (2002), and *Racism, African Americans, and Social Justice* (2005).